Communications in Computer and Information Science 2750

Rationale

The CCIS series is devoted to the publication of proceedings of computer science conferences. Its aim is to efficiently disseminate original research results in informatics in printed and electronic form. While the focus is on publication of peer-reviewed full papers presenting mature work, inclusion of reviewed short papers reporting on work in progress is welcome, too. Besides globally relevant meetings with internationally representative program committees guaranteeing a strict peer-reviewing and paper selection process, conferences run by societies or of high regional or national relevance are also considered for publication.

Topics

The topical scope of CCIS spans the entire spectrum of informatics ranging from foundational topics in the theory of computing to information and communications science and technology and a broad variety of interdisciplinary application fields.

Information for Volume Editors and Authors

Publication in CCIS is free of charge. No royalties are paid, however, we offer registered conference participants temporary free access to the online version of the conference proceedings on SpringerLink (http://link.springer.com) by means of an http referrer from the conference website and/or a number of complimentary printed copies, as specified in the official acceptance email of the event.

CCIS proceedings can be published in time for distribution at conferences or as post-proceedings, and delivered in the form of printed books and/or electronically as USBs and/or e-content licenses for accessing proceedings at SpringerLink. Furthermore, CCIS proceedings are included in the CCIS electronic book series hosted in the SpringerLink digital library at http://link.springer.com/bookseries/7899. Conferences publishing in CCIS are allowed to use our online conference service (Meteor) for managing the whole proceedings lifecycle (from submission and reviewing to preparing for publication) free of charge.

Publication process

The language of publication is exclusively English. Authors publishing in CCIS have to sign the Springer CCIS copyright transfer form, however, they are free to use their material published in CCIS for substantially changed, more elaborate subsequent publications elsewhere. For the preparation of the camera-ready papers/files, authors have to strictly adhere to the Springer CCIS Authors' Instructions and are strongly encouraged to use the CCIS LaTeX style files or templates.

Abstracting/Indexing

CCIS is abstracted/indexed in DBLP, Google Scholar, EI-Compendex, Mathematical Reviews, SCImago, Scopus. CCIS volumes are also submitted for the inclusion in ISI Proceedings.

How to start

To start the evaluation of your proposal for inclusion in the CCIS series, please send an e-mail to ccis@springer.com

Kevin Brown · Esteban Meneses · Kyle Felker ·
Antônio Tadeu Azevedo Gomes ·
José Manuel Monsalve Diaz ·
Katherine Rasmussen
Editors

High Performance Computing

12th Latin American High Performance Computing Conference, CARLA 2025
Kingston, Jamaica, September 22–26, 2025
Proceedings

Springer

Editors
Kevin Brown
Argonne National Laboratory
Lemont, IL, USA

Kyle Felker
Argonne National Laboratory
Lemont, IL, USA

José Manuel Monsalve Diaz
Advanced Micro Devices, Inc. (AMD)
Santa Clara, CA, USA

Esteban Meneses
Centro Nacional de Alta Tecnología
San José, Costa Rica

Antônio Tadeu Azevedo Gomes
Laboratório Nacional de Computação Científica (LNCC)
Petrópolis, Brazil

Katherine Rasmussen
Lawrence Berkeley National Laboratory
Berkeley, CA, USA

ISSN 1865-0929 ISSN 1865-0937 (electronic)
Communications in Computer and Information Science
ISBN 978-3-032-24922-7 ISBN 978-3-032-24923-4 (eBook)
https://doi.org/10.1007/978-3-032-24923-4

This Springer imprint is published by the registered company Springer Nature Switzerland AG
The registered company address is: Gewerbestrasse 11, 6330 Cham, Switzerland

Preface

CARLA, the Latin America High-Performance Computing Conference, is an international academic meeting that provides a forum to foster the growth and strength of the High-Performance Computing (HPC) community in Latin America and the Caribbean. The conference has been running since 2014 and has become a leading event for HPC in the region. A key objective of the CARLA conference is to disseminate the latest breakthroughs in HPC and HPC&AI (the intersection of HPC and Artificial Intelligence) to the global community, reflecting the significance of these domains in driving innovation and progress.

The 12th edition of CARLA marked a significant moment in its history, as for the first time the conference was held in the Caribbean. The location of the CARLA conference rotates each year to broaden participation and foster local engagement. The first edition held in the Caribbean showed the increasing maturity and reach of the CARLA conference and allowed new participants to attend and new collaborations to develop.

CARLA 2025 was held on September 22-26 in Kingston, Jamaica. The conference brought together individuals from an ever-growing network of HPC practitioners throughout Latin America and the Caribbean. For twelve consecutive editions, this network has come together to share ideas, strengthen collaborations, and drive insightful discussions in the field. That network of contacts is embodied and sustained by the SCALAC consortium.

The CARLA 2025 conference program consisted of the presentations of the academic publications presented in this document, in addition to much more. There were two full-day workshops accompanied by four half-day workshops. The full-day workshops tackled issues critical to both the region and the world: "Latin America and Caribbean Advances on Weather Forecasting" and "Energy Efficiency and Sustainability in AI, HPC, and Quantum Computing." The half-day workshops spanned pressing and compelling topics around advanced computing techniques and architectures, bioengineering, HPC practices, and HPC communities and inclusivity. Furthermore, it offered three tutorials on advanced topics in HPC and AI. The website (https://carlaconference.org/previo us_editions/2025 contains complete information about the conference and its schedule.

CARLA 2025 had 192 registered attendees from 26 countries that span the globe. The majority of attendees came from Latin America and the Caribbean, the primary community of the CARLA conference. Attendees also came from as far as Europe and Asia, a representation of the global reach and collaborations fostered by the conference. Assistance with registration was provided to 26 individuals to foster Women in STEM and the participation of the weather and climate forecasting community. The upcoming generation of HPC practitioners also participated as 28 student volunteers from the University of the West Indies, Mona Campus and the University of Technology, Jamaica helped make the conference a success.

The CARLA 2025 committee included professionals from institutions throughout the world. The event was sponsored and supported by SCALAC, RedCLARA, the University of the West Indies, Mona Campus, the Scientific Research Council (Jamaica), and Phase 3 Productions. In addition, CARLA 2025 received sponsorship from 8 companies. The committee also recognizes the role and support of Parris Lyew-Ayee, Jr, Ministerial Advisor to the Minister of Science, Energy, Telecommunications and Transport, Jamaica, for coordinating the collaborations between the CARLA conference and local institutions. Additionally, the committee recognizes the role and support of Charah T. Watson, Executive Director, Scientific Research Council, Jamaica, and the SRC team for providing promotion, logistics, and execution support for the event.

CARLA 2025 featured a total of two keynote speakers, Kate Keahy of Argonne National Laboratory and University of Chicago and Felix Wolf of the Technical University of Darmstadt. Furthermore, the conference included two invited talks by Rupak Biswas of NASA and Ricardo Baeza-Yates of KTH Royal Institute of Technology, in addition to six industry talks given by different sponsors. The conference also encouraged the participation of and discussion with the attendees through three panels, "HPC Everyday and Everywhere", "European Union — Latin America and Caribbean Collaborations", and "AI, National Sovereignty, and Sustainability".

This book contains 16 papers selected from 28 submissions. All manuscripts were peer-reviewed by at least three members of the Program Committee. The work by Daniel Salmun and Esteban Mocskos titled "Fast Sorting for the RISC-V 'V' Vector Extension" was selected for the Best Paper Award. Additionally, the poster by Diego Santibáñez Oyarce, Esteban Gómez Terán, Jorge Vergara-Quezada and Ana Moya-Beltrán titled "Comparative Performance Analysis of DNA Sequence Encoding Methods for Machine Learning-Based Bacterial Classification" was selected for the Best Poster award.

November 2025

Kevin Brown
Esteban Meneses
Kyle Felker
Antônio Tadeu Azevedo Gomes
José Manuel Monsalve Diaz
Katherine Rasmussen

Organization

General Chairs

Kevin Brown	Argonne National Laboratory, USA
Esteban Meneses	Centro Nacional de Alta Tecnología, Costa Rica

Program Committee Chairs

Kyle Felker	Argonne National Laboratory, USA
Antônio Tadeu Azevedo Gomes	Laboratório Nacional de Computação Científica, Brazil
José M. Monsalve Diaz	Advanced Micro Devices, Inc., USA
Katherine Rasmussen	Lawrence Berkeley National Laboratory, USA

Program Committee

Amarís, Marcos	Universidade Federal do Pará, Brazil
Baldassin, Alexandro	Universidade Estadual Paulista, Brazil
Barbosa-Santillán, Liliana Ibeth	Universidad de Guadalajara, Mexico
Caino-Lores, Silvina	INRIA, France
Cardoso, Douglas	University of Coimbra, Portugal
Carretero, Jesus	Universidad Carlos III De Madrid, Spain
Castro, Harold	Universidad de los Andes, Colombia
Castro, Márcio	Federal University of Santa Catarina, Brazil
Catabriga, Lucia	Universidade Federal do Espírito Santo, Brazil
Cazar Ramírez, Dennis	Universidad San Francisco de Quito, Ecuador
Colavecchia, Flavio	National Atomic Energy Commission and Universidad Nacional de Cuyo, Argentina
Cordeiro, Daniel	Universidade de São Paulo, Brazil
Coutinho, Alvaro	Federal University of Rio de Janeiro, Brazil
Dorsch, Juan Pablo	Swiss National Supercomputing Centre, Switzerland
Drummond, Lúcia	Universidade Federal Fluminense, Brazil
Dufrechou, Ernesto	Universidad de la República, Uruguay
Felker, Kyle	Argonne National Laboratory, USA
Galvez, Jorge	Universidad de Guadalajara, Mexico

Gitler, Isidoro	CINVESTAV, Mexico
Goldman, Alfredo	University of São Paulo, Brazil
Gomes, Antônio, Tadeu Azevedo	Laboratório Nacional de Computação Científica, Brazil
Gordillo, José Luis	Universidad Nacional Autónoma de México, Mexico, México
Griebler, Dalvan	Pontifícia Universidade Católica do Rio Grande do Sul, Brazil
Jiménez Vargas, Diego	Max Planck Computing and Data Facility, Germany
Kunas, Cristiano	Universidade Federal do Rio Grande do Sul, Brazil
Lozoya, Jorge	Universidad de Guadalajara, Mexico
Martinez Abaunza,\Victor Eduardo	Universidade Estadual de Campinas, Brazil
Mayo-García, Rafael	CIEMAT, Spain
Mello Schnorr, Lucas	Universidade Federal do Rio Grande do Sul, Brazil
Mocskos, Esteban	Universidad de Buenos Aires & CONICET, Argentina
Monsalve Diaz, Jose M.	Advanced Micro Devices, Inc., USA
Moya, Eduardo Ulises	IIEG Gobierno de Jalisco, Mexico
Navaux, Philippe	Universidade Federal do Rio Grande do Sul, Brazil
Nesmachnow, Sergio	Universidad de la República, Uruguay
Netto, Marco	Microsoft, USA
Orizaga Trejo, Jose Antonio	Universidad de Guadalajara, México
Padoin, Edson Luiz	Regional University of Northwestern Rio Grande do Sul, Brazil
Pantoja, Maria	California Polytechnic State University, USA
Pedemonte, Martín	Universidad de la República, Uruguay
Raffin, Bruno	INRIA, France
Raskar, Siddhisanket	Argonne National Laboratory, USA
Sanoja, Andres	Universidad Central de Venezuela, Venezuela
Senger, Hermes	Universidade Federal de São Carlos, Brazil
Serpa, Matheus	Federal University of Rio Grande do Sul, Brazil
Silva, Romulo	Federal University of Rio de Janeiro, Brazil
Steffenel, Luiz Angelo	Université de Reims Champagne-Ardenne, France
Tadonki, Claude	Mines Paris — PSL, France
Wolovick, Nicolás	UNC Supercómputo, Argentina

Contents

High-Performance Computing (HPC)

Evaluating Malleable Job Scheduling in HPC Clusters Using Real-World Workloads

Patrick Zojer[1], Jonas Posner[1](✉), and Taylan Özden[2]

[1] University of Kassel, Kassel, Germany
patrick.zojer@student.uni-kassel.de, jonas.posner@uni-kassel.de
[2] Technical University of Darmstadt, Darmstadt, Germany
taylan.oezden@tu-darmstadt.de

Abstract. Optimizing resource utilization in high-performance computing (HPC) clusters is essential for maximizing both system efficiency and user satisfaction. However, traditional rigid job scheduling often results in underutilized resources and increased job waiting times.

This work evaluates the benefits of resource elasticity, where the job scheduler dynamically adjusts the resource allocation of malleable jobs at runtime. Using real workload traces from the Cori, Eagle, and Theta supercomputers, we simulate varying proportions (0–100%) of malleable jobs with the ElastiSim software.

We evaluate five job scheduling strategies, including a novel one that maintains malleable jobs at their preferred resource allocation when possible. Results show that, compared to fully rigid workloads, malleable jobs yield significant improvements across all key metrics. Considering the best-performing scheduling strategy for each supercomputer, job turnaround times decrease by 37–67%, job makespan by 16–65%, job wait times by 73–99%, and node utilization improves by 5–52%. Although improvements vary, gains remain substantial even at 20% malleable jobs.

This work highlights important correlations between workload characteristics (e.g., job runtimes and node requirements), malleability proportions, and scheduling strategies. These findings confirm the potential of malleability to address inefficiencies in current HPC practices and demonstrate that even limited adoption can provide substantial advantages, encouraging its integration into HPC resource management.

Keywords: Dynamic Resources · Malleability · Job Scheduling

1 Introduction

High-Performance Computing (HPC) clusters (*supercomputers*) enable the solution of complex problems in various scientific fields. Supercomputers comprise multiple interconnected *nodes*, each executing submitted *jobs*. A job is a program submitted to a *job scheduler* (e.g., Slurm [20]) with user-defined metadata such as runtime limits and required nodes. A collection of jobs constitutes a *workload*.

K. Brown et al. (Eds.): CARLA 2025, CCIS 2750, pp. 3–18, 2026.
https://doi.org/10.1007/978-3-032-24923-4_1

Traditionally, jobs are *rigid* and are allocated a fixed number of nodes for their entire execution. Schedulers assign jobs to nodes based on availability and fairness.

Maximizing node utilization is crucial, yet often unattainable in practice. Job size heterogeneity and scheduler constraints inhibit optimal system packing, resulting in idle nodes even when jobs remain queued. This inefficiency leads to extended job wait times and wasted computational resources.

Supercomputers such as THETA [2], CORI [12], and EAGLE [13] exhibit average node utilization between 30% and 80% [3,6,14]. These low values result from both scheduling inefficiencies and factors such as empty queues or system maintenance.

Resource elasticity offers a promising approach to address underutilization by allowing jobs to change their number of allocated nodes at runtime. Elastic jobs include variants [8] such as *evolving* jobs that request resource changes from the scheduler. In contrast, for *malleable* jobs, the scheduler initiates resource changes. This requires schedulers capable of *expanding* and *shrinking* jobs and applications that support dynamic resource allocation. While resources may include storage or GPUs, this study focuses solely on CPU nodes.

However, introducing elasticity into real HPC environments poses significant challenges. It requires not only schedulers with elasticity support but also applications capable of adapting to dynamic node counts. Many applications cannot efficiently handle such variability, necessitating changes at both the system and application levels. Therefore, elasticity adoption requires modifications at both system administration and application development levels. Additionally, the dominant inter-node parallel programming model Message Passing Interface (MPI) [11] offers limited support for elasticity.

Given these constraints, many studies on elasticity rely on simulations, e.g. [1,10,18]. This approach is practical given the cost and complexity of real testbeds, but requires accurate modeling of input parameters.

This work evaluates the impact of malleable jobs using real workload traces from CORI, THETA, and EAGLE. For simulations, we use the ElastiSim simulation software [15]. Using a speedup model and efficiency thresholds, we transform rigid jobs into malleable ones, with malleability proportions varying from 0% to 100%. In addition to the conventional rigid EASY-backfilling [19], we evaluate four malleable strategies. Three are from prior work [18], while the fourth—introduced in this work—aims to preserve each job's preferred number of nodes. The preferred number of nodes reflects a reasonable speed and efficiency tradeoff [5].

We evaluate multiple performance metrics: job turnaround time, job makespan, job wait time, and node utilization. Results show that, compared to fully rigid workloads, malleability consistently yields significant improvements. Considering the best-performing scheduling strategy for each supercomputer, job turnaround times decrease by 37–67%, job makespan by 16–65%, job wait times by 73–99%, and node utilization improves by 5–52%. However, the improvement varies considerably depending on workload characteristics and scheduling strategy.

The remainder of this work is structured as follows. Section 2 outlines the scheduling strategies, workload preparation, and experimental design. Section 3 presents and analyzes the simulation results across different workloads and scheduling configurations, while Sect. 4 outlines limitations. Section 5 situates this study within the context of existing research, and Sect. 6 summarizes key insights and concludes this work.

2 Methodology

This section describes the methodological foundation of our study. We begin by detailing the job scheduling strategies in Sect. 2.1, including both baseline and malleable strategies. Section 2.2 explains the preprocessing steps applied to real-world HPC workload traces, such as cleaning, filtering, and transformation into simulation-ready formats. Section 2.3 outlines our experimental setup, including malleability proportions, simulation parameters, and the metrics used to evaluate performance. Together, these components form a reproducible framework for evaluating the impact of malleable job scheduling in realistic HPC scenarios.

2.1 Job Scheduling Strategies

We evaluate the following job scheduling strategies in our simulations.

Rigid EASY-Backfill [19]: In traditional rigid scheduling, each job requests a fixed number of nodes for its entire runtime. Jobs are placed in a queue and selected for execution according to scheduling policies.

EASY-Backfill extends the well-known *First-Come, First-Served (FCFS)* strategy, which schedules jobs strictly in submission order. While fair, pure FCFS often results in poor node utilization when the first job in the queue cannot start due to insufficient available nodes. EASY-Backfill addresses this by allowing limited reordering. If enough nodes are available, the first job starts as usual. If not, the scheduler scans the queue for smaller jobs that can be started without delaying the first job. This approach increases node utilization while preserving fairness. In this work, EASY-Backfill serves as our rigid baseline.

Malleable Avg, Min, and Pref [18]: Based on Iserte *et al.* [9] and extended in our prior work [18], these strategies use malleable jobs that define minimum and maximum numbers of nodes. Scheduling proceeds in three steps:

Step 1: Waiting jobs are started using EASY-Backfill. The number of nodes for starting a malleable job is determined by Avg, Min, and Pref.
Step 2: If there are idle nodes but not enough to start jobs, running malleable jobs are shrunk. A priority order (described below) determines the order in which jobs are considered for shrinking, starting with the highest-priority job.
Step 3: Any remaining idle nodes are distributed to expand running malleable jobs. Again, a priority order is used, but in this case, the lowest-priority job is considered first.

MIN prioritizes jobs based on the surplus of allocated over minimum nodes:

$$\text{priority}_{\text{job}} = \textit{current-nodes}_{\text{job}} - \textit{min-nodes}_{\text{job}} \tag{1}$$

In Step 1, all jobs are started at their minimum number of nodes. In Steps 2 and 3, resizing is limited to the smallest number of jobs needed to achieve the target allocation.

PREF introduces the additional job attribute *preferred number of nodes*, reflecting a reasonable speedup-efficiency trade-off [5]:

$$\text{priority}_{\text{job}} = \textit{current-nodes}_{\text{job}} - \textit{preferred-nodes}_{\text{job}} \tag{2}$$

In Step 1, jobs attempt to start with their preferred nodes; if that is not possible, fewer nodes are assigned. Resizing behavior in Steps 2 and 3 mirrors that of MIN.

AVG evaluates the relative utilization within the node range:

$$\text{priority}_{\text{job}} = \frac{\textit{current-nodes}_{\text{job}} - \textit{min-nodes}_{\text{job}}}{\textit{max-nodes}_{\text{job}} - \textit{min-nodes}_{\text{job}}} \tag{3}$$

In Step 1, jobs start with their minimum nodes. In Steps 2 and 3, all malleable jobs are eligible for resizing, enabling a more balanced redistribution of resources.

Malleable KEEPPREF: Proposed in this work, it is based on Eq. 2 but explicitly aims to preserve each job's preferred number of nodes. In Step 1, jobs are always started with their preferred nodes. In Step 2, only jobs currently running with more than their preferred nodes are considered for shrinking.

Metrics: We evaluate scheduling performance using the following metrics:

- **Job Wait Time**: Time from job submission to job start.
- **Job Makespan**: Execution time from job start to completion.
- **Job Turnaround Time**: Total time from submission to completion (Wait Time + Makespan).
- **Node Utilization**: Proportion of nodes actively used during the simulation.

2.2 Workload Preparation

We utilize real-world workload traces from the following supercomputers:

- **Theta** [2]: Operated by ALCF (2017–2023) with 4,392 Xeon Phi 7230 nodes, reaching 11.7 PetaFLOPS (Top500 rank 16, 06/2017). 24 GPU nodes excluded.
- **Eagle** [13]: Operated by NREL (2018–2024) with 2,618 Skylake 6154 nodes, delivering 8 PetaFLOPS (Top500 rank 35, 11/2018). 50 GPU nodes excluded.
- **Cori** [12]: Operated by NERSC (2015–2023) with two partitions: HASWELL (2,388 Xeon E5-2698 nodes, 2.81 PetaFLOPS) and KNL (9,688 Xeon Phi 7250 nodes, 29.5 PetaFLOPS).

The CORI datasets required substantial preprocessing due to structural inconsistencies. Jobs were recorded in daily segments, artificially inflating node utilization due to split entries and shared-node (oversubscribed) execution. As shown in Fig. 1a, raw HASWELL data showed utilization exceeding 4,000 nodes, well above the actual capacity of 2,388. To correct this, we merged split entries and removed all shared-node jobs, resulting in the utilization shown in Fig. 1b.

Table 1 summarizes our job filtering results. HASWELL experienced the largest reduction, primarily due to the exclusion of shared-node jobs. Although this significantly reduced the job count, the removed jobs typically consumed only partial node resources while contributing disproportionately to total runtime, and their removal provides a more accurate picture of actual system utilization. In contrast, KNL and EAGLE required minimal filtering, and THETA remained unmodified, as it contained no shared-node jobs, GPUs, or structural anomalies.

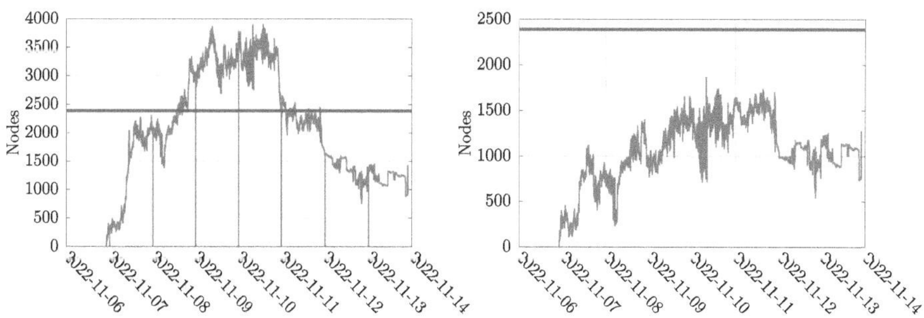

(a) Raw data (b) After cleaning and merging

Fig. 1. HASWELL: Raw data (a) shows artifacts from shared-node jobs and daily splits (vertical blue lines). The red line shows the capacity of 2,388 nodes. After cleaning and merging, the data looks realistic (b). (Color figure online)

Table 1. Raw jobs and cleaned jobs (* = jobs with shared nodes)

Dataset	Raw Jobs	Cleaned Jobs	Runtime Loss
EAGLE	7,390,585	72,580	~165,000 h (~1.275%)
KNL	55,587	14,063	~41 h (~0.004%)*
HASWELL	119,781	91,200	~33,370 h (~13.680%)*

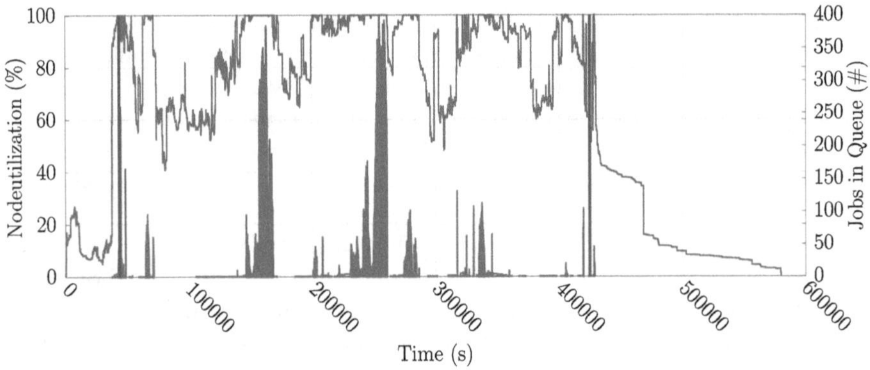

Fig. 2. KNL: Node utilization (blue line) with 100% rigid jobs. Red lines mark warm-up and final submission; metrics are computed in between. Green areas illustrate the number of jobs in the queue. (Color figure online)

Table 2. Simulation configurations

Dataset	Start	Duration	Jobs	Tick	Nodes
THETA [2]	2023-08-01	28 d	2.550	1 s	4,392
EAGLE [13]	2022-09-01	28 d	143,829	10 s	2,568
KNL [12]	2022-11-06	5 d	41,524	10 s	9,688
HASWELL [12]	2022-11-07	5 d	28,259	1 s	2,388

For simulations, we used ElastiSim [15], an open-source simulator for malleable job scheduling ElastiSim takes a set of jobs as input and simulates their execution on a supercomputer using a given scheduling algorithm. To integrate with ElastiSim, job data were converted to JSON with metadata (job ID, submission time, nodes, runtime, etc.). Missing time limits were set to 125% of runtime based on empirical averages. Based on previous work, malleable jobs received min/max/preferred node counts using a speedup model with efficiency thresholds to ensure realistic scaling behavior [17].

For THETA and EAGLE, we selected representative time windows to balance data quality and simulation feasibility. Anomalous periods, including scheduled maintenance, end-of-year test jobs, or irregular submission spikes, were excluded. Segment selection was guided by statistical analysis and visual inspection of job and utilization distributions. The final time windows are detailed in Sect. 2.3, with workload characteristics discussed in Sect. 3.

2.3 Experimental Design

Each workload is simulated with increasing proportions of malleable jobs: 0%, 20%, ..., 100%. For each proportion, we perform 10 simulation runs using different pseudo-random seeds to determine which jobs are converted to malleable variants. All metrics reported in Sect. 3 are averaged over these 10 runs. We report interquartile ranges (IQR) as error bars, as real workload metrics often exhibit non-normal distributions, making IQR preferable to standard deviation.

To ensure fair comparisons, we exclude the first 12 h of each simulation as a warm-up phase, which builds a representative job queue but behaves atypically. We also exclude the time after the last job submission to avoid skewing metrics due to drain-down. Figure 2 illustrates this approach for KNL, where only data between the red lines (after warm-up, before drain-down) are used for analysis.

Table 2 summarizes simulation parameters: start time, duration, job count, node count, and simulator tick rate. The tick rate defines the interval between scheduling points and directly impacts simulation runtime. For larger workloads like EAGLE, a 10 s tick is used. Smaller workloads such as HASWELL are simulated at 1 s for finer granularity. These values have a negligible impact on results but enable practical completion times. Reconfiguration costs are not explicitly modeled, but the tick rate introduces idle times that approximate overheads based on prior work [16] (i.e., 2–4 s for add/remove 8 nodes).

3 Evaluation

This section presents simulation results, analyzing how real HPC workloads respond to varying malleability proportions under different scheduling strategies. Sections 3.1–3.4 examine each workload individually. Section 3.5 discusses trends across all workloads and schedulers.

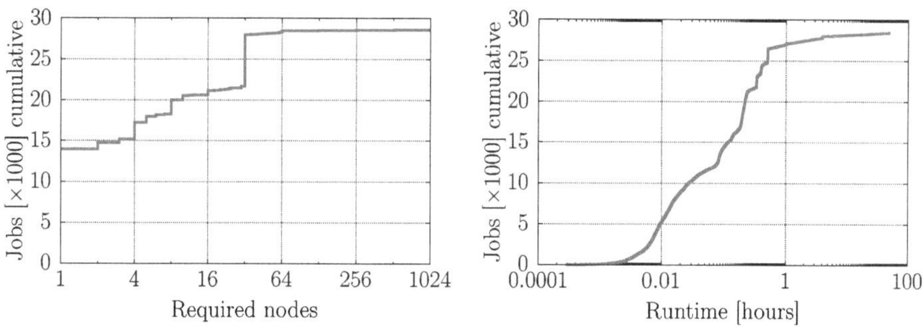

(a) Number of nodes required by jobs (b) Runtime of jobs

Fig. 3. HASWELL: Node counts and runtimes—most jobs are small and short.

3.1 Cori Haswell

Figure 3 illustrates the characteristics of the HASWELL workload. The distribution is dominated by small-scale jobs: 97.8% request ≤ 32 nodes, with 50% requesting a single node (Fig. 3a). In terms of runtime, 75% of jobs complete within 1,000 s (Fig. 3b), consistent with the high throughput of 28,259 jobs over the five-day simulation period.

Figure 4 shows node utilization under the rigid baseline. A job burst at 300,000 s leads to elevated queue pressure and corresponding increases in wait times.

Figure 6 presents the impact of increasing malleability. Job turnaround time (Fig. 6a) decreases consistently with increasing malleability, dropping from 2,391 s to 792 s—a 66.87% improvement. Job makespan (Fig. 6b) follows a similar trend, improving by up to 65.32%.

Job wait time (Fig. 6c) improves by up to 99.71% and stabilizes below 10 s once malleability reaches 40%. While KEEPPREF shows slightly higher average wait times, the IQR reveals that most jobs wait less than one second even at modest 20% malleability. The previously identified job submission burst (Fig. 4) contributes to occasional high-value outliers.

Node utilization (Fig.,6d) rises from 72.33% to 98.73% with increasing malleability. Variability across seeds decreases, indicating consistent resource usage.

Figures 6e and 6f show expand and shrink operations per job, respectively. Expand operations are most frequent with KEEPPREF, which averages over 11 expand operations per job. In contrast, AVG remains steady at ≈ 5 expand operations. Shrink operations start at ≈ 25 per job across all schedulers at low malleability. Only AVG and PREF show clear declines as malleability increases, while MIN and KEEPPREF maintain higher shrink rates, indicating a more aggressive approach.

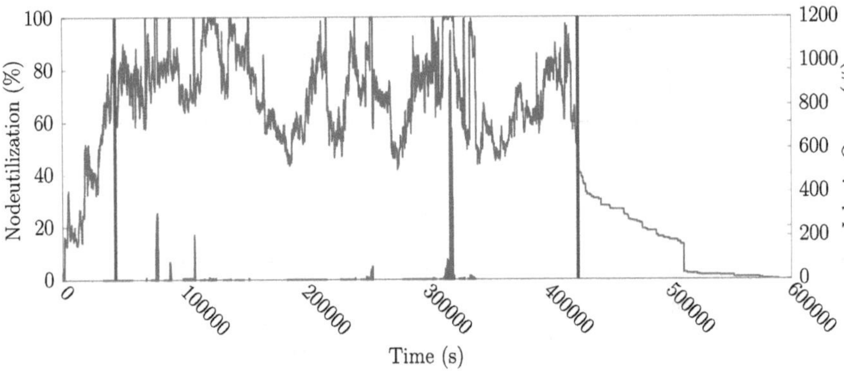

Fig. 4. HASWELL: Node utilization with 100% rigid jobs. Red lines mark warm-up and final submission; metrics are computed in between. (Color figure online)

3.2 Cori KNL

Like HASWELL, KNL is dominated by small jobs: 94.4% request ≤ 32 nodes, with 63% requesting exactly four nodes (Fig. 5a). Job runtimes are similarly compact, with 80% of jobs completing within 1h increasing malleability, dropping from000 s and a visible cluster between 600–800 s (Fig. 5b). The simulation window includes 41,524 jobs submitted over five days.

Figure 7 presents the impact of increasing malleability. Job turnaround time (Fig. 7a) improves with increasing malleability, dropping from 4,551 s to 1,696 s—a 62.74% improvement. Job makespan (Fig. 7b) follows a similar trend, improving by up to 60.87%.

Job wait time (Fig. 7c) improves by up to 98.81% and falls below 20 s at $\geq$ 40% malleability. Notably, KeepPref shows higher averages and wider IQRs, particularly at 40% and 60% malleability. This behavior correlates with job submission spikes observed in node utilization (see Fig. 2 in Sect. 2.3).

Node utilization (Fig. 7d increases from 85.5% to $\approx$95% at 60% malleability, with minimal additional gains thereafter. The progressively narrowing IQR indicates more consistent system usage as malleability increases.

Figures 7e and 7f show expand and shrink operations per job, respectively. Expand operations decrease steadily as malleability increases, with KeepPref and Avg exhibiting more than twice the frequency of other strategies. Shrink operations remain fairly stable at $\approx$20 per job, except for Min, which increases slightly—indicating more aggressive downscaling as malleability increases.

3.3 Eagle

Figures 5c and 5d show that the Eagle workload is homogeneous: 96.6% of jobs request exactly one node, and 86.8% complete within 10,000 s.

Job turnaround time (Fig. 8a) improves by 65.55%, dropping from 6,138 s to 2,114 s. Although the bars appear similar due to axis scaling, the large IQR in the rigid case (29,377 s) highlights a wide spread in job turnaround times. Job makespan (Fig. 8b) follows a similar pattern, decreasing by up to 65.43%.

Job wait time (Fig. 8c) decreases from 330 s to 89 s—a 73.17% improvement. The reduced IQR indicates that this benefit extends beyond the average case.

Node utilization (Fig. 8d) increases from 28.71% to 43.61%. The low initial value suggests that underutilization is primarily due to workload structure rather than scheduling inefficiencies.

Figures 8e and 8f show expand and shrink operations per job, respectively. Expand operations decrease moderately with increasing malleability: KeepPref and Avg drop from 8–9 expands per job to 6–7, while Pref and Min drop from 3 to 1–2. Shrink operations decline slightly across all strategies, with the most notable reduction occurring between 20% and 40% malleability.

3.4 Theta

For Theta, node requests concentrate at 1 (34.8%), 8 (20.3%), and 256 nodes (12.6%) (Fig. 5e). A total of 84.7% of jobs complete within 10,000 s (Fig. 5f).

Job turnaround time (Fig. 9a) improves by up to 36.91% for three of the four strategies, while Pref shows a slight increase for $\geq$ 60% malleability—an anomaly unique to this workload. Job makespan (Fig. 9b) follows a similar pattern: only KeepPref achieves consistent improvements (up to 16.3%), while the remaining strategies *degrade* performance by up to 60.85%.

Job wait time (Fig. 9c) decreases by up 99.98% for all strategies except KeepPref, which achieves only a 16.53% reduction. This suggests limited adaptability of KeepPref to the workload's heterogeneity. Node utilization (Fig. 9d) further confirms this divergence. KeepPref slightly increases utilization (72.67% to 76.26%), whereas other strategies exhibit minor drops (up to 3.82%).

Figures 9e and 9f show expand and shrink operations per job, respectively. Expand operations remain stable across all malleability proportions, with KeepPref maintaining 6 expand operations per job. Shrink operations also vary little, but KeepPref consistently triggers about 50% fewer shrink operations than the other strategies, reflecting its more conservative reallocation policy.

3.5 Cross-Workload Summary

To enable meaningful comparisons across workloads with differing timeframes, Table 3 reports job submission rates in *jobs per hour*. Among the four supercomputers, the Theta workload exhibits the lowest job submission rate, reflecting a workload dominated by fewer, longer-running jobs with higher node requirements. In contrast, the Eagle workload consists of many short, single-node jobs, yet having a moderate job submission rate, which explains its persistently low node utilization. The Haswell and KNL workloads show both high job submission rates and the most consistent improvements across all evaluation metrics.

Although this work primarily aims to evaluate the impact of malleability on real workloads, we also propose KeepPref, a novel strategy that preserves each job's number of preferred nodes where feasible. The differences observed among strategies yield valuable insights into malleable scheduling behavior.

EASY-Backfill serves as the rigid baseline and, as expected, performs worst in malleable settings. The three malleable strategies (Avg, Min, and Pref) differ in how they redistribute nodes: either based on average, minimum, or preferred number of nodes. In contrast, KeepPref applies a more conservative approach, shrinking only when necessary and prioritizing stability in resource allocation.

Across all workloads except Theta, malleability results in substantial gains in job turnaround time, job wait time, job makespan, and node utilization. While KeepPref occasionally shows slightly higher job wait times, these remain within acceptable limits for production systems. Notably, KeepPref performs best on Theta, which features a diverse job mix, while Pref consistently triggers the fewest shrink and expand operations.

In summary, three key findings emerge: (1) even modest malleability proportions (e.g., 20%) deliver notable improvements; (2) workload characteristics strongly impact the effectiveness of the job scheduling strategy; and (3) the consistent gains across varied configurations demonstrate benefits, given the applicability of malleability.

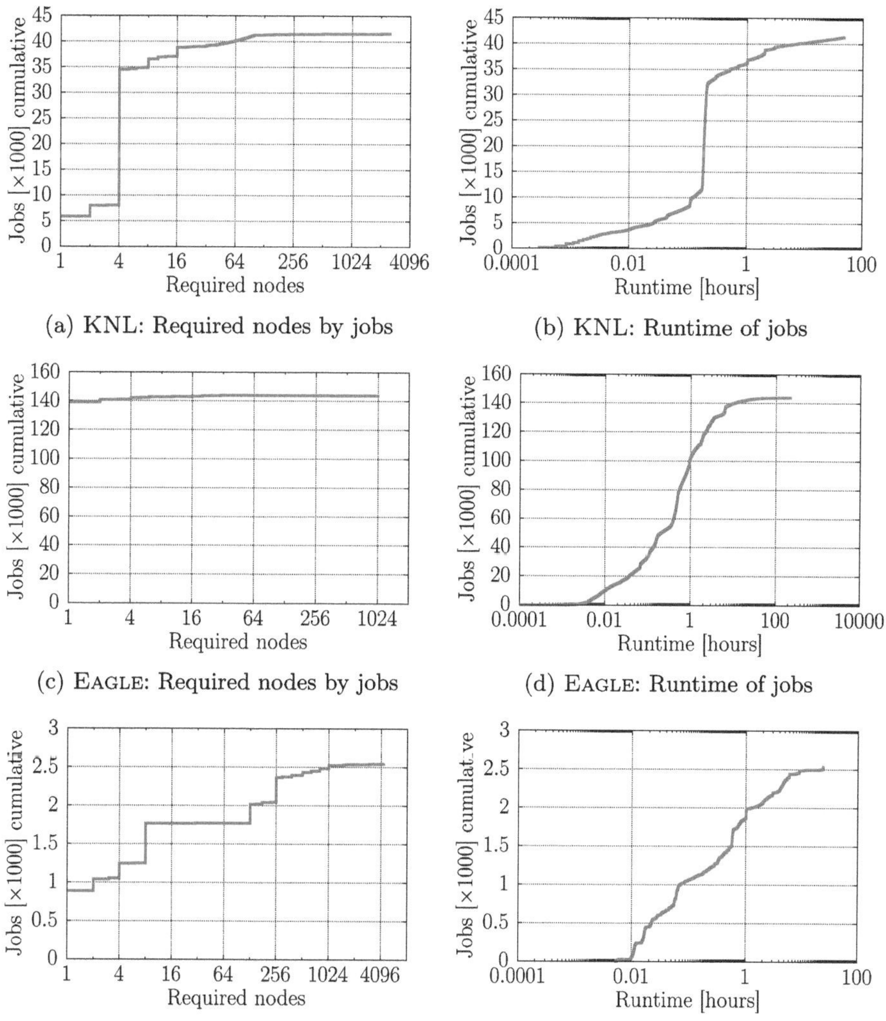

(a) KNL: Required nodes by jobs

(b) KNL: Runtime of jobs

(c) EAGLE: Required nodes by jobs

(d) EAGLE: Runtime of jobs

(e) THETA: Required nodes by jobs

(f) THETA: Runtime of jobs

Fig. 5. Distribution of job sizes and runtimes. KNL: Most jobs use 4 or fewer nodes and run under 1,000 s. EAGLE: Jobs are nearly all single-node and short-lived. THETA: More even distribution, with peaks at 1, 8, and 256 nodes.

Table 3. Job submission rates in *jobs per hour*

Dataset	HASWELL	KNL	EAGLE	THETA
Job submission rate [jobs/hour]	235.49	340.36	214.03	3.79

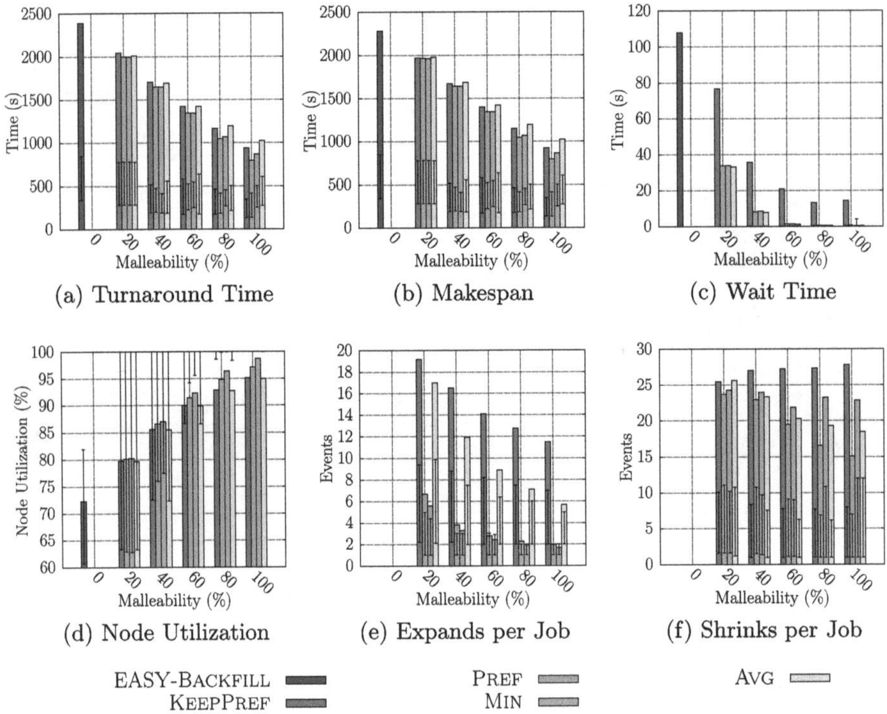

Fig. 6. HASWELL: Simulation results with IQR error bars

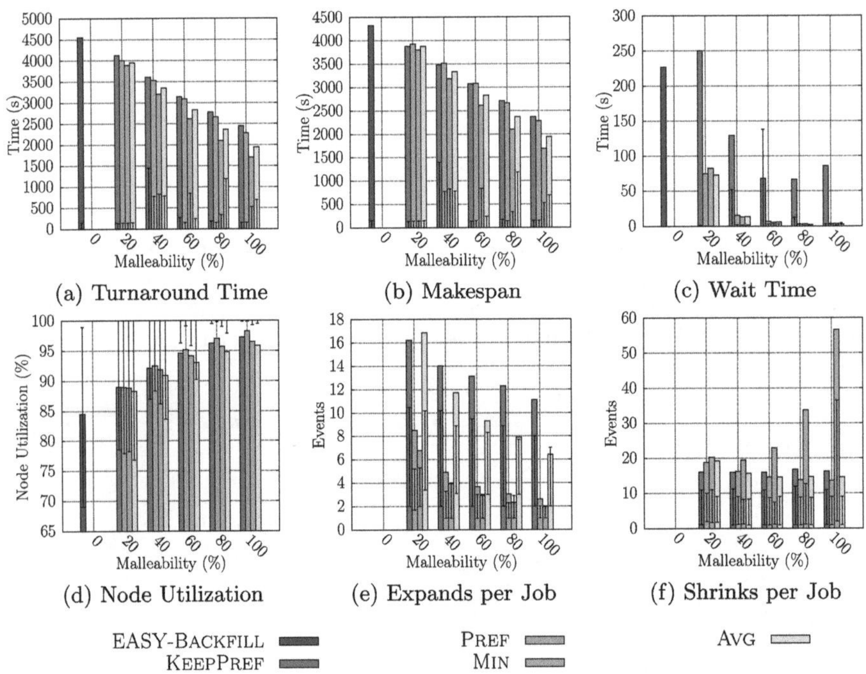

Fig. 7. KNL: Simulation results with IQR error bars

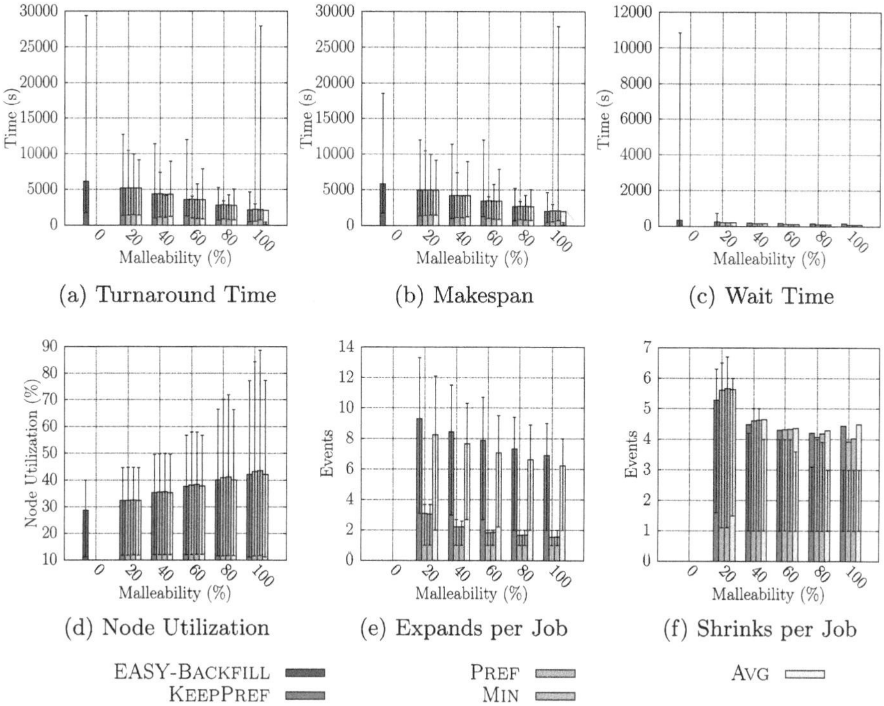

Fig. 8. EAGLE: Simulation results with IQR error bars

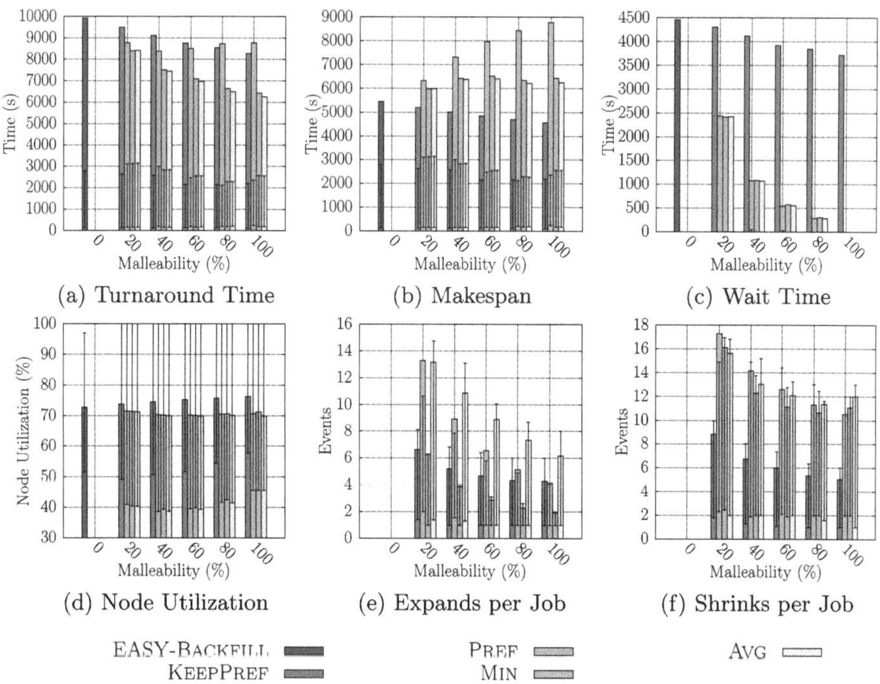

Fig. 9. THETA: Simulation results with IQR error bars

4 Limitations

Simulating the impact of malleability in real HPC clusters remains inherently challenging due to the complexity of modeling workloads, system architectures, and scheduling behavior. While our simulations reveal clear trends, several limitations should be addressed in future work to further enhance accuracy.

First, more comprehensive and longer-duration workload traces would improve simulation fidelity and support stronger generalizations. Our current simulations do not account for data movement or I/O, which is a notable omission, as such phases can significantly limit scheduling flexibility.

As GPUs are now widespread in modern HPC architectures, supporting heterogeneous workloads that use both CPUs and GPUs is a critical next step. This study focuses solely on CPU-based workloads.

Additionally, the transformation of rigid into malleable jobs was based on a heuristic model. Developing a systematic, empirically grounded method for this conversion would increase the realism and generalizability of simulation results.

The M100 dataset [4] from the Marconi100 supercomputer provides hundreds of performance and sensor data, offering strong potential for future enhancements such as phase-based workload modeling and improved performance profiling.

Furthermore, schedulers could target consistent node utilization levels to enable selective node shutdowns for energy savings, maintenance, or workload-aware scaling. This aligns with the growing focus on sustainability and system availability in HPC infrastructure planning.

5 Related Work

Numerous studies have demonstrated the benefits of job malleability in HPC, e.g. [1,7,10,18]. Their findings align roughly with our results, particularly that even modest proportions of malleable jobs yield significant improvements.

In the following, we compare our work to that of Eberius *et al.* [7], who also use simulations to evaluate the impact of malleable jobs on the CORI workloads. However, the methodological approach differs in several respects. Notably, the rigid node utilization differs significantly, especially for the HASWELL workload. We merged split jobs and excluded shared-node jobs (see Sect. 2.2), which Eberius *et al.* appear not to do. After merging, the original 119,781 jobs were reduced to 110,555, while Eberius *et al.* reported 118,818. Their rigid simulations consistently demonstrate higher node utilization, frequently approaching 100%, likely due to unfiltered shared-node jobs.

Our approach differs in several additional aspects. We explicitly exclude warm-up and drain-down periods to avoid analytical artifacts and employ variable tick rates (1 s for HASWELL, 10 s for KNL) to balance simulation runtime and temporal resolution. We support fine-grained expand/shrink operations, while their malleable schedulers rely on doubling/halving the number of nodes, either conservatively (one change per tick) or aggressively (unlimited).

Despite methodological differences, the KNL results show consistency across both studies, with similar trends and utilization gains (35% at 100% malleability). This convergence—despite differing assumptions and implementations—underscores the robustness and practical value of malleability.

6 Conclusion

This work evaluated the impact of malleable jobs using real-world workload traces from HASWELL, KNL, EAGLE, and THETA. Each workload was preprocessed and simulated in both rigid and malleable configurations using ElastiSim. In addition to the rigid EASY-Backfill job scheduling strategy, we evaluated four malleable strategies, including a novel preference-nodes–preserving strategy.

Across all experiments, malleability consistently yielded substantial performance gains. With the best-performing scheduler for each supercomputer, job turnaround times improved by 37–67%, job makespan by 16–65%, job wait times by 73–99%, and node utilization by 5–52%. Although the extent of improvement varied with workload characteristics and scheduling strategy, significant benefits were already evident at low malleability ratios (e.g., 20%).

Overall, this work demonstrates the potential of malleability to enhance both resource efficiency and user experience.

References

1. Almaaitah, N.O., Singh, D.E., Özden, T., Carretero, J.: Performance-driven scheduling for malleable workloads. J. Supercomput. (2024). https://doi.org/10.1007/s11227-023-05882-0
2. Argonne Leadership Computing Facility (ALCF): Theta System. https://www.alcf.anl.gov/alcf-resources/theta
3. Argonne Leadership Computing Facility (ALCF): Theta Workload. https://reports.alcf.anl.gov/data/theta.html
4. BorgheAsi, A., et al.: M100 ExaData: a data collection campaign on the CINECA's Marconi100 Tier-0 supercomputer. Scientific Data (2023). https://doi.org/10.1038/s41597-023-02174-3
5. Downey, A.B.: A parallel workload model and its implications for processor allocation. In: Cluster Comput. (1998). https://doi.org/10.1023/A:1019077214124
6. Eberius, D.: elastic-sim. https://github.com/davideberius/elastic-sim
7. Eberius, D., Wasi-Ur-Rahman, M., Ozog, D.: Evaluating the potential of elastic jobs in HPC systems. In: Supercomputing (SC) Workshops (PMBS). ACM (2023). https://doi.org/10.1145/3624062.3624199
8. Feitelson, D.G., Rudolph, L.: Toward Convergence in Job Schedulers for Parallel Supercomputers. In: Job Scheduling Strategies for Parallel Processing (JSSPP). Springer (1996). https://doi.org/10.1007/BFb0022284
9. Iserte, S., Mayo, R., Quintana-Ortí, E.S., Peña, A.J.: DMRlib: Easy-Coding and Efficient Resource Management for Job Malleability. Transactions on Computers (TC) (2020). https://doi.org/10.1109/TC.2020.3022933

10. Lina, D.H., Ghafoor, S., Hines, T.: Scheduling of elastic message passing applications on HPC systems. In: Job Scheduling Strategies for Parallel Processing (JSSPP). Springer (2023). https://doi.org/10.1007/978-3-031-22698-4_9
11. MPI Forum: MPI: A Message-Passing Interface Standard Version 4.1. https://www.mpi-forum.org/docs/mpi-4.1/mpi41-report.pdf
12. National Energy Research Scientific Computing Center (NERSC): Cori System. https://web.archive.org/web/20231001013828/https://docs.nersc.gov/systems/cori/
13. National Renewable Energy Laboratory (NREL): Eagle System. https://web.archive.org/web/20221128214549/https://www.nrel.gov/hpc/eagle-system-configuration.html
14. National Renewable Energy Laboratory (NREL): Eagle Workload. https://catalog.data.gov/dataset/nrel-eagle-supercomputer-jobs
15. Özden, T., Beringer, T., Mazaheri, A., Fard, H.M., Wolf, F.: ElastiSim: a batch-system simulator for malleable workloads. In: International Conference on Parallel Processing (ICPP). ACM (2022). https://doi.org/10.1145/3545008.3545046
16. Posner, J., Bietendorf, N., Huber, D., Schreiber, M., Schulz, M.: Dynamic Resource Management: Comparison of Asynchronous Many-Task (AMT) and Dynamic Processes with PSets (DPP). In: WAMTA Springer (2025). https://doi.org/10.1007/978-3-031-97196-9_2
17. Posner, J., Fohry, C.: Transparent resource elasticity for task-based cluster environments with work stealing. In: International Conference on Parallel Processing (ICPP) Workshops (P2S2). ACM (2021). https://doi.org/10.1145/3458744.3473361
18. Posner, J., Hupfeld, F., Finnerty, P.: Enhancing supercomputer performance with malleable job scheduling strategies. In: Euro-Par Workshops (PECS). Springer (2023). https://doi.org/10.1007/978-3-031-48803-0_14
19. Wong, A.K., Goscinski, A.M.: Evaluating the EASY-backfill job scheduling of static workloads on clusters. In: CLUSTER (2007). https://doi.org/10.1109/CLUSTR.2007.4629218
20. Yoo, A.B., Jette, M.A., Grondona, M.: SLURM: simple linux utility for resource management. In: Feitelson, D., Rudolph, L., Schwiegelshohn, U. (eds.) JSSPP 2003. LNCS, vol. 2862, pp. 44–60. Springer, Heidelberg (2003). https://doi.org/10.1007/10968987_3

NUMA-Aware FIFO Scheduling: Optimizing Data Movement for the Montage Workflow

Aurelio Vivas(✉) and Harold Castro

Universidad de los Andes, Bogotá, Colombia
{aa.vivas,hcastro}@uniandes.edu.co

Abstract. High-performance computing systems are essential for efficient scientific workflow execution. However, integrating workflow scheduling algorithms with non-uniform memory access (NUMA) architectures remains largely unexplored. This work extends an existing FIFO scheduling algorithm by incorporating NUMA awareness to reduce data movement. The approach leverages a runtime system that uses the Portable Hardware Locality (hwloc) library to map memory topology and collect task execution metadata, such as core and memory locality, which the scheduler uses to make NUMA- and data locality-aware decisions. The proposed scheduler achieved 64.72%, 65.79%, and 70.17% local read accesses for the 619-, 310-, and 58-task Montage workflows, respectively, improving average task read times and balancing the distribution of tasks, data, and memory accesses. These results demonstrate the effectiveness of the strategy, particularly for larger workflows.

Keywords: Scheduling · Algorithm · Workflow · Runtime · NUMA

1 Introduction

Scientific workflow scheduling has largely targeted uniform memory access (UMA) systems, such as cloud virtual machines [22]. However, modern HPC platforms increasingly rely on non-uniform memory access (NUMA) architectures, where memory access latency depends on the proximity between cores and memory regions [15]. This architecture requires schedulers to consider core and data locality not only across the distributed infrastructure but also within individual computing nodes.

Contribution. This work extends a traditional FIFO scheduling algorithm by incorporating NUMA awareness to mitigate the impact of data movement on the performance of data-intensive workflows. First, it is shown that NUMA memory architectures significantly affect the behavior of conventional, non-NUMA-aware FIFO scheduling. Then, the benefits of the NUMA-aware extension are quantified across several key metrics: (a) workflow execution time (distinct from makespan), (b) data access performance, and (c) load balancing of tasks and memory accesses across NUMA domains.

K. Brown et al. (Eds.): CARLA 2025, CCIS 2750, pp. 19–33, 2026.
https://doi.org/10.1007/978-3-032-24923-4_2

Organization of This Work. Sect. 2 reviews related work on scheduling algorithms that optimize data movement in scientific workflows executed on NUMA memory architectures. Section 3 describes the methodology, including the workflow and computing system models, as well as the evaluation strategy for the proposed scheduling algorithm. Section 4 presents the experimental results assessing the performance of this algorithm. Section 5 discusses the findings and compares them with related work. Finally, Sect. 6 provides concluding remarks and outlines directions for future work.

2 Related Work

While many studies address data movement in scientific workflows through scheduling algorithms for diverse environments, they largely overlook the specific challenges posed by NUMA memory architectures. Most studies focus on cloud environments [4,12,16,17], workstations [20], and clusters [6,19] [2,11,14], with fewer works targeting HPC systems [7,18]. These approaches often optimize data movement through workflow partitioning and task clustering [22], but rarely address the characteristics of NUMA memory architectures [1]. While some related studies do consider NUMA, such as those by Amela et al. and Drebes et al., they target numerical applications whose data access patterns and computation granularity differ substantially from those in scientific workflows. Nevertheless, we describe these studies because, despite addressing different application domains, scientific workflows and numerical parallel applications, they share methodological aspects relevant to our approach.

Amela et al. (2017) [1] extended the PyCOMPSs task-based programming model to support multi-threaded tasks in numerical libraries, such as MKL, with three scheduling strategies: a data locality scheduler, a FIFOData scheduler, and a NUMA-aware task allocation mechanism. The data locality scheduler scores each task based on the amount (in bytes) of its input data residing on a specific computing node. It prioritizes and assigns tasks with the most locally available data to the node that holds it. The FIFOData scheduler offers an alternative task prioritization strategy. It prioritizes tasks that share dependencies with the most recently completed task, scheduling them immediately in first-in-first-out (FIFO) order, otherwise defaulting to the data locality policy. The NUMA-aware strategy minimizes cross-socket communication among the threads of a multi-threaded task by binding those threads to a particular NUMA node.

Drebes et al. (2014) [5] extended an existing random work-stealing algorithm with three key mechanisms: work-pushing, dependence-aware data allocation, and topology-aware work stealing. The work-pushing mechanism aims to improve data locality for read accesses. When a task's dependencies are met, it is first added to the deque of the worker that resolved the last dependency. An attempt is then made to transfer this task to the MPSC FIFO queue of another worker on the NUMA node that holds the task's input buffer. The MPSC FIFO is drained by moving its back element to the worker's local deque. The dependence-aware data allocation mechanism focuses on improving the locality of write accesses. The NUMA node for an output buffer is selected based on the largest data contribution from its producer (predecessor) tasks. Task buffers are logically allocated before all producer tasks execute, but the actual physical memory pages are only committed upon the first write operation (copy-on-write), typically triggered by the initial producer task, aiming to allocate physical pages close to the primary data producers. The topology-aware work-stealing mechanism prioritizes stealing tasks from cores that are topologically close to the thief.

Our FIFO scheduling algorithm adopts similar concepts to the data locality scheduler proposed by Amela et al. [1], such as data locality score computation, task prioritization, and node selection, but there are significant methodological distinctions: *Computing System Model*: Their approach is designed for scheduling in HPC systems with multiple computing nodes. In contrast, our work focuses on scheduling across multiple NUMA nodes within a single HPC system computing node. This reflects a difference in granularity for data locality tracking and resource management. *Workflow Model*: They consider workflows composed of multi-threaded tasks, primarily targeting numerical applications. Our work, however, deals with workflows consisting of single-threaded tasks. *Optimization Objectives*: Their primary optimization goal is to minimize cross-socket communication among the threads of a single task, aiming to indirectly improve numerical execution performance in terms of FLOPs. In contrast, our work directly quantifies data access performance and its impact on makespan, providing a more direct measure of data locality effects on NUMA systems.

Our work also shares methodological similarities with Drebes et al. [5], including workflow awareness through the utilization of producers' communication payload information for buffer allocation, data locality awareness by pushing tasks to nodes where their data resides, NUMA awareness by prioritizing task stealing from neighboring cores based on memory topology, and a focus on measuring and improving data access performance. However, key differences exist in the workflow model. Their model assumes a single buffer for all writing predecessors and successors (consumers) reading from single locations, implying a centralized data location. In contrast, our model allows predecessors to write to different NUMA domains and successors to read from various ones. This reflects a distributed data access pattern in which producers write data locally, while consumers gather it from multiple locations.

3 Methodology

This section describes the workflow and computing system model, the proposed scheduling algorithm, and the evaluation methodology.

3.1 Workflow

The workflow is represented as a directed acyclic graph (DAG) $G = (V, E)$, where $V = \{v_1, v_2, \ldots, v_n\}$ is the set of tasks and $E \subset V \times V$ is the set of directed edges representing data dependencies between tasks. Each task $v_i \in V$ is characterized by a fixed computational cost, defined as the number of double-precision floating-point operations required for its execution. Each edge $(v_i, v_j) \in E$ corresponds to a data item produced by task v_i and consumed by task v_j, with its size denoted as $d_{i,j}$ bytes. This formulation implies that each task produces a distinct data item for each of its successors. At the start of each task's execution, all its input data items $(v_k, v_i) \in E$ must be present in memory, where they are consumed and then deallocated. The task then generates its output data items $(v_i, v_j) \in E$, which are written to memory for consumption by its successors. This strict data handling rule ensures that no task simultaneously holds both its input and output data in memory, aligning with the data flow constraints defined in [13].

3.2 Machine

The target computing system follows a non-uniform memory access (NUMA) architecture, consisting of P homogeneous physical cores, organized into M NUMA nodes. Each node N_m (for $m = 1, \ldots, M$) contains a set of cores and a dedicated local memory region M_m with high-bandwidth, low-latency access for its resident cores. The memory model assumes direct main memory access, ignoring intermediate caches. Each core $c_p \in N_m$ accesses data items from its local memory with latency L_m and bandwidth B_m. If a core $c_p \in N_m$ needs to access a data item $d_{i,j}$ located in a remote node N_n (where $m \neq n$), the access incurs a higher latency $L_{m,n}$ and is constrained by the interconnect bandwidth $B_{m,n}$ linking the nodes.

3.3 Algorithm

A FIFO queue manages ready tasks. When a task releases multiple successors, the newly released tasks are ordered using a level-order traversal of the task graph. Each of these tasks is then assigned a data locality score, defined as the total volume (in bytes) of its input data across all NUMA nodes. This score is used to prioritize the newly released tasks, which are inserted at the end of the queue without altering the order of existing tasks. Level-order traversal is preserved when tasks at the same graph level have identical locality scores. The task at the front of the queue is scheduled on the NUMA node that holds the largest share of its input data. When scores are equal, NUMA node priorities are applied and rotated to ensure balanced task distribution across nodes.

3.4 nFlows

The NUMA-Aware Workflow Execution Runtime System (nFlows) [21] was employed to evaluate the proposed scheduling algorithm. The system uses `pthreads` to enable asynchronous task execution and binding to specific cores, while `hwloc` is leveraged to monitor task placement and data locality across

NUMA nodes. Tasks are executed non-preemptively, with their behavior emulated as follows: compute-intensive operations are modeled using fused multiply-add (FMA) instructions, data writes with `memset`, and data reads by sequentially accessing a buffer byte-by-byte in a `for` loop.

3.5 Experiment

This section describes the experimental setup, including the system configuration, workloads, tests, and parameters used to evaluate the proposed scheduling algorithm's performance.

System. Experiments were conducted on the Chameleon Cloud testbed [9] using a single node from an HPC system. This node comprises two sockets, each housing a multi-core Intel® Xeon® Gold 6240R CPU @ 2.40 GHz (24 cores, 2 threads per core). In this configuration, each socket corresponds to a distinct NUMA node, each equipped with 93 GB of main memory and a three-level cache hierarchy, including a 36 MB L3 cache. The latency and bandwidth matrices were measured using the Intel® Memory Latency Checker (v3.11). On average, local memory access exhibits a latency of 71.2ns and a bandwidth of 121,431.6 MB/s, while remote access incurs an average latency of 135.95ns and a bandwidth of 34,397 MB/s.

Workloads. The Montage workflow was selected to evaluate the proposed scheduling strategy, as it has been extensively studied and characterized in the literature [3,8,22]. Montage captures all basic workflow data movement structures, including process, pipeline, data distribution, data aggregation, and data redistribution [3]. Six real execution traces were considered: 2mass-025d-001 (619 tasks), dss-10d-001 (472 tasks), 2mass-015d-001 (310 tasks), dss-075d-001 (178 tasks), 2mass-01d-001 (103 tasks), and dss-05d-001 (58 tasks). The variation in task count directly reflects the input dataset size. Larger datasets generate more tasks, which result in increasingly complex dependency structures and higher communication demands. Parallel dependencies were consolidated following the dataflow model. To isolate communication effects, the compute payload of all tasks was fixed to 1 GFLOP, ensuring performance variations (e.g., makespan) could be attributed primarily to data movement efficiency.

For each workflow trace, communication payloads were scaled across three configurations: Constant Set (all payloads fixed at 40 MB), Small Set (4050 MB), and Large Set (40100 MB). A minimum payload size of 40 MB, larger than the L3 cache, was enforced to target main memory rather than cache-level effects, facilitating generalization to distributed systems where non-uniform memory access is also present. For the Small and Large sets, payload sizes were adjusted to fit the defined ranges while preserving the original statistical distribution. This preserved the characteristics of real workflows while enabling controlled evaluation of the scheduling strategy under varying communication demands.

Tests. The evaluation considered four configurations of the FIFO scheduling algorithm: **M**, non-NUMA-aware operation across multiple NUMA domains; **MA**, NUMA-aware operation across multiple NUMA domains; **SL**, single NUMA domain execution with only local memory access (best case); and **SR**, single NUMA domain execution with forced remote memory access (worst case). The primary comparison focuses on **M** (baseline) and **MA** (NUMA-aware extension), while **SL** and **SR** serve as control scenarios representing performance bounds. These configurations were evaluated under the workloads described in Sect. 3.5, considering different levels of core availability: 8, 16, and 24 cores (corresponding to 4, 8, and 12 cores per NUMA domain, respectively).

Parameters. (i) *Processor-memory interaction*: Data sizes were chosen to exceed the L3 cache capacity, preventing data caching effects. (ii) *Exclusive execution on physical cores*: Hyper-threading and core migrations were disabled. (iii) *NUMA balancing control*: Disabled to prevent data page migration during read operations, allowing for precise tracking of data locality. (iv) *NUMA data spreading*: The maximum resident data size was kept smaller than the NUMA node memory capacity to avoid page spreading across nodes. (v) *Hardware and compiler prefetching*: Both hardware prefetchers and compiler prefetching optimizations were disabled to eliminate prefetch-induced variability in read accesses and target memory access performance. (vi) *Thread memory binding policy*: The first-touch policy was used, binding memory pages to the NUMA node where the thread executing a workflow task first accesses them. This policy ensures that all write, buffer, and data allocation operations occur locally.

4 Results

The results are organized into six analyses: makespan distribution, impact of NUMA architecture, NUMA-aware (MA) vs. non-aware scheduling (M), workflow execution time (distinct from makespan), data access performance, and balance of tasks, data, and memory accesses. The first three analyses consider the full set of experiments, including all FIFO scheduling configurations (M, MA, SL, SR), all workflow sizes (619, 472, 310, 178, and 58 tasks), communication payloads (constant, small, and large), and core availability scenarios (8, 16, and 24 cores). The remaining three analyses focus on the M (baseline) and MA (NUMA-aware extension) configurations, using a fixed workflow size (619 tasks) and core availability of 24 cores.

4.1 Makespan Distribution

Figure 1 shows the makespan distribution across all experiments. As the number of cores increases, the makespan consistently decreases, with a more pronounced reduction observed when scaling from 8 to 16 cores compared to the smaller gain from 16 to 24 cores. This diminishing return indicates increasing memory contention caused by higher parallelism and the resulting surge in concurrent memory accesses. Among the evaluated strategies, SL consistently achieves the lowest makespan. However, its strict locality constraints can exacerbate memory contention at higher core counts. A similar issue arises with SR, which enforces strict remote memory access. For workflows with constant and small communication payloads, maximum makespan values remain relatively close across strategies. This pattern suggests that NUMA-aware strategies provide limited performance gains under low communication demands, but become increasingly beneficial as communication costs grow. In contrast, for large communication payloads, the differences become more pronounced. In this case, a clear ordering emerges across all core counts: SL, MA, M, and SR, when ranked from lowest to highest maximum makespan.

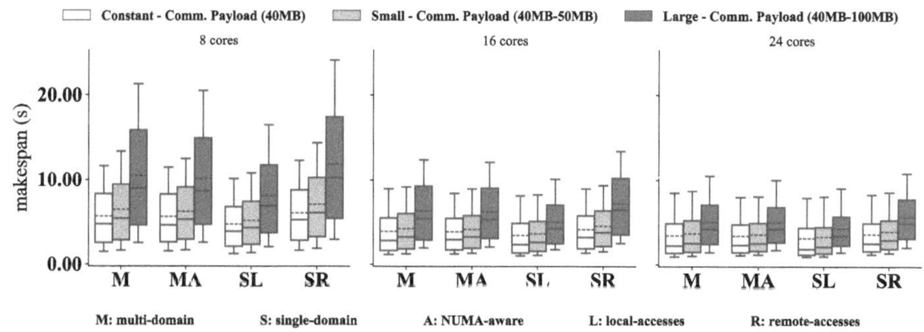

Fig. 1. Makespan: median (solid line) and average (dotted line). Error bars represent the minimum and maximum values across six workflows (58, 103, 178, 310, 472, and 619 tasks).

4.2 Impact of NUMA Memory Architecture

Figures 2 and 3 report relative makespan, [M/SL] and [MA/SL], across workflow instances with 58, 103, 178, 310, 472, and 619 tasks, for the constant, small, and large workflow sets as the number of cores increases. A solid purple line at 1 denotes the threshold of no impact, representing cases where the evaluated configuration performs equivalently to the baseline. A red dotted line highlights the workflow instance with the highest observed performance impact relative to SL, while a green dotted line marks the instance with the lowest impact.

As the core count increases, both M and MA configurations exhibit a reduction in their highest and lowest observed performance impacts relative to the SL baseline, as shown in Figs. 2 and 3, respectively. This trend indicates that performance differences diminish at higher levels of parallelism. Notably, MA consistently demonstrates a lower maximum impact than M, with reductions of

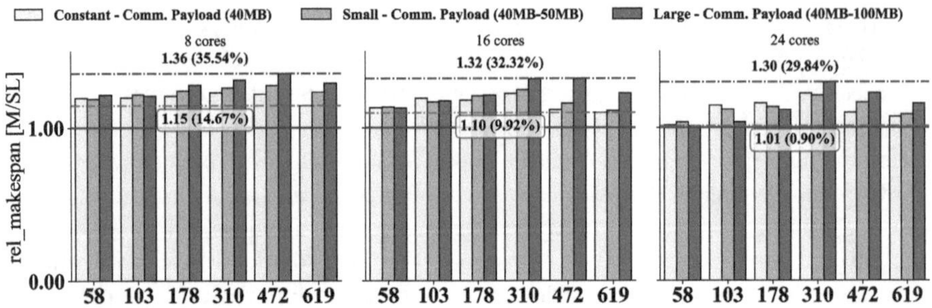

Fig. 2. NUMA Impact [M/SL].

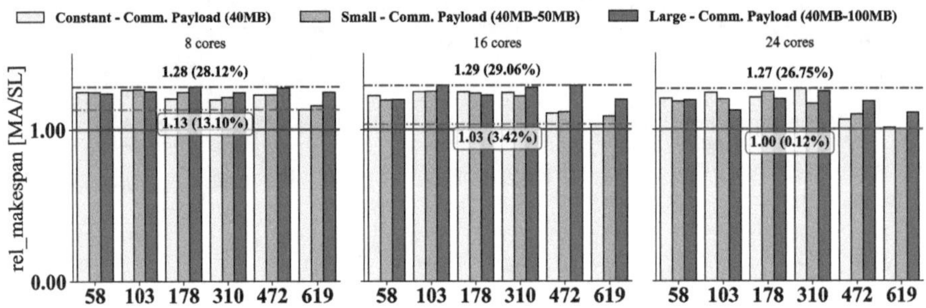

Fig. 3. NUMA Impact [MA/SL].

7.42%, 3.26%, and 3.09% at 8, 16, and 24 cores, respectively. At 24 cores, M achieves equivalent performance to SL for the 58-task workflow instance, while MA does so for the 619-task instance. For the 58-instance, M benefits from memory locality by scheduling tasks predominantly on the first NUMA node, allowing M to achieve performance nearly identical to SL, which enforces strict local memory usage. In summary, M generally shows lower performance impact than MA in smaller workflow instances (58, 103, 178 tasks), exhibits similar impact in the 310-task instance, and is outperformed by MA in larger workflows (472 and 616 tasks), where load balancing across NUMA nodes becomes more beneficial.

4.3 NUMA-Aware (MA) vs Non-aware Scheduling (M)

Figure 4 presents the speedup of M relative to MA [M/MA]. MA consistently achieves higher performance than M in large workflow instances (310, 472, and 619 tasks), whereas M outperforms MA in smaller instances. This trend is consistent with the observations reported in Sect. 4.2. Notably, for the 58-task instance at 24 cores, the speedup is negative, indicating that MA is 15.62% slower than M. Equivalently, MA achieves only 84% of M's performance in this scenario. In other words, the reciprocal of 0.84 (i.e., $\frac{1}{0.84} \times 100 \approx 19\%$) shows that M is approximately 19% faster than MA for this particular workflow instance.

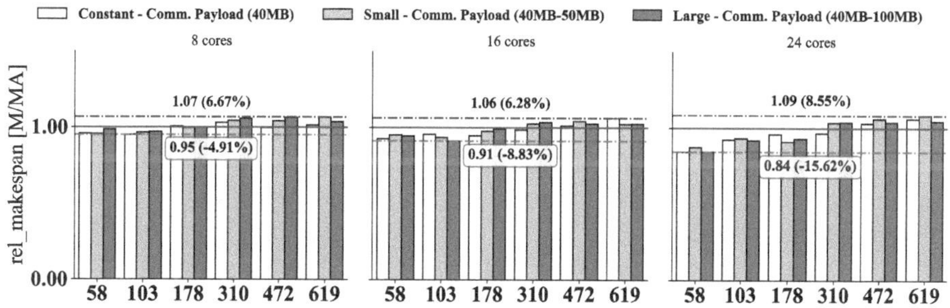

Fig. 4. Speedup [M/MA].

4.4 Workflow Execution Time

Figure 5 breaks down the execution time for the 619-task Montage workflow, showing how it's distributed among compute, read (local and remote), and write operations. We have specifically focused on this workflow, as it demonstrated the most representative and relevant speedup in MA configuration of FIFO (see Sect. 4.3). The total execution time is calculated as the sum of all 619 individual task durations. Each task's duration encompasses its compute, read, and write times. It's assumed that read and write operations within a task occur sequentially, allowing for a precise analysis of how changes in these individual components affect the overall sum.

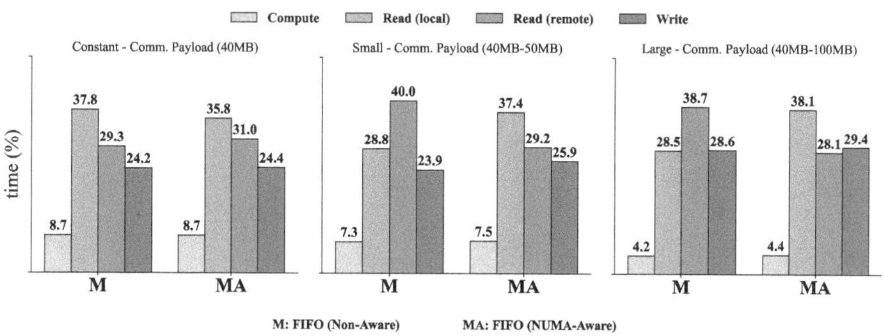

Fig. 5. Time distribution across read (remote/local), write, and compute.

As expected, compute times are similar across both M and MA configurations, since all workflow tasks involve a fixed compute payload of 1 GFLOP. Write operations are also consistent and are expected to be approximately twice as fast as reads due to their strictly local nature, ensured by the first-touch memory policy, and the presence of write buffers (see Sect. 3.5). Read operations dominate total execution time. This is due to the large communication payloads, the variability in read locality (local vs. remote), and the explicit disabling of hardware and software prefetchers to expose raw memory access performance (see Sect. 3.5). These factors highlight the data-intensive nature of the workflow.

The communication payload strongly influences the time spent on local and remote read operations within the workflow. With a constant 40MB payload for all dependencies, M and MA show similar proportions of local and remote read times, differing by less than 2%. This is attributed to the highly parallel structure of the Montage workflow at the first (mProject) and second (mDiffFit) levels, along with the scheduling behavior of both strategies. Under constant payloads, M assigns tasks in a round-robin manner across all cores. Since tasks within the same level have identical locality scores, MA behaves similarly. In contrast, with varying payloads, MA leverages these scores to improve data locality and significantly outperforms M.

4.5 Data Access Performance

Figures 6 and 7 illustrate the workflow makespan and the duration of the critical read path, respectively, for the 619-task Montage workflow executed on 24 cores, comparing the MA and M configurations of the FIFO scheduler. The critical read path is defined as the path, considering only read operations, with the longest cumulative duration. As this path may vary across experimental runs, the figures report the average duration. This metric is used to estimate the impact of the data locality strategy on the makespan, based on the strong correlation observed between the workflow makespan and the traditional critical path. This correlation holds in our case, as task compute times and write operations exhibit constant performance, while significant variations can be attributed to read performance, which may vary depending on the scheduling algorithm configuration and the workflow communication payloads (see Sect. 4.4).

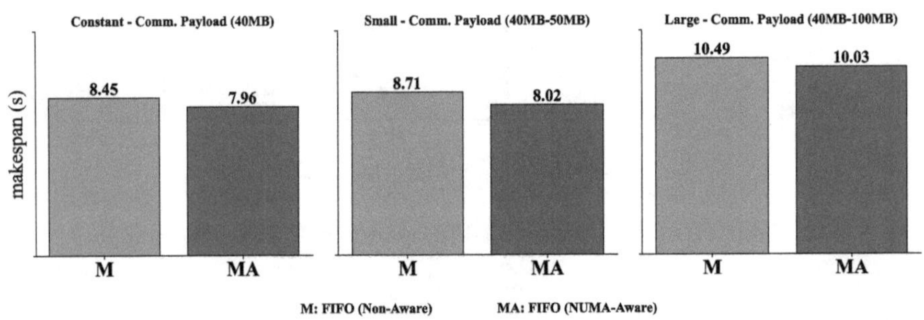

Fig. 6. Workflow makespan.

Table 1 shows that the MA configuration reduces total makespan by 0.49, 0.69, and 0.46 s (5.80%, 7.92%, and 4.36%) for constant, small, and large payloads, respectively, compared to M. However, it increases the duration of the

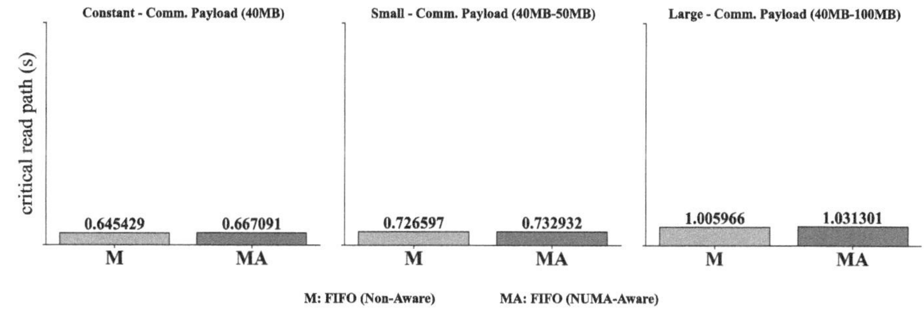

Fig. 7. Critical read path duration.

critical read path (CRP) by 4.42%, 0.92%, and 7.63% in the same scenarios. Although MA improves overall read locality across tasks, as demonstrated in Sect. 4.4, the critical read path is particularly sensitive to the longest individual data access operation. If this dominant access is remote, the benefits of improved locality across other tasks' dependencies are effectively diminished.

Table 1. Contribution of NUMA-aware scheduling in the workflow makespan.

	Makespan (M) [s]			Critical Read Path (CRP) [s]			Contribution CRP to M [%]
Comm. Payload	M	MA	M-MA	M	MA	M-MA	CRP.(M-MA) / M.(M-MA) [%]
Constant	8,45	7,96	0,49	0,645429	0,667091	-0,021662	-4,420816
Small	8,71	8,02	0,69	0,726597	0,732932	-0,006335	-0,918116
Large	10,49	10,03	0,46	1,005966	1,041083	-0,035117	-7,634130

4.6 Balance of Tasks, Data, and Memory Accesses

Figures 8, 9, and 10 compare M and MA in terms of task, data, and memory access distribution across NUMA domains for the 619-, 310-, and 58-task Montage workflows, respectively. These workflows represent MA's best-, equivalent-, and worst-performing cases relative to M (Fig. 4).

MA's performance gains stem mainly from its even distribution of tasks across NUMA nodes, enabled by the regular and symmetric structure of Montage. The first two workflow levels (mProject and mDiffFit) exhibit high parallelism. Tasks at the first level, being root tasks, receive identical locality scores. This results in balanced task placement across NUMA domains and ensures that their output data are placed locally due to the first-touch memory policy. Tasks in subsequent levels receive varied scores based on data distribution, and the symmetry in Montage.'s dependencies helps maintain an even spread across NUMA nodes. In contrast, M tends to concentrate tasks on the first NUMA node. While this may offer short-term locality benefits, it causes load imbalance

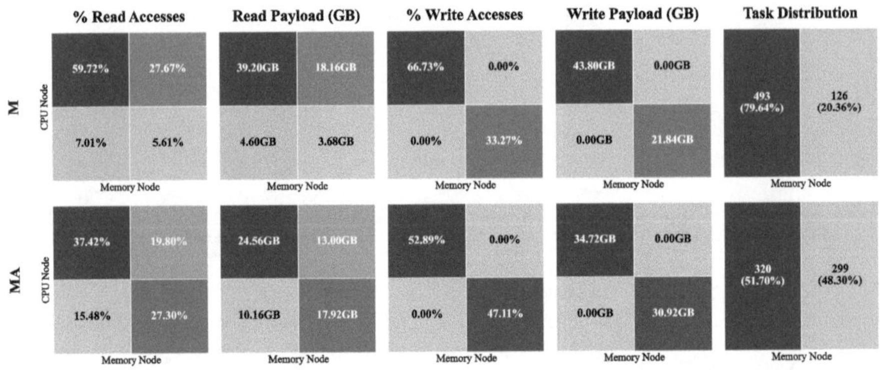

Fig. 8. Montage workflow with 619 tasks (MA's best-performing instance).

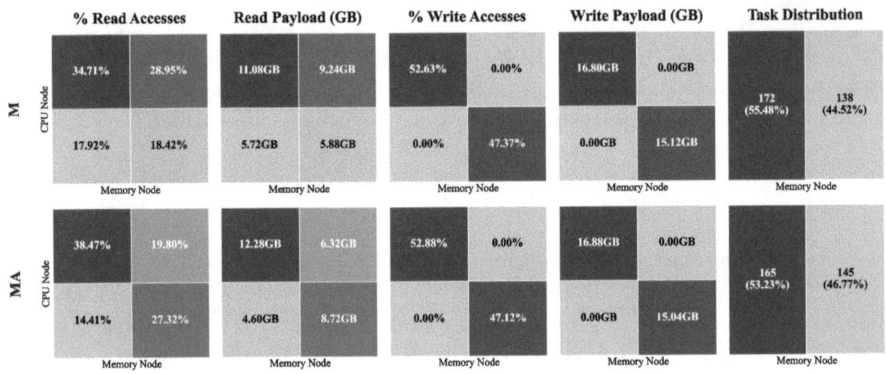

Fig. 9. Montage workflow with 310 tasks (MA's equivalent-performing instance).

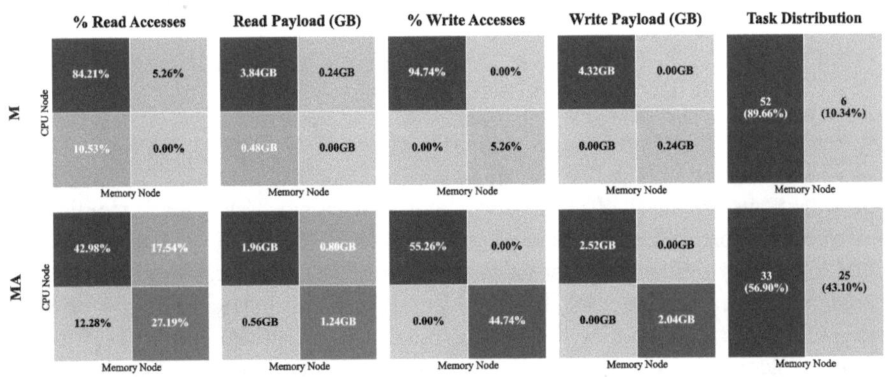

Fig. 10. Montage workflow with 58 tasks (MA's worst-performing instance).

and longer makespans, as M favors the first available core over the one with the earliest projected start time.

5 Discussion

The results highlight three key findings: (i) the symmetric and regular structure of the Montage workflow enables a balanced distribution of tasks, data, and memory accesses across NUMA domains, reducing contention and improving overall makespan; (ii) while NUMA-aware scheduling significantly improves the read access times of individual tasks, these improvements have limited impact on the total workflow makespan; and (iii) the NUMA-aware strategy performs best for workflows with more than 310 tasks regardless of communication payload (constant, small, or large), while smaller workflows tend to achieve better results with the non-NUMA-aware M strategy.

The regularity and symmetry of workflow structures enhance memory access locality when effectively leveraged. This observation is consistent with the findings of Drebes et al. [5], who showed that structured workflows such as Seidel and Bitonic benefit from topology-aware scheduling, achieving 92% and 66% local read/write accesses, respectively. In our case, the first-touch memory policy guarantees local writes, and our MA configuration achieves 64.72%, 65.79%, and 70.17% local read accesses for the 619-, 310-, and 58-task Montage workflows, respectively. A key contribution of our work, not addressed by Drebes et al., is the insight that workflow structural regularity facilitates balanced distribution of data and memory accesses, contributing not only to improved locality but also to load balancing across NUMA domains.

Although improvements in individual task read times have limited impact on overall makespan in highly parallel workflows, they offer significant advantages for workflows whose tasks access dependencies sequentially—similar to programs that read input files one after another rather than in parallel. In such cases, reducing remote read times directly lowers both task execution time and overall workflow makespan. Our approach achieves this by reducing the time spent on remote reads from 40% to 29.2%, and from 38.7% to 28.1% (see Sect. 4.4).

Finally, in workflows with fewer than 310 tasks, M benefits from concentrating task execution on the first NUMA node, providing short-term locality advantages. However, for workflows larger than 310 tasks, this causes notable load imbalance and longer makespans, making the MA strategy more effective in these cases.

In closing, although the proposed algorithm shows promising results, further validation is necessary. The current evaluation is limited to a system with only two NUMA nodes, which may restrict conclusions about scalability. Additionally, experiments were conducted on a single structured workflow (Montage); further analysis on both structured and unstructured workflows is needed to assess the generalizability of the approach.

6 Conclusions

This work presents a NUMA-aware extension to a FIFO scheduling algorithm designed to reduce data movement and improve scientific workflow execution on NUMA systems. Leveraging the hwloc library, the scheduler collects task and data locality information to guide informed task placement. Experiments with the Montage workflow on 24-core systems yielded local read access rates of 64.72%, 65.79%, and 70.17% for the 619-, 310-, and 58-task cases, respectively. These improvements stem from a more balanced distribution of tasks, data, and memory accesses across NUMA domains. While reductions in workflow makespan were modest, the approach demonstrates clear advantages for structured and larger workflows by preventing contention and avoiding the concentration of tasks and memory usage on a single NUMA node.

These results contribute to related research in several ways, including enabling in-memory workflow execution [10], reducing contention in NUMA architectures, and improving memory bandwidth utilization. Additionally, understanding data movement in NUMA systems becomes increasingly relevant as large-scale high-performance computing platforms introduce heterogeneous memory hierarchies, such as high-bandwidth memory and burst buffers. In this context, capturing and exploiting memory locality in workflow scheduling will be essential. Future work will address the limitations discussed, including broader validation across diverse workflows and NUMA configurations.

Acknowledgments. Results presented in this paper were obtained using the Chameleon testbed supported by the National Science Foundation.

References

1. Amela, R., Ramon-Cortes, C., Ejarque, J., Conejero, J., Badia, R.M.: Enabling python to execute efficiently in heterogeneous distributed infrastructures with pycompss. In: Proceedings of the 7th Workshop on Python for High-Performance and Scientific Computing, pp. 1–10 (2017)
2. Aniello, L., Baldoni, R., Querzoni, L.: Adaptive online scheduling in storm. In: Proceedings of the 7th ACM International Conference on Distributed Event-based Systems, pp. 207–218 (2013)
3. Bharathi, S., Chervenak, A., Deelman, E., Mehta, G., Su, M.H., Vahi, K.: Characterization of scientific workflows. In: 2008 Third Workshop on Workflows in Support of Large-scale Science, pp. 1–10. IEEE (2008)
4. Choi, J., Adufu, T., Kim, Y.: Data-locality aware scientific workflow scheduling methods in hpc cloud environments. Int. J. Parallel Prog. **45**, 1128–1141 (2017)
5. Drebes, A., Heydemann, K., Drach, N., Pop, A., Cohen, A.: Topology-aware and dependence-aware scheduling and memory allocation for task-parallel languages. ACM Trans. Architect. Code Optimizat. (TACO) **11**(3), 1–25 (2014)
6. Eskandari, L., Huang, Z., Eyers, D.: P-scheduler: adaptive hierarchical scheduling in apache storm. In: Proceedings of the Australasian Computer Science Week Multiconference, pp. 1–10 (2016)
7. Huang, M., Narayana, V.K., Simmler, H., Serres, O., El-Ghazawi, T.: Reconfiguration and communication-aware task scheduling for high-performance reconfigurable computing. ACM Tran. Reconfigurable Technol. Syst. (TRETS) **3**(4), 1–25 (2010)

8. Juve, G., Chervenak, A., Deelman, E., Bharathi, S., Mehta, G., Vahi, K.: Characterizing and profiling scientific workflows. Futur. Gener. Comput. Syst. **29**(3), 682–692 (2013)
9. Keahey, K., et al.: Lessons learned from the chameleon testbed. In: Proceedings of the 2020 USENIX Annual Technical Conference (USENIX ATC 2020). USENIX Association (July 2020)
10. Kulagina, S., Meyerhenke, H., Benoit, A.: Mapping large memory-constrained workflows onto heterogeneous platforms. In: Proceedings of the 53rd International Conference on Parallel Processing, pp. 305–316 (2024)
11. Li, B., Sun, D., Chau, V.L., Buyya, R.: A topology-aware scheduling strategy for distributed stream computing system. In: Xiang, W., Han, F., Phan, T.K. (eds) BROADNETS 2021. LNICST, vol. 413. Springer, Cham (2022). https://doi.org/10.1007/978-3-030-93479-8_8
12. Lin, J.W., Arul, J.M., Lin, C.Y.: Joint deadline-constrained and influence-aware design for allocating mapreduce jobs in cloud computing systems. Clust. Comput. **22**, 6963–6976 (2019)
13. Marchal, L., Nagy, H., Simon, B., Vivien, F.: Parallel scheduling of dags under memory constraints. In: 2018 IEEE International Parallel and Distributed Processing Symposium (IPDPS), pp. 204–213. IEEE (2018)
14. Pang, J., Wang, W., Zhang, Z.: Communication-efficient task scheduling for real-time distributed computing. In: 2021 13th International Conference on Wireless Communications and Signal Processing (WCSP), pp. 1–5. IEEE (2021)
15. Perdomo, D.A.R., Hernandez, E., Li, X.: Parallel computing strategies in wrf: The role of mpi, openmp, & numa. In: n: Guerrero, G., San Martín, J., Meneses, E., Barrios Hernández, C.J., Osthoff, C., Monsalve Diaz, J.M. (eds.) CARLA 2024. CCIS, vol. 2270. Springer, Cham.(2025). https://doi.org/10.1007/978-3-031-80084-9_21
16. Qi, T., Rodriguez, M.: A traffic and resource aware online storm scheduler. In: Proceedings of the 2021 Australasian Computer Science Week Multiconference, pp. 1–10 (2021)
17. Samandi, V., Tiňo, P., Bahsoon, R.: Duplication scheduling with bottom-up top-down recursive neural network. In: International Conference on Intelligent Data Engineering and Automated Learning, pp. 170–178. Springer (2022). https://doi.org/10.1007/978-3-031-80084-9_21
18. Selvitopi, O., Demirci, G.V., Turk, A., Aykanat, C.: Locality-aware and load-balanced static task scheduling for mapreduce. Futur. Gener. Comput. Syst. **90**, 49–61 (2019)
19. Tanaka, M., Tatebe, O.: Workflow scheduling to minimize data movement using multi-constraint graph partitioning. In: 2012 12th IEEE/ACM International Symposium on Cluster, Cloud and Grid Computing (ccgrid 2012), pp. 65–72. IEEE (2012)
20. Tang, J., Xu, M., Fu, S., Huang, K.: A scheduling optimization technique based on reuse in spark to defend against apt attack. Tsinghua Sci. Technol. **23**(5), 550–560 (2018)
21. Vivas, A.: Donaurelio/nflows: v4.6.1 (Aug 2025). https://doi.org/10.5281/zenodo.16749046
22. Vivas, A., Tchernykh, A., Castro, H.: Trends, approaches, and gaps in scientific workflow scheduling: a systematic review. IEEE Access (2024)

ACCLAIM: Accelerating Long Context LLM Inference on Heterogeneous Edge Platforms

Rakshith Jayanth[1(✉)], Yi Chien Lin[1], Souvik Kundu[2], Deepak A. Mathaikutty[2], and Viktor Prasanna[1]

[1] University of Southern California, Los Angeles, USA
{jayanthr,yichienl,prasanna}@usc.edu
[2] Intel Labs, Santa Clara, USA
{souvikk.kundu,deepak.a.mathaikutty}@intel.com

Abstract. With the growing deployment of Large Language Models (LLMs) on edge platforms, supporting long-context inference has become increasingly important. However, achieving low inference latency remains challenging due to high computational and data transfer demands, combined with limited compute and memory resources. In this work, we present ACCLAIM, a novel system designed for long-context inference on heterogeneous edge platforms. ACCLAIM addresses key challenges by: **(1)** segmenting the prefill stage to generate and access KV cache in chunks, reducing memory footprint; **(2)** leveraging the inherent sparsity in self-attention to lower computational complexity; and **(3)** performing offline profiling to determine optimal chunk size and generate an efficient load-balancing strategy across heterogeneous cores. These optimizations significantly reduce Time To First Token (TTFT). We evaluate ACCLAIM on two state-of-the-art heterogeneous platforms, showing up to 23× speedup in TTFT over standalone chunked prefill and up to 1.5× average speedup over state-of-the-art mapping algorithms.

Keywords: Edge Computing · Long Context LLM Inference · Heterogeneous Edge Platform

1 Introduction

Large Language Models (LLMs) have gained significant popularity in recent years for their exceptional performance across a wide range of natural language processing tasks. Recently, there has been growing interest in long-context inference, which is increasingly essential for applications [8] such as document summarization, conversational AI, and real-time decision making. While cloud-based solutions offer the computational resources needed for long-context LLM inference, they often incur high costs, limited offline accessibility, and potential privacy concerns. Enabling long-context inference on edge platforms addresses these limitations by ensuring offline access, preserving user privacy, and reducing

K. Brown et al. (Eds.): CARLA 2025, CCIS 2750, pp. 34–48, 2026.
https://doi.org/10.1007/978-3-032-24923-4_3

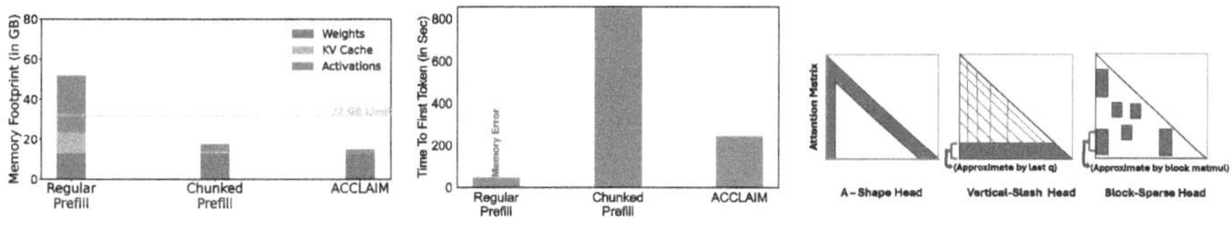

(a) (b) (c)

Fig. 1. (a) Estimated Memory Footprint (b) TTFT comparison [Model: Llama3.2-3B (FP-32), Platform: Intel Core Ultra 7 258V, Context Length: 16K] (c) Sparsity Patterns [7] in ACCLAIM

costs. Modern edge devices-such as Intel and AMD AIPCs [4]-are equipped with heterogeneous cores, enhancing their computational potential and making them well-suited for on-device LLM inference.

However, performing long-context LLM inference on edge platforms remains challenging due to the high computational demand and large memory footprint—requirements that exceed the limited compute and memory resources typically available on such devices. This challenge is most pronounced during the prefill stage, where the entire input prompt is processed, making it the most compute- and memory-intensive phase of inference. For instance, processing a 300K-token context with the LLaMA3-8B model on an NVIDIA A100 GPU can take up to 6 min [7] and require nearly 60 GB of memory. A similar trend is observed on edge platforms: for example, the LLaMA3.2-3B model, which is compatible with edge devices, takes nearly 4 min to process an 8K token input. Context lengths beyond 8K exceed the typical 32 GB memory limit on edge platforms, causing memory overflows and program crashes (Fig. 1b).

Challenges: In this work, we identify three challenges in accelerating long-context LLM inference on edge platforms. (1) **Large memory requirement of KV cache**: In LLMs, the KV cache is a memory optimization technique that stores key and value tensors from self-attention layers across decoding steps. Its size grows linearly with context length. For long-context inference on edge platforms, the KV cache storage can exceed system memory capacity, as illustrated in Fig. 1a. (2) **Quadratic complexity in Self-Attention**: Self-attention is central to LLMs, where each token interacts with all previous tokens to capture contextual dependencies. However, its computational complexity grows quadratically with context length [14], making long-context processing much more time-consuming than short prompts. (3) **Load balancing on a heterogeneous platform**: Optimizing performance on a heterogeneous system requires effective load balancing across diverse compute cores, each with varying compute capabilities. This makes load distribution non-trivial, necessitating careful mapping of computational tasks to the most suitable hardware to maximize performance.

Our Approach: To address the challenges of long-context LLM inference on edge platforms with heterogeneous compute cores, we propose ACCLAIM, a novel system that integrates efficient techniques for self-attention computation, KV cache management, and parallel execution. ACCLAIM performs *chunked* *prefill* [3] to address the memory footprint challenge. This approach segments the input and stores the computed KV cache of each segment on the Solid State Drive (SSD) and ensures that only the required segments of the cache are loaded into memory. This significantly reduces memory usage, enabling inference on edge systems with limited memory. To reduce the computational complexity of self-attention, ACCLAIM incorporates sparsity-aware attention. Prior work [7] has shown that attention matrices for long contexts are highly sparse, with sparsity patterns differing across attention heads and layers. By exploiting these patterns, ACCLAIM accelerates the prefill stage to lower Time To First Token (TTFT), as shown in Fig. 1b. Additionally, sparsity reduces memory overhead by minimizing the number of KV vectors retrieved from SSD (Fig. 1a). ACCLAIM also introduces a sparsity-guided mapping strategy. Attention heads are assigned to compute cores based on their sparsity patterns and the core's computational characteristics. For example, heads with unstructured sparsity—where values are irregularly distributed—could be mapped to CPUs, which are better suited for such irregular workloads than GPU [16]. In contrast, structured sparsity patterns could be mapped to GPUs, which excel at regular computation. Finally, ACCLAIM ensures efficient load balancing by using offline profiling to estimate the computational cost of executing attention heads on different cores. This profiling guides optimal workload distribution across heterogeneous hardware. It should be noted that the focus of ACCLAIM is to exploit sparsity in self-attention and not FFN sparsity. As context lengths increase, the compute bottleneck shifts from the FFN to self-attention, since the computational complexity of FFN grows linearly with context length, while self-attention scales quadratically. Our key contributions are:

- We propose ACCLAIM, a novel system for long-context LLM acceleration on edge heterogeneous platforms.
- We enable long-context LLM inference on edge devices using *chunked prefill*, which incrementally processes input to reduce memory footprint and overcome platform memory limits.
- Our system exploits the inherent sparsity in self-attention to greatly reduce the computation overhead and the memory footprint of the prefill stage.
- We design a profiler and load balancer that analyze the target edge platform to generate an efficient parallelization strategy for mapping operations to its compute cores.
- We conduct comprehensive experiments comparing our parallelization strategy with state-of-the-art mapping algorithms, demonstrating its optimality and achieving up to 1.5× speedup.

2 Background

2.1 Stages in LLM Inference

LLMs handle inference requests in two compute stages: the prefill stage and the decode stage. In the prefill stage, the model processes the full input sequence by

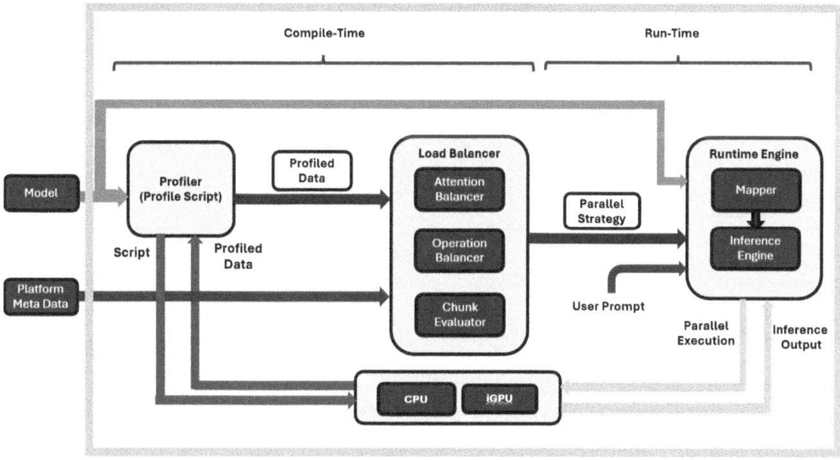

Fig. 2. System Overview of ACCLAIM

converting it into tokens, populating the Key-Value (KV) cache, and generating the first output token. The first step involves computing the token embeddings E(X), where X is the input token sequence. The second step involves generating the Key (K) and Value (V) caches, along with the Query matrix Q, as follows:

$$Q = W_Q.E(X), \quad K = W_K.E(X), \quad V = W_V.E(X) \tag{1}$$

The third step is to compute self-attention using Q and the complete KV cache. The computation of self-attention during LLM inference is done as follows:

$$A = Softmax(\frac{Q.K^T}{\sqrt{d}})V \tag{2}$$

The final step involves computing the Feed-Forward Network (FFN) and generating the first output token. As shown in Eq. 2, the prefill stage is computationally intensive, with self-attention having a complexity of O($T^2\,d$) where T is the input context length and d is the model dimension. Moreover, the KV cache incurs a space complexity of O(Td), growing linearly with the input length. In the decode stage, the model autoregressively generates tokens beyond the first one, appending new KV vectors to the cache at each step.

2.2 Sparsity in Self Attention

Prior work [7,17] on long-context inference has shown that self-attention exhibits inherent sparsity during the prefill stage. Here, sparsity refers to the observation that each token depends strongly on only a subset of the input tokens. These sparsity patterns can be categorized into three types [7]: A-shape, Vertical-Slash, and Block-Sparse, each capturing a unique dependency structure as shown in

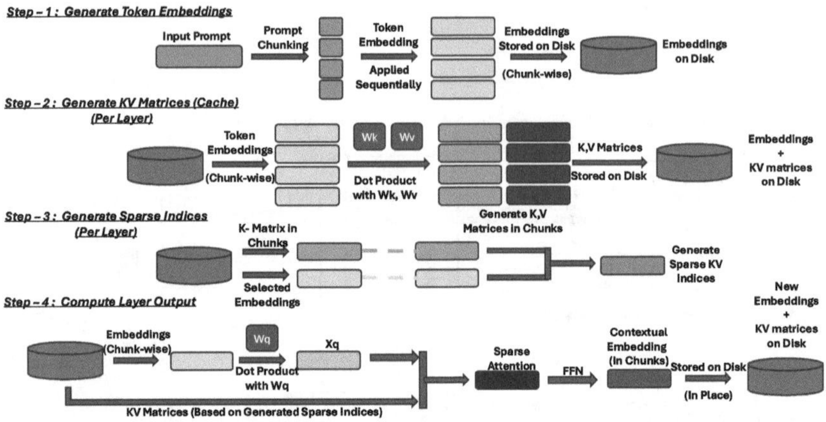

Fig. 3. Prefill Stage Workflow (With steps-2,3,4 repeating for each layer)

Fig. 1c. Moreover, in Multi-Head Attention (MHA), each head may adopt a different sparsity pattern. With sparsity, the self-attention equation is as follows:

$$A_{inter} = Softmax(\frac{sparse(Q.K^T, I)}{\sqrt{d}}) \tag{3}$$

$$A = sparse(A_{inter}.V, I) \tag{4}$$

Here, I denotes the list of sparse indices. Exploiting sparsity in self-attention not only reduces computation but also significantly lowers memory footprint, as only a subset of the KV cache corresponding to the sparse indices is needed—unlike standard self-attention, which requires the full KV cache.

3 System Workflow

3.1 Overall Workflow

Our system, ACCLAIM, enables long-context LLM inference on heterogeneous edge platforms, focusing on accelerating prefill stage, the most compute and memory-intensive stage. The workflow of ACCLAIM is shown in Fig. 2.

Overview of ACCLAIM: ACCLAIM addresses the three key challenges of the prefill stage outlined in Sect. 1: large memory footprint, computational intensity, and efficient load balancing across heterogeneous cores. It does so through three core components: the Profiler, the Load Balancer, and the Runtime Engine, which work together as shown in Fig. 2. The Profiler and Load Balancer are executed once per model-platform pair, with their execution time categorized as compilation time. In contrast, the Runtime Engine runs for each prompt, and its execution time is considered runtime.

Reduction in Memory Footprint Through Chunked Prefill: To reduce memory footprint, ACCLAIM employs chunked prefill, where the input context is divided into chunks, which are processed sequentially. This limits in-memory storage to the KV vectors and embeddings of the current chunk, while KV vectors from earlier chunks are offloaded to SSD. During self-attention, prior KV vectors are read in chunks as needed. A key aspect of this approach is determining the optimal chunk size, which is computed by the Profiler and Load Balancer. The Runtime Engine then uses this chunk size to process the input prompt.

Decrease in Computational Complexity Through Sparse Attention: To mitigate the computational complexity of self-attention, ACCLAIM employs sparse attention using the sparsity patterns proposed in [7]. These include A-shape, Vertical-Slash, and Block-Sparse patterns, as illustrated in Fig. 1c, which highlights the valid regions of the causal attention mask. Each attention head may adopt a distinct sparsity pattern. Through sparsity-aware self-attention, ACCLAIM significantly reduces computational complexity and lowers Time To First Token (TTFT). It also decreases memory footprint by requiring only a subset of KV vectors to be fetched from SSD. The Runtime Engine performs chunked prefill with sparsity-aware attention to optimize inference.

Achieve Efficient Load Balancing Through Heterogeneity-Aware Mapping: Efficient load balancing across the compute cores is a key performance factor on heterogeneous platforms. ACCLAIM achieves load balancing through Tensor Parallelism of Multi-Head self-attention (MHA) and the Feed Forward Network (FFN). Load balancing on a homogeneous system is trivial as the workload gets equally distributed across the compute cores. In contrast, load balancing is non-trivial in heterogeneous systems due to varying core characteristics. To achieve optimal load balancing, ACCLAIM maps MHA and FFN uniquely. ACCLAIM maps MHA by analyzing sparsity patterns across attention heads—if a pattern has affinity towards a specific core, the mapping accounts for relative core performance to redistribute heads. For FFN, the attention output is chunked and distributed across cores proportionally to their performance, with partial results aggregated using all-reduce. The Profiler evaluates relative core performance by measuring the latency of operations like matrix-matrix and matrix-vector multiplication, using sizes derived from model dimensions. The Profiler is also responsible for reporting the relative performance of the sparsity patterns across the compute cores. The Load Balancer considers all the values reported by the Profiler to generate an optimal mapping strategy. Since ACCLAIM accounts for all the key parameters in its mapping strategy, it aligns with Service Level Objective (SLO)-aware scheduling principles [12].

3.2 Profiler and Load Balancer

The Profiler is run once per model-platform pair and performs three key tasks. First, it measures the relative performance of compute cores by executing matrix and matrix-vector multiplications across dimensions based on input length and model size. Second, it evaluates sparsity pattern performance by running sparsity kernels across various input lengths. Third, it assesses the sparse kernel performance across different chunk sizes to identify the optimal chunk size, stopping at the point of memory overflow. All results are given to the Load Balancer, which, using this data, determines the optimal chunk size and generates an optimal mapping strategy across heterogeneous cores. We describe the algorithm of the Load-Balancer in Algorithm 1.

Mapping Strategy Based on Relative Performance: To generate the mapping strategy, the algorithm uses latency values for operations like matrix-matrix and matrix-vector multiplication, as reported by the Profiler. For each operation, latencies across the p cores are aggregated into *p_list*. From these, performance ratios are computed, which define the strategy for mapping operations across cores.

Algorithm 1. Load Balancer for efficient mapping of operations

Input: Profiled data from the Profiler, Platform metadata x
Output: Parallel execution strategy, optimal chunk size

```
strategy = [ ], p_list = [ ], a_list = [ ], type_list = [ ], chunk_list = [ ]
p = number_of_compute_cores
   (1) Mapping based on relative performance of the p cores
for each entry e in Profiled_data do
    latency = get_time(p_list(op, core)) + e(op, core)
    p_list.update(op, core, latency)
end for
for each op in p_list do
    r = get_ratio(op, p_list)                      ▷ Mapping ratio on compute cores
    strategy.append(op, r)
end for
   (2) Mapping of Attention Heads based on Sparse-kernels
for each attention head entry a in Profiled_data do
    latency = get_time(a_list(sparsity_type, core)) + a(sparsity_type, core)
    a_list.update(sparsity_type, core, latency)
end for
for each layer a in a_list do
    agr = aggregate(number of heads of each sparsity_type)
    type_list.append(agr)
end for
for type in type_list do
    for heads in type_list(each layer) do
        r = get_ratio(op = atten, a_list)          ▷ Mapping ratio on p compute cores
        strategy.append(layer, op = attention, type, r)
    end for
end for
   (3) Determining Optimal Chunk Size
for each input_length len in Profiled_data do
    opt_chunk = get_min_latency_chunk(len, Profiled_data)
    chunk_list.append(opt_chunk)
end for
Optimal_Chunk_Size = Median(chunk_list)
```

Table 1. Specifications of the platforms

Platforms	Intel Meteor Lake Core Ultra 9 185H	Intel Lunar Lake Core Ultra 7 258V
# of CPU cores	16	8
Memory Size	32 GB	32 GB
CPU Peak Perf. (FP32)	1 TFLOPS	1 TFLOPS
GPU Peak Perf. (FP32)	4.81 TFLOPS	6.24 TFLOPS

Mapping of Attention Heads Based on Sparse Kernels: To generate the mapping strategy for attention heads, the algorithm uses latency values for each sparsity kernel across the p compute cores. For each sparsity pattern, latencies are aggregated into *a_list*. Using the number of heads per pattern (from *type_list*), the algorithm computes performance ratios across cores to determine the optimal mapping. This ensures a balanced distribution of attention heads, avoiding core overload from sparsity-pattern affinity while preserving performance through pattern-aware assignments.

Determining Optimal Chunk Size. To determine the optimal chunk size, the algorithm evaluates sparse kernel performance across different chunk sizes and input lengths. For each input, it selects the chunk size with the lowest latency and stores it in *chunk_list*. The median of this list is chosen as the optimal size, as it is a reliable estimate across varied context lengths.

3.3 Runtime Engine

The Runtime Engine begins by taking the parallel execution strategy and chunk size from the Load Balancer. It maps operations to the available compute cores based on this strategy. Once mapping is complete, the engine starts processing user prompts. The complete prefill stage workflow is illustrated in Figure 3.

Step 1: The prompt is tokenized and segmented into chunks based on the Load Balancer's chunk size. Each chunk is embedded, and the token embeddings are stored on SSD to manage memory, as they are large tensors.

Step 2: This step processes the token embeddings chunk-by-chunk to generate the full KV matrices for the current layer, which are then stored on SSD.

Step 3: The third step generates sparse keys for attention, which are the row indices of the K and V matrices. Using the stored KV matrices and, if needed, segments of contextual embeddings (e.g., the last 64 tokens for vertical-slash pattern), sparse keys are inferred for all attention heads.

Step 4: The fourth step performs self-attention and feed-forward network (FFN) computations chunk-wise. Each chunk computes attention using the relevant KV matrix rows indicated by the sparse keys and applies the corresponding sparse mask. After FFN, the output embeddings for the chunk are written to SSD. Steps two through four are repeated until the first token is generated.

Table 2. Performance of Prefill Stage - (Precision: FP-32 — Batch Size: 1) [3] **Comparing Time To First Token (TTFT) values (Sec.) across the baseline Chunked Prefill (CP) on iGPU, Sparsity-Aware (SA) Prefill on CPU, SA Prefill with SLB and HEFT based Tensor Parallelism, and ACCLAIM**

Platform - 1: Intel Core Ultra 7 258V

Model	Context Length	CP - iGPU	SA - CPU	SA - SLB	SA - HEFT	ACCLAIM
Llama3.2 - 1B	16,000	1392.90	556.07	118.64	110.37	**108.47**
	32,000	5286.70	1897.78	343.6	312.93	**229.30**
	64,000	10575.8	3988.67	1028.40	855.02	**813.52**
	100,000	15860.1	6920.42	1709.99	1635.76	**1602.34**
Gemma2 - 2B	16,000	1447.89	641.55	238.18	210.35	**192.56**
	32,000	5725.64	2372.61	477.57	428.17	**405.37**
	64,000	10938.33	4975.92	1253.34	1103.45	**1023.96**
	100,000	16252.49	7918.56	2584.22	2177.52	**2107.14**
Llama3.2 - 3B	16,000	1532.49	683.14	273.35	260.06	**255.58**
	32,000	5936.64	2546.37	608.53	552.03	**541.72**
	64,000	11170.58	5197.08	1468.73	1147.68	**1126.41**
	100,000	16760.33	8970.95	2909.47	2509.39	**2415.03**

Platform - 2: Intel Core Ultra 9 185H

Model	Context Length	CP - iGPU	SA - CPU	SA - SLB	SA - HEFT	ACCLAIM
Llama3.2 - 1B	16,000	1478.01	671.96	362.74	300.52	**292.67**
	32,000	6219.91	2043.88	607.25	594.07	**539.45**
	64,000	11021.63	4581.54	1314.52	1186.80	**1207.75**
	100,000	16199.50	7300.96	2176.60	2063.55	**2005.36**
Gemma2 - 2B	16,000	1522.04	798.11	408.18	343.26	**303.40**
	32,000	7317.28	2713.42	794.76	710.00	**684.56**
	64,000	11441.70	5867.94	1801.45	1694.88	**1657.71**
	100,000	16831.19	8937.46	3675.99	3602.41	**3580.5**
Llama3.2 - 3B	16,000	1641.83	834.90	423.87	380.55	**343.74**
	32,000	7959.49	3349.64	803.59	750.43	**717.03**
	64,000	11847.03	6142.58	2134.77	2103.80	**2078.65**
	100,000	17580.42	10829.06	4101.65	3998.72	**3935.31**

Note: The results may vary across different software stacks and configurations. The results presented here are specific to the evaluation framework used in this study for representative academic purpose

Table 3. Comparison of Memory Footprint for Llama 3.2–3B model across context lengths on Intel Core Ultra 7 258V

Context Length	8K	16K	32K	64K	100K
Standard Inference	27 GB	–	–	–	–
Chunked Prefill (Chunk size = 2000)	18 GB	18 GB	18 GB	18 GB	18 GB
ACCLAIM	16 GB	16.3 GB	16.8 GB	17.1 GB	17.6 GB

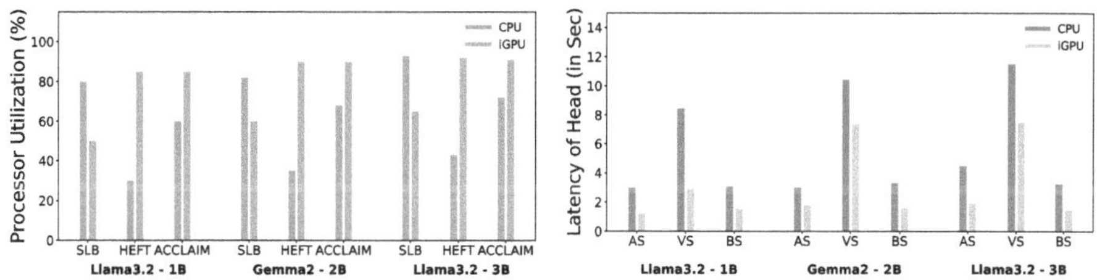

Fig. 4. Evaluation of Latency of Sparsity Patterns and Processor Utilization (FP-32, Context Length = 32K) on Intel Core Ultra 7 258V

4 Experiments

4.1 Experimental Setup

Hardware Platform: We conduct our experiments on Intel Meteor Lake Core Ultra 9 185H and Intel Lunar Lake Core Ultra 7 258V—state-of-the-art heterogeneous platforms featuring multi-core CPUs and integrated Intel Arc GPUs (iGPUs). Platform specifications are detailed in Table 1.

Software Frameworks and Models: We use Python v3.11 and PyTorch v2.5.1 for CPU, with Intel Extension for PyTorch [1] for integrated GPU support. Multi-threading is managed via Python's concurrent thread pool. Evaluation is performed on prompt lengths from 8K to 100K using FP32 precision, for LLaMA-3.21B, Gemma22B, and LLaMA 3.23B—state of the art on device LLMs. Quantization is excluded to analyze the raw performance of inference. We use Time To First Token (TTFT) to evaluate prefill efficiency and compare processor and memory usage against state-of-the-art mapping algorithms, Static Load Balancing (SLB) [13] and Heterogeneous Earliest Finish Time (HEFT) [11].

ACCLAIM Intial Setup: The Profiler is run with the LLM model and a configuration file specifying sparsity patterns from [7]. It processes prompts ranging from 8K to 100K tokens and sends performance data to the Load Balancer, which generates optimal chunk size and mapping strategy. The Profiler runs for about 20–30 minutes and Load Balancer takes under a minute, both run once for a model-platform pair. Inference runs with a *batch size of 1*, as edge platforms typically handle only one inference request at a time. The Profiler and Load Balancer are run once for the given model and platform. The mapping strategy generated by the Load Balancer is stored in a configuration file which is later utilized by the Runtime engine. The Profiler and Load Balancer are not re-run for a given model on the same platform.

4.2 Performance Evaluation

In this section, we evaluate ACCLAIM's performance by comparing it against baseline chunked prefill, sparsity-aware (SA) prefill on CPU, and SA prefill with Tensor Parallelism using SLB and HEFT strategies. *Chunked prefill* is our baseline as the state-of-the-art edge platforms result in memory overflow (Table 3).

Note that the TTFT results reported in this section is the average of three runs of the system. The maximum difference in TTFT from the average across the runs is 5 s.

Comparison with the Baseline - Chunked Prefill on iGPU and SA Prefill on CPU: Table 2 presents the Time To First Token (TTFT) for chunked prefill on iGPU and sparsity-aware (SA) prefill on CPU. Comparing with the CPU-based SA highlights the raw performance gains from applying sparsity. SA prefill achieves up to 23× speedup over chunked prefill, primarily due to: (1) reduced computation from sparse self-attention (Sect. 2.2), and (2) lower memory footprint, as shown in Table 3, since fewer KV vectors are fetched from SSD, reducing SSD-to-memory traffic. Table 2 further shows that ACCLAIM achieves up to 4.5× speedup over the CPU-based SA prefill, attributed to its heterogeneity-aware Tensor Parallelism (evaluated in the following section).

Comparison with Classic Mapping techniques for Tensor Parallelism: To evaluate ACCLAIM's effectiveness, we compare it against two classic mapping strategies of SLB and HEFT. SLB distributes workload equally across compute cores, mapping attention heads in a fixed 1:1 ratio to CPU and iGPU. As shown in Table 2, ACCLAIM achieves up to 1.2× speedup over sparsity-aware (SA) SLB prefill, as SLB fails to account for both hardware and sparsity-pattern heterogeneity. HEFT, in contrast, is an affinity-based strategy that maps each task to the core with the lowest execution latency. For attention heads, this means mapping all heads of a given sparsity pattern to the core with the fastest execution time. However, from Table 2, ACCLAIM still achieves up to 1.2× speedup over HEFT. This is because HEFT lacks load balancing, Fig. 4a shows iGPU performs best for all patterns, causing HEFT to map all heads to the iGPU, leading to a bottleneck. In contrast, ACCLAIM performs heterogeneity-aware mapping by leveraging profiling data on both core performance and sparsity patterns (Fig. 4b), enabling the Load Balancer to generate an optimized execution plan, as detailed in Sect. 3.1.

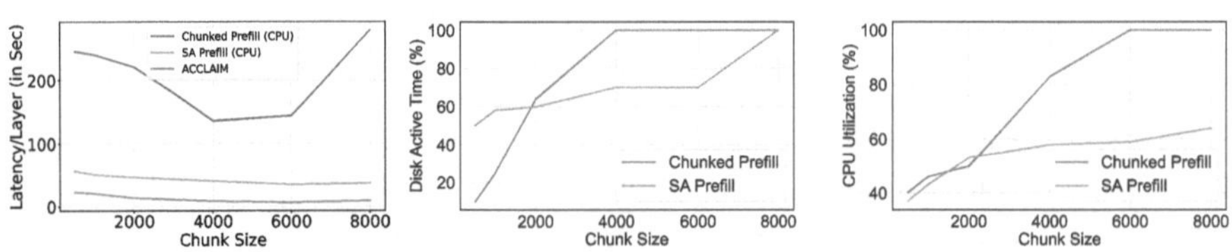

Fig. 5. Effect of chunk size on per-layer latency, SSD and CPU utilization for Llama3.2-1B model (FP-32, Context Length = 16K) on Intel Core Ultra 7 258V

5 Ablation Study

5.1 Selection of Optimal Chunk Size

We study the impact of chunk size across three cases: chunked prefill, SA prefill without Tensor Parallelism, and ACCLAIM. As shown in Fig. 5a, all three exhibit

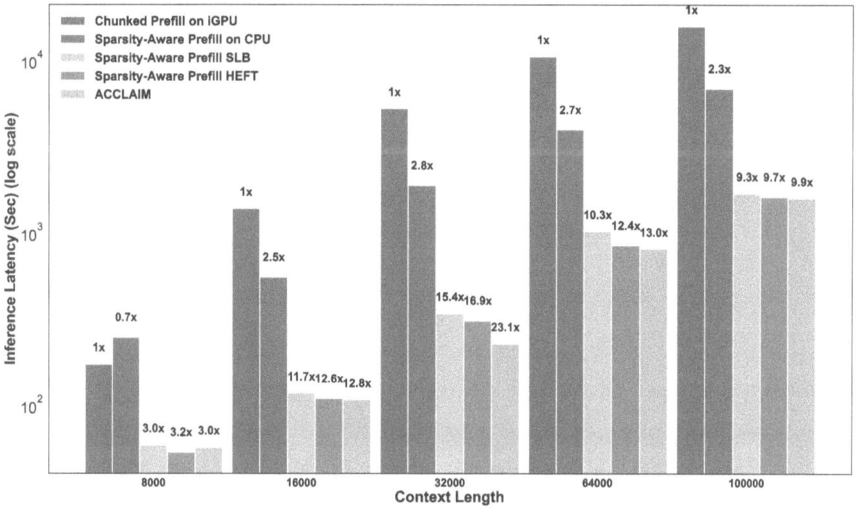

Fig. 6. Comparison of Inference Latency of ACCLAIM with the Baselines for Llama-3.2-1B model with FP-32 precision

a similar trend: latency per layer decreases with larger chunk sizes up to a point, then increases due to SSD communication overhead (Fig. 5b), indicating the optimal chunk size. Figure 5a shows that SA prefill has a larger optimal chunk size than chunked prefill, due to reduced self-attention computation and lower processor utilization at smaller chunk sizes, as seen in Fig. 5c.

5.2 Performance of Sparsity-Aware Prefill on Medium Context Lengths

We conduct a study to analyse the performance of SA prefill on medium context lengths such as 8K. From Fig. 6 it can be seen that for context length of 8K, chunked prefill on iGPU performs better than SA prefill on CPU. This can be attributed to the initial overhead of generating sparse attention masks and synchronization of attention heads implementing different sparsity patterns.

6 Discussion

6.1 Extending to Other Heterogeneous Platforms

We evaluate ACCLAIM on Intel Meteor Lake and Lunar Lake platforms, but it is not restricted to them. ACCLAIM generalizes to other edge platforms, such as AMD AIPCs and Apple's M-series, by abstracting the hardware as a set of compute cores during profiling and load balancing. Platform-specific adaptations are limited to core-level execution calls in the Profiler and Runtime Engine, using platform-specific tools.

6.2 Accuracy Evaluation

ACCLAIM incorporates several optimizations. Chunked prefill and heterogeneity-aware tensor parallelism preserve model accuracy, as they operate layer by layer, ensuring full execution of all required operations per layer. The only optimization that alters model semantics is the use of sparsity, which follows the approach in [7]. This introduces minimal accuracy drop while significantly improving inference latency. As our method adopts the same algorithms as [7], we do not separately evaluate model accuracy in this work.

7 Related Works

7.1 Long Context LLM Inference at the Edge

Previous work has explored edge LLM inference by distributing computation across edge platforms, optimizing for ARM CPUs [15], and extending frameworks like Llama.cpp [1] for FPGA inference [5]. However, these approaches struggle with long-context inference due to unaddressed memory constraints and reliance on single-core execution, leading to resource under-utilization. Current literature has works such as [10], that target consumer-grade GPUs with offloading some data and compute to the CPU. Other works such as [18] target CPU-NPU compute on mobile devices. Among these, [10] addresses long-context inference. However, its setup relies on discrete edge accelerators like the Nvidia RTX 4090, which boasts a peak performance of 82 TFLOPS for FP-32, significantly surpassing the performance of integrated GPUs like the Intel Arc GPU, which offers only 4 TFLOPS. [18] do not target long-context inference. In contrast, our work supports long-context inference through *chunked prefill* and heterogeneity-aware Tensor Parallelism.

7.2 Chunking of Prefill Stage

Chunked prefill was initially designed to improve serving performance on server-grade GPUs, with prior works [3] using it to overlap decode and prefill. Recent efforts [19] apply it for long-context memory efficiency but often reduce accuracy and target only server hardware. In contrast, our work uses *chunked prefill* to address edge platform memory limits without sacrificing accuracy.

7.3 Accelerating Long Context Inference by Exploiting Sparsity

Existing works reduce TTFT during long-context inference by exploiting sparsity in self-attention. Methods like [9] limit attention to token windows, while others [7] assign attention heads to predefined sparsity patterns, reducing computation. However, they still compute complete KV matrices, leading to memory issues on edge platforms. Our work addresses this by combining sparsity patterns from [7] with *chunked prefill* to stay within memory limits. We further reduce TTFT by leveraging the computational characteristics of each sparsity pattern, enabling Tensor Parallelism across heterogeneous compute cores.

8 Conclusion

In this work, we proposed ACCLAIM, a novel system for accelerating long-context LLM inference on heterogeneous edge platforms. ACCLAIM enables long-context inference by addressing memory constraints through *chunked prefill* and reduces computation via sparsity-aware self-attention, achieving up to 23× speedup in TTFT over standalone *chunked prefill*. It further exploits hardware heterogeneity through optimized Tensor Parallelism, delivering up to 1.5× speedup over state-of-the-art parallelization methods.

The current ACCLAIM system focuses on full-precision FP-32 to showcase raw performance improvements. Applying quantization can further enhance performance without affecting ACCLAIM's effectiveness, as both optimizations are orthogonal and can be implemented simultaneously. Furthermore, we plan to expand ACCLAIM to include dynamic attention architectures, where a distinct sparsity pattern is identified for each input prompt. Recent study [20] have shown that this approach outperforms static sparsity patterns in attention, resulting in an approximate 4% increase in accuracy. Additionally, we aim to explore energy-efficient techniques for long-context inference by extending ACCLAIM to balance performance and energy consumption.

Acknowledgments. This work is supported by Intel Labs, the Semiconductor Research Corporation (SRC), and the National Science Foundation(NSF) IDEAS Center [2] grants under the award numbers SaTC-2104264 and CNS-2009057.

References

1. Llama.cpp. https://github.com/ggerganov/llama.cpp
2. Nsf-iucrc-ideas-center. https://iucrc.nsf.gov/centers/
3. Agrawal, A., Panwar, A., Mohan, J., Kwatra, N., Gulavani, B.S., Ramjee, R.: Sarathi: efficient llm inference by piggybacking decodes with chunked prefills (2023). https://arxiv.org/abs/2308.16369
4. Gomes, W., Morgan, S., Phelps, B., Wilson, T., Hallnor, E.: Meteor lake and arrow lake intel next-gen 3d client architecture platform with foveros. In: 2022 IEEE Hot Chips 34 Symposium (HCS), pp. 1–40 (2022)
5. Haris, J., Saha, R., Hu, W., Cano, J.: Designing efficient llm accelerators for edge devices. arXiv preprint arXiv:2408.00462 (2024)
6. Huseynli, F., Raoofy, A., Schulz, M.: Leveraging cpu-fpga co-design for matrix profile computation. In: Guerrero, G., San Martín, J., Meneses, E., Barrios Hernández, C.J., Osthoff, C., Monsalve Diaz, J.M. (eds.) High Performance Computing, pp. 127–141. Springer Nature Switzerland, Cham (2025). https://doi.org/10.1007/978-3-031-80084-9_9
7. Jiang, H., et al.: MInference 1.0: accelerating pre-filling for long-context LLMs via dynamic sparse attention. In: The Thirty-eighth Annual Conference on Neural Information Processing Systems (2024)
8. Kulkarni, P., Mahabaleshwarkar, A., Kulkarni, M., Sirsikar, N., Gadgil, K.: Conversational ai: an overview of methodologies, applications & future scope. In: 2019 5th International Conference On Computing, Communication, Control and Automation (ICCUBEA), pp. 1–7 (2019)

9. Li, Y., et al.: Snapkv: Llm knows what you are looking for before generation (2024). https://arxiv.org/abs/2404.14469
10. Luo, C., et al.: Headinfer: memory-efficient llm inference by head-wise offloading. arXiv preprint arXiv:2502.12574 (2025)
11. Samadi, Y., Zbakh, M., Tadonki, C.: E-heft: enhancement heterogeneous earliest finish time algorithm for task scheduling based on load balancing in cloud computing. In: 2018 International Conference on High Performance Computing & Simulation (HPCS), pp. 601–609 (2018)
12. Seo, W., Cha, S., Kim, Y., Huh, J., Park, J.: Slo-aware inference scheduler for heterogeneous processors in edge platforms. ACM Trans. Archit. Code Optim. **18**(4) (Jul 2021)
13. Tantawi, A.N., Towsley, D.: Optimal static load balancing in distributed computer systems. J. ACM **32**(2), 445–465 (1985)
14. Vaswani, A., et al.: Attention is all you need (2023). https://arxiv.org/abs/1706.03762
15. Wang, Z., et al.: Mnn-llm: a generic inference engine for fast large language model deployment on mobile devices. In: Proceedings of the 6th ACM International Conference on Multimedia in Asia Workshops. MMAsia 2024 Workshops. Association for Computing Machinery, New York (2024)
16. Wang, Z.: Sparsert: accelerating unstructured sparsity on gpus for deep learning inference. In: Proceedings of the ACM International Conference on Parallel Architectures and Compilation Techniques, PACT 2020, pp. 31–42. Association for Computing Machinery, New York (2020)
17. Xiao, G., et al.: Duoattention: efficient long-context llm inference with retrieval and streaming heads. arXiv preprint arXiv:2410.10819 (2024)
18. Xue, Z., Song, Y., Mi, Z., Zheng, X., Xia, Y., Chen, H.: Powerinfer-2: fast large language model inference on a smartphone (2024). https://arxiv.org/abs/2406.06282
19. Zeng, Z., et al.: Memorize step by step: efficient long-context prefilling with incremental memory and decremental chunk. In: Al-Onaizan, Y., Bansal, M., Chen, Y.N. (eds.) Proceedings of the 2024 Conference on Empirical Methods in Natural Language Processing, pp. 21021–21034. Association for Computational Linguistics, Miami, Florida, USA (Nov 2024)
20. Zhang, H., Fan, H., Sha, K., Huang, Y., Feng, Y.: Dam: dynamic attention mask for long-context large language model inference acceleration (2025). https://arxiv.org/abs/2506.11104

Parallel/Distributed Computing for Optimizing Investment Planning in Electricity Markets

Santiago Freire[1(✉)], Pedro Moreno[2], and Sergio Nesmachnow[1]

[1] Universidad de la República, Montevideo, Uruguay
{sfreire,sergion}@fing.edu.uy

[2] Universidad Autónoma del Estado de Morelos, Cuernavaca, Mexico
pmoreno@uaem.mx

Abstract. This article presents a parallel and distributed computing strategy for optimizing investment planning in electricity markets. An implementation is developed for a stochastic dynamic programming model used by the Uruguayan electrical company to determine investment strategies in generation assets. The sequential execution of thousands of solver instances results in high computing times, rendering the process inefficient for large-scale scenarios. A distributed architecture based on Message Passing Interface is proposed to enable parallel execution across multiple computing resources. The solution includes modular components organized in a layered architecture, load balancing and fault recovery features. Performance results indicate that the parallel implementation allows addressing complex scenarios with high computing demands. Significant reductions in execution time were obtained, with high speedup values (up to 98×) and efficiency up to 0.86 for a full-scale scenario executed on distributed nodes of a high-performance computing cluster.

Keywords: Investment planning in electricity markets · parallel computing · cluster

1 Introduction

The emergence of the novel smart grid paradigm has brought significant transformations in electricity markets [2,8]. The smart grid paradigm involves specific infrastructure components for the electrical grid, to incorporate advanced communication, control, monitoring, and processing technologies to solve relevant problems related to electricity. Smart grids have reshaped the way electricity is generated, distributed, and consumed [13,15] and specific efforts are performed to optimize the three main phases of generation, distribution, and consumption of electricity. The smart grid paradigm represents a significant shift from traditional electricity grids to take advantage of information and communication technologies to develop more interconnected, automated, and intelligent systems.

K. Brown et al. (Eds.): CARLA 2025, CCIS 2750, pp. 49–64, 2026.
https://doi.org/10.1007/978-3-032-24923-4_4

Electricity markets are being transformed by the smart grid paradigm, including the integration of renewable energy sources (solar, wind, and thermal) into the electricity grid, the implementation of demand response programs to promote consumers to adjust their electricity usage based on real-time information about price or grid conditions, and the analysis of relevant data to gain insights into grid performance, usage patterns, and system optimization. These features allow for a more diverse energy mix, enhancing flexibility, resilience, and efficiency of the electricity grid, while promoting long-term sustainability.

Optimizing investment planning in electricity markets under the smart grid paradigm is crucial. A proper planning allows resource efficiency, cost reductions, improved reliability, and provides a basis for implementing strategies for meeting the evolving needs of the energy sector and society. In the ever changing energy production and distribution ecosystem, the optimization of investment strategies is vital for companies seeking to improve efficiency, reliability, and profitability. In recent years, disruptive technologies have emerged as contributions in that field, including sophisticated numerical models, stochastic simulation approaches, and computational intelligence and data analytics. Although identifying the key factors influencing smart grid investments has a great impact, there is a lack of research in this area, and a need for new studies and approaches to provide valuable insights for decision-making in uncertain scenarios [4].

In this line of work, this article presents a parallel/distributed approach for an optimization model for generation investments in electrical systems. The studied model explores large graphs of states to find minimum-cost expected strategies for the design of resource parks, taking into account stochastic variables and decision-making investments on energy centrals, contracts, and other business-related operations. The underlying optimization problem is solved applying dynamic stochastic programming, but the large dimension of the search space demands significantly large execution times, even prohibitive for large scenarios. A specific case study is addressed, considering the energy market in Uruguay and the operational decisions to be taken by the Planning and Environmental Investment Management Department (Gerencia de Planificación de Inversiones y Medio Ambiente) of the Uruguayan state-owned electricity company, UTE.

The proposed parallel/distributed approach applies a hierarchical master-slave architecture. A specific protocol is applied for communication between the different components of the parallel/distributed implementation. A load balancing scheme is applied to distribute the load for each dynamic stochastic programming solver. Fault recovery mechanisms are implemented by persisting intermediate results and verifying the existence of previous outputs before executing a simulation. Further enhancements are applied to improve efficiency after performing a memory usage analysis.

The efficiency analysis was conducted on two representative scenarios: a small case executed on a single node and a full-scale case executed on a distributed platform. The developed parallel implementation showed capable of handling the complexity of the full-scale scenario, which demands high computing time. Significant reductions in execution time were achieved. A proper speedup behavior was shown for the full-scale scenario, with efficiency up to 0.82 when using three distributed nodes of the high-performance computing cluster.

The article is organized as follows. The next section describes the problem of optimization of electricity investment planning and reviews related works. Section 3 describes the proposed parallel/distributed design and implementation. The experimental evaluation is reported in Sect. 4. Finally, Sect. 5 presents the conclusions and formulates the main lines for future work.

2 Optimization of Electricity Investment Planning

This section describes the problem of optimizing investment planning in electricity markets and reviews relevant related works.

2.1 Optimization of Investment Planning in Electricity Markets

The Optimal Generation Investments Model (in Spanish, Modelo de Inversiones en Generación Óptimas, MINGO) [14] is a program that allows for finding strategies of minimum expected cost in the design of the electricity resource park (power plants, power purchase agreements, etc.) to meet the generation demand.

The main goal of the model is to optimize (minimize) an expected updated generalized cost, which takes into account the current value of the annual disutility of costs, including fuel and failure costs, and other contributions such as environmental impacts. The concept of disutility is based on a convex function of annual costs to reflect the risk aversion in the decision-making process.

The underlying optimization problem is solved using a stochastic dynamic programming algorithm. The main control variables are associated with the generation resources to be constructed or contracted and the transformations of existing resources to be evaluated in a given planning period. The search space is determined by a tunnel including a set of feasible states defined by the user through heuristic constraints. The proposed approach is similar to the one applied in other software models and tools for planning of electrical systems, such as the Wien Automatic System Planning (WASP) package [7].

For planning and simulation, MINGO needs to iteratively apply an operational optimization model (MOP) to determine the optimal operational strategy for a planning horizon of one year within a given generation resource park and specific values for natural variables that define the availability of renewable energy sources. The process involves computing the costs and operational outcomes for the year across many scenarios of pertinent random variables, such as hydrological inputs and wind power generation potential.

MOP applies an stochastic dynamic programming algorithm to explore a graph of states that define different configuration of the electricity infrastructure. The dynamic programming algorithm involves three stages: i) generating the graph of states in the future considering real information and heuristic constraints; ii) determining the optimal investment decision on each node of the graph of states; and iii) validation and possibly relaxation of heuristic constraints. The sequence is repeated until a feasibility criterion is met.

The optimization problem demands a large amount of computational resources (CPU and memory). In a standard computing node the maximum dimension of the graph of states solvable using MINGO is about 30 000 nodes. Each execution of MOP demands up to 20 h to complete. Further scaling the dimension of scenarios is impossible on a single computing resource. Thus, an implementation applying parallel/distributed computing over a large supercomputing infrastructure is needed for solving complex scenarios.

Overall, MINGO offers a comprehensive and optimized approach for decision-making in energy generation investment, taking into account aspects of cost, risk, and sustainability. The parallel/distributed implementation is needed to achieve a proper scalability and enhancement of results for large scenarios.

2.2 Related Work

Recent research in the literature has advanced parallel stochastic optimization methods for energy planning, management, and investment. Particularly, there has been interest in parallelized stochastic dynamic programming methods using different parallel schemes to achieve efficiency. Next, related work is described.

Dias et al. [3] proposed a parallel approach to enhance long-term operational planning in electrical power systems. The approach used stochastic dynamic programming and a convex hull algorithm to estimate operation and functions costs, employing static and dynamic task assignment strategies within a Single Program Multiple Data model. The implementation used open-source libraries (CLP, Qhull and MPICH2). The proposed parallel approach was validated over a data of a Brazilian hydrothermal system. Two case studies were conducted using historical water inflow data and discrete reservoir levels, with simulations run on a 10-node computer cluster with Intel Quad-Core Xeon processors and 8 GB RAM. The proposed approach achieved peak performance with 128 processors, yielding 55% efficiency for static and 69% for dynamic scheduling.

Machado et al. [10] proposed an asynchronous stochastic dual dynamic programming (SDDP) approach for long-term hydrothermal energy planning, formulated as a multistage linear stochastic optimization problem. Two strategies were adopted: asynchronous SDDP strategy to divide the problem into subproblems to be solved independently by stage (time step) and gathering results at the end of each step, and totally asynchronous SDDP that waits for incoming data to a given processor to proceed to the next step without full synchronization before each step, allowing processors to operate simultaneously at different stages. The approach was implemented in C++ using Boost, COIN-OR, and MPICH2, and the simulations were performed on a Beowulf cluster with AMD Opteron Processors (12 cores) with 98 GB of RAM. Two case studies—mid-term (24 stages, five scenarios) and long-term (120 stages, 20 scenarios)—demonstrated near-linear speedup and high efficiency with up to 120 processors.

Gil and Araya [6] proposed a parallel stochastic mixed-integer linear programming approach for short-term hydrothermal generation scheduling under uncertainty. The approach employed a Progressive Hedging algorithm to decompose the problem by scenario to enable parallel processing. The method was implemented in FORTRAN with CPLEX and used OpenMP and MPI on a two-node cluster (12 cores). The case study was the Central Interconnected System of Chile. Problem instances considering a weekly horizon with hourly resolution. Results showed that shared memory architecture was efficient for up to 6 scenarios, while distributed memory offered better performance for larger instances, making it more suitable for scalable optimization.

Pedrini et al. [12] proposed a parallel Stochastic Dual Dynamic Programming method using a two-period decomposition to solve the long-term hydrothermal scheduling problem. The model minimized expected operational costs over a 59-month horizon, integrating synchronous, asynchronous, and hybrid parallelization strategies. The case study was the Brazilian power system. Problem instances were created with 53 hydro and 30 thermal plants. The parallel method was developed in Python 3.7, and the optimization was performed using Gurobi 9.11 on a computer cluster with two server computers with Intel Xeon 2.6 GHz with 128 GB of RAM. The proposed approach showed up to a 26% reduction in the confidence interval of the optimality gap. The hybrid asynchronous strategy further improved scalability, achieving up to a 40% reduction.

Ávila et al. [1] proposed parallel scheme for the stochastic dual dynamic programming method applied to a Brazilian hydrothermal scheduling problem. The schemes differ by distributing computation per scenario (Monte Carlo samples) or node (value function cuts), with synchronous and asynchronous variants. The method was implemented in Julia v0.6 using JuMP v0.18 and Gurobi 8. Experiments were performed on the Lemaitre3 cluster composed of 80 computing nodes with two 12-core Intel SkyLake 5118 processors (2.3 GHz, 95 GB RAM). Two case studies were addressed: inventory control and hydrothermal scheduling problems. Results showed that the node-based parallelization was more efficient in early iterations and scaled better, though it required shared memory. Increasing Monte Carlo samples in scenario-based schemes reduced performance, emphasizing the need for scalable SDDP methods for distributed systems.

Lara et al. [9] proposed a parallel stochastic dual dynamic integer programming approach for long-term power infrastructure planning under uncertainty, integrating strategic (fuel prices, carbon tax) and operational (renewable availability, load demand) factors. The method distributed subproblems using nested Benders decomposition. The approach was implemented using Pyomo 5.6, Gurobi 8, and PyMP for parallel processing, and validated on a MacBook Pro with a 2.3 GHz quad-core 8th-generation Intel Core i5 processor with 8GB of RAM. Three problem instances were solved, varying the number of stages (years) in the planning horizon based on the Electric Reliability Council of Texas. Results showed that the proposed method efficiently solved large-scale instances up to 15 stages and quadrillions of variables with 76% parallel efficiency.

The analysis of related works highlights the growing effectiveness and scalability of parallel stochastic methods in energy systems optimization. In this line of work, this article contributes with a parallel/distributed implementation of an investment planning model currently in use by UTE, Uruguay.

3 Design and Implementation of the Parallel Solution

This section describes the architectural design, implementation, and operational mechanisms of the distributed optimization system, including its parallelization strategy, load balancing, and fault recovery features.

3.1 Architectural Design of the Solution

The architecture for the proposed solution is organized following a hierarchical master-slave model, with multiple interconnected components that interact in a layered structure. Each layer communicates exclusively with the layers directly above or below it. Figure 1 presents a diagram of the proposed architecture for parallel/distributed MINGO.

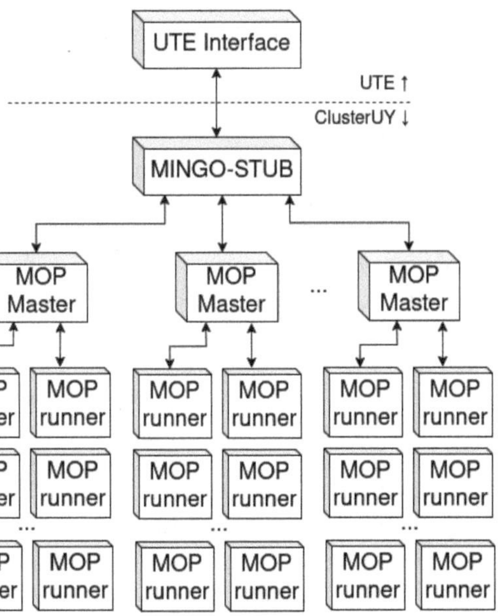

Fig. 1. Architecture of the solution.

The architecture was conceived for the implementation to be executed in a distributed environment. The UTE Interface layer runs locally on the computers of the operators, and the rest of the layers execute on the high performance computing of National Supercomputing Center, ClusterUY [11]. The components of the layered architecture are described in the following subsections.

UTE Interface. The UTE Interface layer is designed to offer a friendly and simplified user experience for UTE operators who use MINGO and MOP in their work. Users interact with a graphical application installed on their personal computers, which allows them to start the optimization process, view the final results, adjust input parameters, and modify remote and local settings. The interface acts as a bridge between users and the optimization system, ensuring that the process is accessible and understandable without the need for technical knowledge of internal components.

MINGO-STUB. MINGO-STUB generates the MOP input files in Extensible Markup Language (XML) format based on a provided scenario, which specifies a possible temporal evolution of the relevant random variables (such as fuel prices and demands) as represented in the nature graph. The generated input files are distributed among the MOP Masters, with MINGO-STUB managing the load balancing to ensure an equitable distribution of work. Once the parallel MOP executions are completed, MINGO-STUB performs the dynamic programming stage of MINGO, which determines the optimal investment decisions across the entire planning horizon by minimizing the expected discounted cost under uncertainty. Finally, it collects and sends the final results to the UTE Interface.

MOP Master. A MOP Master is responsible for receiving input files for MOP executions from MINGO-STUB and managing the sending of XML files to its various assigned MOP runners. It monitors the execution of each scenario and, as they complete, notifies MINGO-STUB to receive new XML files for processing.

MOP Runner. A MOP runner receives input XMLs from the MOP Master and executes the MOP optimization model with the received XMLs as input. At the end of each execution, MOP stores the result (two small Microsoft Office template files, with the XLT extension) in a directory defined in the configuration file on disk and then notifies the MOP Master of its completion. If there are more unprocessed XMLs either in MINGO-STUB or its MOP Master, it waits for the reception of more XMLs. The relationship between a MOP Master and its MOP runner is master-slave: a MOP Master oversees executions and sends data to its MOP runners for processing, while the MOP runners execute them. There are no dependencies between slaves on the tasks that other slaves execute.

3.2 Implementation

The system was implemented in Java, using existing tools and libraries developed by UTE [14], tuned to support parallelism, and new modules such as the MOP Master and the graphical interface. The OpenMPI wrapper for Java was used to support message passing.

The graphical interface was developed in Java Swing, which provides a visual application that allows operators to initiate processing and adjust the input parameters necessary for optimization. Once the process is started from the interface, an instruction is sent via SSH to activate the distributed work in the MINGO runtime environment.

The MINGO and MOP programs were previously developed by UTE in Java and are packaged in JAR files containing both the executable code and its dependencies. To implement parallelization, the parallelism functionality was also developed in Java. Communication between distributed processes is handled through Message Passing Interface, with the existing wrapper for Java, which avoids the need to port a large codebase to a new language such as C and facilitates the integration of parallelism with existing programs.

MINGO-STUB is derived from the original MINGO program developed by UTE, with modifications to optimize input file management for MOPs. Originally, all XML files were written to disk; however, to improve performance, they are now stored in main memory and sent to the MOP Masters via MPI. Since each XML file is approximately 200 KB in size and due to the large amount of communication required, the `deflate` compression algorithm is used, which reduces file sizes by up to 90%. Given the highly repetitive structure of XML files, they are good candidates for compression. Compressed files are packaged into another compressed file with a defined number of XMLs.

Initially, each MOP Master receives a defined number of entries from each MOP, and then the MINGO-STUB sends smaller execution packets to it. The number of MOP Masters (N_M), runners per MOP Master (N_R), and the initial (I_P) and upcoming (U_P) sizes of the XML packets sent are configurable in a configuration file read at program startup. Each process evaluates its MPI rank to determine which section of code to execute. The process with rank 0 executes MINGO-STUB, while processes with rank 1 to N_M execute the code corresponding to the MOP Masters. Processes with ranks from $N_M + 1$ to $N_M + N_M \times N_R$ are responsible for executing the code of the MOP runners.

When MINGO-STUB has no remaining XML packets to send, it sends a termination signal to the MOP Masters. Each MOP Master then instructs its MOP runners to complete the processing of their current XML file, if any, and subsequently terminate. Once all MOP Masters and MOP runners have completed their tasks and reported their completion, the resulting data from all MOP runs is loaded using pre-existing methods in MINGO. Finally, the dynamic programming algorithm is applied, the results of the MINGO iteration are written to disk, a completion notification email is sent, and the results become available for visualization and input parameter modification through the UTE interface, allowing new simulations to be launched.

The communication protocol between MINGO-STUB, MOP Masters, and MOP Runners is illustrated in Fig. 2. A MOP Master cannot complete its execution until all its runners have completed their simulations, since not all simulations may be complete by the time it receives the finish signal from MINGO-STUB. Similarly, MINGO-STUB cannot move on to the next execution phase (loading MOP results and applying dynamic programming) because there may still be MOP runners processing inputs. Therefore, finish signals are sent from a higher layer to a lower layer and also from a lower layer to a higher layer; this way, each process can finish its execution (or, in the case of MINGO-STUB, move on to a next phase) when it is certain that there is no work left to do.

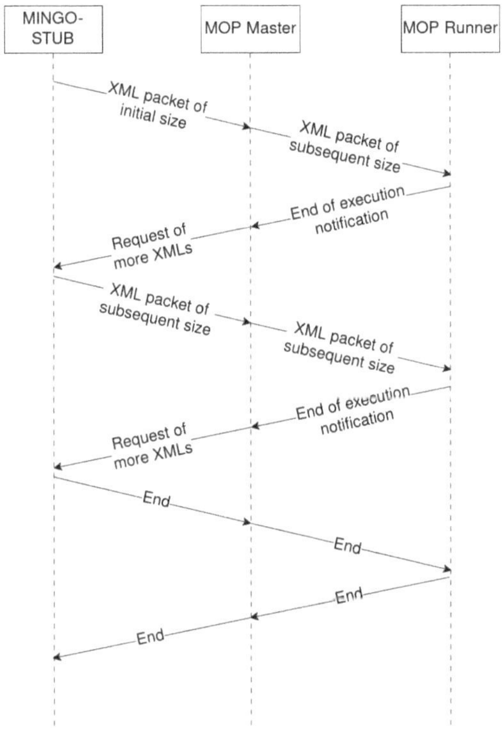

Fig. 2. Communication protocol between layers.

A MOP Master ends its execution, first sending a finish signal to MINGO-STUB, when the number of finish signals received by its MOP runners equals the number of MOP runners assigned to it. Similarly, MINGO-STUB moves to the next phase of execution when the number of end signals received from the MOP Masters equals the total number of MOP Masters. A MOP runner terminates, having previously sent the end signal to its MOP Master, as soon as it finishes processing the last XML received before receiving the end signal.

The specific implementation details for each layer are described in the following subsections.

MINGO-STUB. Upon receiving the start signal from the UTE Interface, MINGO-STUB begins generating the XML files using its own algorithm. Unlike the original implementation, XML files are not written directly to disk. Instead, each XML file is stored as a text string in a collection of strings in memory. Once all the XML files are generated, they are distributed to the MOP Masters using a Round Robin scheduling algorithm. The size of the initial packets is defined in the variable I_P. When a MOP Master notifies that a runner has completed its execution, MINGO-STUB performs the load balancing algorithm described in Sect. 3.3 and sends a new XML packet of the size specified by U_P to the MOP Master with the lowest load and available runners for the packet to be sent. This packet is then sent by the MOP Master to one of its available runners.

MOP Master. A MOP Master initially receives a packet of XML files of size I_P from MINGO-STUB. Then, it distributes the XML packets to the MOP runners in new packets of size U_P. Once a MOP runner completes processing its packet, it sends a notification to the MOP Master, which in turn notifies MINGO-STUB to request more XML packets. The MOP Master assigns new packages to its available MOP Runners using a random selection strategy.

MOP Runner. The MOP runner modifies the original implementation by UTE. The new implementation receives XML files directly via MPI instead of read them from disk. Once it receives an XML file, the MOP runner runs the corresponding simulation and saves the results, two small XLT files that together add up to approximately 85 KB. The results are persisted on disk in a directory specified in the configuration file, from which MINGO-STUB will then load the data from all runs to execute the dynamic programming algorithm.

3.3 Load Balancing

The system implements a load balancing mechanism to ensure that work is distributed equitably among the MOP Masters. MINGO-STUB manages load balancing by saving the current load of each MOP Master, defined as the number of XML files being processed at a given time. Initially, each MOP Master starts with a load equal to I_P, which represents the maximum load to handle. Upon receiving notification that a MOP runner has completed a packet, the load record of the respective MOP Master is updated, and MINGO-STUB evaluates which MOP Master is able to receive more work.

If a MOP Master can accept a new packet without exceeding the maximum load (i.e., current load $+ U_P \leq I_P$), MINGO-STUB selects the MOP Master with the lowest load to send the new packet. This approach aims at distributing work evenly, even if some MOP executions are slower than others, thus optimizing resource usage and minimizing total execution time.

3.4 Fault Recovery

The fault recovery adopted is based on avoiding unnecessary duplication of work, persisting the results of each MOP runner on disk. Before processing an XML file, the MOP runner checks whether the two corresponding output files already exist. If both files are present, it is assumed that the processing of the XML file has already been completed, so the MOP runner notifies the MOP Master of its completion without repeating the processing. If only one of the two output files is present, it is deleted, and the XML is reprocessed from the beginning to ensure data consistency. It is assumed that the output directory does not contain data from MINGO runs of cases other than the current one.

The verification mechanism allows processing to resume quickly in the event of interruptions anywhere in the system (for example, a job preemption in ClusterUY). MOP runners that encounter already processed inputs will skip their execution, significantly reducing recovery time compared to a complete system restart. The fault-recovery strategy used aims to keep the execution time of all simulations as short as possible in the event of failures, avoiding rework.D

3.5 Memory Usage Analysis

To increase resource efficiency, the memory usage of the program was studied during an execution of the full scenario. Each MOP runner, due to a (previously present) code fragment, stored each result in a HashTable of Java objects in memory. When each MOP runner ran the runs in the full scenario the HashTable grew significantly, causing the runners to fail due to a lack of memory.

The analysis of the code indicated that the HashTable was never consulted; it was only used to add the results to the object. Therefore, the problem was solved by removing the use of the HashTable. The 4 GB of RAM used by the HashTable occurred after running simulations associated with approximately 97 XMLs. The full MINGO scenario consists of 14,323 XMLs, so if the memory usage trend continued, almost 600 GB of RAM would eventually be consumed across all the runners on objects that are never used.

4 Performance Evaluation

This section describes the performance evaluation of the proposed solution.

4.1 Evaluation Methodology

The performance evaluation varied the number of MOP Masters (N_M) and the number of MOP runners per Master (N_R) used in the parallel implementation. For each configuration, traditional metrics to evaluate the performance of parallel algorithms were evaluated: execution time, speedup, and the efficiency. The speedup is the ratio of the execution times of the sequential algorithm (T_1) and the parallel version executed on N computing elements (T_N) (Eq. 1). The ideal case for a parallel/distributed algorithm is to achieve linear speedup ($S_N = N$). However, the common situation is to achieve sublinear speedup ($S_N < N$), due to the times required to communicate and synchronize the parallel/distributed processes or threads. The efficiency is the normalized value of the speedup, regarding the number of computing elements used for execution (Eq. 2). The linear speedup corresponds to $E_N = 1$, and usually $E_N < 1$ [5].

$$S_N = \frac{T_1}{T_N} \quad (1) \qquad\qquad E_N = \frac{S_N}{N} \quad (2)$$

Computational experiments were performed on high performance computing servers with two AMD EPYC 7763 processors and 64 cores each (3.5 GHz, 512 GB RAM) from the National Supercomputing Center, Uruguay [11]

Two problem instances were solved by varying the number of XML files: a reduced case study involving 151 XML input files, executed in a single node; and a full case study comprising 14,323 XML input files, executed in several distributed nodes from ClusterUY. The single-node execution used up to 23 cores (maximum available in the computing node) and the distributed execution used up to 120 cores (maximum available for a single job in ClusterUY).

Five independent executions of each experiment were performed to avoid bias in the results due to unpredictable situations in the computing infrastructure.

4.2 Performance Results

The performance results are reported and discussed next.

Reduced Case Study: Single-Node Execution. Table 1 reports the execution time, speedup, and efficiency for different numbers of MOP Masters (N_M) and MOP runners by master (N_R). MOP Masters were excluded from the number of computing elements since they do not perform calculations.

Table 1. Performance evaluation of the parallel/distributed MINGO implementation for the reduced case study (single-node execution).

#	N_M	N_R	*execution time*	*speedup*	*efficiency*
1	1	1	01:39:18 (5 958 s)	1.00	0.50
2	1	2	00:50:05 (3 005 s)	1.98	0.66
3	2	1	00:52:44 (3 614 s)	1.65	0.55
4	2	2	00:30:46 (1 846 s)	3.23	0.65
5	2	4	00:20:23 (1 223 s)	4.87	0.54
6	4	2	00:21:07 (1 267 s)	4.70	0.52
7	4	4	00:15:43 (943 s)	6.31	0.37
8	1	16	00:13:12 (792 s)	7.52	0.44
9	2	10	00:13:44 (824 s)	7.23	0.34
10	1	20	00:13:34 (814 s)	7.32	0.35

The standard deviation for experiment number 10 was very small (7.11 s). Performance results in Table 1 indicate that increasing the number of MOP runners significantly reduced the execution time and improved the speedup up to a maximum speedup value of 7.52. However, efficiency tended to decrease as more resources were added. The highest efficiency was 0.66, using one MOP Master and two MOP runners. Results suggest that parallelism boosts performance and introduces coordination overhead that affects efficiency.

Small differences in execution times were detected when using the same number of MOP runners and varying the number of MOP Masters. Differences are attributed to the increased communication time between MOP Masters and their runners, required to notify completions and send new XMLs, and the communications required for the MOP Master to request more XMLs from MINGO-STUB.

For the considered problem size, increasing the number of MOP Masters to more than one did not improve performance, even degrading the execution time due to the additional coordination and communication overhead. The coordination between MOP Masters and their runners, added to the load balancing and data distribution operations performed by MINGO-STUB, introduces synchronization delays that increase as the number of controlling processes grows. Thus, better efficiency is achieved using a single MOP Master and assigning the available runners directly under its control. Figure 3 presents the graphics of execution time, speedup, and efficiency for the reduced case study (single-node execution).

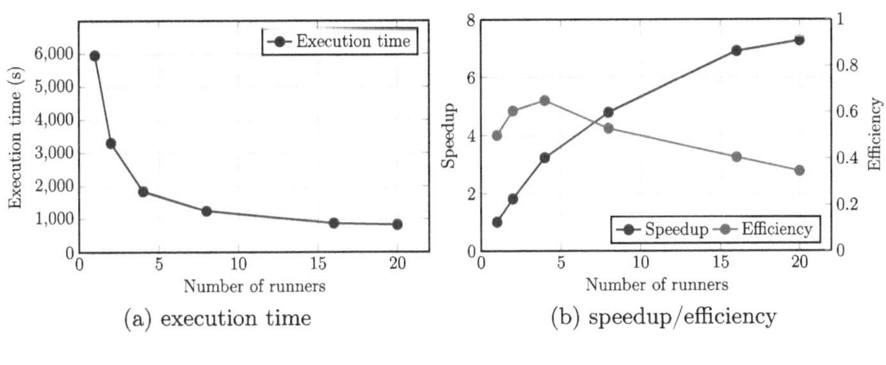

Fig. 3. Performance evaluation of the parallel/distributed MINGO implementation for the reduced case study (single-node execution): speedup and efficiency.

The graphics in Fig. 3 clearly show that the execution time decreased as the number of runners increased, whereas the efficiency tended to decrease for larger numbers of runners due to the parallelization overhead.

Full Case Study: Distributed Execution. Each computing node in the platform was set to execute up to 40 MPI processes. Since each process has one core assigned, when the number of MPI processes (MINGO-STUB + MOP Masters + MOP runners) was over 40, more than one node was used.

Table 2 reports the results of the performance metrics for the full scenario (distributed execution).

Results in Table 2 indicate that the execution time greatly decreased when using more runners. The overall reduction in execution time was significant: from more than nine and a half days (sequential implementation) to just below two and a half hours using 118 computing resources. The best speedup value was 97.99 using 118 computing resources, and efficiency values remained high for most configurations. Unlike the reduced case study, efficiency values did not degrade when using more computing resources. Figure 4 presents the graphics of execution time, speedup, and efficiency for the full case study (distributed execution).

Table 2. Performance evaluation of the parallel/distributed MINGO implementation for the full case study (distributed execution)

#	N_M	N_R	*execution time*	*speedup*	*efficiency*
1	1	1	9 D 14:04:38 (828 278 s)	1.00	0.50
2	1	5	1 D 23:09:25 (169 765 s)	4.88	0.81
3	1	15	16:38:29 (59 909 s)	13.83	0.86
4	1	30	13:18:39 (47 919 s)	17.29	0.56
5	1	60	6:17:39 (22 659 s)	36.55	0.60
6	1	118	2:20:53 (8 453 s)	97.99	0.82

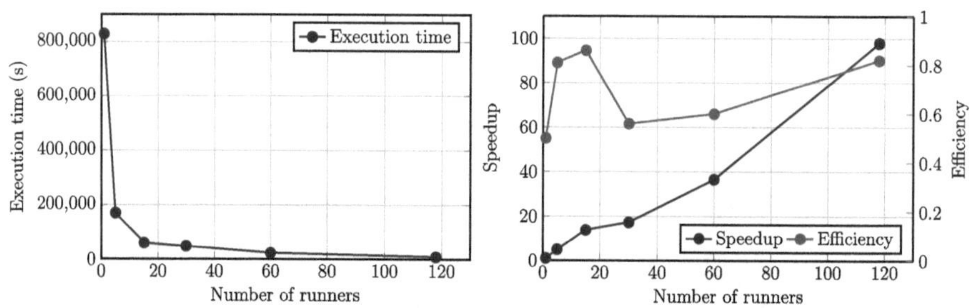

(a) execution time (b) speedup/efficiency

Fig. 4. Performance evaluation of the parallel/distributed MINGO implementation for the full case study (distributed execution): speedup and efficiency.

The performance results show that the proposed implementation showed a proper speedup behavior and scaled reasonably, taking advantage of more computing resource to address the larger scenario. The reduced execution time and reasonable efficiency through the use of parallelism enable solving large-scale instances that are infeasible for a sequential execution.

5 Conclusions and Future Work

This article presented a parallel and distributed implementation of MINGO, an investment planning model, using process coordination, load balancing, and parallel task execution to address large-scale stochastic optimization instances.

The proposed architecture defined a hierarchical and layered organization that separates the user interface, coordination, task distribution, and scenario execution while maintaining clear responsibilities for each component. The main performance results showed significant reductions in execution time for both single-node and distributed executions, achieving a maximum speedup of 97.99 and efficiency values up to 0.86 in the full scenario.

The main lines for future work include exploring alternative architectures to address the problem, optimizing each component to minimize idle time, and evaluating the solution on computing platforms with more available resources.

Acknowledgment. The research was partly developed in a joint project with UTE. S. Freire was partly funded by PEDECIBA (First Experience on Research program).

References

1. Avila, D., Papavasiliou, A., Löhndorf, N.: Parallel and distributed computing for stochastic dual dynamic programming. CMS **19**, 199–226 (2022)
2. da Costa, V., et al.: Electricity markets in the context of distributed energy resources and demand response programs: main developments and challenges based on a systematic literature review. Energies **15**(20) (2022)
3. Dias, B., et al.: Parallel computing applied to the stochastic dynamic programming for long term operation planning of hydrothermal power systems. Eur. J. Oper. Res. **229**(1), 212–222 (2013)
4. Dinçer, H., Krishankumar, R., Yüksel, S., Ecer, F.: Evaluating smart grid investment drivers and creating effective policies via a fuzzy multi-criteria approach. Renew. Sustain. Energy Rev. **208**, 115052 (2025)
5. Foster, I.: Designing and Building Parallel Programs: Concepts and Tools for Parallel Software Engineering. Addison-Wesley Longman Publishing Co., Inc. (1995)
6. Gil, E., Araya, J.: Short-term hydrothermal generation scheduling using a parallelized stochastic mixed-integer linear programming algorithm. Energy Procedia **87**, 77–84 (2016)
7. International Atomic Energy Agency: Wien Automatic System Planning (WASP) Package: A Computer Code for Power Generating System Expansion Planning Version WASP-IV. Technical report, IAEA/CMS/16 (2001)
8. Kumar, R., Datta Ray, P., Reed, C.: Smart grid: an electricity market perspective. In: Innovative Smart Grid Technologies Conference Europe, pp. 1–8 (2011)
9. Lara, C., Siirola, J., Grossmann, I.: Electric power infrastructure planning under uncertainty: stochastic dual dynamic integer programming (SDDIP) and parallelization scheme. Optim. Eng. **21**(4), 1243–1281 (2020)
10. Machado, F., Diniz, A., Borges, C., Brandão, L.: Asynchronous parallel stochastic dual dynamic programming applied to hydrothermal generation planning. Electric Power Syst. Res. **191**, 106907 (2021)

11. Nesmachnow, S., Iturriaga, S.: Cluster-UY: collaborative scientific high performance computing in Uruguay. In: Torres, M., Klapp, J. (eds.) ISUM 2019. CCIS, vol. 1151, pp. 188–202. Springer, Cham (2019). https://doi.org/10.1007/978-3-030-38043-4_16
12. Pedrini, R., Beltrán, F., Finardi, E.: Innovative approaches to stochastic dual dynamic programming: two-period decomposition and parallelization in a hydrothermal scheduling case study. J. Water Resour. Plan. Manag. **150**(12), 05024014 (2024)
13. Razon, A., Thomas, T., Banunarayanan, V.: Advanced distribution management systems: connectivity through standardized interoperability protocols. IEEE Power Energ. Mag. **18**(1), 26–33 (2020)
14. Tasende, D.: Power generation investment: an algorithm to get a good feasible solution from operation simulations. Facultad de Ingeniería, Universidad de la República (Uruguay), Tesis de Maestría en Ingeniería Matemática (2002)
15. Wang, X., et al.: Design strategy of electricity purchase and sale combination package based on the characteristics of electricity prosumers in power system. Processes **12**(12) (2024)

Fast Sorting for the RISC-V "V" Vector Extension

Daniel Salmun[1] and Esteban Mocskos[1,2(✉)]

[1] Universidad de Buenos Aires. Facultad de Ciencias Exactas y Naturales. Departamento de Computación. Pabellón 0+inf Ciudad Universitaria, Ciudad Autónoma de Buenos Aires (C1428EGA), Buenos Aires, Argentina
{dsalmun,emocskos}@dc.uba.ar

[2] CONICET. Centro de Simulación Computacional para Aplicaciones Tecnológicas (CSC-CONICET). Godoy Cruz 2390. Ciudad Autónoma de Buenos Aires (C1425FQD), Buenos Aires, Argentina

Abstract. The increasing adoption of the RISC-V instruction set architecture (ISA), particularly its "V" Vector (RVV) extension, introduces new opportunities and challenges for software optimization. This paper tackles high-performance sorting on RISC-V processors by developing a native, in-place, single-threaded vectorized Quicksort algorithm specifically optimized for the RVV extension. We investigate key optimization techniques, including (1) LMUL-aware register grouping to maximize throughput, (2) arithmetic workarounds for RVV's lack of interleaving instructions, and (3) strategic instruction reordering to mitigate hazards. Comprehensive experimental evaluations on a `SpacemiT K1` processor (RV64GCVB, 256-bit VLEN) demonstrate superior performance: for large datasets of 32-bit integers, our implementation significantly outperforms all compared state-of-the-art sorting implementations, achieving a speedup of up to 1.89 times over the fastest alternative. These findings highlight RVV's potential for computationally intensive tasks and offer insights into overcoming its unique architectural challenges, such as implementation-defined register widths and variations in available vector instructions compared to other SIMD platforms.

Keywords: RISC-V Vector Extension · Vectorized Sorting · Quicksort Optimization · SIMD Algorithms

1 Introduction

RISC-V is an open, modular, extensible, royalty-free instruction set architecture (ISA) based on the principles of reduced instruction set computer (RISC) design [2]. This ISA has attracted great interest from both industry and academia, leading to a proliferation of new implementations [12], extensions [11], and software applications [21].

As a modular ISA, RISC-V includes optional extensions to its base specification that enhance the instruction set. This flexibility allows each RISC-V

K. Brown et al. (Eds.): CARLA 2025, CCIS 2750, pp. 65–79, 2026.
https://doi.org/10.1007/978-3-032-24923-4_5

implementation to support a chosen subset of extensions, enabling manufacturers to create custom processors optimized for specific applications by balancing performance and power consumption.

This work focuses primarily on the RISC-V "V" Vector (RVV) extension [1], which adds vector instructions to the ISA, enabling simultaneous processing of multiple data elements with a single instruction. Most modern processors feature this capability, called Single Instruction Multiple Data (SIMD). A key feature of the RVV extension is that the ISA does not predefine the SIMD register size; instead, its design allows each manufacturer to define it according to their needs, provided they comply with the minimum and maximum size restrictions. Consequently, the vector instructions are agnostic to the SIMD register length, a design choice that differentiates RVV from most other SIMD extensions that specify a fixed register size. A notable exception is the ARM SVE extension, which also features a vector-length agnostic design [27].

This work applies the unique features of the RVV extension to one of the fundamental problems of Computer Science: sorting. Solutions to the sorting problem have appeared since the 1950s, and the literature has extensively studied them [19] due to the strong impact that sorting techniques have on application performance. Specifically, this work develops an efficient sorting algorithm capable of exploiting the parallel processing capabilities of the RVV extension.

One sorting algorithm that is well-suited for this purpose is Quicksort [16]. The literature first mentioned Quicksort's vectorization in the 1970s, where researchers implemented it on the CDC STAR supercomputer [28]. However, it was not until the late 2000s that vectorized hybrid sorting algorithms for general-purpose processors became the subject of study. Furtak et al. [14] present vectorized sorting networks as an optimization to the base cases of recursive sorting algorithms. Subsequently, Inoue et al. [17] and Chhugani et al. [9] provide hybrid vectorized implementations of MergeSort for the PowerPC 970MP and Intel SSE extension, respectively. In 2015, Gueron et al. [15] provide a vectorized implementation of Quicksort for the Intel AVX2 extension. With the advent of AVX-512, Bramas [7] improves upon this work by performing the array partition in-place.

These techniques and improvements have proven effective in the industry, as Intel's official sorting library and Google's Highway `vqsort` [30] currently employ them. The underlying Highway library provides portable SIMD intrinsics for various ISAs—including support for the RVV extension as a backend—making its `vqsort` implementation platform-independent. However, while `vqsort`'s authors tested its functionality on an emulator, they did not, to our knowledge, conduct benchmarks on actual RVV hardware.

Therefore, this paper presents a native, single-threaded vectorized Quicksort for the RISC-V "V" Vector extension by combining Bramas's partition algorithm, using sorting networks as Quicksort's base case, and employing a simple yet robust pivot selection [20]. We analyze its performance against the vectorized `vqsort`. Moreover, we compare it against a selection of state-of-the-art scalar implementations: LLVM's `std::sort`, `boost::pdqsort`, `boost::integer_sort`, and `IPS`^{4}`o`. The first two implementations are based on variations of Quicksort [22,23], the third is an implementation of Spreadsort [25], and the last derives from Samplesort [3,13].

2 Implementation

2.1 Overview

As a Divide & Conquer algorithm, Quicksort divides the process of sorting a subarray $A[p:r]$ into three stages [10]:

1. **Divide**: Select any element $A[q]$, which serves as the **pivot**, and **partition** (rearrange) the array $A[p:r]$ into two subarrays $A[p:q-1]$ and $A[q+1:r]$, such that all elements in $A[p:q-1]$ are less than or equal to the pivot, and all elements in $A[q+1:r]$ are greater than or equal to the pivot.
2. **Conquer**: Recursively call Quicksort to sort the subarrays $A[p:q-1]$ and $A[q+1:r]$ until they are trivially sorted (i.e., they contain zero or one element).
3. **Combine**: From the previous stage, the subarray $A[p:q-1]$ is sorted and less than or equal to $A[q]$, and the subarray $A[q+1:r]$ is sorted and greater than or equal to $A[q]$. Therefore, the subarray $A[p:r]$ is sorted and requires no further processing.

This work focuses on three key aspects of the algorithm: selecting a pivot, partitioning the array, and replacing the base case with sorting networks when the subarray size is below a threshold.

2.2 Pivot Selection

In Quicksort, proper pivot selection is essential for a high-performing implementation, as it ensures the workload is evenly distributed between the two recursively processed subarrays. In the worst-case scenario, if the pivot is consistently chosen as the largest or smallest array element, the algorithm degrades significantly. This occurs because the partition step repeatedly divides the array into highly unbalanced subarrays–one empty and the other containing $n-1$ elements–resulting in an overall complexity of $\mathcal{O}(n^2)$. Conversely, when pivots are selected such that they consistently yield subarrays of similar sizes, Quicksort achieves its expected time complexity of $\mathcal{O}(n \log n)$. Therefore, a pivot selection method that is robust across various data distributions is essential [10].

The most direct way to meet this requirement is to obtain the median of the subarray. However, this results in a complexity of $\mathcal{O}(n)$ for the pivot selection, while the expected complexity is $\mathcal{O}(1)$ for this procedure. Therefore, a good trade-off is to take a constant-size sample of the subarray we want to partition. Nevertheless, taking the median of three or five elements, a common practice in the literature, may not be sufficient to obtain a good pivot. In the `pdqsort` paper, Peters [23] recommends using the technique called `ninther` [29] for sufficiently large inputs. This technique involves taking nine elements from the array, computing the median of each of the three subarrays of three elements, and then obtaining the median of the three resulting medians. In this way, we obtain a value that is a highly accurate approximation of the true median of the array [20]. LLVM's `std::sort` currently uses this method: it employs the median of three elements for arrays of up to 128 elements, while it uses `ninther` for larger arrays. We adopt this strategy in our implementation to ensure the fairest possible comparison between our implementation and LLVM's `std::sort`.

2.3 Partition

The partitioning step is asymptotically the most expensive stage of the algorithm, as it is linear in the size of the array. A common way to solve this problem is to use two iterators, one that traverses the array from the beginning and another from the end. Iterators swap elements to satisfy the Quicksort invariant, meaning that all elements less than or equal to the pivot are on the left, and all elements greater than or equal to the pivot are on the right. However, this scalar implementation cannot take advantage of the vector capabilities available to us.

Therefore, we adopt Bramas's vector partitioning procedure [7]. The algorithm first establishes four pointers: a read and a write pointer for both the left and right sides of the array. To create an initial buffer, it pre-loads a full vector of elements from each end, while also broadcasting the pivot $A[q]$ into a dedicated vector register for the upcoming comparisons. In each loop iteration, it loads a vector from the side with less available write space to keep the buffers balanced. The data vector is compared against the pivot to generate masks, which the `vcompress` instruction then uses to compact the smaller ($\leq A[q]$) and larger ($\geq A[q]$) elements into separate vector registers. These compacted vectors are subsequently written to memory at the locations indicated by the write pointers. This loop continues until the gap between the left and right read pointers becomes too small to load a full vector. Afterwards, a cleanup phase handles all remaining elements, including the two initially pre-loaded vectors. Finally, the pivot $A[q]$ is swapped into the location of the left write pointer, completing the partition.

2.4 Sorting Networks

Quicksort's logic is inherently more complex than simpler algorithms like Insertion Sort or Selection Sort–an added complexity that comes at a cost. While this cost is amortized over large inputs, it can be significant for small arrays.

This issue is exacerbated by Quicksort's recursive nature: as the array is partitioned, the sizes of the resulting subarrays shrink, leading to a large number of recursive calls on increasingly smaller segments. To mitigate this, a common optimization introduces a fixed-size threshold. Subarrays smaller than this threshold are then sorted using a simpler algorithm that is more efficient for small inputs–typically Insertion Sort [26].

However, is Insertion Sort indeed the best choice? Despite its conceptual simplicity, its inner loop contains numerous data-dependent swaps and unpredictable conditional branching. These characteristics negatively impact performance on modern CPUs with deep instruction pipelines.

As an alternative, we propose using sorting networks, a well-studied construct with two key advantages: they are easily vectorizable and employ a data-oblivious sequence of comparisons. These properties make sorting networks particularly attractive for architectures with SIMD support [9] and for GPU implementations [18].

Researchers originally described sorting networks in the 1950s as a way to sort fixed-size arrays using a fixed number of comparisons and data movement operations. Subsequently, significant academic interest has focused on discovering the minimum number of comparisons necessary to sort a constant-size array with sorting networks [19].

Figure 1 illustrates a common way to represent sorting networks. These diagrams consist of horizontal lines, called *wires*, to represent array elements, and vertical lines, called *comparators*, to connect two wires. If a comparator's upper wire holds an element greater than its lower wire (assuming ascending order), it exchanges the elements. The diagram is interpreted from left to right. Input values enter the wires on the left and move through the network, where they are swapped by any comparator they encounter if they are in the wrong order. On the right side of the diagram, we obtain the sorted array.

(a) Trivial processing of two elements (b) Processing three elements

Fig. 1. Sorting networks. Each horizontal line represents an element from the input array, while the vertical lines represent compare-and-exchange operations between elements. The diagram is read from left to right.

Unfortunately, no general method is known for constructing optimal sorting networks for arbitrary fixed-size arrays. However, recursive approaches can approximate optimality. Batcher introduced two such methods: Odd-Even Merge Sort and Bitonic Merge Sort [4], both requiring $\mathcal{O}(n \log^2 n)$ comparisons. In practice, Odd-Even Merge Sort typically uses fewer comparisons than Bitonic Merge Sort. However, it does not perform comparisons between all elements at each stage, which complicates its implementation. On processors with SIMD extensions, Bitonic Merge Sort often outperforms Odd-Even Merge Sort due to its simpler and more regular structure, which reduces the cost of masking and data movement [9].

Vectorization. The idea of using SIMD instructions to accelerate sorting networks in general-purpose processors originates from the work of Furtak et al. [14]. Their research details how to vectorize sorting networks, provided the SIMD extension offers at least one instruction for element movement within a register (e.g., permutation or shuffle), along with instructions for element-wise minimum and maximum.

Then, Inoue et al. [17] and Chhugani et al. [9] provide more details on how to use SIMD instructions to optimize sorting networks for the IBM PowerPC 970MP processor and Intel's SSE extension, respectively. Their method consists of modeling each register as a row of a matrix, and then sorting the matrix column-wise by using a sequence of predefined min/max and shuffle instructions, followed by transposing it and merging the rows. In contrast, Bramas implements a more direct approach: creating different sorting networks based on the number of SIMD registers required to contain the subarray. His implementation supports sorting up to a maximum of 16 SIMD registers at a time, equivalent to 256 elements for 32-bit integer sorting using AVX-512 registers [7].

In all previously discussed works, a known SIMD register width at compile time enables the use of statically defined permutation values to create sorting networks. This is not possible in RVV due to implementation-defined SIMD register widths. However, Bramas's follow-up work on ARM SVE [8] proposes modifications to his original AVX-512 implementation to make the procedure vector length agnostic. Instead of predefined permutation vectors, he proposes a loop-based scheme that dynamically generates a permutation vector in each iteration for each level of the sorting network based on Bitonic Merge Sort.

Figure 2 shows the Bitonic Merge Sort sorting network for 16 elements. The network employs a bottom-up divide-and-conquer approach, where the first subnetworks (marked in blue) merge two trivially sorted sequences of size 1 and output a sorted sequence of size 2, as in Fig. 1(a). The second subnetworks merge two sorted sequences of size 2 and output a sorted sequence of size 4. This process continues until we reach the final sorted sequence of size 16. Our solution iteratively recreates each of these subnetworks by constructing at runtime the masks that define the element movements for each stage.

Our initial implementation takes inspiration from Bramas's ARM SVE implementation. However, manually rewriting the implementation from ARM SVE to RVV is not entirely straightforward, as ARM SVE includes instructions that lack similar counterparts in RVV. In these cases, we must emulate the instruction's behavior.

Two instructions are particularly problematic: `zip1` and `uzp2`. The first takes two vectors and returns the result of interleaving the elements from the lower halves. The second takes two vectors and returns the result of interleaving the elements with odd indices from the inputs. RVV has no instruction that allows such interleaving; the closest is the `vrgather` instruction, which tends to be costly. This problem worsens because we want to perform these operations on masks. Masks are special cases in RISC-V because they do not account for the width of

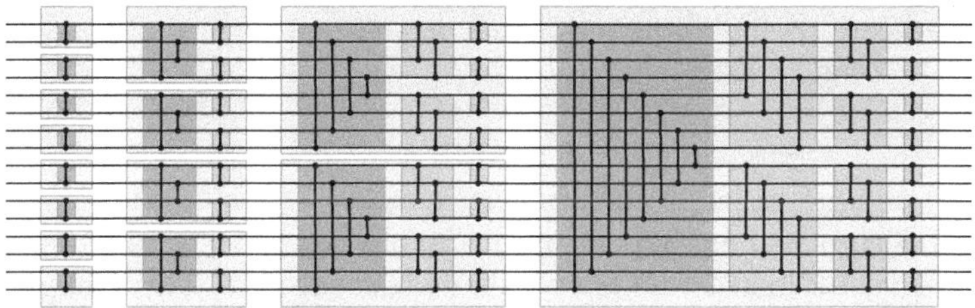

Fig. 2. Bitonic Merge Sort for 16 elements. Each subnetwork (marked in blue) merges two sorted sequences of equal size; the leftmost subnetworks merge two trivially sorted sequences of size 1 to output a sorted sequence of size 2 (reproduced from the public domain). (Color figure online)

the element we are processing; instead, each bit of the mask represents a vector element. Therefore, we must first widen the mask bits to the width of the element, and then perform a shuffle to obtain the result. The lack of interleaving and mask modification instructions in RISC-V is a problem that members of the RISC-V International organization have already noted and analyzed [5,31]. Fortunately, they propose alternative arithmetic methods for performing interleaving operations for non-mask elements, potentially using fewer cycles than shuffle instructions. These methods involve element *widening* as a `zip` replacement, and *narrowing* as an `unzip` replacement.

As in Bramas's work, we define different specialized functions at compile time, each targeting a specific count of SIMD registers needed to hold the array, for register counts ranging up to 16. For instance, if a partition fits into eight SIMD registers, we call the function designed for that specific size. When a subarray's elements do not completely fill the registers, we pad the remaining lanes with the maximum value for that data type. These padding values are then filtered out when writing the sorted results back to memory.

Reducing Impact of Data Hazards. Our initial implementation suffered considerably from data hazards in both the sorting network and partitioning procedures. To reduce these, we reordered instructions to ensure sufficient separation between data-dependent instructions. This optimization minimizes potential pipeline stalls and is particularly significant for our target hardware, an in-order processor, which cannot reorder instructions to reduce data hazards.

Bramas's sorting networks implementation for ARM SVE [8] includes this optimization. To understand it, consider the naive approach: sorting one subarray completely, then sorting the second, and finally merging them, as detailed in our explanation of Bitonic Merge Sort. In contrast, the optimized approach sorts both subarrays simultaneously by interleaving their corresponding instructions. The approach uses different SIMD registers for each subarray, as they contain data from distinct subarrays. By interleaving operations on these independent SIMD registers, we create a sequence of instructions with fewer immediate data dependencies, thus mitigating data hazards. Moreover, this approach reduces overhead by combining multiple loops into one, which also allows for the efficient reuse of generated mask values.

Vector Register Grouping. The RISC-V "V" Vector extension specification details a technique called *vector register grouping.* This feature allows multiple SIMD registers to be grouped to functionally act as a single, larger register, enabling one vector instruction to operate on them at once. This grouping is configured by setting the Vector Length Multiplier (LMUL) using the `vset[i]vl[i]` instruction. According to the specification, this functionality's original purpose was to operate on a consistent number of elements across different data type widths. However, our work focuses on an observation from the specification's authors: they note its potential to increase the throughput of vector instruction execution in some workloads, an advantage we leverage in our implementation.

The possible values for LMUL are 1, 2, 4, 8, $\frac{1}{2}$, $\frac{1}{4}$, and $\frac{1}{8}$. Fractional LMUL values only use a fraction of each SIMD register, while integer LMUL values use contiguous SIMD registers as a single vector. We must note that increasing LMUL is not always an optimization: defining an LMUL>1 reduces the number of usable SIMD registers from 32 to $\frac{32}{LMUL}$. This increases the register pressure considerably, which can cause problems with our implementation. Furthermore, the latency of essential instructions for our algorithm, such as `vrgather` and `vcompress`, can grow exponentially with LMUL [6,24].

Consequently, we implement both the partitioning and sorting networks subalgorithms using different LMUL values that we hypothesize are high-performing. Our experiments then determine the optimal LMUL value for each procedure on the target processor.

3 Experimental Evaluation

We conduct the experiments on the `Banana Pi BPI-F3` board, which features a `SpacemiT K1` processor with 8 `SpacemiT X60 RISC-V` cores (1.6 GHz, 8-stage dual-issue in-order pipeline). It adheres to the `RV64GCVB` ISA and the `RVA22` profile standard, featuring 256-bit wide SIMD registers and 8 GB of LPDDR4 RAM. To run and compile the software, we use `Bianbu OS 2.1.2` and `LLVM 19.1.1`. Unless the library's authors specify otherwise, we compile all implementations with `-stdlib=libc++ -march=rva22u64_v -O3`. No significant differences are observed when compiling with the `-O2` flag.

For all experiments, we use random uniform distributions of 32-bit signed integers. The number of test repetitions varies with the input size: smaller arrays are tested up to 10 000 times, while larger arrays are tested at least 10 times. In each repetition, a new seed is used to generate the array. We measure the median time for each data point, and calculate the *Million Elements Per Second* (MEPS) metric, which represents the number of elements processed per second. This metric is useful as a way to normalize performance across arrays of different sizes. We opted for the median time over the mean to avoid the impact of outliers, which were common when evaluating small array sizes on the platform. The shaded areas in the figures represent the interquartile range (IQR) of the time measurements.

In all experiments, we validate our results: for the full sort implementation, we compare our output against that of LLVM's `std::sort` to ensure they are identical. For the partitioning procedure, we verify that the output array correctly satisfies the partition invariant.

3.1 Partition

Figure 3 presents the performance evaluation of the partitioning procedure using different LMUL values and the comparison to LLVM's `std::partition`. It is important to emphasize that this evaluation focuses solely on the partitioning step, not the full Quicksort implementation.

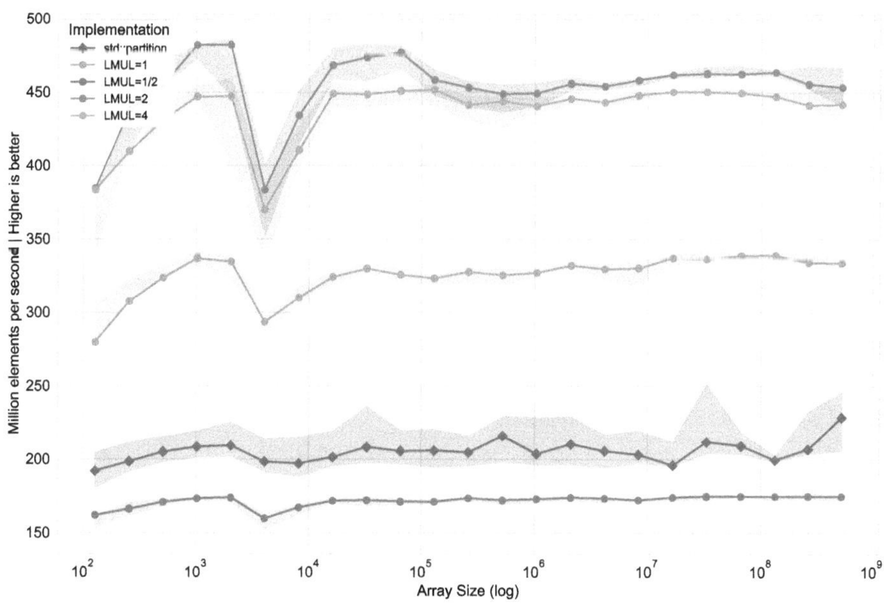

Fig. 3. Performance of the partitioning procedure implemented with different LMUL values, compared to LLVM's `std::partition`.

The pivot element is selected using the strategy described in Sect. 2.2. We benchmark performance across a range of array sizes, each a power of two and bounded by the platform's memory size. To improve readability, the X-axis of the figure uses a logarithmic scale.

Despite some variability, the implementation using LMUL = 2 consistently achieves the best performance across all tested sizes. We believe this is because the procedure does not use a significant number of instructions that slow down exponentially with LMUL (such as those listed in Sect. 2.4). Therefore, increasing the LMUL value to LMUL = 2 doubles the number of elements processed per instruction, reduces the number of instructions decoded and executed, and reduces the iterations needed to process the array. The only instruction in the procedure that slows down exponentially with LMUL is the `vcompress` instruction, whose increased latency might be the reason why LMUL = 4 performs slightly worse than LMUL = 2. Conversely, the fractional LMUL values perform poorly. For LMUL = $\frac{1}{2}$, the benefit of a lower-latency `vcompress` instruction does not compensate for processing half as many elements per instruction. The same behavior is less significantly observed for LMUL = 1.

Compared to LLVM's `std::partition`, our LMUL = 2 implementation achieves a speedup of up to 2.36 times, measured in MEPS.

A sharp performance drop is observed across all implementations when partitioning arrays of size 8192. We attribute this to the fact that 8192 32-bit elements occupy 32 kB, which matches the L1D cache size of the `SpacemiT X60` core–likely resulting in frequent cache misses. However, it is not clear why subsequent array sizes are not affected by the considerably slower L2 cache: public information regarding the `SpacemiT K1`'s microarchitecture is limited, and Linux `perf` tools are not fully supported on the platform. Nevertheless, we speculate that an effective hardware prefetcher might be responsible for the observed behavior.

3.2 Sorting Networks

As discussed in Sect. 2.4, our sorting networks are designed to sort arrays that fit within 16 SIMD registers. On our platform, which has SIMD registers of 256 bits, this corresponds to array sizes of up to 128 32-bit elements. In the case of LMUL = $\frac{1}{2}$, we test all array sizes up to 64 elements, as only half the register width is available. We compare our sorting network implementations against LLVM's `std::sort`, as shown in Fig. 4.

For all LMUL values, we observe higher throughput when sorting up to 8 SIMD registers at a time instead of 16 SIMD registers. A possible reason is that while the procedure benefits from the use of multiple SIMD registers, larger sorting networks are negatively affected by high register pressure.

Our implementations using LMUL = 1 and LMUL = $\frac{1}{2}$ significantly outperform LLVM's std::sort, achieving speedups of up to 2.04 times and 1.92 times, respectively. For small arrays (32 elements or fewer), the LMUL = $\frac{1}{2}$ implementation delivers the highest throughput. We believe this is because the vrgather instruction, whose latency increases with the LMUL setting, becomes the primary bottleneck. This issue is more pronounced in the LMUL = 2 and LMUL = 4 variants, which are hampered not only by the high latency of `vrgather` but also by high register pressure. As a result, while the LMUL = 2 implementation can occasionally beat `std::sort`, it remains consistently slower than the LMUL = 1 and LMUL = 1/2 versions in all tested cases.

The clear sawtooth pattern visible in Fig. 4 is expected. This effect occurs when the array size is not perfectly divisible by the number of elements in a SIMD register. In these cases, the algorithm pads the final vector with the data

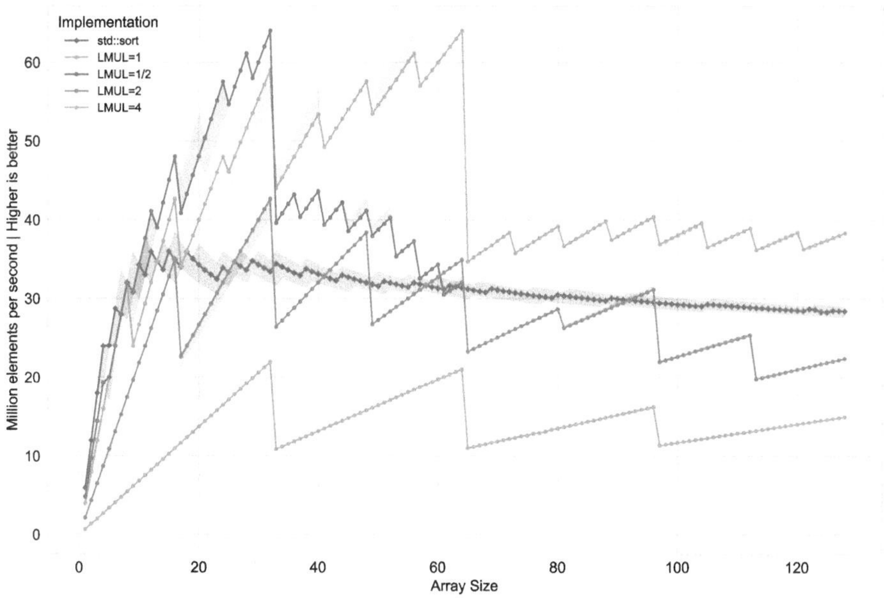

Fig. 4. Performance of the sorting networks procedure implemented with varying LMUL values, compared to LLVM's `std::sort`.

type's maximum value. Although it contains filler, this vector requires the same computational effort as one entirely filled with valid data, causing a relative drop in performance.

3.3 Overall

Selecting the best LMUL value is challenging, as performance varies significantly with array size. Based on our results, we made the following choices for our Quicksort implementation:

- For the partitioning procedure, we selected LMUL = 2, which consistently delivered the best performance across all tested inputs.
- For the sorting networks, we chose LMUL = 1, using a cutoff point corresponding to the capacity of eight SIMD registers. While the LMUL = $\frac{1}{2}$ variant shows higher throughput for very small arrays (32 elements or fewer, as seen in Fig. 4), we opted for the simpler LMUL = 1 implementation to avoid the overhead of additional branching.

We benchmark our optimized implementation against several state-of-the-art solutions, using array sizes that span powers of two and powers of ten and bounded by the platform's memory size. The results are presented in Fig. 5, which uses a logarithmic scale for the X-axis to cover the wide range of inputs. The figure indicates that our implementation consistently achieves the highest throughput among all tested solutions.

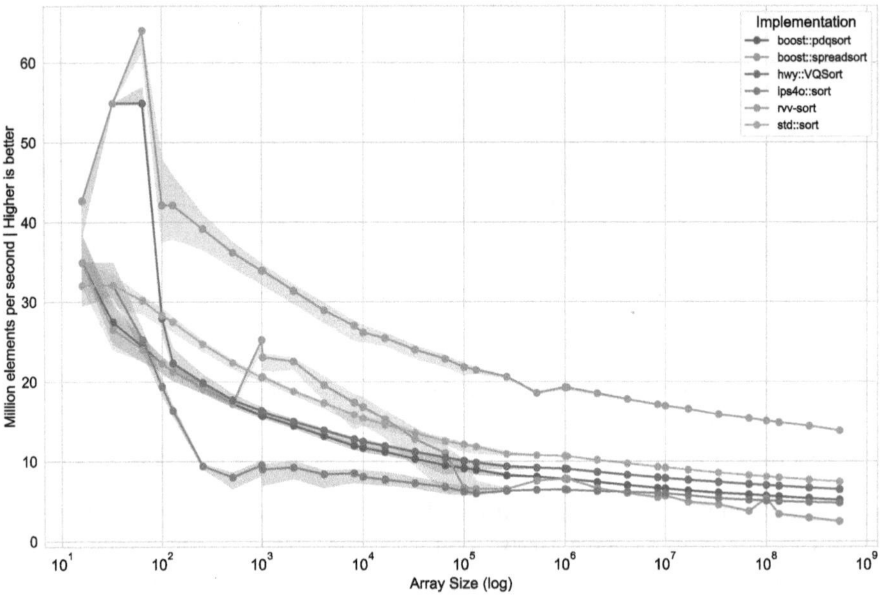

Fig. 5. Performance of our optimized implementation compared to state-of-the-art implementations.

Figure 6 shows the speedup of our implementation relative to the second-fastest method, LLVM's `std::sort`. While our algorithm is faster across all inputs, the performance gain varies with the array size.

The peak speedup of 2.12 times is achieved with 64-element arrays. This is the ideal size for our implementation, as it fits entirely within the in-register sorting network that serves as our Quicksort's base case.

Beyond this point, the speedup temporarily decreases, narrowing to 1.49 times for moderately sized arrays, before recovering and increasing again as the input size grows larger. Performance for smaller arrays showed higher variability, as evidenced by a large IQR in the measurements. This is likely due to the disproportionate impact of a few unbalanced partitions, an effect that is amortized as the array size increases.

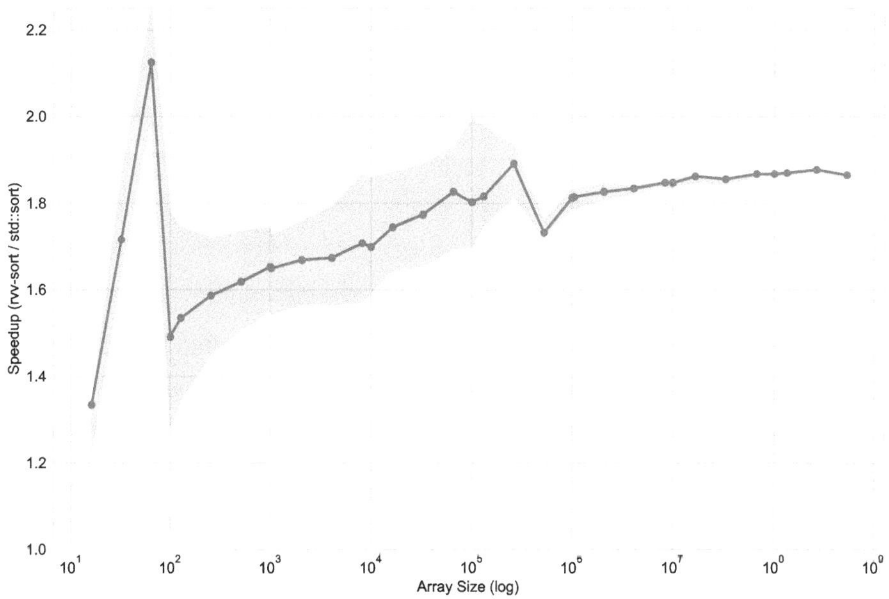

Fig. 6. Speedup of our optimized implementation compared to the second overall fastest implementation, LLVM's `std::sort`.

4 Conclusions

In this work, we present a high-performance, vectorized Quicksort algorithm optimized for the RISC-V "V" Vector Extension (RVV). By porting and adapting established techniques from other SIMD architectures to the RVV ISA, our implementation outperforms all other sorting algorithms evaluated, achieving speedups of up to 1.89 times on large arrays.

The performance gains stem from several key optimizations: the use of Bramas's in-place partitioning algorithm, vectorized sorting networks for small subarrays, careful fine-tuning of LMUL values across subprocedures, and strategic instruction reordering to reduce data hazards. Our experiments show that LMUL = 2 yields optimal results for partitioning, while LMUL = 1 is better suited for sorting networks, underscoring the importance of tailoring vector register configuration to specific workloads.

Moreover, we addressed RVV-specific challenges, including its implementation-defined vector register width and the absence of certain SIMD instructions commonly available in other architectures. Despite these constraints, our results demonstrate that RVV can deliver competitive performance for sorting through careful algorithmic adaptation and tuning.

Beyond advancing the state of the art in sorting for RISC-V, our work offers general insights into writing high-performance vectorized code for this emerging platform. As the RISC-V ecosystem continues to evolve, we hope these techniques will aid future efforts to optimize a broader class of algorithms on RVV-enabled processors.

Acknowledgments. This work is partially supported by grants from Universidad de Buenos Aires (UBA) UBACYT 20620190100001BA, and CONICET PIP 11220220100027CsO.

References

1. Amid, A., et al.: RISC-V "V" vector extension 1.0. GitHub Release (2021). https://github.com/riscvarchive/riscv-v-spec/releases/download/v1.0/riscv-v-spec-1.0.pdf. Accessed 29 Apr 2026
2. Asanović, K., Patterson, D.A.: Instruction sets should be free: the case for RISC-V. Technical report, UCB/EECS-2014-146, University of California, Berkeley (2014). http://www2.eecs.berkeley.edu/Pubs/TechRpts/2014/EECS-2014-146.html
3. Axtmann, M., Witt, S., Ferizovic, D., Sanders, P.: In-place parallel super scalar samplesort (IPSSSSo). In: Pruhs, K., Sohler, C. (eds.) Proc of the Annual European Symposium on Algorithms (ESA). Leibniz Int Proc in Informatics (LIPIcs), vol. 87, pp. 9:1–9:14. Schloss Dagstuhl - Leibniz-Zentrum für Informatik, Dagstuhl, Germany (2017). https://doi.org/10.4230/LIPIcs.ESA.2017.9
4. Batcher, K.E.: Sorting networks and their applications. In: Proceedings of the Spring Joint Computer Conference. AFIPS '68, pp. 307–314 (Spring), ACM, New York, NY, USA (1968). https://doi.org/10.1145/1468075.1468121
5. Bernstein, O.: RISC-V vector extension for integer workloads: an informal gap analysis. GitHub Gist (2024). https://gist.github.com/camel-cdr/99a41367d6529f390d25e36ca3e4b626. Accessed 29 Apr 2026
6. Bernstein, O.: RVV benchmark (2024). https://camel-cdr.github.io/rvv-bench-results. Accessed 29 Apr 2026
7. Bramas, B.: A novel hybrid quicksort algorithm vectorized using AVX-512 on Intel Skylake. Int. J. Adv. Comput. Sci. App. **8** (2017). https://doi.org/10.14569/IJACSA.2017.081044
8. Bramas, B.: A fast vectorized sorting implementation based on the ARM scalable vector extension (SVE). PeerJ Comput. Sci. **7**, e769 (2021). https://doi.org/10.7717/peerj-cs.769
9. Chhugani, J., et al.: Efficient implementation of sorting on multi-core SIMD CPU architecture. Proc. VLDB Endow. **1**(2), 1313–1324 (2008). https://doi.org/10.14778/1454159.1454171
10. Cormen, T., Leiserson, C., Rivest, R., Stein, C.: Introduction to Algorithms, 4 edn. MIT Press, Cambridge (2022)
11. Cui, E., Li, T., Wei, Q.: RISC-V instruction set architecture extensions: a survey. IEEE Access (2023). https://doi.org/10.1109/ACCESS.2023.3246491
12. Dörflinger, A., et al.: A comparative survey of open-source application-class RISC-V processor implementations. In: Proceedings of the 18th ACM International Conference on Computing Frontiers. CF '21, pp. 12–20. ACM, New York, NY, USA (2021). https://doi.org/10.1145/3457388.3458657
13. Frazer, W.D., McKellar, A.C.: SampleSort: a sampling approach to minimal storage tree sorting. J. ACM **17**(3), 496–507 (1970). https://doi.org/10.1145/321592.321600

14. Furtak, T., Amaral, J.N., Niewiadomski, R.: Using SIMD registers and instructions to enable instruction-level parallelism in sorting algorithms. In: Proceedings of the Nineteenth Annual ACM Symposium on Parallel Algorithms and Architectures. SPAA ’07, pp. 348–357. ACM, New York, NY, USA (2007). https://doi.org/10.1145/1248377.1248436
15. Gueron, S., Krasnov, V.: Fast quicksort implementation using AVX instructions. Comput. J. **59**(1), 83–90 (2015). https://doi.org/10.1093/comjnl/bxv063
16. Hoare, C.A.R.: Quicksort. Comput. J. **5**(1), 10–16 (1962). https://doi.org/10.1093/comjnl/5.1.10
17. Inoue, H., Moriyama, T., Komatsu, H., Nakatani, T.: AA-Sort: a new parallel sorting algorithm for multi-core SIMD processors. In: 16th International Conference on Parallel Architecture and Compilation Techniques. PACT ’07, pp. 189–198 (2007). https://doi.org/10.1109/PACT.2007.4336211
18. Kipfer, P., Westermann, R.: Improved GPU sorting. In: Pharr, M. (ed.) GPU Gems 2: Programming Techniques for High-Performance Graphics and General-Purpose Computation, chap. 46. Addison-Wesley Professional, Upper Saddle River, NJ (2005). https://developer.nvidia.com/gpugems/gpugems2/part-vi-simulation-and-numerical-algorithms/chapter-46-improved-gpu-sorting
19. Knuth, D.E.: The Art of Computer Programming, 2 edn, vol. 3. Addison Wesley Longman Publishing Co., Inc. (1998)
20. Kurosawa, N.: Quicksort with median of medians is considered practical (2016). https://doi.org/10.48550/arXiv.1608.04852
21. Mezger, B.W., Santos, D.A., Dilillo, L., Zeferino, C.A., Melo, D.R.: A survey of the RISC-V architecture software support. IEEE Access **10**, 51394–51411 (2022). https://doi.org/10.1109/ACCESS.2022.3174125
22. Musser, D.R.: Introspective sorting and selection algorithms. Softw. Pract. Exp. **27**(8), 983–993 (1997). https://doi.org/10.1002/(SICI)1097-024X(199708)27:8<983::AID-SPE117>3.0.CO;2-#
23. Peters, O.R.L.: Pattern-defeating quicksort (2021). https://doi.org/10.48550/arXiv.2106.05123
24. RISE: RISC-V optimization guide (2024). https://riscv-optimization-guide.riseproject.dev/. Accessed 29 Apr 2026
25. Ross, S.J.: The spreadsort high-performance general-case sorting algorithm. In: Proceedings of the International Conference on Parallel and Distributed Processing Techniques and Applications. PDPTA ’02, vol. 3, pp. 1100–1106. CSREA Press (2002)
26. Sedgewick, R., Wayne, K.: Algorithms, 4 edn. Addison-Wesley Professional (2011)
27. Stephens, N., et al.: The ARM scalable vector extension. IEEE Micro **37**(2), 26–39 (2017). https://doi.org/10.1109/MM.2017.35
28. Stone, H.S.: Sorting on STAR. IEEE Trans. Softw. Eng. **4**(2), 138–146 (1978). https://doi.org/10.1109/TSE.1978.231484
29. Tukey, J.W.: The ninther, a technique for low-effort robust (resistant) location in large samples. In: David, H.A. (ed.) Contributions to Survey Sampling and Applied Statistics, pp. 251–257. Academic Press (1978). https://doi.org/10.1016/B978-0-12-204750-3.50024-1
30. Wassenberg, J., Blacher, M., Giesen, J., Sanders, P.: Vectorized and performance-portable quicksort. Softw. Pract. Exp. **52**(12), 2684–2699 (2022). https://doi.org/10.1002/spe.3142
31. Yin, T., Jiayan, Q., Agrawal, P.: RISCV64 new vector instructions requirements for video / multimedia. RISE Project Confluence (2024). https://lf-rise.atlassian.net/wiki/x/5AyD. Accessed 29 Apr 2026

Good Sustainability Practices for Data Centers: A Systematic Literature Review

Josiany Brito Guimarães[2], Felipe Barbosa[1(✉)], Erick Damasceno[2], Fellipe Queiroz[2], and Marcos Amaris[1]

[1] Amazon Development Center in Engineering, Federal University of Para, Tucuruí, Brazil
felipe.barbosa@icen.ufpa.br, amaris@ufpa.br

[2] Institute of Exact and Natural Sciences, Federal University of Pará, Belém, Brazil
{josiany.guimaraes,erick.silva,fellipe.queiroz}@tucurui.ufpa.br

Abstract. The search for sustainable practices and energy efficiency in data centers has become a top priority in today's world, driven by the rapid growth in internet use and online traffic. This highlights the urgent need for research that focuses on practical strategies to reduce the environmental impact of these vital facilities. This article reviews 10 relevant studies that examine the primary methods used to enhance energy efficiency in data centers, including emerging technologies, resource management techniques, and sustainable policies. Additionally, the paper discusses the environmental impacts of data centers, including high energy consumption, greenhouse gas emissions, and intensive use of natural resources. The findings indicate that implementing good sustainability practices can bring several benefits, such as lowering operating costs and reducing the carbon footprint, while maintaining service quality.

Keywords: Energy Efficiency · Sustainability · Data Storage Center · Carbon Footprint · Best Practices

1 Introduction

The exponential growth in global data consumption has led to a continuous increase in the energy demand of data centers, raising significant concerns about their environmental sustainability. As pillars of the digital infrastructure, these centers are responsible for storing, processing, and transmitting large volumes of information, which results in higher energy consumption and CO_2 emissions. Intelligence applications will further aggravate their ecological footprint.

Without the adoption of sustainable practices, the growing dependence on these facilities (driven by increased internet traffic, cloud computing, and artificial intelligence applications) tends to make their ecological footprint even worse. This urgency is reinforced by a European Union report, published in 2023, which highlights the persistent growth in greenhouse gas (GHG) emissions since the early 2000s, with only a temporary reduction of 3.7% during the COVID-19 Pandemic [5].

K. Brown et al. (Eds.): CARLA 2025, CCIS 2750, pp. 80–93, 2026.
https://doi.org/10.1007/978-3-032-24923-4_6

In this context, the adoption of sustainable practices in data centers is no longer optional, but necessary, as it contributes simultaneously to mitigating environmental impacts and improving operational efficiency by reducing costs. Among the strategies analyzed, DevOps (a methodology that integrates software development practices and IT operations) has been explored as an alternative to promote sustainability [3].

By automating infrastructure management tasks such as server configuration, virtual machine provisioning, and energy monitoring, DevOps tools enable energy efficiency gains in organizations of different sizes. However, despite these advances, the adoption of sustainable practices in data centers remains fragmented, characterized by gaps in systematic implementation and a lack of affordable solutions, particularly for smaller institutions.

This article presents a systematic literature review to analyze current research on energy efficiency and sustainability in *data centers*, structured along three principal axes. Firstly, it seeks to identify best practices for *green data centers* and assess their environmental impacts. Next, it examines the role of automation tools, such as DevOps, in enhancing energy efficiency and improving its economic viability, particularly when applied through open-source solutions.

Finally, it highlights gaps in the literature, providing input for the development of a practical framework for the design of sustainable *data centers*. By synthesizing existing studies, this review aims to guide future research and offer practical recommendations for reducing the ecological footprint of *data centers*, without compromising performance or accessibility.

The article is organized into six sections: Sect. 1 presents the introduction; Sect. 2 discusses the theoretical framework; Sect. 3 describes the methodological procedures adopted; Sect. 4 presents and analyzes the results; and Sect. 5 brings together the findings and directions for future research.

2 Theoretical Background

This section presents the fundamental concepts that underpin the studies analyzed, focusing on the relationships between CO_2 emissions, energy efficiency, and data center infrastructure. Relevant approaches and technologies are also discussed, such as *DevOps*, green computing, virtualization, and *Machine Learning*, which contribute to sustainability in IT environments.

Carbon dioxide (CO_2) is a colorless gas made up of two oxygen atoms and one carbon atom, released mainly during the burning of fossil fuels (such as oil, coal, and natural gas). Its accumulation in the atmosphere intensifies the greenhouse effect and contributes to climate change [20].

Energy efficiency refers to the ability to achieve maximum performance using the least amount of energy possible. In data centers, this means reducing consumption without compromising the quality of the services provided, contributing directly to the reduction of CO_2 emissions.

Data centers, which are responsible for storing, processing, and distributing large volumes of data, are among the biggest energy consumers in the technology sector. These environments comprise a complex IT infrastructure consisting of servers, storage systems, and network equipment, including routers, switches, firewalls, and Wi-Fi access points [6]. In addition, they use cooling systems and redundant power sources (such as batteries and generators) to guarantee the constant availability of services.

The **DevOps** methodology integrates software development and IT operations practices, promoting process automation, continuous integration, and collaboration between teams [2,24]. This approach enables faster and more efficient deliveries, with reduced waste of computing resources, and is being explored as an alternative support method to enhance sustainability in IT operations.

These strategies are part of the concept of green computing, an approach that extends beyond the technical and assumes a strategic role by aligning technological innovation with sustainability. Green computing aims to minimize the environmental impact of technology through practices such as virtualization, automation, intelligent monitoring, and the efficient use of energy resources.

Thus, the interconnection between CO_2 emissions control, energy efficiency, the operation of *data centers*, development methodologies, and emerging technologies forms a cycle of continuous improvement. This systematic review will analyze these relationships, highlighting their implications for sustainability and the efficient management of technological resources.

3 Methodology

This article adopts a descriptive and analytical approach to examining energy systems in data centers, with a focus on their relevance, efficiency, modernization, and strategies for promoting sustainability. The research was conducted through a literature review, analyzing academic articles, research reports, and technical publications, to gather information on the main components, challenges, and strategies for making data center energy systems more sustainable.

3.1 Search Strategies

In this literature review, the tool *Parsifal*[1] was utilized to filter and extract data, following a review protocol. This enabled data to be collected from three databases: *Google Scholar*, *Scopus*, and *Capes Digital Library* from Brazil.

The searches used the following key expressions, covering publications from 2018 to 2023. The keywords selected were: **Energy Efficiency, Sustainability, Data Centers, Carbon, Best Practices**. These terms were chosen to encompass the primary topics related to energy efficiency and sustainability in data centers.

To extract the data from Google Scholar, we used the software *Publish or Perish*[2], which facilitates the retrieval of structured academic citations.

[1] https://parsif.al/about/.
[2] https://harzing.com/resources/publish-or-perish.

3.2 Article Selection

After the searches, the articles were downloaded and uploaded to the Parsifal platform for cataloging. Duplicates were identified and removed, and inclusion (IC) and exclusion (EC) criteria were applied to verify relevance. The texts were then read in full to select those that answered the proposed research questions.

Table 1 shows the criteria used:

Table 1. Inclusion Criteria (IC) and Exclusion Criteria (EC) used to select articles for the study

Inclusion Criteria (IC)		Exclusion Criteria (EC)	
IC1	Addresses the topic to be studied	EC1	Does not address the topic to be studied
IC2	The text is complete and accessible	EC2	Before 2018
IC3	It is after 2018	EC3	It is not an article
		EC4	The article is not complete or accessible

3.3 Data Extraction

A total of 131 articles were cataloged. Of these, 9 were duplicates and were removed, and 10 were selected for the systematic review after applying the criteria, as shown in Table 2.

Table 2. Summary of article retrieval and selection across academic databases

Database	Results	Duplicated	Excluded	Included
Scopus	20	4	16	0
Capes Brasil	9	1	6	1
Google Scholar	102	3	90	9
Total	131	8	112	10

During the screening process, the 131 records were analyzed in detail. Based on the exclusion criteria in Table 1, 111 articles were discarded: EC1 (87 articles), EC2 (5 articles), EC3 (7 articles), and EC4 (12 articles). Thus, 10 articles were included in the review, according to Table 3.

3.4 Questions Raised

The questions raised are intended to facilitate understanding of the subject. When it comes to energy efficiency, approaches are generally found in various sectors, and the computing sector should be included in the global carbon

Table 3. Articles included in the systematic review with respective references

ID	A1	A2	A3	A4	A5	A6	A7	A8	A9	A10
Ref.	[17]	[4]	[15]	[16]	[1]	[18]	[21]	[19]	[27]	[8]

Source: author's elaboration based on selected references

dioxide reduction targets. This is because equipment, data centers, laboratories, and other infrastructure generally require significant amounts of electricity. For example, these centers require power 24 h a day. Therefore, the following questions are presented to enhance understanding of the topic in Table 4:

Table 4. Research questions and motivations related to energy efficiency and sustainability in data centers

Research Question	Motivation
Q1: Strategies—What strategies can be adopted for energy efficiency in *data centers*?	Driven by the need to highlight the importance of energy efficiency and identify effective approaches to achieve it.
Q2: Impact—What is the environmental impact of *data centers*?	Emphasizes the relevance of understanding and mitigating the environmental effects caused by these infrastructures.
Q3: Need—What is the need for a green *data center*?	Supports a broader understanding of why adopting sustainable practices in building and operating data centers is essential.

Source: elaborated by the author.

4 Analysis of Results

4.1 Q1 What Strategies Can Be Adopted for Energy Efficiency in Data Centers?

Through 5 Elements: Energy and Operational Efficiency, Green Energy, Recycling, and Social Impact.

For the authors to Lykou *et al.* [17] present a proposal that aims to assess the feasibility of making data centers more sustainable through five key elements, each consisting of a variety of factors that influence this sustainability. These key elements include energy efficiency, operational efficiency, renewable energy adoption, resource recycling, and social impact. Various factors, including the consumption and reuse of energy from renewable sources, the use of recycled materials, and the effective management of resources influence them. Figure 1 clearly illustrates these five elements.

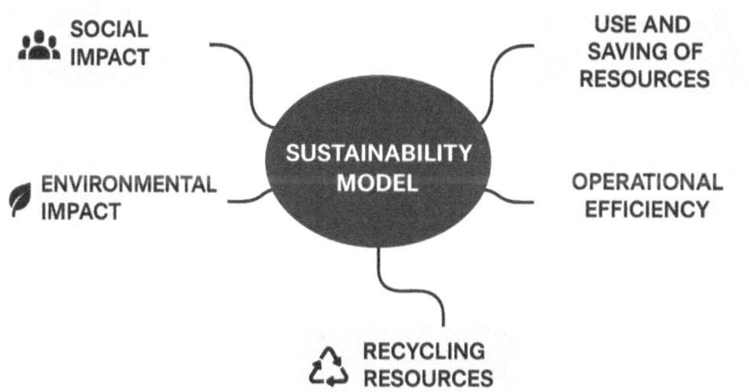

Fig. 1. Key elements for sustainable data centers: energy and operational efficiency, renewable energy, recycling, and social impact. Source: Adapted from Lykou et al. [17].

The evaluation factors were weighted based on the five pillars of sustainability, resulting in a comprehensive analysis of sustainability in data centers [17]. The **environmental impact** pillar highlights the use of renewable energy sources and the adoption of recycling policies as priority measures.

The dimension of **efficient use of resources and cost-effectiveness** considers the rational use of energy, water, and materials, as well as the economic viability of operations. In terms of **operational efficiency**, criteria such as the adoption of efficient equipment, ensuring operational safety, continuity of services, maintenance management, and energy control were taken into account.

The **recycling of resources** was assessed based on the ability to reuse inputs (such as wastewater), combined with the implementation of systematized recycling policies. Finally, the **social impact** dimension addresses corporate social and environmental responsibility, adequate occupational health and safety conditions, and incentives for sustainable mobility, including the promotion of electric vehicles and the construction of cycle paths.

Through the Implementation of *Devops Green*:

According to Muppala [19], the adoption of sustainable DevOps practices in banking data centers resulted in significant reductions in energy consumption. Among the strategies evaluated, adopting microservices and containerization reduced monthly energy use from 1,200 kWh to 800 kWh (a savings of 33.33%), and process automation achieved a similar reduction. Advanced monitoring with real-time analysis tools reduced consumption from 1,500 kWh to 900 kWh (a 40% savings).

Moving to cloud services powered by renewable energy resulted in the highest savings, decreasing consumption from 1,500 kWh to 800 kWh (46.67%), reducing CO_2 emissions from 1,000 kg to 400 kg.

These results are associated with the technical characteristics of each solution: *containers* and microservices promote on-demand allocation and reduce server idleness; automation tools such as Jenkins and Ansible dynamically deactivate inactive resources in periods of low demand; continuous monitoring with predictive analysis allows for the intelligent shutdown of underutilized equipment; and cloud computing with renewable sources takes advantage of efficient infrastructure based on solar and wind energy.

The research employed a mixed-methodological approach, combining the analysis of energy metrics with qualitative data collected through questionnaires administered to IT professionals, DevOps teams, and data center managers.

The instruments aimed to assess perceptions of the effectiveness of the adopted practices, the obstacles encountered, and the impact on operational efficiency. Although the exact number of respondents was not specified, the data contributed to validating the effectiveness of the interventions in the practical context of the banking sector.

Thus, the case study presented by Muppala et al. [19] demonstrates how sustainable DevOps practices can be strategically implemented to improve energy efficiency in critical computing environments, such as banking data centers.

Through Energy Optimization:

In the case study carried out by Basmadjian *et al.* [1], an energy management system was implemented in a Hewlett Packard Enterprise (HPE) data center in Milan. The initiative focused on dynamic optimization techniques, combining load forecasting with intelligent resource control to improve energy efficiency.

The architecture implemented (illustrated in Fig. 2) was composed of three main components. First, a **predictor** applied mathematical models to estimate future consumption based on usage patterns. Second, an **optimizer** was responsible for making decisions about efficient resource allocation, such as turning servers on or off and migrating workloads between nodes. Finally, an **orchestrator** executed these decisions while coordinating and monitoring the system's resources.

The results of this implementation highlighted substantial energy savings. Peak reductions reached up to **50%**, and total energy consumption decreased by **25%**, demonstrating the relevance of this approach for promoting sustainability in data center environments.

Through the Use of Containers:

According to Minxian *et al.* [27], the use of container-based techniques such as *brownout* represents an alternative to improve energy efficiency in cloud data centers. This approach enables the dynamic deactivation of optional application components during peak demand periods, contributing to energy reduction without significantly compromising service quality.

The experiments were conducted in a real environment using the Grid'5000 infrastructure, with physical servers monitored by energy consumption APIs. The proposed system demonstrated the ability to save between 10% and 40% of energy compared to baseline algorithms such as NPA and HS, while maintaining acceptable levels of average response time and SLA violations.

Integrated Strategy Approach:

Among the recommendations presented by the authors are different measures aimed at energy efficiency in data centers. **Hardware and air management optimization** involves both upgrading equipment and improving air circula-

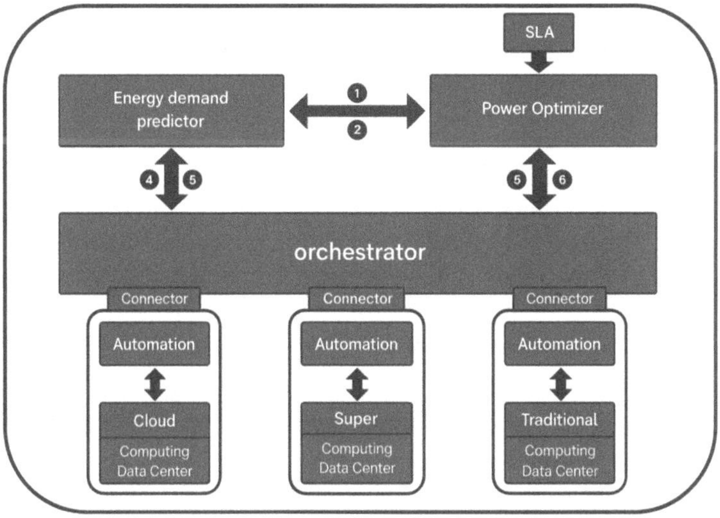

Fig. 2. Energy Management System (EMS) architecture for dynamic energy optimization in data centers. Fonte: Adaptado de Basmadjian *et al.* [1].

tion and cooling systems, which can include solutions such as economizers, free-cooling techniques, or heat recovery.
temperature control suggests adjusting operating points to recommended upper limits, seeking to reconcile energy efficiency with maintaining suitable conditions for the equipment. Another practice covered is **consolidation and virtualization**, which consists of transforming physical servers into virtual machines, reducing the number of active devices and, consequently, energy consumption, as well as optimizing the use of *hardware* resources.

Energy management must also be improved to avoid wastage during periods of idleness, and it is possible to integrate **Data Center Infrastructure Management** (GIDC) software for more precise monitoring and control. Finally, the **selective deactivation** of inactive infrastructure components, as well as the activation of backup systems only when necessary, contributes to a further reduction in energy consumption. The author illustrates these measures [4] through a case study of a medium-sized data center located in Bucharest, which has been operational since 2005. In this case, the optimization involved implementing the above-mentioned strategies, resulting in positive outcomes in reducing energy consumption and improving operational efficiency.

In addition to the practices previously discussed, adopting standardized metrics is crucial. Commonly used indicators include Power Usage Effectiveness (PUE), which measures the ratio of total energy used to the energy effectively utilized by IT equipment; Water Usage Effectiveness (WUE), which gauges the volume of water used per kWh of energy delivered to IT devices; and Carbon Usage Effectiveness (CUE), which associates CO_2 emissions with the energy consumption of IT systems. These three indicators constitute the "sustainability triangle" of data centers, offering a solid foundation for ongoing monitoring and improvements in energy, water, and carbon efficiency [17,26].

Furthermore, several practical steps should be taken into consideration. Lykou et al. [17] suggest upgrading cooling systems and replacing equipment with more energy-efficient hardware, while Dumitrescu et al. [4] emphasize the importance of temperature control, server consolidation, virtualization, and integrated management systems. Prasanna et al. [23] recommend adopting container-based architectures and implementing brownout techniques to adjust computing resources according to demand dynamically. When aligned with standardized sustainability metrics, these practices offer a strong and measurable approach to creating greener and more efficient data centers.

4.2 Q2 What is the Environmental Impact of *Data Centers*?

Carbon Dioxide Emissions:

It is estimated that data centers account for approximately 2% of global electricity consumption and about 1% of energy-related greenhouse gas (GHG) emissions [14,17]. According to the International Energy Agency (IEA), data centers and data transmission networks together emitted around 330 million tons of CO_2 equivalent ($MtCO_2e$) in 2020, accounting for about 1% of global energy-related GHG emissions. In the same year, the electricity consumption of these infrastructures ranged from 240 to 340 TWh, representing 1–1.3% of global electricity demand [14].

Although this percentage may appear modest compared to sectors such as transportation or agriculture, it becomes increasingly relevant in the context of the digitalization of the economy, the centralization of computing in hyperscale infrastructures, and the growing demand for digital services, artificial intelligence, and cloud computing. Moreover, the environmental impact varies depending on the energy sources used, with higher emissions in regions that still rely heavily on fossil fuels.

Thus, the estimated 1% figure not only reflects the current environmental footprint of data centers but also emphasizes their strategic role in climate mitigation policies, particularly in alignment with the goals set by the Paris Agreement.

Beyond energy use, water consumption also represents a significant environmental concern in data centers, particularly when open or evaporative cooling systems are employed. The study by Lykou et al. [17] highlights sustainable practices implemented in various infrastructures worldwide, such as *rainwater harvesting*, the adoption of *low-energy evaporative cooling systems*, and *chiller-free cooling using seawater*, which reduce both potable water consumption and energy usage.

Conversely, the same study reports on data centers that do not implement specific water reuse or recycling measures, revealing substantial variation in sustainability strategies across the analyzed infrastructures.

Among the most relevant technological alternatives to minimize water-related impacts are *air-based cooling systems*, which eliminate direct water use; *closed-*

loop liquid cooling systems, which enable water recirculation; and *waste heat reuse*, which allows recovered heat to be redirected for purposes such as heating office areas.

Beyond water and energy consumption, the environmental impact of data centers also extends to the extraction of raw materials used in their infrastructure and equipment. Metals such as aluminum, copper, lithium, and cobalt are essential for servers, batteries, and cooling systems. However, their extraction and processing are associated with emissions, water use, and ecological damage. For example, producing one ton of aluminum emits around 16 tons of CO_2eq, with global emissions reaching 1.1 gigatons in 2018 [13]. Sustainable alternatives include metal recycling and circular economy strategies to reduce the pressure on natural resources [11,12,25].

High Energy Consumption

The article *How much energy do data centers really use* emphasizes that the lack of public data on energy consumption and carbon emissions from *data centers*makes it hard to determine the sector's environmental impact [18] Only a few major companies, such as Google, Apple, Switch, and Facebook, share this information, which underscores the overall lack of transparency.

The authors note that this scarcity of data, especially regarding location and the carbon intensity of the electricity grid used, hinders proper quantification of emissions. They also compare the emissions from existing data centers to those of the aviation industry and warn about the increasing influence of emerging technologies—such as artificial intelligence and 5G—in boosting data traffic and, consequently, energy consumption.

To improve transparency, the article suggests developing and sharing reliable data on infrastructure and energy use, enhancing modeling capabilities through predictive and collaborative methods, and creating techniques for analyzing emerging trends in technological advancements [18].

Dioxide Emissions in Machine Learning Training

The article in question, published by the renowned technology company Google, addresses energy consumption in Machine Learning training [21]. Carbon dioxide emissions in this process are classified as operational and life cycle. Operational emissions refer to the energy costs associated with operating the hardware, including overhead, whereas life cycle emissions occur during the manufacturing of components.

The article primarily focuses on operational emissions, citing studies that have identified an overestimation of the cost and carbon footprint associated with machine learning training. This is due to a lack of access to accurate information, data extrapolation, and failure to take into account hardware and algorithm improvements. More accurate numbers are crucial to properly assessing climate change challenges.

The paper proposes best practices, including selecting efficient model architectures and utilizing optimized hybrid approaches for machine learning and cloud computing training. These practices can significantly reduce energy consumption and carbon emissions, contributing to a smaller carbon footprint over time.

4.3 Q3 What Is the Need for a *green Data Center*?

Reducing Energy Use and Environmental Impact

According to [15], the information technology industries are among the primary users of *data centers*, mainly because of the need for scalable infrastructure and global connectivity. However, more recent studies, such as the one by Pilz and Heim [22], indicate that these facilities also support vital applications in sectors like finance, government, health, e-commerce, media, and science, which rely on large-scale computing for their operations.

The *Data Age 2025* report, prepared by IDC in partnership with Seagate, highlights that sectors such as manufacturing, financial services, digital health, media, and entertainment hold nearly half of the world's corporate data volume. This increasing demand fuels the need for strong data center infrastructure, especially to meet requirements for storage, real-time processing, and applications based on artificial intelligence [9,10].

The questionnaire used by Jnr *et al.* [15] was developed based on the descriptive nature of the study and the methodological procedures of Hair *et al.* [7]. Validated by green computing experts, the instrument was answered by 133 IT professionals from Malaysian industries with their data centers. Reliability, assessed by Cronbach's alpha, was 0.986. The responses analyzed five strategies of the green computing life cycle: green design, green production, green purchasing, green operations, and green disposal. Each of these phases involves actions such as utilizing renewable energy, virtualization, resource consolidation, cooling optimization, and recycling, to reduce CO_2 emissions.

Despite the benefits of adopting sustainable practices in data centers, the study identified challenges to the full implementation of the proposed strategies. These include **difficulty in balancing multiple objectives**, such as accuracy, efficiency, and cost reduction with sustainability, as well as lapses in environmental consideration during the initial design phase. Added to this is cultural and organizational resistance, reflected in a low level of awareness and a limited focus on specific practices, with incomplete metrics. It should also be noted that the generalization of findings is limited to the regional context of Malaysia.

High Energy Consumption and Low Utilization:

According to Kotowski *et al.*, address the increase in internet use and the consequent demand for *data centers* [16]. With the annual growth of the Internet exceeding 10%, the demand for these Data Centers is expected to increase by 20%. However, this increase in use also raises cost concerns, primarily due to the high cost of energy storage systems.

Energy efficiency stands out as a crucial issue. Large data centers often operate at less than 10% of their capacity, resulting in excessive energy costs. This inefficiency is also linked to carbon emissions, which makes the adoption of sustainable practices essential.

The authors suggest the strategic adoption of Green Cloud Computing as a solution. This would enable optimized resource sharing, promoting energy efficiency and infrastructure automation. In summary, optimizing the use of data centers, adopting sustainable practices, and exploring cloud computing are crucial steps to deal with the growing demand, reduce costs, and minimize environmental impacts.

Sustainability and Economics:

According to Heikkinen and Daan, the relevance of adopting sustainable approaches in *data centers*, referred to as *Green Data Centers* [8]. The authors emphasize not only the importance of implementing renewable energy but also address critical issues related to greenhouse gas emissions, water conservation, waste management, responsible land use, and the preservation of ecosystems and biodiversity, all of which are essential to building a sustainable future.

The modern context, characterized by the increased use of mobile devices and computing technologies, results in a significant increase in energy and water consumption, accompanied by the rise in carbon dioxide emissions in each data center implemented. In this sense, it becomes imperative to adopt more environmentally friendly approaches in data centers, to effectively contribute to the goals of reducing CO_2 emissions.

In addition to environmental considerations, the economic aspect also stands out. Research demonstrates that companies reap substantial benefits from adopting sustainable practices. Therefore, there is a fruitful intersection between sustainability and financial benefit.

A driving factor for building green data centers is the exponentially growing demand for data storage. In this context, energy efficiency is crucial for meeting evolving needs and minimizing environmental impact.

Therefore, green data centers play a fundamental role in contemporary society. However, it is crucial that these initiatives not only align with reducing environmental impact but also generate operational efficiency. To meet both the demand for data storage and the adoption of renewable energy, these practices make significant contributions to the environment and the financial health of organizations.

In summary, when analyzing studies on energy efficiency and sustainability in data centers, it becomes clear that there are still essential solutions to be explored, such as the use of automation tools, DevOps, and Artificial Intelligence, which have not received sufficient attention. Several studies have addressed these topics. Most research to date has focused on solutions such as cooling server rooms, reducing energy consumption by deactivating servers through energy management systems, and recycling materials. However, it is crucial to focus on the possibility of achieving efficiency through the use of automation tools.

5 Conclusions and Future Works

This systematic literature review examined the main strategies for improving energy efficiency in data centers through sustainable practices. The results show that adopting methodologies such as DevOps, energy optimization techniques, advanced energy management systems, and resource virtualization contributes to reducing energy consumption and improving operational sustainability. These practices not only optimize the use of resources, but also align with global efforts to mitigate environmental impacts.

The study points to relevant implications for the information technology (IT) industry. The integration of green practices, such as the adoption of renewable energy sources, energy management based on artificial intelligence, and the principles of the circular economy (e.g. resource recycling), can reduce operating costs and carbon emissions. The transition to renewable sources and the implementation of intelligent cooling systems stand out as important strategies for the sustainability of data centers.

However, this research has some limitations. Firstly, the scope was restricted to publications in English, which may have excluded relevant studies in other languages. In addition, several articles reviewed pointed out difficulties in accurately quantifying greenhouse gas (GHG) emissions, highlighting the lack of standardized measurement methodologies. Another limitation is the scarcity of empirical studies on the application of DevOps for energy efficiency, especially in large-scale data center infrastructures.

To overcome these gaps, future research should investigate DevOps in depth, especially its role in automating energy-efficient workflows in large data centers, as well as evaluating the scalability of renewable energy solutions in different geographical and climatic contexts.

References

1. Basmadjian, R.: Flexibility-based energy and demand management in data centers: a case study for cloud computing. Energies **12**(17), 3301 (2019)
2. Beck, K., et al.: Manifesto for agile software development (2001). https://agilemanifesto.org/
3. Debois, P.: Agile infrastructure and operations: How infra-gile are you? In: Agile 2008 Conference, pp. 202–207. IEEE (2008)
4. Dumitrescu, C., Plesca, A., Adam, M., Nituca, C., Dragomir, A.: Methods for reducing energy consumption, optimization in operational data centers. In: 2018 International Conference and Exposition on Electrical And Power Engineering (EPE), pp. 0483–0486. IEEE (2018)
5. Europeia, C., et al.: GHG emissions of all world countries (2023). Serviço das Publicações da União Europeia (2023)
6. Geng, H.: Data Center Handbook. Wiley (2014)
7. Hair, J.F., Black, W.C., Babin, B.J., Anderson, R.E., Tatham, R.L.: Análise multivariada de dados. Bookman Editora (2009)
8. Heikkinen, D.: The need for green data centers in modern society: technology, economy and environmental sustainability. MPRA (2023)
9. i-SCOOP: Data age 2025: the datasphere and data-readiness from edge to core (2018). https://www.i-scoop.eu/big-data-action-value-context/data-age-2025-datasphere/

10. IDC, Seagate: Data age 2025: the digitization of the world from edge to core (2018). https://www.seagate.com/files/www-content/our-story/trends/files/Seagate-WP-DataAge2025-March-2017.pdf, white Paper
11. International Organization: Mining and the green energy transition (2023). https://www.oxfam.org/en/research/mining-and-green-energy-transition. Accessed 16 July 2025
12. International energy agency: The role of critical minerals in clean energy transitions (2021). https://www.iea.org/reports/the-role-of-critical-minerals-in-clean-energy-transitions. Accessed 16 July 2025
13. International energy agency: Aluminium – analysis (2023). https://www.iea.org/reports/aluminium. Accessed 16 July 2025
14. International energy agency: Data centres and data transmission networks. Online: IEA (2023). https://www.iea.org/energy-system/buildings/data-centres-and-data-transmission-networks. Accessed 15 July 2025
15. Jnr, B.A., Majid, M.A., Romli, A.: A descriptive study towards green computing practice application for data centers in it based industries. In: MATEC Web of Conferences, vol. 150, p. 05048. EDP Sciences (2018)
16. Kotowski, J., Oko, J., et al.: Green computing and energy storage systems. In: E3S Web of Conferences, vol. 44. EDP Sciences (2018)
17. Lykou, G., Mentzelioti, D., Gritzalis, D.: A new methodology toward effectively assessing data center sustainability. Comput. Secur. **76**, 327–340 (2018). https://doi.org/10.1016/J.COSE.2017.12.008
18. Masanet, E., Lei, N.: How much energy do data centers really use. Aspen Global Change Institute (2020)
19. Muppala, P.K.: Sustainable Devops: minimizing the carbon footprint of banking data centers. Int. J. Sci. Res. Arch. **14**(1), 1780–1793 (2025)
20. National Oceanic and Atmospheric Administration (NOAA): Carbon toolkit - basics (2022). https://gml.noaa.gov/education/carbon_toolkit/basics.html. Acesso 24 July 2023
21. Patterson, D., et al.: The carbon footprint of machine learning training will plateau, then shrink. Computer **55**(7), 18–28 (2022)
22. Pilz, K., Heim, L.: Compute at scale: a broad investigation into the data center industry. arXiv preprint arXiv:2311.02651 (2023)
23. Prasanna, T., Singh, K.P.: Improving energy efficiency in cloud data centers through an brownout software system strategy based on containers. eurchembull.com (2023)
24. Redhat: Introdução ao devops (2022). https://www.redhat.com/pt-br/topics/devops#:~:text=DevOps%20%C3%A9%20uma%20abordagem%20de,r%C3%A1pidas%20e%20de%20alta%20qualidade. Acesso 10 Jun 2023
25. United nations economic commission for Europe: united nations framework classification for resources (UNFC) (2023). https://unece.org/sustainable-energy/unfc-and-unrms. Accessed 26 July 2025
26. Vertiv: Words to go: 6 key data center sustainability metrics (2023). https://www.techtarget.com/searchdatacenter/feature/Words-to-go-6-key-data-center-sustainability-metrics. Acesso 15 Jul 2025
27. Xu, M., Buyya, R.: BrownOutcon: a software system based on brownout and containers for energy-efficient cloud computing. J. Syst. Softw. **155**, 91–103 (2019)

Subgroup and SIMD Optimization of RTM Kernels in Intel SYCL for Portable Performance

Cristiano Künas[1(✉)], Gabriel Freytag[1], Alexandre Sardinha[2], Philippe O. A. Navaux[1], Alexandre Carissimi[1], Everton Paulino[3], and Fabio Zuvanov[4]

[1] Federal University of Rio Grande do Sul (UFRGS), Porto Alegre, Brazil
{cakunas,gfreytag,navaux,asc}@inf.ufrgs.br
[2] Petroleo Brasileiro S.A., Rio de Janeiro, Brazil
alexandre.sardinha@petrobras.com.br
[3] Intel Corporation, Michigan, USA
everton.paulino@intel.com
[4] Intel Corporation, Rio de Janeiro, Brazil
fabio.zuvanov@intel.com

Abstract. Reverse Time Migration (RTM) is a key method for seismic imaging, but it demands substantial computational power and memory. With the growing diversity of GPU architectures, ensuring performance portability while maintaining energy efficiency has become a major challenge. This work evaluates RTM simulations on the Intel Max 1100 GPU, comparing three implementations: a baseline version, a SIMD-optimized version tailored for Intel's architecture, and a subgroup-based version designed for portability. Experiments across multiple 3D grid sizes and simulation durations assess performance, energy consumption, and computational efficiency. Results show that SIMD optimizations offer the best performance (up to 4.6×) and energy savings (up to 36%) but limit portability. In contrast, subgroup-based optimizations strike a balance, delivering speedups over the baseline while maintaining broader hardware compatibility. These findings suggest practical strategies for deploying efficient and portable RTM simulations, particularly valuable for heterogeneous HPC environments in cloud platforms and collaborative industrial workflows where code sustainability and adaptability are critical.

Keywords: RTM · HPC · Seismic Simulation · Performance Portability · Energy Efficiency

1 Introduction

Reverse Time Migration (RTM) is a seismic imaging method widely used in oil and gas exploration [29]. It reconstructs subsurface structures by numerically

K. Brown et al. (Eds.): CARLA 2025, CCIS 2750, pp. 94–108, 2026.
https://doi.org/10.1007/978-3-032-24923-4_7

solving the two-way wave equation in reverse time, producing high-fidelity images of geological formations. Due to its computational complexity, RTM typically requires large 3D grids, thousands of time steps, and high memory throughput, making it one of the most demanding algorithms in seismic processing pipelines.

As survey resolutions and domain sizes grow, ensuring efficient RTM execution on modern HPC systems becomes increasingly important. Recent hardware trends have moved toward heterogeneous architectures that combine general-purpose CPUs with a range of accelerators, such as GPUs [27]. While this opens new opportunities for performance optimization, it also introduces challenges in adapting RTM implementations to different devices. Efficient use of these platforms requires careful management of parallelism, memory hierarchy, and data movement [3,25].

In this context, the concept of performance portability has gained traction. It refers to the ability of a codebase to deliver high performance across diverse architectures with minimal modifications. For RTM simulations, which often include low-level numerical kernels and fine-tuned memory access patterns, achieving performance portability can be particularly difficult. Rewriting these kernels for each target architecture increases maintenance costs and slows down adoption on new platforms [18].

Among emerging accelerators, the Intel Max Series GPUs offer new capabilities for scientific computing. The Intel Max 1100, in particular, provides high memory bandwidth and a large number of vector processing units, making it a promising target for RTM workloads. However, to benefit from this architecture, simulation codes must be optimized to exploit its vector units and execution model [17,30].

This work evaluates the performance and energy efficiency of RTM simulations on the Intel Max 1100 GPU. We compare three implementations of the same RTM algorithm: a baseline version with minimal GPU-specific tuning, a version optimized with Explicit SIMD (ESIMD) for Intel's vector units, and a portable version based on GPU subgroups to enable broader compatibility with other vendors [22]. All versions are implemented using SYCL and tested across a range of simulation scenarios.

The goal is to analyze the trade-offs between hardware-specific optimization and code portability. By measuring performance, energy consumption, and computational efficiency across different configurations, we provide insights into how different GPU programming strategies impact RTM execution on modern heterogeneous systems.

The rest of the paper is organized as follows. Section 2 presents related work that provides a context for our contributions. Section 3 describes the tools and methods used, including the background on RTM and performance portability, our methodology, and the evaluation platform used. Section 4 presents the experimental results, focusing on performance, energy consumption, and computational efficiency. Section 5 provides a discussion of these results, analyzing their implications for portability. Finally, Sect. 6 concludes the paper with directions for future work.

2 Related Work

The pursuit of performance portability has become a defining challenge in high-performance computing (HPC) due to the proliferation of heterogeneous architectures, including CPUs, GPUs, and FPGAs. As Moore's Law slows and architectural diversity grows, developers are increasingly pressured to maintain high performance across platforms without sacrificing software maintainability. Numerous studies underscore this tension between portability and peak optimization. Frameworks like Kokkos, OpenMP, OpenCL, and data-centric abstractions such as Stateful DataFlow Graphs (SDFGs) have been proposed to address these issues, with varying degrees of success. Recent contributions highlight the need for hardware-agnostic programming approaches that can match–or at least approach–the performance of platform-specific solutions, particularly in scientific and simulation-intensive domains [4,16,19,23,24].

In response to these issues, a number of portable programming models have been developed to streamline the development process across both CPU and GPU architectures. Among them, SYCL has gained traction as a modern C++ abstraction for heterogeneous programming. Its effectiveness has been demonstrated across various domains, including fluid dynamics and plasma physics, often showing competitive performance with CUDA while significantly improving code portability [6,28]. Comparative evaluations have positioned SYCL as a viable alternative to OpenCL, Kokkos, and OpenMP in both scientific and high-energy physics workloads, although fine-grained tuning is still often required to achieve peak performance [7,11,14].

Seismic imaging, particularly through Reverse Time Migration (RTM) and Full Waveform Inversion (FWI), exemplifies performance portability challenges in real-world, computationally intensive applications. RTM is a memory- and compute-intensive algorithm that benefits significantly from GPU acceleration. Various studies have demonstrated RTM's scalability across CUDA, OpenMP, and OpenACC implementations, each offering trade-offs between performance and maintainability [20,26]. Further developments have explored task-based runtime frameworks like StarPU [1] and high-bandwidth memory strategies for RTM checkpointing and I/O bottlenecks [2]. Multi-GPU strategies continue to play a key role in scaling RTM kernels, often relying on low-level CUDA primitives like streams and peer-to-peer memory transfers [15].

While performance remains a major focus in RTM optimization, energy efficiency is gaining importance, particularly in large-scale deployments. FPGA-based RTM implementations have shown dramatic reductions in energy use compared to GPUs, albeit at the cost of portability and higher development effort [5]. Recent comparisons between CUDA, OpenMP, and OpenACC for RTM highlight that portable models can, in some cases, outperform architecture-specific implementations in both performance and energy use [19,26].

Despite the growing number of studies on portable HPC frameworks and RTM acceleration, little work has been done to combine these two threads, particularly using emerging models like SYCL. To the best of our knowledge, no existing study has systematically evaluated the trade-offs between hardware-specific vectorization (e.g., SIMD) and portable subgroup abstractions (e.g., SYCL) in RTM on Intel GPUs. Furthermore, no published work explicitly benchmarks such implementations on Intel Max 1100 architectures focusing on energy efficiency, maintainability, and portability.

In summary, while substantial research has explored RTM acceleration and performance portability across heterogeneous systems, existing studies often focus on architecture-specific solutions or general-purpose frameworks without directly comparing their effectiveness in a unified context. Notably, the use of SYCL for seismic imaging workloads remains underexplored, particularly in balancing fine-grained performance tuning with cross-platform compatibility. This paper addresses this gap by providing a comparative evaluation of SIMD and subgroup optimization strategies using SYCL on Intel Max 1100 GPUs. By focusing on both performance and energy metrics, it contributes novel insights into the trade-offs faced when aiming for efficient yet portable implementations of computationally intensive geophysical applications.

3 Tools and Methods

This section presents the main tools, models, and optimization strategies used in this work. We begin with an overview of the seismic modeling technique employed (Sect. 3.1), followed by a discussion on performance portability challenges (Sect. 3.2). We then describe our experimental methodology, including the simulation structure and the three RTM kernel implementations analyzed (Sect. 3.3).

3.1 Fletcher Modeling

Seismic modeling plays a crucial role in subsurface exploration, particularly in identifying oil and gas reserves. One widely adopted method for simulating seismic wave propagation is the approach proposed by Fletcher [10]. This technique numerically solves the wave equation to model how seismic energy travels through heterogeneous geological structures. Figure 1 illustrates a typical marine seismic acquisition setup, where the dynamic behavior of seismic waves is captured during their interaction with subsurface layers.

In practice, the data collection process begins with a survey vessel that tows an array of acoustic sources and receivers–similar in concept to sonar systems. The sources emit seismic pulses into the Earth, which then reflect and refract at interfaces between different geological layers. These returning signals are recorded by the receivers, enabling the construction of a detailed image of the subsurface. The accuracy and resolution of these signals are vital for assessing the potential of hydrocarbon reservoirs.

The computational core of Fletcher's method is grounded in solving the acoustic wave equation across a discretized 3D spatial domain. This equation incorporates the medium's elastic properties, including variations in propagation speed, which are critical for capturing realistic wave behavior. The simulation advances iteratively, computing the wavefield at each point in the grid

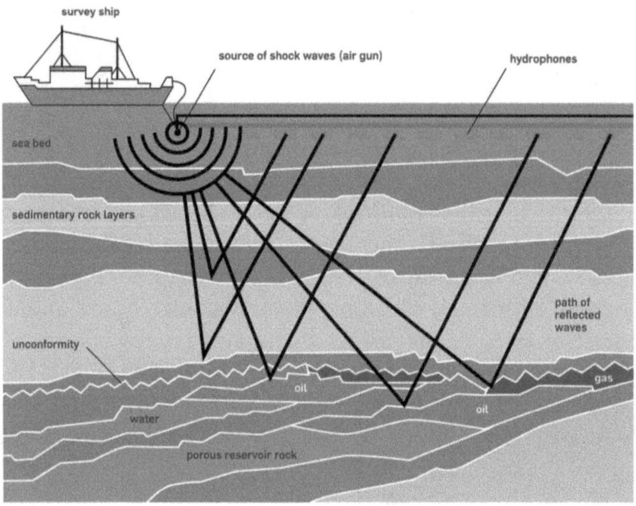

Fig. 1. Data collection in a marine seismic survey [13].

by considering the state of the previous time step. This recursive nature allows the model to capture complex phenomena such as scattering, diffraction, and energy loss as waves traverse different geological layers. Such iterative modeling provides valuable insight into how seismic energy propagates in realistic Earth models. By accounting for spatial variability and physical discontinuities, Fletcher's approach supports detailed and high-fidelity simulations essential for modern geophysical workflows.

3.2 Performance Portability

The increasing heterogeneity of HPC systems has made performance portability a relevant challenge for scientific applications [8,24]. In many research and production environments, applications are expected to run efficiently across different hardware backends, including GPUs from multiple vendors. Ensuring good performance without rewriting large parts of the code for each new architecture is essential to maintain productivity and reduce development costs [12].

In the context of seismic wave simulations, such as reverse time migration (RTM), which involve memory- and compute-intensive calculations, adapting to multiple architectures requires attention to details such as the parallelism model, efficient memory utilization, and the exploitation of the vector or subgroup units offered by each hardware [21]. Specific optimization strategies, such as SIMD on Intel GPUs or warps on NVIDIA GPUs, can provide high performance, but compromise portability.

The search for portable solutions, such as the use of parallelism abstractions (e.g. SYCL or Kokkos), aims to balance performance and code maintainability in the long term [9]. However, this portability often implies a loss of performance in specific architectures, creating a trade-off that must be evaluated according to the objectives and execution environment of the application.

3.3 Methodology

This study evaluates three implementations of the same Reverse Time Migration (RTM) simulation kernel, each designed with a distinct optimization strategy targeting the Intel Max 1100 GPU. The objective is to analyze trade-offs in performance, energy efficiency, and portability.

All implementations follow the same high-level execution flow, as described in Listing 1:

```
main()
    Initialize grid and simulation parameters.
    Initialize device and host arrays.
    for each time step
        Compute source value.
        Call Propagate() for computation.
        Swap pressure fields.
        Output results if needed.
    Finalize simulation and report metrics.

Propagate()
    Define kernel configuration.
    Run kernel.
    kernel()
        for each grid point
            Compute derivatives using scalar operations.
            Update pressure fields.
```

Listing 1. RTM simulation execution flow (shared by all implementations).

The main differences between the implementations lie in the kernel body within the *Propagate()* routine. All versions follow the same execution flow presented in Listing 1; however, in the ESIMD and Subgroups variants, the core propagation kernel is restructured to exploit specific GPU execution models. Listings 2, 3, and 4 highlight the key differences in a single representative operation–namely, the computation of spatial derivatives and pressure updates. These snippets do not represent the full kernel body but rather illustrate the most important changes required to adapt the original implementation to each target model.

RTM Implementations

- **original**: A baseline implementation using direct array indexing and scalar operations. It is portable and straightforward, but lacks architecture-specific optimizations. The absence of data-level parallelism results in lower throughput on modern GPUs.

```
const int i = ind(ix, iy, iz);

// Compute derivative in x direction
const float pxx = 1.6f * pc[i + strideX] - 0.2f * pc[i + 2 * strideX];

// Update pressure field
pp[i] = 2.0f * pc[i] - pp[i] + pxx * dt * dt;
```

Listing 2. Original RTM kernel (baseline).

- **original-esimd**: Optimized with Intel's Explicit SIMD (ESIMD), this version uses vectorized intrinsics to load and store data, increasing memory throughput and arithmetic intensity. While efficient on Intel hardware, it relies on vendor-specific extensions.

```
using namespace sycl::ext::intel::esimd;

const int simdlen = 16;
const int i = ind(ix, iy, iz);

// Load data with SIMD intrinsic
auto pci = lsc_block_load<float, simdlen>(pc + i);

// Compute derivative in x direction
auto pxx = 1.6f * (pci + strideX) - 0.2f * (pci + 2 * strideX);

// Update pressure field
lsc_block_store<float, simdlen>(pp + i, pci * dt * dt + pxx);
```

Listing 3. RTM kernel using Intel ESIMD.

- **original-subgroups**: This version adopts SYCL subgroups to achieve portable data-level parallelism. It offers improved performance on various GPU architectures while preserving maintainability and cross-platform support.

```
sycl::sub_group sg = item.get_sub_group();
const int i = ind(ix, iy, iz);

// Load data with subgroup memory operation
auto pci = sg.load((sycl::global_ptr<float>)(pc + i));

// Compute derivative in x direction
auto pxx = 1.6f * (pci + strideX) - 0.2f * (pci + 2 * strideX);

// Update pressure field
sg.store((sycl::global_ptr<float>)(pp + i), pci * dt * dt + pxx);
```

Listing 4. RTM kernel using SYCL subgroups.

All three versions apply the same numerical stencil computation over a 3D grid. However, they differ in how data movement and parallelism are exposed to the GPU, reflecting distinct trade-offs between performance tuning, energy efficiency, and code portability.

Experimental Setup. All experiments were conducted on a computational node equipped with an Intel Max 1100 GPU, made available through the Santos Dumont Supercomputer (SDumont)[1] at the National Laboratory for Scientific Computing (LNCC)[2]. The Intel Max 1100 features many vector processing cores and integrated high-bandwidth memory (HBM2e), optimized for scientific high-performance computing workloads. The software environment included Intel's oneAPI toolkit, with compiler support for DPC++ programming models targeting ESIMD and subgroup functionalities. Performance and energy profiling were performed using Intel-provided tools capable of runtime sampling and measurement.

Simulation Configuration. RTM simulations were executed on four different 3D grid sizes: $216x216x216$, $408x408x408$, $600x600x600$, and $792x792x792$ points. Each configuration was tested using three normalized simulation durations (tmax): 0.2, 1.0, and 2.0. These durations correspond to increasing numbers of time steps and workload sizes. For every combination of grid size and simulation duration, three key metrics were measured:

- **Performance**: Reported in millions of samples processed per second (MSamples/s)
- **Energy consumption**: Measured in kilojoules (kJ)
- **Computational efficiency**: Defined as MSamples processed per kJ (MSamples/kJ)

Each test was executed multiple times to ensure statistical consistency, minimizing variability, and average results are reported. The same input models and parameters were used across all runs. Energy measurements were considered reliable only for simulations lasting longer than one second, due to sampling constraints of the monitoring tools.

All executions were performed in isolated GPU environments to minimize the impact of background processes and ensure accurate measurements.

4 Experimental Results

This section presents the comparative results of three RTM implementations executed on the Intel Max 1100 GPU. Evaluations are organized around three key metrics: computational performance, energy consumption, and computational efficiency. Section 4.1 examines the throughput across varying grid sizes

[1] https://sdumont.lncc.br.
[2] https://www.lncc.br.

and simulation durations; Sect. 4.2 analyzes energy usage per configuration; and Sect. 4.3 explores the efficiency trade-offs by normalizing performance to energy consumption. Collectively, these results illuminate the performance-portability landscape for RTM workloads in heterogeneous environments.

4.1 Performance Results

Performance was quantified as the average number of mega samples processed per second (MSamples/s) for each RTM implementation, across multiple 3D grid sizes and normalized time steps (tmax). Results are visualized in Fig. 2.

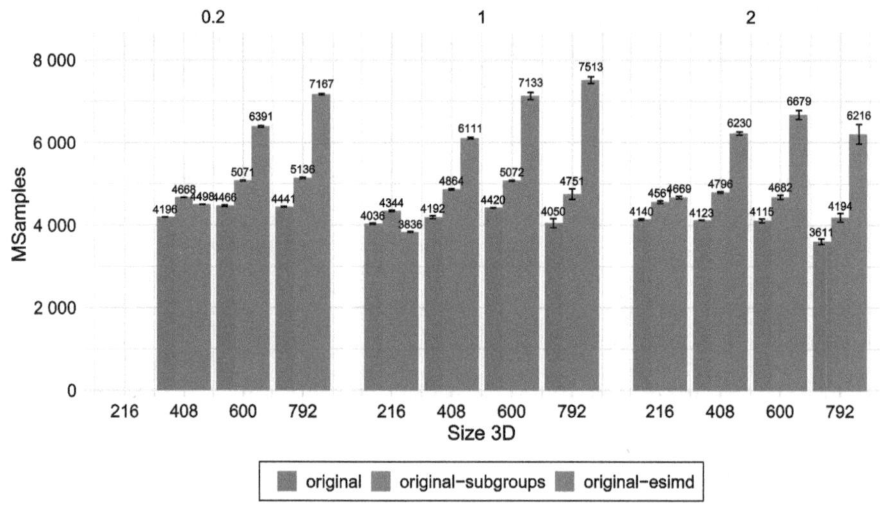

Fig. 2. Performance (MSamples/s) with different parallelism techniques in SYCL (Intel Max 1100).

The SIMD-optimized version ("original-esimd") delivered the highest throughput across all configurations. On smaller grids (e.g., 216^3) and shorter simulations (tmax = 0.2), it achieved up to 4.6× speedup over the baseline. As grid sizes increased, absolute gains remained significant, though slightly tempered by increased memory traffic and synchronization overheads.

The subgroup-based version ("original-subgroups") showed consistent improvements over the baseline, particularly on larger grids (e.g., 600^3 at tmax = 2.0), where cooperative subgroup execution effectively utilized GPU parallelism. In this scenario, it delivered up to 15% higher throughput than the baseline.

Despite its gains, the subgroup strategy did not match the SIMD variant in raw performance, illustrating the inherent trade-off between portability and peak optimization. Across all test cases, the baseline version remained the least performant due to its lack of architecture-specific tuning. These results underscore that while SIMD optimization provides maximal throughput, subgroup abstractions offer a practical compromise for developers prioritizing cross-platform code reuse.

4.2 Energy Consumption Results

Energy consumption, measured in kilojoules (kJ), provides insight into the cost-effectiveness of each optimization strategy (see Fig. 3).

The SIMD-optimized implementation not only excelled in performance but also proved to be the most energy-efficient, consuming up to 36% less energy than the baseline on the 600^3 grid at tmax = 2.0. This dual benefit highlights the synergy between fine-grained vectorization and reduced runtime overhead.

The subgroup-optimized version demonstrated intermediate energy performance. While not as efficient as the SIMD variant, it consistently consumed less energy than the baseline–especially for larger grid sizes where idle thread overhead was mitigated by efficient subgroup coordination.

Note that measurements for the smallest grid configuration (216^3 at tmax = 0.2) are excluded from energy analysis due to the limited temporal resolution of the profiling tools, which impacted the reliability of readings on sub-second workloads.

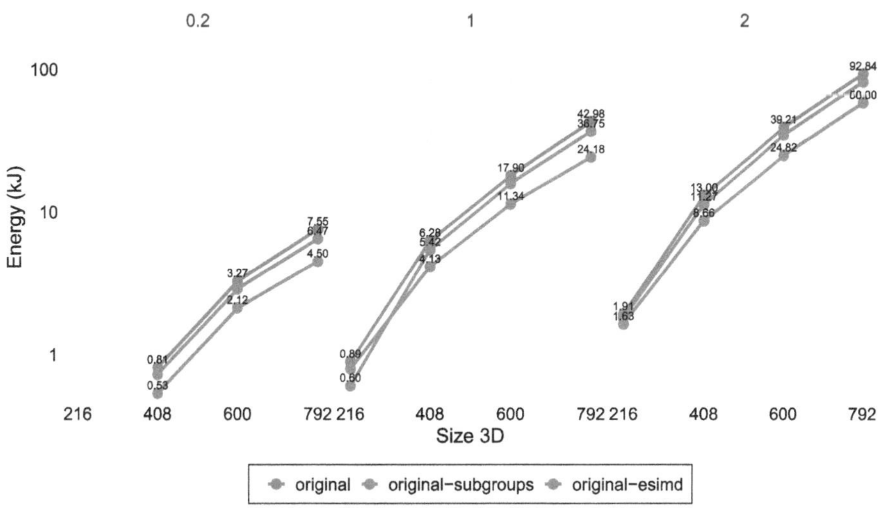

Fig. 3. Power consumption (kJ) for SYCL implementations (Intel Max 1100).

4.3 Computational Efficiency

To assess the performance-energy balance, we calculated computational efficiency as MSamples processed per kilojoule (MSamples/kJ). Figure 4 summarizes these results.

The SIMD-optimized version exhibited the highest efficiency across all configurations. For the 600^3 grid at tmax = 2.0, it reached approximately 269 MSamples/kJ–more than double the baseline's 105 MSamples/kJ and substantially ahead of the subgroup version's 135 MSamples/kJ. Similar trends held for the largest test case (792^3 at tmax = 2.0), reinforcing SIMD's superior energy-to-throughput ratio.

While the subgroup approach did not match SIMD in raw or normalized terms, it consistently outperformed the baseline. This suggests that portable optimizations–when carefully implemented–can yield meaningful efficiency gains without resorting to hardware-specific tuning.

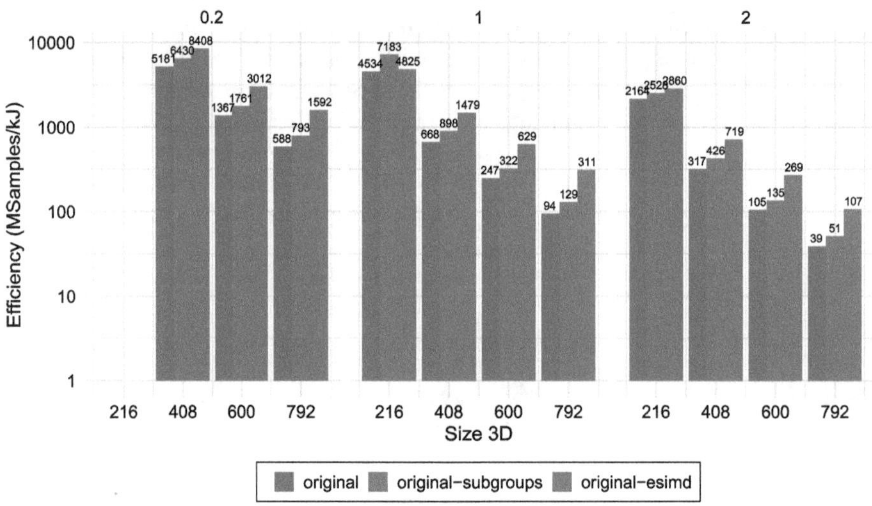

Fig. 4. Absolute performance difference (MSamples/kJ) between parallelism techniques.

Overall, the results confirm that SIMD strategies unlock peak performance and efficiency but at the cost of reduced portability. Subgroup abstractions, while less optimal, strike a favorable balance between execution efficiency and platform compatibility, making them suitable for diverse HPC ecosystems.

5 Discussion

The experimental results emphasize the trade-offs between maximizing performance through architecture-specific optimizations and ensuring code portability across heterogeneous systems. The SIMD-optimized implementation ("original-esimd") consistently delivered the highest performance, energy efficiency, and computational throughput. These benefits affirm the effectiveness of low-level tuning in exploiting the full capabilities of specialized architectures like the Intel Max 1100 GPU.

However, the portability of such solutions is a key concern, particularly for industry developers who often need to deploy and maintain seismic applications across diverse environments, from on-premises HPC clusters to cloud-based infrastructures. The reliance on Intel-specific constructs in the ESIMD implementation creates significant barriers to reuse, requiring additional engineering effort to support alternative platforms like NVIDIA or AMD GPUs.

In contrast, the subgroup-optimized version ("original-subgroups") offers a more sustainable and flexible approach. Although it falls short of the SIMD version in absolute performance, its ability to run efficiently on multiple GPU architectures makes it an attractive option for long-term maintainability. This is especially valuable in collaborative industrial workflows, where hardware heterogeneity is common, and deployment flexibility is critical.

Furthermore, both optimized versions demonstrated clear energy efficiency gains over the baseline, reinforcing the principle that performance tuning can also drive sustainability. As energy use becomes a cost and regulatory factor in industrial-scale simulations, energy-aware code design will increasingly influence adoption decisions.

Looking ahead, future work should explore the integration of auto-tuning frameworks that can dynamically adapt execution parameters to the target hardware. Such tools can help bridge the gap between performance and portability without requiring manual tuning for each platform. Additionally, incorporating AI-based optimization strategies–such as machine learning models that predict optimal kernel configurations–could further automate performance tuning and enhance adaptability across devices. These directions hold significant promise for scaling RTM workloads on emerging exascale platforms, while maintaining portability and developer productivity.

6 Conclusion

This work presented a comparative analysis of three Reverse Time Migration (RTM) implementations on the Intel Max 1100 GPU: a baseline version, a SIMD-optimized version using ESIMD, and a portable version utilizing SYCL subgroups. Through a systematic evaluation across various 3D grid sizes and simulation durations, we demonstrated how different GPU programming strategies impact performance, energy consumption, and computational efficiency.

Our findings confirm that architecture-specific tuning via ESIMD delivers superior performance–achieving up to 4.6× speedups–and notable energy savings of up to 36%. However, this comes at the cost of limited portability, requiring vendor-specific programming constructs that hinder adoption on other platforms. In contrast, the SYCL subgroup-based version offers a compelling middle ground, achieving meaningful improvements over the baseline while preserving cross-vendor compatibility. This trade-off is particularly relevant for developers targeting diverse HPC environments, such as academic clusters, industrial simulations, and cloud-based platforms.

As energy efficiency and maintainability become increasingly critical in large-scale scientific applications, our results underscore the value of portable abstractions that offer a favorable balance between performance and sustainability. Moving forward, extending this study to other GPU architectures–including those from NVIDIA and AMD–will be crucial for validating the generality of SYCL-based optimization strategies. Additionally, exploring hybrid programming models and scaling across multi-node configurations will be essential steps toward enabling exascale-ready seismic imaging workflows.

Acknowledgment. This study was partially supported by Petrobras grant n.o 2020/00182-5, by CNPq/MCTI/FNDCT - Universal 18/2021 under grants 406182/2021-3, National Laboratory for Scientific Computing (LNCC/MCTI, Brazil) for providing HPC resources of the SDumont supercomputer, which have contributed to the research results reported within this paper. URL: http://sdumont.lncc.br, and by the Coordenação de Aperfeiçoamento de Pessoal de Nível Superior Brasil (CAPES) Finance Code 001.

References

1. Alonazi, A., Ltaief, H., Keyes, D., Said, I., Thibault, S.: Asynchronous task-based execution of the reverse time migration for the oil and gas industry. In: 2019 IEEE International Conference on Cluster Computing (CLUSTER), pp. 1–11 (2019). https://doi.org/10.1109/CLUSTER.2019.8891054
2. Alturkestani, T., Ltaief, H., Keyes, D.: Maximizing I/O bandwidth for reverse time migration on heterogeneous large-scale systems. In: Euro-Par 2020: Parallel Processing, pp. 263–278 (2020). https://doi.org/10.1007/978-3-030-57675-2_17
3. Assis, Í.A., Fernandes, J.B., Barros, T., Xavier-De-Souza, S.: Auto-tuning of dynamic scheduling applied to 3D reverse time migration on multicore systems. IEEE Access **8**, 145115–145127 (2020)
4. Ben-Nun, T., Licht, J.D.F., Ziogas, A., Schneider, T., Hoefler, T.: Stateful dataflow multigraphs: a data-centric model for performance portability on heterogeneous architectures. In: SC19: International Conference for High Performance Computing, Networking, Storage and Analysis, pp. 1–14 (2019). https://doi.org/10.1145/3295500.3356173
5. Bittencourt, J.C., et al.: Performance and energy efficiency analysis of reverse time migration on a FPGA platform. In: 2019 IEEE/ACM International Workshop on Heterogeneous High-performance Reconfigurable Computing (H2RC), pp. 50–58. https://doi.org/10.1109/H2RC49586.2019.00012
6. Büttner, M., Alt, C., Kenter, T., Köstler, H., Plessl, C., Aizinger, V.: Enabling performance portability for shallow water equations on CPUS, GPUS, and FPGAS with SYCL. In: Proceedings of the Platform for Advanced Scientific Computing Conference (2024). https://doi.org/10.1145/3659914.3659925
7. Cabrera, A., et al.: Toward evaluating high-level synthesis portability and performance between intel and XILINX FPGAS. In: Proceedings of the 9th International Workshop on OpenCL (2021). https://doi.org/10.1145/3456669.3456699
8. Davis, J.H., et al.: An evaluative comparison of performance portability across GPU programming models. Tech. rep, Lawrence Livermore National Laboratory (LLNL), Livermore, CA (United States) (2024)

9. Ding, Y., et al.: Evaluating performance portability of SYCL and KOKKOS: a case study on LBM simulations. In: 2023 IEEE Intl Conf on Parallel & Distributed Processing with Applications, Big Data & Cloud Computing, Sustainable Computing & Communications, Social Computing & Networking (ISPA/BDCloud/SocialCom/SustainCom), pp. 328–335. IEEE (2023)
10. Fletcher, R.P., Du, X., Fowler, P.J.: Reverse time migration in tilted transversely isotropic (TTI) media. Geophysics **74**(6), WCA179–WCA187 (2009)
11. Fujita, N., et al.: Charm-SYCL & IRIS: a tool chain for performance portability on extremely heterogeneous systems. In: 2024 IEEE 20th International Conference on e-Science (e-Science), pp. 1–10 (2024). https://doi.org/10.1109/e-Science62913.2024.10678717
12. Harrell, S.L., et al.: Effective performance portability. In: 2018 IEEE/ACM International Workshop on Performance, Portability and Productivity in HPC (P3HPC), pp. 24–36. IEEE (2018)
13. Kukreja, N., Louboutin, M., Lange, M., Luporini, F., Gorman, G.: Rapid development of seismic imaging applications using symbolic math. In: Third EAGE Workshop on High Performance Computing for Upstream, vol. 2017, pp. 1–4. European Association of Geoscientists & Engineers (2017)
14. Kwok, K., et al: Application of performance portability solutions for GPUS and many-core CPUS to track reconstruction kernels. In: EPJ Web of Conferences (2024). https://doi.org/10.1051/epjconf/202429511003
15. Liu, G., Meng, X., Yu, Z., Liu, D.: An efficient scheme for multi-GPU TTI reverse time migration. Appl. Geophys. **16**, 56–63 (2019). https://doi.org/10.1007/s11770-018-0743-8
16. Liu, W., Wu, L., Xu, X., Wang, Y.: Implementing performance portability of high performance computing programs in the new golden age of chip architecture. ArXiv:abs/2308.13802 (2023). https://doi.org/10.48550/arXiv.2308.13802
17. Lueh, G.Y., et al.: C-for-metal: high performance SIMD programming on intel GPUS. In: 2021 IEEE/ACM International Symposium on Code Generation and Optimization (CGO), pp. 289–300. IEEE (2021)
18. Milthorpe, J., Wang, X., Azizi, A.: Performance portability of the chapel language on heterogeneous architectures. In: 2024 IEEE International Parallel and Distributed Processing Symposium Workshops (IPDPSW), pp. 6–13. IEEE (2024)
19. Olivier, S.L., Ellingwood, N.D., Berry, J.W., Dunlavy, D.M.: Performance portability of an spmv kernel across scientific computing and data science applications. In: 2021 IEEE High Performance Extreme Computing Conference (HPEC), pp. 1–8 (2021). https://doi.org/10.1109/HPEC49654.2021.9622869
20. Qawasmeh, A., Hugues, M., Calandra, H., Chapman, B.: Performance portability in reverse time migration and seismic modelling via OPENACC. Int. J. High Perform. Comput. Appl. **31**, 422–440 (2017). https://doi.org/10.1177/1094342016675678
21. Qu, L., Abdelkhalak, R., Ltaief, H., Said, I., Keyes, D.: Exploiting temporal data reuse and asynchrony in the reverse time migration. Int. J. High Perform. Comput. Appl. **37**(2), 132–150 (2023)
22. Reguly, I.Z.: Evaluating the performance portability of SYCL across CPUS and GPUS on bandwidth-bound applications. In: Proceedings of the SC 2023 Workshops of the International Conference on High Performance Computing, Network, Storage, and Analysis, pp. 1038–1047 (2023)
23. Riera, M., Tavakoli, E.B., Quraishi, M.H., Ren, F.: Halo 1.0: a hardware-agnostic accelerator orchestration framework for enabling hardware-agnostic programming with true performance portability for heterogeneous HPC. ArXiv (2020)

24. Ruzicka, J., Asch, C., Meneses, E., Rampp, M., Laure, E.: A study of performance portability in plasma physics simulations. In: Latin American High Performance Computing Conference, pp. 19–35. Springer (2024). https://doi.org/10.1007/978-3-031-80084-9_2
25. Salamanca, W.A., Ramirez, A.B., Vivas, F.A.: Comparative analysis of 3D RTM implementation strategies for an efficient use of memory in a single GPU. CT&F-Ciencia, Tecnología y Futuro **8**(2), 75–82 (2018)
26. Serpa, M., et al.: Energy efficiency and portability of oil and gas simulations on multicore and graphics processing unit architectures. Concurr. Comput. Pract. Exp. **33** (2021). https://doi.org/10.1002/cpe.6212
27. Sharma, G., Poudel, P.: Current trends in heterogeneous systems: a review. Trends Comput. Sci. Inf. Technol. **7**(3), 086–090 (2022)
28. Vasileska, I., Tomšič, P., Kos, L., Bogdanovic, L.: Unveiling performance insights and portability achievements between CUDA and SYCL for particle-in-cell codes on different GPU architectures. In: 2024 47th MIPRO ICT and Electronics Convention (MIPRO), pp. 1115–1120 (2024). https://doi.org/10.1109/MIPRO60963.2024.10569866
29. Zhou, H.W., Hu, H., Zou, Z., Wo, Y., Youn, O.: Reverse time migration: a prospect of seismic imaging methodology. Earth Sci. Rev. **179**, 207–227 (2018)
30. Zubair, M., Walden, A., Nastac, G., Nielsen, E., Bauinger, C., Zhu, X.: Optimization of ported CFD kernels on intel data center GPU max 1550 using oneapi esimd. In: Proceedings of the SC 2023 Workshops of the International Conference on High Performance Computing, Network, Storage, and Analysis, pp. 1705–1712 (2023)

Machine Learning for Predicting Job States and CPU Power on a Supercomputer

Dylan Benavides[1(✉)], Fabricio Quirós-Corella[1], and Esteban Meneses[1,2]

[1] National High Technology Center, San José 10109, Costa Rica
{dbenavides,fquiros,emeneses}@cenat.ac.cr, esmeneses@tec.ac.c
[2] Costa Rica Institute of Technology, Cartago 159-7050, Costa Rica
https://www.cenat.ac.cr/es/, https://www.tec.ac.cr/

Abstract. Efficient resource management in high-performance computing (HPC) is essential for optimizing costs, reducing energy consumption, and improving system productivity. However, job variability and failures introduce uncertainties that complicate scheduling and resource allocation. Accurately predicting job failures and estimating energy consumption can enhance planning and operational efficiency.

This study analyzes data from the Simple Linux Utility for Resource Management (SLURM) on the Kabré supercomputer at Costa Rica's National High Technology Center (CeNAT). After selecting and preprocessing relevant variables, a dataset was created to train a two-stage machine learning model comprising a binary classifier and a regression model.

Using 10-fold cross-validation, multiple models were evaluated, with Random Forest emerging as the best performer in both stages. The classification model was assessed using the confusion matrix and ROC curve, while the regression model was evaluated through residual analysis and metrics such as Root Mean Square Error (RMSE) and the Coefficient of Determination (R^2). This approach can support users and administrators by improving job scheduling decisions and reducing energy waste in HPC systems.

1 Introduction

High Performance Computing (HPC) systems have become essential tools across various fields, including industry and scientific research, enabling users to perform complex computational tasks that require substantial resources such as memory, processing power, and storage. These tasks encompass simulations, large-scale data analyses, and the training of artificial intelligence models. HPC systems have become increasingly accessible, particularly to users affiliated with universities and research centers [10].

Given the rising demand in recent years, optimizing HPC performance has become a critical priority, as it directly impacts operational costs, energy consumption, and overall infrastructure sustainability. A common challenge is the

K. Brown et al. (Eds.): CARLA 2025, CCIS 2750, pp. 109–124, 2026.
https://doi.org/10.1007/978-3-032-24923-4_8

misestimation of resource requirements, as users often overestimate or underestimate the necessary memory, number of processing units, or execution time. Overestimation leads to inefficient resource utilization and energy waste, while underestimation may cause premature job termination, forcing users to resubmit tasks and thereby increasing delays and computational costs [11]. For instance, a long-running simulation may fail after consuming thousands of CPU hours due to underestimated memory requirements, or conversely, an analysis may reserve far more CPUs than necessary, leaving parts of the cluster idle.

These inefficiencies underscore the importance of predicting, immediately after job submission, whether a job is likely to fail and estimating its energy consumption if it completes successfully. Such predictions enable HPC systems to improve job scheduling, reduce wasted energy, and provide users with actionable recommendations to adjust their submissions, ultimately promoting more sustainable and efficient resource usage [5].

To address this challenge, we propose a supervised two-stage machine learning approach tailored to HPC workloads. The first stage predicts whether a job will complete successfully or fail, while the second stage estimates its average CPU power consumption exclusively for jobs classified as likely to succeed. Using historical data from the SLURM logs of the Kabré supercomputer at the National Center for High Technology (CeNAT) in Costa Rica, we conducted extensive data preprocessing and feature engineering to build robust predictive models. Among the algorithms evaluated, the Random Forest model achieved the best performance in both classification ($\texttt{AUC} = 0.95$) and regression ($R^2 = 0.98$).

This methodology facilitates more efficient decision-making for resource allocation, enhances job scheduling, and reduces energy waste in HPC systems. Moreover, the developed implementation is publicly available, ensuring reproducibility and ease of adaptation to other cluster environments.

2 Problem Description

Efficiently allocating computational resources in High Performance Computing (HPC) environments remains a significant challenge. When submitting jobs to a cluster, users must estimate parameters such as memory, number of CPUs, and execution time. These estimates are often inaccurate, leading to two main issues. First, overestimation occurs when users reserve significantly more resources than required, causing CPUs to remain idle and wasting energy that could have been utilized by other jobs. Second, underestimation may result in premature job failure, causing loss of progress, project delays, and the need to resubmit the job, which further increases energy consumption and reduces overall system efficiency.

For instance, a common scenario arises when a data analysis task requests more CPUs than necessary, leading to inefficient scheduling and restricting other users' access to those resources. Conversely, a researcher running a multi-day simulation may experience job failure near completion due to underestimated memory allocation. The job must then be resubmitted with adjusted parameters, repeating much of the computation and consuming additional energy.

This study addresses these challenges by developing a supervised two-stage machine learning approach. The first stage predicts whether a job will complete successfully or fail, enabling early identification of potentially problematic submissions. The second stage focuses on jobs predicted to succeed and estimates their average CPU power consumption, facilitating more precise resource allocation. By leveraging historical job data from the Kabré supercomputer at the National Center for High Technology (CeNAT) in Costa Rica, the proposed models provide actionable insights that help reduce job failures, optimize scheduling, and minimize unnecessary energy consumption in HPC systems.

3 Background and Related Work

3.1 Machine Learning for Resource Estimation in HPC

The use of machine learning techniques to predict resource requirements in HPC tasks has been a central topic in numerous previous studies, as discussed in [1,2], and [4]. These works agree that accurate resource estimation is critical for improving system efficiency, reducing operational costs, and optimizing overall cluster performance. In particular, the analysis of energy consumption, specifically CPU power consumption (`CPUPower`), has gained relevance due to growing concerns regarding the sustainability of supercomputer usage. In this context, forecasting CPU power consumption not only enhances job scheduling but also supports the design of energy-aware management strategies tailored to the constraints and dynamics of each HPC system.

Specifically, Leon-Vega *et al.* [5] emphasize that traditional methods for estimating energy consumption in HPC environments rely primarily on reports generated by power supply units. However, these approaches typically assume exclusive node usage, an assumption that becomes increasingly inadequate in modern scenarios where computational resources are shared among multiple users and tasks. To address this limitation, the authors collected detailed metrics on both CPU usage and server energy consumption to identify patterns under varying workload conditions. By employing a nonnegative linear regression model, they estimated parameters describing the relationship between CPU utilization and energy consumption, thereby achieving a more precise understanding of how different workload types impact energy demand. Moreover, they noted that few studies estimate CPU power consumption based on the instructions executed by programs or workloads. In contrast, predominant approaches estimate energy consumption at the system level, whether for an individual computer or a server.

Tanash *et al.* [10] developed machine learning models to predict and determine the resources required to run jobs on a supercomputer. They also compared the effects of overestimating memory versus execution time in resource allocation, aiming to identify which type of overestimation is more detrimental to system performance and efficiency. This approach provides valuable insights into improving resource allocation in HPC environments.

Dash *et al.* [2] analyzed data from the Titan computing cluster, including job scheduler logs, GPU failure data, and project-specific information. Their study focused on scheduler performance over time and on how users adjust their behavior following system failures. The primary goal was to generate actionable insights for better understanding system behavior and optimizing resource allocation, which is crucial for efficiently managing system failures and improving stability and performance.

Furthermore, Lowell *et al.* [6] developed a model called TROUT, based on neural networks, to predict job wait times in the Anvil HPC cluster. They used SLURM data, which were transformed during feature engineering to provide information about work priorities, partitions, and states. Their study explores various prediction methods for wait times in HPC environments and concludes that deep learning models are viable solutions for such predictions.

Our approach stands out by jointly addressing two key predictive tasks in HPC environments: forecasting the final state of a job (completed or failed) and estimating its CPU energy consumption in the case of successful completion. Unlike previous studies, which typically address these stages separately or without system-specific adaptation, we propose a two-phase supervised learning model tailored to the characteristics of the Kabré supercomputer, leveraging historical job data stored in SLURM. This strategy enables anticipating energy requirements prior to execution, which is essential for improving scheduling efficiency, reducing operational costs, and promoting sustainable resource utilization [1]. Our approach can be readily adapted to other supercomputer or cluster environments.

3.2 SLURM: Simple Linux Utility for Resource Management

SLURM [15] is an open-source cluster management system for Linux. It is extensively popular across supercomputing installations in the world. Its main functions include:

- Allocating users exclusive or shared access to compute nodes for a specified period so they can execute their jobs.
- Providing a framework for starting, executing, and monitoring those jobs on the assigned nodes.
- Managing resource contention by controlling a queue of pending jobs.

One of the most relevant tools for users is `sacct`, which provides detailed information about jobs and job steps that are currently running or have already completed. In this study, we utilize the variables managed by SLURM, specifically via the `sacct` tool, to obtain information that enables a comprehensive analysis of the supercomputer's usage and efficiency across multiple dimensions. In particular, we focus on logs from the partitions of the Kabré supercomputer that contain only CPUs, with the aim of studying CPU power consumption in completed jobs.

3.3 Machine Learning Models

The purpose of this research was to predict job states, either completed or failed, and to estimate CPU power consumption (`CPUPower`) exclusively for completed jobs, based on variables such as memory required per CPU, CPU time requested, job priority, reserved time, among others, which are detailed in Sect. 4.

The models considered for the classification and regression tasks are described according to [3].

Support Vector Machine (SVM). This model aims to find a hyperplane that maximizes the margin between classes while allowing some flexibility to handle non-separable data. The solution relies on a subset of points known as support vectors, which define the precise position of the decision boundary.

K-Nearest Neighbors (KNN). This model bases its predictions on the proximity of observations in the feature space. To make a prediction, it identifies the k closest points to the test instance according to a distance metric. In classification tasks, it assigns the most frequent class among the neighbors, while in regression, it estimates the output value as their average.

Random Forest (RF). This ensemble model builds multiple decision trees from bootstrap samples of the dataset. At each split, a random subset of variables is selected to determine the best split, which reduces the correlation between trees.

Neural Networks (NNET). This method is used for classification and regression and represents complex functions through nonlinear combinations of linear transformations of the inputs. It is composed of layers of neurons that apply activation functions to weighted combinations of variables.

Extreme Gradient Boosting (XGB). This model employs a sequential combination of multiple decision trees, where in each iteration a new tree is fitted to correct the residual errors of the previous trees using the gradient of the loss function.

Generalized Linear Model (GLM). The objective of *GLM* is to extend linear regression to accommodate response variables that do not necessarily follow a normal distribution. In this study, a logistic regression model was specifically used within the *GLM* framework.

Linear Model (LM). This model was applied only to the regression task in this research. Its objective is to predict a numerical value based on a set of explanatory variables, assuming that the relationship between the response variable and the inputs is linear with respect to the parameters.

To evaluate the classification models, we primarily used metrics derived from the confusion matrix, such as overall accuracy and category precision. Additionally, model performance was assessed using the Receiver Operating Characteristic (`ROC`) curve and the corresponding Area Under the Curve (`AUC`).

For the evaluation of the regression models, we considered various metrics, including Root Mean Squared Error (`RMSE`), Residual Standard Error (`RSE`), Mean Absolute Error (`MAE`), Relative Error (`RE`), the Pearson Correlation Coefficient (r), and the Coefficient of Determination (R^2). The metrics Percentage Increase in Mean Squared Error (`%IncMSE`) and Increase in Node Purity (`IncNodePurity`) were also employed to evaluate the importance of the variables in the selected final model.

4 Methodology

This section describes the processing of the dataset obtained from the SLURM[1] logs, as well as the selection, calibration, and parameter tuning of the two-stage machine learning model.

4.1 Data Preparation and Feature Analysis

The set of observations and variables was obtained using the `sacct` command[2], extracted from the SLURM logs of the Kabré supercomputer. Kabré is the supercomputing infrastructure at the National High Technology Center in Costa Rica and is accessible to the entire academic community of public universities in the country. The system consists of several partitions, each with unique architectural features. The partitions used in this study were: *Andalan* (general purpose), *Dribe* (high memory), *Nu* (massively parallel), and *Kura* (general purpose). The hardware characteristics of each partition are shown in Table 1.

Table 1. Hardware specifications of the partitions used in the experiments

Partition	Hardware Specifications
Andalan	5 nodes: 2 nodes with Intel Xeon 24 cores @ 2.20 GHz, 2 threads/core, 64 GB RAM; 1 node with Intel Xeon 16 cores @ 2.10 GHz, 2 threads/core, 64 GB RAM; 1 node with 10 cores @ 2.20 GHz, 2 threads/core, 32 GB RAM; 1 node with 24 cores @ 2.40 GHz, 2 threads/core, 128 GB RAM. Runs AlmaLinux 8 OS, requires SLURM script adjustment for modules.
Dribe	7 nodes: 1 node with Intel Xeon 36 cores @ 3.00 GHz, 2 threads/core, 1024 GB RAM; remaining nodes with 18 cores @ 3.00 GHz, 2 threads/core, 512 GB RAM. Optimized for memory-intensive applications.
Nu	27 nodes Intel Xeon Phi KNL, each with 64 cores at 1.3 GHz and 96 GB RAM; each core has two AVX units. Suitable for highly parallel and vectorized applications.
Kurá	12 nodes: Intel Xeon 20 cores @ 2.30 GHz, 2 threads/core, 256 GB RAM. Runs AlmaLinux 8 OS, requires SLURM script adjustment for modules.

An initial selection of twelve variables deemed relevant to the research was performed. These features are described in Table 2.

[1] The SLURM version used was 20.11.9.

[2] The actual command line used was `sacct -o consumedenergyraw, cputimeraw, reqcpus, reqmem, reqnodes, resvcpuraw, submit, timelimitraw, partition, priority, qos, state -S 2024-07-01T00:00:00 -E 2025-05-01T00:00:00 -P -L -X > sacct_test.csv`.

Table 2. Variables selected for analysis.

Feature	Type	Description
`ConsumedEnergyRaw`	int	Total energy consumed by all tasks in job, in joules.
`CPUTimeRAW`	int	Time used (Elapsed time * CPU count) by a job or step in seconds.
`ResvCPURAW`	int	How many seconds were used as reserved time for this job.
`TimelimitRaw`	chr	What the timelimit was/is for the job (in minutes).
`ReqMem`	chr	Minimum required memory for the job (in MB or GB per CPU or node).
`ReqNodes`	int	Requested minimum number of nodes.
`ReqCPUS`	int	Number of requested CPUs.
`QOS`	chr	Name of Quality of Service.
`Partition`	chr	Identifies the partition on which the job ran.
`Priority`	int	Slurm priority.
`State`	chr	The job status.
`Submit`	chr	The time the job was submitted.

The log file, containing records of jobs executed between July 1, 2024, and May 1, 2025, for a total of approximately 40 837 observations, was processed using the selected variables in the R programming language through three main stages: data filtering, handling of missing values, and outlier treatment with feature transformation.

The data are distributed across the four aforementioned partitions, with *Andalan* registering the highest number of executed jobs. After applying feature engineering, the reduced number of jobs is also presented in Table 3.

Table 3. Distribution of completed and failed jobs by partition.

Partition	Completed	Failed
Andalan	1 096	14 865
Dribe	5 040	3 252
Nu	4 237	3 576
Kura	2 912	1 752

The distribution of `ConsumedEnergyRaw` by partition and job state is shown in Table 4. The *Dribe* partition exhibits the highest energy consumption for both completed and failed jobs, whereas the *Andalan* partition shows the lowest consumption in both states. In all partitions, failed jobs include cases in which no energy consumption was reported; additionally, in *Dribe*, some completed jobs also show no recorded energy consumption. Numerous outliers are evident across all analyzed combinations, and the distributions display pronounced positive skewness.

Table 4. Energy consumption distribution by state and partition.

Partition	State	Min	1st Qu.	Median	Mean	3rd Qu.	Max
Andalan	Completed	51	659	2 654	178 453	13 133	10 829 071
Dribe	Completed	0	8 398	57 193	2 545 809	616 390	784 918 802
Nu	Completed	59	368	2 835	1 247 195	77 188	315 905 325
Kura	Completed	16	1 070	12 933	788 150	131 498	72 705 718
Andalan	Failed	0	7 192	16 639	737 035	39 026	31 433 295
Dribe	Failed	0	289	2 144	668 580	19 599	284 753 855
Nu	Failed	0	105	517	989 858	4 367	85 858 016
Kura	Failed	0	76	338	157 387	4 647	49 047 874

Data Filtering. An initial filter was applied to select records with a `CPUTimeRAW` value greater than 0, after which a new variable called `CPUPower` was defined. This variable is calculated as the ratio between `ConsumedEnergyRaw` and `CPUTimeRAW`. Its unit of measurement is watts (W), and it represents the average CPU power consumption of the jobs submitted to the system.
Missing Values and Outlier Treatment. A total of 2562 null values were removed. The highest number of null entries was found in the *Kura* partition, with 1425 records. All null records corresponded to canceled or timed-out jobs, which were not considered in this study. To mitigate the influence of outliers, a five percent winsorization was applied to the variables `CPUPower`, `ReqMem`, `TimelimitRaw`, `ResvCPURAW`, and `Priority`, replacing values below the fifth percentile with the respective percentile value and similarly for the upper tail, replacing values above the ninety-fifth percentile with the corresponding cut-off value.
Feature Transformation. First, the variable `TimelimitRAW` was converted into seconds, and the variable `ReqMem` was converted into bytes. The `Submit` variable was transformed into date format, and from it, two new variables were created: `SubmitHour` and `SubmitWeekday`, which represent, respectively, the hour and the day of the week when the jobs were submitted to the system. Next, three additional variables were defined: `CPUs.per.node`, which indicates the number of CPUs per node; `Mem.per.CPU`, which represents the memory used per CPU; and `CPU.time.requested`, which reflects the total time limit requested by all CPUs.

Logarithmic transformations were then applied to the variables `Mem.per.CPU` and `CPU.time.requested` to reduce the positive skewness and high kurtosis exhibited by their distributions. These results indicate that the initial distributions of these variables were leptokurtic and positively skewed. Finally, min-max normalization was applied to scale the numerical variables to the range

[0, 1]. This transformation preserves the relationships between the original values while preventing variables with larger ranges from dominating the model training. Furthermore, the `QOS` and `Partition` variables were converted into factors to appropriately handle their categorical nature during model training.

4.2 Two-Stage Machine Learning Model

A two-stage machine learning model is proposed, comprising a classification phase followed by a regression phase. The classification model was trained on a filtered dataset containing only instances labeled as completed or failed jobs. For this model, 80% of the data were used for training, and 20% were reserved for testing. Similarly, the regression model was trained exclusively using records corresponding to completed jobs, also with 80% of the data for training and 20% for testing.

In the classification phase, Welch's t-tests were performed for each numerical predictor variable to assess differences in means between the two classes while accounting for potential heteroscedasticity. Subsequently, a 10-fold cross-validation was conducted to evaluate the predictive performance of various candidate models. Key metrics derived from the confusion matrix, such as overall accuracy and true positive rates for failed and completed jobs, were analyzed. Furthermore, the classification threshold was optimized to balance sensitivity and specificity, and the discriminative ability of the selected model was assessed through the `ROC` curve and its corresponding `AUC` value.

For the regression phase, a Pearson correlation matrix was computed to identify the numerical variables most strongly associated with the target variable, `CPUPower`. A 10-fold cross-validation procedure was applied to evaluate model performance using metrics including Root Mean Squared Error (`RMSE`), Residual Standard Error (`RSE`), Mean Absolute Error (`MAE`), Relative Error (`RE`), and the Coefficient of Determination (R^2). Based on these criteria, the most robust model was selected. Finally, hyperparameter tuning was performed using a 5-fold cross-validation to minimize `RMSE`[3].

5 Results and Discussion

Classification Model. The results of Welch's t-tests are summarized in Table 5. The analysis revealed significant differences for most variables. Failed jobs typically use more CPUs per node and request longer CPU time, whereas completed jobs tend to have more memory per CPU, higher priority values, and are generally submitted later in the day. These findings indicate distinct patterns in resource utilization and submission behavior associated with job outcomes. However, the `ResvCPURAW` and `SubmitWeekday` variables did not show statistically significant differences between the two groups. Consequently, these variables were excluded from the classification model due to their limited discriminative power.

[3] The two-stage machine learning model codes are available at https://github.com/DylanBC09/Project-1-CeNAT.git.

Table 5. Summary of Welch's t-test results.

Variable	t-value	p-value	Mean Completed	Mean Failed	Significance
`ResvCPURAW`	1.71	>0.05	0.10	0.09	Not significant
`Priority`	11.45	<0.05	0.30	0.26	Significant
`CPUs.per.node`	−85.99	< 0.05	0.22	0.50	Significant
`Mem.per.CPU`	62.79	<0.05	0.53	0.38	Significant
`CPU.time.requested`	−86.98	<0.05	0.53	0.76	Significant
`SubmitHour`	16.41	<0.05	0.57	0.53	Significant
`SubmitWeekday`	−0.99	>0.05	0.48	0.49	Not significant

These results are further illustrated in Fig. 1, which shows the distribution of each variable according to job status. The `ResvCPURAW` and `SubmitWeekday` variables display similar distributions across completed and failed jobs, whereas the remaining variables exhibit clear differences, reinforcing their relevance for modeling.

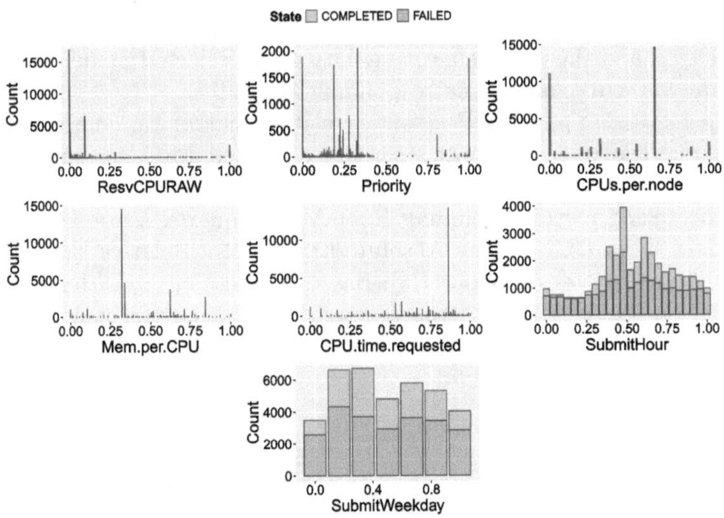

Fig. 1. Distributions of selected numerical variables for jobs classified as Completed and Failed. The variables `ResvCPURAW` and `SubmitWeekday` show similar distributions between both classes, which is confirmed by Welch's t-tests indicating no significant differences ($p > 0.05$), as summarized in Table 5.

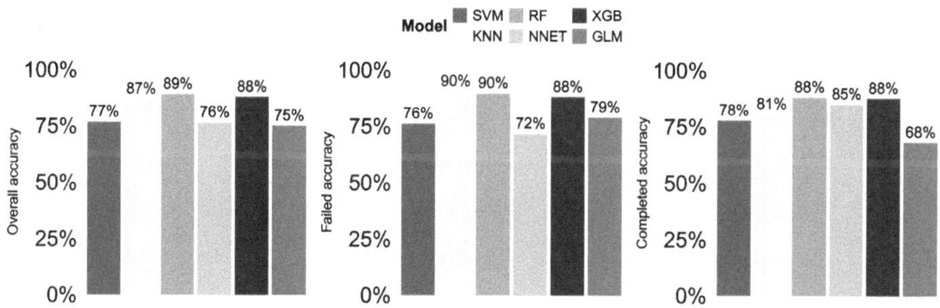

Fig. 2. Overall accuracy and category-specific accuracy of the considered models, averaged over 10-fold cross-validation.

The results of the ten-fold cross-validation are presented in Fig. 2, which shows the key metrics for each model. According to the results, the highest overall accuracy was achieved by the Random Forest (*RF*) model at 89%, followed by Extreme Gradient Boosting (*XGB*) with 88%, and K-Nearest Neighbors (*KNN*) with 87%. At the lower end of the list were Support Vector Machines (*SVM*) with 77%, Neural Networks (*NNET*) with 76%, and the Generalized Linear Model (*GLM*) with 75%.

Regarding the detection of failed jobs, *KNN* obtained the highest true positive rate at 90%, followed by *RF* at 90% and *XGB* at 88%. The lowest performance for this metric was observed in *NNET*, with 72%. For the classification of completed jobs, *RF* showed the best performance at 88%, tied with *XGB* at 88%, followed by *NNET* at 85%. In this case, *GLM* had the lowest accuracy at 68%.

Considering both overall accuracy and balance in identifying failed and completed jobs, Random Forest (*RF*) was selected as the most suitable model. This algorithm represents the best overall choice, as it combines high total accuracy with strong performance in classifying completed jobs, without significantly compromising the detection of failures.

A probability threshold calibration was performed for the binary classification task to improve the balance between category-specific accuracy rates. After evaluating different threshold values, a threshold of 0.4 was selected to assign observations to the completed or failed classes. This means that a job is classified as completed only if the estimated probability exceeds 40%. Using this threshold, an overall accuracy of 87.11% was achieved, indicating good general performance of the model. When analyzing accuracy by category, the completed class reached 92.02%, while the failed class achieved 84.32%.

As a complement to the confusion matrix analysis, the performance of the Random Forest model was evaluated using the `ROC` curve. Figure 3 shows the resulting curve, and the area under the curve (`AUC`) was 0.95, indicating a high capability of the model to discriminate between completed and failed jobs. Finally, the number of trees in the Random Forest model was tuned, and it was found that fifty trees are sufficient to achieve solid classification performance.

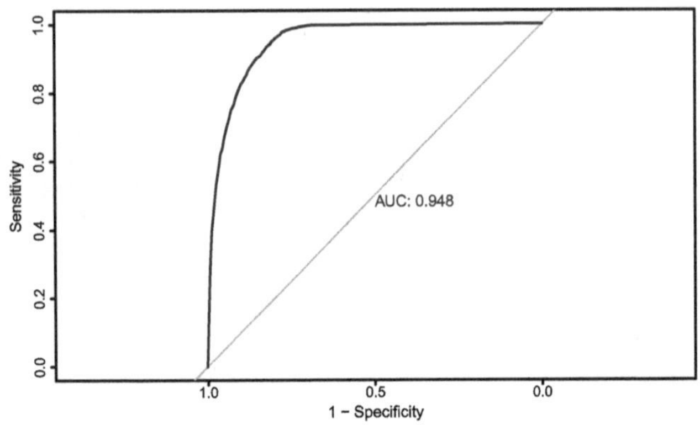

Fig. 3. Receiver Operating Characteristic curve for the Random Forest model used to predict job states.

This configuration offers a good balance between accuracy and computational efficiency, making the Random Forest model with fifty trees the most suitable choice for the problem at hand.

Regression Model. The correlation matrix shown in Fig. 4 reveals a strong positive correlation between `Mem.per.CPU` and `CPUPower`, moderate negative correlations between `ResvCPURAW`, `CPUs.per.node`, and `CPUPower`, a weak negative correlation between `Priority`, `CPU.time.requested`, and `CPUPower`, and a weak positive correlation between `SubmitHour`, `SubmitWeekday`, and `CPUPower`.

After applying a ten-fold cross-validation and evaluating the corresponding metrics for each model, the results presented in Table 6 were obtained. It can be observed that the Random Forest model achieved the lowest `MAE` and `RE`. Additionally, it shares with the *XGB* model the lowest values of `RMSE` and `RSE`. Both models also achieved the highest correlation coefficient of 0.99, indicating a strong association between the predicted and observed values. Finally, the highest coefficient of determination, with a value of 0.98, was obtained by both *RF* and *XGB*, indicating that these models fit the data well. The second column of Table 6 presents a comparison of the average `RMSE` across all models.

After performing a random search to explore different combinations of hyperparameters and applying 5-fold cross-validation, the configuration that yielded the lowest root mean square error (`RMSE`) of 0.047 was selected as optimal. The best model consisted of 100 trees, with the `mtry` parameter set to 3, meaning that at each decision node, three predictor variables were randomly selected to determine the best split. Additionally, the minimum node size was set to 1, allowing nodes to continue splitting as long as they contained at least one observation. This setup enabled the construction of highly detailed trees and contributed to the superior predictive performance observed during validation.

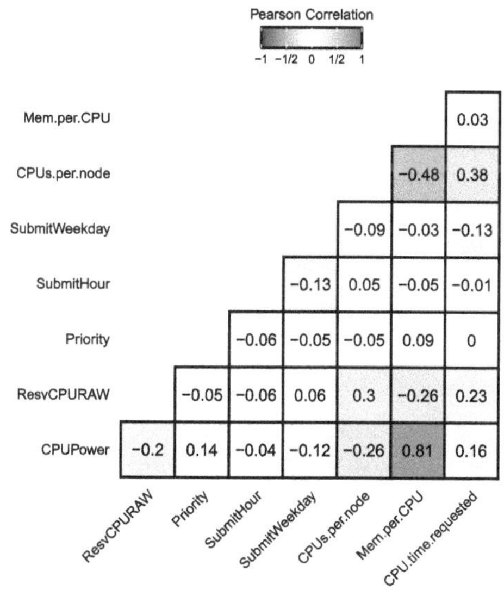

Fig. 4. Pearson correlation matrix of the numerical predictor variables in the regression model.

Table 6. Results of the error metrics for each regression model considered, averaged over 10-fold cross-validation.

Model	RMSE	RSE	MAE	RE	r	R^2
SVM	0.063	0.064	0.038	0.072	0.98	0.97
KNN	0.059	0.059	0.027	0.051	0.98	0.97
RF	0.051	0.051	0.025	0.047	0.99	0.98
NNET	0.072	0.072	0.044	0.084	0.98	0.96
XGB	0.051	0.051	0.027	0.051	0.99	0.98
LM	0.13	0.13	0.10	0.19	0.94	0.89

Figure 5 shows that the predictions closely match the actual values of the test set, as reflected by the Pearson correlation coefficient, which reached $r = 0.98$. The results presented in Table 7 indicate that `Partition` is the most important variable influencing CPU power consumption, followed by `CPUs.per.node` and `Mem.per.CPU`. Variables such as `CPU.time.requested` and `Priority` also have a notable impact. Other factors, including `SubmitHour`, `SubmitWeekday`, `ResvCPURAW`, and `QOS`, play a smaller but still relevant role in model predictions.

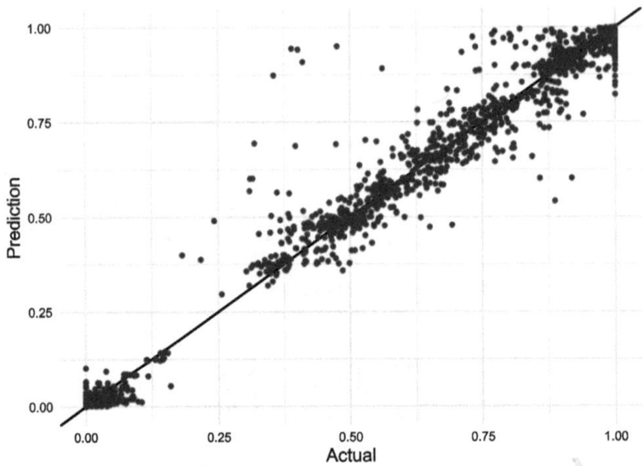

Fig. 5. Scatter plot of actual versus predicted values from the Random Forest regression model with parameters `ntree`=100, `mtry`=3 and `nodesize`=1.

Table 7. Variable importance metrics for the final predictive model

Variable	`%IncMSE`	`IncNodePurity`
`Partition`	43.77	768.04
`CPUs.per.node`	28.01	134.29
`Mem.per.CPU`	10.14	530.83
`CPU.time.requested`	14.26	108.02
`Priority`	16.20	19.66
`SubmitHour`	12.13	7.31
`SubmitWeekday`	9.19	11.79
`QOS`	8.37	4.06
`ResvCPURAW`	10.41	16.27

6 Conclusions and Future Work

Of the different machine learning models evaluated, Random Forest demonstrated the best fit to the computing cluster data, excelling in both prediction and classification tasks. Other models, such as K-Nearest Neighbors and Extreme Gradient Boosting, also produced positive results. It can be concluded that, for this study, nonparametric models were the most effective in explaining the variability of the data.

Regarding the classification problem, the majority of the selected variables exhibited strong discriminative power, as evidenced by the results of Welch's t-test. This is reflected in the model's performance, indicating that it is possible to accurately predict whether a job will fail or succeed based on user-submitted job characteristics. For the regression task, the final predictive model proved robust according to the evaluated error metrics. The results indicate that the most influential variables on CPU power consumption are partition, memory per CPU, and the number of CPUs per node.

For future work, it is recommended to develop a model that jointly analyzes the energy consumption of both CPUs and GPUs. Furthermore, updating the database is essential to improve the robustness of the model, enabling better capture of data variability and detection of relevant behavioral patterns.

Additionally, incorporating a time series analysis of CPU power consumption over time would be beneficial to identify key components such as seasonality and trends. This would allow predictive models to be adjusted according to different times of the year or variations in user behavior.

Finally, the development of an interface that integrates the predictive model into the job submission process of the Kabré supercomputer could also be considered. Such a tool would provide users with real-time feedback on the likelihood of job success and the estimated CPU energy consumption, enabling better resource allocation decisions and reducing the number of failed or inefficient jobs.

Acknowledgments. This research was partially supported by a machine allocation on Kabré supercomputer at the Costa Rica National High Technology Center. We would like to thank Herson Mena, system administrator of Kabré, for his valuable help in accessing and interpreting the data for this study.

Compliance with ethical standards

Disclosure of Interests. The authors have no competing interests to declare that are relevant to the content of this article.

References

1. Andresen, D., Hsu, W., Yang, H., Okanlawon, A.: Machine Learning for Predictive Analytics of Compute Cluster Jobs (2018). http://arxiv.org/abs/1806.01116
2. Dash, S., Paul, A.K., Oral, S., Wang, F.: SMC Data Challenge 2021: Analyzing Resource Utilization and User Behavior on Titan Supercomputer (2021). https://doi.ccs.ornl.gov/ui/doi/334
3. Hastie, T., Tibshirani, R., Friedman, J.: The Elements of Statistical Learning: Data Mining, Inference, and Prediction. Springer Series in Statistics. Springer (2009).
4. León, F., Diaz, G.: Development of a web interface for submitting jobs to SLURM. Revista UIS Ingenierías, 18(4), 95–98 (2019). https://doi.org/10.18273/revuin.v18n4-2019008
5. León-Vega, L. G., Tosato, N., Cozzini, S.: EfiMon: A Process Analyser for Granular Power Consumption Prediction (2024). http://arxiv.org/abs/2409.17368
6. Lovell, A., Wisniewski, P., Rodenbeck, S., Ashish.: A hierarchical deep learning approach for predicting job queue times in HPC systems. In: Proceedings of SC 2024-W: Workshops of the International Conference for High Performance Computing, Networking, Storage and Analysis, pp. 621–628 (2024). https://doi.org/10.1109/SCW63240.2024.00086

7. McSpadden, D., et al.: Dataset for Investigating Anomalies in Compute Clusters (2023). https://doi.org/10.5281/zenodo.10058230
8. Morán, M., Balladini, J., Rexachs, D., Rucci, E.: Towards management of energy consumption in HPC systems with fault tolerance. 2020 IEEE Congreso Bienal de Argentina, ARGENCON 2020 - 2020 IEEE Biennial Congress of Argentina, ARGENCON 2020 (2020, December 1). https://doi.org/10.1109/ARGENCON49523.2020.9505498
9. Tanash, M., Andresen, D., Hsu, W.: AMPRO-HPCC: a machine-learning tool for predicting resources on Slurm HPC clusters HHS public access. In: ADVCOMP International Conference Advance Engineering Computer Applied Science (2021).
10. Tanash, M., Dunn, B., Andresen, D., Hsu, W., Yang, H., Okanlawon, A.: Improving HPC system performance by predicting job resources via supervised machine learning. In: ACM International Conference Proceeding Series (2019, July 28). https://doi.org/10.1145/3332186.3333041
11. Tanash, M., Yang, H., Andresen, D., Hsu, W.: Ensemble prediction of job resources to improve system performance for slurm-based HPC systems. In: ACM International Conference Proceeding Series (2021, July 17). https://doi.org/10.1145/3437359.3465574
12. Taghavi, T., Lupetini, M., Kretchmer, Y.: Compute job memory recommender system using machine learning. In: Proceedings of the ACM SIGKDD International Conference on Knowledge Discovery and Data Mining, 13-17-August-2016, pp. 609–616 (2016).. https://doi.org/10.1145/2939672.2939717
13. Wilcox, R.R.: Applying contemporary statistical techniques (2020).
14. Xu, L., Hong, Y., Morris, M.D., Cameron, K.W.: Prediction for Distributional Outcomes in High-Performance Computing I/O Variability (2022). http://arxiv.org/abs/2205.09879
15. Yoo, A.B., Jette, M.A., Grondona, M.: Slurm: simple Linux utility for resource management. In: Feitelson, D., Rudolph, L., Schwiegelshohn, U., (Eds.), Job Scheduling Strategies for Parallel Processing (pp. 44–60) (2003). Springer. https://slurm.schedmd.com/

Leveraging Local Data Share for Efficient Stencil Computation in the Fletcher Model on AMD MI250X

Arthur Francisco Lorenzon[1(✉)], Alexandre Sardinha[2], Davide Teixeira[3], Alfredo Heiss[3], and Philippe O. A. Navaux[1]

[1] Federal University of Rio Grande do Sul, Porto Alegre, Brazil
{aflorenzon,navaux}@inf.ufrgs.br
[2] Petróleo Brasileiro SA, Rio de Janeiro, Brazil
alexandre.sardinha@petrobras.com.br
[3] AMD - Advanced Micro Devices, Santa Clara, USA
{Davide.Teixeira,Alfredo.Heiss}@amd.com

Abstract. As high-performance computing systems scale, maximizing both performance and energy efficiency has become critical, particularly for memory-bound stencil computations that dominate scientific applications. In this scenario, we investigate optimization techniques for the Fletcher model, a high-order finite-difference seismic wave propagation solver, on AMD GPUs. We consider the impact of two hardware-level strategies: (*i*) exploiting Local Data Share (LDS) memory to reduce redundant global memory accesses in stencil kernels, and (*ii*) applying non-temporal memory instructions to avoid cache pollution from low-reuse coefficient arrays. The optimizations target the two main kernels of the model, `partialDerivatives` and `propagation`, by reusing shared memory in the y- and z-directions, improving spatial locality, and reducing memory traffic. Through a set of experiments performed on an AMD MI250X, we show that using LDS improves performance and energy by 9.3% and 12% compared to the baseline version that exploits the use of global memory. Also, when considering both LDS and non-temporal stores together, the performance gains increase to 31.9% while the energy savings increase to 27%, compared to the baseline version.

Keywords: Performance-Energy Efficiency · RTM · GPU · Memory usage

1 Introduction

Graphics Processing Units (GPUs) have become a central component of modern high-performance computing (HPC) systems, offering massive parallelism and energy-efficient acceleration for a wide range of scientific applications [2,15]. Among these, Reverse Time Migration (RTM) is a key workload in geophysical imaging, widely used for high-resolution subsurface modeling. Due to its

K. Brown et al. (Eds.): CARLA 2025, CCIS 2750, pp. 125–139, 2026.
https://doi.org/10.1007/978-3-032-24923-4_9

compute- and memory-intensive nature, RTM has increasingly been deployed on GPU-accelerated systems, where it can benefit from high throughput and parallelism across large-scale datasets.

Despite the computational power offered by modern GPUs, the performance of RTM applications is often limited not by raw compute throughput but by memory subsystem behavior. These applications exhibit stencil-like access patterns with frequent memory reads and writes, placing significant pressure on memory bandwidth and latency [1,13]. As a result, inefficient use of the memory hierarchy, particularly global memory, can become a critical bottleneck, limiting the performance gains achievable through increased parallelism [12]. In this scenario, memory optimization is a key challenge in achieving high-performance and energy-efficient RTM execution on GPU architectures.

One strategy to mitigate memory bottlenecks in RTM is to leverage low-latency memory spaces provided by GPU architectures, such as shared memory on NVIDIA GPUs or Local Data Share (LDS) on AMD GPUs. These hardware-managed memory regions reside closer to the compute units and offer significantly higher bandwidth and lower latency compared to global memory. In this scenario, by promoting data reuse and enabling fine-grained thread cooperation, these resources can substantially reduce memory access overheads, particularly in stencil-based computations. However, employing these features in the source code typically requires explicit management and restructuring of the application code. This includes redesigning memory access patterns, handling synchronization across threads, and ensuring data consistency, all while maintaining correctness and avoiding resource contention. As a result, optimizing RTM with shared memory or LDS is a non-trivial task.

Considering the aforementioned scenario, we propose the use of local data share memory to optimize the performance and energy efficiency of an RTM application, called the Fletcher model, on one node of the Frontier supercomputer. Fletcher is widely used to simulate seismic wave propagation during subsurface surveys and is a GPU-intensive application where performance is dependent on memory operations. Therefore, by employing the use of LDS, we show that performance can be improved by 9.3% compared to a baseline version that relies on global memory only. This version also reduces the energy consumption by 12%. We also propose the use of non-temporal store operations on the L2 cache to further improve memory usage. With that, we were able to improve the amount of floating-point operations per second due to better hardware usage, resulting in 31.9% of performance improvements and 27% energy savings compared to the baseline implementation.

The remainder of this work is structured as follows. In Sect. 2, we describe the Fletcher model and list the related work. Then, in Sect. 3, we present and discuss the optimizations implemented into the two kernels of the Fletcher model. The methodology employed during the experiments is discussed in Sect. 4. Results are discussed in Sect. 5, while the final considerations and future work are discussed in Sect. 6

2 Background

In this section, we start by describing the implementation of our target application. Then, in Sect. 2.2, we discuss load data sharing in AMD GPUs. Finally, in Sect. 2.3, we list the related work and highlight our contributions.

2.1 Fletcher Modeling

Fletcher modeling is widely used in geophysics to simulate seismic wave propagation during subsurface surveys [4]. It solves the acoustic wave equation over a 3D grid, where each point represents physical properties such as velocity and density. The method updates pressure values over time to simulate how waves reflect, refract, and diffract through geological structures. Given the pressure field $p(x, y, z, t)$, velocity model $V(x, y, z)$, and density $\rho(x, y, z)$, Eqs. 1 and 2 describe the wave propagation and velocity update used in Fletcher's implementation.

$$\frac{1}{V^2}\frac{\partial^2 p}{\partial t^2} = \nabla^2 p \tag{1}$$

$$\frac{1}{V^2}\frac{\partial^2 p}{\partial t^2} = \nabla^2 p - \frac{\nabla \rho}{\rho} \cdot \nabla p \tag{2}$$

Algorithm 1 shows the baseline HIP implementation of the *Fletcher* method, which uses 3D domain decomposition across the x, y, and z axes. We refer to this as the *baseline* during the rest of the paper, and it serves as the basis for developing the variant when exploiting local data shared on AMD GPUs. The algorithm takes as input the grid dimensions (sx, sy, sz), the number of iterations α, and the output interval Θ. The `initData()` routine initializes the required data structures, including derivative coefficient arrays ($chxx$, $chxy$, etc.), wavefield variables (p, q), and velocity-dependent parameters. GPU memory is allocated with `allocDataGPU()`, and input data is transferred using `hipMemcpy`. Each iteration inserts a modulated Gaussian pulse at the center of the domain (`insertPulse()`) and propagates it using a 5-point stencil. The process involves computing first and second-order spatial derivatives (`partialDerivatives()`), followed by wavefield updates in `propagate()`, which performs derivative accumulation, RHS calculation, and wavefield updates in the x, y, and z directions.

During the `partialDerivatives`$(\cdots)$ and `propagate`$(\cdots)$ functions, the implementation considers that the grid is partitioned following a three-dimensional (3D) domain decomposition strategy by extracting a plane along the x, y, and z axes. As there is no dependency between individual points, they can be calculated in parallel in each function. However, there is a data dependency between both functions as the partial derivatives of pc and qc in x and y (pDx, pDy, qDx, and qDy) are inputs of the `propagate` function. Once the point associated with the acoustic wave is computed on the device and there is a need to write to the disk, the grid is updated in the CPU memory via `hipMemcpy`. When the number of iterations reaches the threshold Θ, the wave is written to

Algorithm 1 Baseline HIP implementation

Input: α: number of iterations the wave will propagate.
Θ: number of iterations where the wave will be stored on disk.
sx, sy, sz: size of dimensions x, y, z.

function MAIN(...)
  $initData(grids, sx, sy, sz)$
  $allocDataGPU(\cdots)$
  $copyH2D(\cdots)$
  for each dt in α **do**
    $insertPulse(\cdots)$
    $partialDerivatives(\cdots)$
    $propagate(\cdots)$
    if $dt == \Theta$ **then**
      $update(\cdots)$
      $writeWave()$
    end if
  end for
end function

function PARTIALDERIVATIVES(...)
  $x = threadIdx.x + blockIdx.x * blockDim.x$
  $y = threadIdx.y + blockIdx.y * blockDim.y$
  $z = threadIdx.z + blockIdx.z * blockDim.z$
  $pDx_{xyz} = \frac{\partial p_c}{\partial x}, pDy_{xyz} = \frac{\partial p_c}{\partial y}$
  $qDx_{xyz} = \frac{\partial q_c}{\partial x}, qDy_{xyz} = \frac{\partial q_c}{\partial y}$
end function

function PROPAGATE(...)
  $x = threadIdx.x + blockIdx.x * blockDim.x$
  $y = threadIdx.y + blockIdx.y * blockDim.y$
  $z = threadIdx.z + blockIdx.z * blockDim.z$
  $\frac{\partial p_c}{\partial x}, \frac{\partial p_c}{\partial y}, \frac{\partial p_c}{\partial z}, \frac{\partial^2 p_c}{\partial x^2}, \frac{\partial^2 p_c}{\partial y^2}, \frac{\partial^2 p_c}{\partial z^2}, \frac{\partial^2 p_c}{\partial x \partial y}, \frac{\partial^2 p_c}{\partial x \partial z}, \frac{\partial^2 p_c}{\partial y \partial z}$
  $\frac{\partial q_c}{\partial x}, \frac{\partial q_c}{\partial y}, \frac{\partial q_c}{\partial z}, \frac{\partial^2 q_c}{\partial x^2}, \frac{\partial^2 q_c}{\partial y^2}, \frac{\partial^2 q_c}{\partial z^2}, \frac{\partial^2 q_c}{\partial x \partial y}, \frac{\partial^2 q_c}{\partial x \partial z}, \frac{\partial^2 q_c}{\partial y \partial z}$
  $h1p = \left(\frac{\partial p_c}{\partial x} + \frac{\partial^2 p_c}{\partial x^2} + \cdots\right); h2p = \left(\frac{\partial^2 p_c}{\partial x^2} + \cdots\right) - h1p$
  $h1q = \left(\frac{\partial q_c}{\partial x} + \frac{\partial^2 q_c}{\partial x^2} + \cdots\right); h2q = \left(\frac{\partial^2 q_c}{\partial x^2} + \cdots\right) - h1q$
  $rhsp = v2px_{xyz} * h2p + v2pz_{xyz} * h1q + v2sz_{xyz} * (h1p - h1q)$
  $rhsq = v2px_{xyz} * h2p + v2pz_{xyz} * h1q + v2sz_{xyz} * (h2p - h2q)$
  $pp_{xyz} = 2.0 * pc_{xyz} - pp_{xyz} + rhsp * dt * dt$
  $qp_{xyz} = 2.0 * qc_{xyz} - qp_{xyz} + rhsq * dt * dt$
end function

the disk. It is worth mentioning that it is needed to ensure that the values x, y, *and* z are within the boundaries of the grid (sx, sy, and sz, respectively).

2.2 Local Data Share on AMD GPUs

AMD GPUs provide a fast, low-latency on-chip memory space known as Local Data Share (LDS), which is designed to enable efficient data exchange and reuse among threads within the same workgroup. LDS is functionally analogous to shared memory on NVIDIA GPUs, offering significantly higher bandwidth and lower latency than global memory. Each Compute Unit (CU) contains its own LDS region, typically ranging from 64 KB to 128 KB, which is shared across all wavefronts executing concurrently on that CU[1].

[1] amd.com/pt/products/accelerators/instinct/mi200/mi250x.html.

Exploiting LDS can yield performance benefits for memory-bound applications, particularly those with regular data access patterns or opportunities for data reuse, such as stencil computations. By staging frequently accessed data in LDS, it is possible to reduce global memory traffic, mitigate memory latency bottlenecks, and increase arithmetic intensity. In HIP, LDS is managed through statically declared memory using the `__shared__` keyword with specific address space qualifiers. A typical usage pattern involves the following steps:

- Declare LDS buffers using `__shared__` within the kernel scope to allocate memory that is visible to all threads in a block.
- Cooperatively load data from global memory into LDS using threads in the workgroup.
- Synchronize threads with `__syncthreads()` to ensure that all data transfers are complete before computation begins.
- Perform computations using the LDS-resident data to minimize redundant global memory accesses.
- Optionally write results back to global memory.

2.3 Related Work

Different works have been proposed to optimize the execution performance of RTM applications, by either tuning the execution configuration of GPU kernels, the number of compute nodes that run the application, or the data movement across CPU and GPU. Liu et al., [10] explore using GPUs to accelerate the Reverse Time Migration (RTM) algorithm. The parallelization scheme focuses on using two GPUs by employing a workload division strategy. The authors also consider a version that relies on the unified memory scheme available in CUDA. The results suggest that the workload division strategy presents better results than unified memory in a multi-GPU environment. Serpa et al., [20] address optimizing the Fletcher method on multicore and single-GPU architectures, focusing on portability. The paper analyzes the performance, energy consumption, and energy efficiency of two versions of the code, an original version and an optimized version for OpenMP, OpenACC, and CUDA.

Liu et al., [11] discuss the implementation of the GPU-accelerated RTM algorithm. It also addresses specific issues such as uneven topography and anisotropic environment, i.e., it focuses on various technical aspects of implementing GPU-accelerated RTM. Pearson et al., [17] explore techniques to improve 3D stencil communication on heterogeneous supercomputers using strategies such as hierarchical partitioning and optimization of data exchange between GPUs. Okamoto et al., [16] describe how the use of multiple GPUs can significantly speed up simulations of seismic wave propagation. A particular challenge faced when using multiple GPUs is non-contiguous memory alignment in the overlapping regions between subdomains processed by different GPUs.

Distinct works have evaluated the impact of Unified Memory management and data prefetching on RTM applications. Knap and Czarnul [9] evaluate the performance of Unified Memory with data prefetching and memory oversubscription on Pascal and Volta architecture GPUs. Jung et al., [8] exploit Unified Memory to overlap communication with computation. Subway [19] is a solution to optimize the performance of GPU graph processing applications by only loading active edges of the graph to the GPU memory instead of employing a Unified Memory technique. Riahi et al., [18] propose machine-learning-based models to estimate data transfer time between CPUs and GPUs.

Grus [22] is a system framework to improve the space efficiency of GPU graph applications via a Unified Memory trimming scheme tailored to the data access behaviors of graph workloads. Bienz et al., [3] propose a strategy for communicating large amounts of data between GPUs on different nodes. Montella et al., [14] propose a solution to support CUDA Unified Memory in open-source GPGPU virtualization devices. Jin and Vetter [6] evaluate the impact of data migration methods, including Unified Memory, pageable memory, pinned memory, and zero-copy, on the matrix multiplication and vector addition performance. Jung et al., [7] implement a framework called DeepUM that exploits CUDA Unified Memory to allow GPU memory over-subscription for Deep neural networks. Garvey and Abdelrahman [5] propose a machine learning strategy to tune the execution configurations of kernels to improve the performance of stencil computations on GPUs. Zhang et al., [23] evaluate the performance and power consumption of ATI GPUs while running different applications, including stencil-based. Tabbakh et al., [21] aim to reduce data movement and increase effective cache space in GPUs. For that, a sharing-aware scheduler is proposed that attempts to assign threads with data sharing to the same shared memory.

Although many works have focused on optimizing the performance of RTM applications on GPUs by finding ideal configurations to execute them or optimizing data movement across GPU and CPU memories, there is still a lack of works that consider optimizing the memory usage of the Fletcher model. Therefore, our contribution relies on filling this research gap, focusing on optimizing the Fletcher model through the use of local data sharing and non-temporal store operations on AMD GPUs. Furthermore, our work is orthogonal to the other proposed strategies and can be applied together to the optimization strategies to further improve the performance and energy efficiency of RTM applications.

3 Exploiting Local Data Share to Improve Memory Performance

In the baseline implementation of the `partialDerivatives` kernel, the spatial derivatives $\frac{\partial pc}{\partial x}$, $\frac{\partial pc}{\partial y}$, $\frac{\partial qc}{\partial x}$, and $\frac{\partial qc}{\partial y}$ are computed using values fetched directly from global memory. While this approach is straightforward, it introduces redundant memory transactions, especially in the y-direction, where each stencil operation repeatedly loads neighboring data points across iterations. This results in inefficient use of memory bandwidth and limited exploitation of spatial locality. To reduce these overheads, we redesigned the kernel to cache a vertical slice of the `pc` and `qc` arrays into LDS, focusing on the y-axis stencil computation.

Algorithm 2 Leveraging LDS for the PartialDerivative Function

1: **function** PARTIALDERIVATIVESLDS(...)
2: $x = threadIdx.x + blockIdx.x * blockDim.x$
3: $y = threadIdx.y + blockIdx.y * blockDim.y$
4: $z = threadIdx.z + blockIdx.z * blockDim.z$
5: __shared__ float $lds_{pc}[lds_x][lds_y][lds_z]$
6: __shared__ float $lds_{qc}[lds_x][lds_y][lds_z]$
7:
8: *load content into shared variables*
9:
10: __syncthreads();
11: $pDx_{xyz} = \frac{\partial pc}{\partial x}$, $pDy_{xyz} = \frac{\partial lds_{pc}}{\partial y}$
12: $qDx_{xyz} = \frac{\partial qc}{\partial x}$, $qDy_{xyz} = \frac{\partial lds_{qc}}{\partial y}$
13: **end function**

Algorithm 2 lists the modifications performed in the baseline function. First, the shared arrays are defined in lines 5 and 6, one for the pc (lds_{pc}) and the other for the qc array (lds_{qc}). Each array has the dimensions defined by the variables lds_x, lds_y, and lds_z, which define the number of elements that will be loaded into each dimension. This optimization targets the y-axis because of its alignment with the thread-block decomposition, which allows threads within a warp to collectively load contiguous regions of memory, improving coalescence. Specifically, each thread loads the center and halo points required for a high-order finite-difference stencil into shared memory. Then, after loading the content into the shared variables, the synchronization barrier (`__syncthreads()`) ensures that all threads have completed loading their data before any computation begins.

Once the data is cached, the stencil operation is applied using only LDS values, significantly reducing the number of global memory reads. It is worth mentioning that to use the shared variables, each thread calculates the right index value according to its global index. Also, the x-derivative computation remains unchanged in this version, continuing to rely on global memory. This decision stems from a trade-off between complexity and performance benefit: the reuse potential in the x-direction is lower given the memory access stride, and introducing LDS along this axis would impose higher register pressure and occupancy constraints.

In the baseline implementation of the `propagate` kernel, first-order cross-derivatives in the xz and yz planes, such as $\frac{\partial^2 p}{\partial x \partial z}$ and $\frac{\partial^2 p}{\partial y \partial z}$, are computed directly using values fetched from global memory. This implementation leads to excessive and redundant memory accesses across stencil iterations, particularly in the z-direction, where spatial locality is inherently limited due to memory access strides. As a result, memory bandwidth is poorly utilized, and cache efficiency is reduced. To alleviate these limitations, we modified the kernel to preload the necessary stencil regions of the arrays `pDx`, `pDy`, `qDx`, and `qDy` into LDS, following the same style of code modification done in Algorithm 2. The modification consists of allocating shared arrays, each covering the halo region and center values required for the stencil computation along the z-axis. Threads within a block cooperatively load their respective values into LDS, following a structured access pattern that maximizes memory coalescence and minimizes bank conflicts. The synchronization barrier, `__syncthreads()`, is placed immediately after the data loading phase to ensure that all values are correctly staged in LDS before any computation begins.

Once the input arrays are cached, the kernel computes the cross-derivatives $\frac{\partial^2}{\partial x \partial z}$ and $\frac{\partial^2}{\partial y \partial z}$ from lines 29 and 30 from Algorithm 1, using the LDS-resident values. This redesign reduces global memory access traffic and enhances temporal locality by reusing data across multiple stencil evaluations within a block. This optimization is selectively applied to the z-axis because we found it exhibits a high degree of data reuse and aligns well with the thread-block structure. On the other hand, cross-derivatives in the xy-plane, such as $\frac{\partial^2 p}{\partial x \partial y}$, are still computed directly from global memory. Extending LDS usage to these dimensions would increase shared memory demand, raise register pressure, and reduce occupancy, offering a less favorable trade-off.

To further optimize memory behavior, we apply non-temporal memory operations to coefficient and velocity arrays that exhibit low spatial and temporal locality. Specifically, arrays such as `ch1dxx`, `ch1dyy`, `ch1dzz`, `ch1dxy`, `ch1dxz`, `ch1dyz`, `v2px`, `v2pn`, `v2pz`, and `v2sz` are accessed using `__builtin_nontemporal_store` to avoid cache pollution. These arrays are read once per thread and are not reused within the same iteration, making them poor candidates for caching. With that, we bypass the L1 and L2 caches, preventing these rarely reused values from displacing frequently accessed data, such as the wavefield variables `pc`, `qc`, and their derivatives.

4 Methodology

The experiments were performed on 1 node of the Frontier supercomputer. Each node has a 64-core AMD-optimized 3rd Gen EPYC 7763 CPU featuring two hardware threads per physical core and 512 GB of DDR4 memory. Each node has 4x AMD MI250X accelerators, each containing two graphics compute dies (GCDs), resulting in eight GCDs per node. Each GCD is paired with 64 GB of high-bandwidth memory (HBM2E). For the purpose of these experiments to only evaluate the impact of using local data share and non-temporal store feature, we fixed the application to run on only one node. The GPU operates with a thermal design power (TDP) of 560W, at a peak engine clock speed of 1,700MHz (the min clock speed is 500MHz). To perform the experiments, we considered the default configurations of the GPU and CPU operating frequency. We compiled the application with the AMD *ROCm hipcc* 5.7.1, using the *-O3* and *-offload-arch=gfx90a* flags. For reproducibility, the following modules were loaded for the experiments: *craype-accel-amd-gfx90a* and *rocm/5.7.1*.

In the following sections, we evaluate three configurations:

- *Baseline*, which is the standard implementation of the Fletcher model without the use of local data sharing and non-temporal store.
- *LDS-Only*, where the `partialDerivatives` and `propagate` kernels leverage the use of local data share.

- *LDS-NTS*, the same as the previous, but exploiting the non-temporal memory operations (e.g., `__builtin_nontemporal_store`).

For each configuration, we have executed the Fletcher model with the following input set: grid size of 768 × 768 × 768. Each combination of input set and configuration was executed 30 times, and the results presented in the next subsections are the average of these executions, with a standard deviation lower than 0.5%. To get the metrics from the GPU hardware throughout the execution, we used the *AMD Rocprof* tool.

5 Evaluation

5.1 Arithmetic Intensity and FLOPs/s Evaluation

To quantify the impact of the optimizations described in Sect. 3, we analyze the arithmetic intensity (measured in FLOPs/byte) and achieved performance (measured in FLOPs/s) for both the `partialDerivatives` and `propagation` kernels. Table 1 summarizes these metrics for the three configurations: *Baseline*, which uses global memory only; *LDS-Only*, which caches selected stencil components in local data share (LDS); and *LDS-NTS*, which combines LDS with non-temporal store operations for coefficient and velocity arrays.

The arithmetic intensity of the `partialDerivatives` kernel remains unchanged across all configurations at 1.71 FLOPs/byte. This invariance is expected, as both the total number of floating-point operations and the volume of memory accesses remain constant. The introduction of LDS optimizations modifies the location of memory accesses, shifting from global memory to on-chip shared memory, but does not alter the number of bytes transferred or operations executed per grid point. Despite the unchanged arithmetic intensity, the *LDS-Only* implementation achieves a substantial performance increase, reaching 1.95×10^{12} FLOPs/s compared to 1.56×10^{12} FLOPs/s in the *baseline*. This improvement arises from a more efficient utilization of the memory subsystem. By staging input wavefield values in local data share (e.g., shared memory), the kernel reduces redundant global memory accesses in the y-dimension stencil computations, minimizing latency and increasing memory coalescing efficiency. As discussed in Sect. 3, the LDS buffers are loaded cooperatively by the threads in a wavefront, aligning with the thread-block layout and improving access granularity.

In the `propagation` kernel, we observe a more significant change in the ratio of computation to memory access, depending on how memory is handled. In the *LDS-Only* version, this ratio drops slightly from 1.09 to 0.93 FLOPs/byte. This small decrease happens because loading data into shared memory (LDS) adds some overhead, such as extra memory transfers that do not directly contribute to calculations. Even so, performance improves: the kernel is able to do more floating point operations per second, increasing from 9.46×10^{11} to 1.10×10^{12} FLOPs/s, thanks to more efficient access to data, especially along the z-axis. When we also apply non-temporal memory stores in the *LDS-NTS* version, we avoid using the cache for some data that is used only once. This helps keep frequently accessed data in the cache, improving overall memory efficiency. With this adjustment, the computation-to-memory ratio returns to 1.09 FLOPs/byte, and performance increases further to 1.35×10^{12} FLOPs/s. This shows that carefully controlling how data is stored and accessed can lead to better use of memory and higher execution speed.

Table 1. Comparison of arithmetic intensity (FLOPs/byte) and performance (FLOPs/s) for each evaluated configuration on each HIP kernel

Versão	FLOPs/byte		FLOPs/s	
	`PartialDerivatives`	`Propagate`	`PartialDerivatives`	`Propagate`
Baseline	1.71	1.09	1.56×10^{12}	9.46×10^{11}
LDS-Only	1.71	0.93	1.95×10^{12}	1.10×10^{12}
LDS-NTS	1.71	1.09	1.95×10^{12}	1.35×10^{12}

5.2 Analysis of Hardware-Level Metrics on AMD MI250X

To better understand the impact of the memory optimizations introduced in the `partialDerivatives` and `propagation` kernels, as discussed in Sect. 3, we analyzed hardware-level metrics collected using `rocprof` on the AMD MI250X GPU. The metrics examined include `MemUnitStalled`, `L2CacheHit`, `VALUBusy`, and `SALUBusy`, each of which provides information about different stages of the memory hierarchy and compute pipeline utilization. Figure 1 illustrates these results, which are discussed next.

`MemUnitStalled` measures the percentage of GPU cycles during which the memory subsystem is stalled due to requests. High values typically indicate that memory bandwidth or latency is limiting performance. As observed in Fig. 1a, in the baseline configuration of the `partialDerivatives` kernel, this metric reaches $\approx$ 45.30%, showing substantial memory bottlenecks caused by redundant global memory accesses in the stencil computations. With the introduction of LDS caching in the *LDS-Only* and *LDS+NTS* configurations, this value drops significantly to $\approx$ 25.6%, demonstrating the effectiveness of LDS in alleviating memory pressure. It is worth mentioning that the use of non-temporal store is only applied to the `propagation` kernel. Similarly, in the `propagation` kernel, `MemUnitStalled` decreases from $\approx$ 11.51% in the baseline to $\approx$ 7.90% in the *LDS+NTS* version, confirming that staging data in LDS reduces memory subsystem wait times even in kernels with inherently lower memory stress.

`L2CacheHit` reports the percentage of memory requests that are served by the L2 cache. Figure 1bshows the results for each configuration. In `partialDerivatives`, the baseline L2 hit rate is high ($\approx$ 80.50%), as repeated global accesses to the same data result in strong cache reuse. However, when using

LDS, this metric drops to approximately $\approx$ 62.8%. This decrease is expected as replacing many global memory accesses with shared memory transactions, the application issues fewer L2-relevant requests, thus naturally reducing the hit rate. In the `propagation` kernel, the L2 hit rate increases from $\approx$ 60.30% to $\approx$ 67.60% in the *LDS-Only* configuration due to improved memory access patterns when staging data. On the other hand, in the *LDS+NTS* configuration, the hit rate drops slightly to $\approx$ 62.60%, reflecting the intentional bypass of cache via non-temporal stores for low-reuse coefficient arrays.

`VALUBusy` represents the percentage of time that the Vector Arithmetic Logic Units (VALU) are actively executing instructions. We illustrate these results in Fig. 1c. In `partialDerivatives`, this metric increases slightly from $\approx$ 53.80% in the baseline to $\approx$ 55.5% in both optimized versions. This indicates that reducing memory stalls allows the compute units to stay active more consistently. The `propagation` kernel shows a more significant increase, from $\approx$ 23.54% in the baseline to $\approx$ 30.95% in the *LDS+NTS* configuration, highlighting the benefits of reduced memory latency and better scheduling of computation when memory bottlenecks are alleviated.

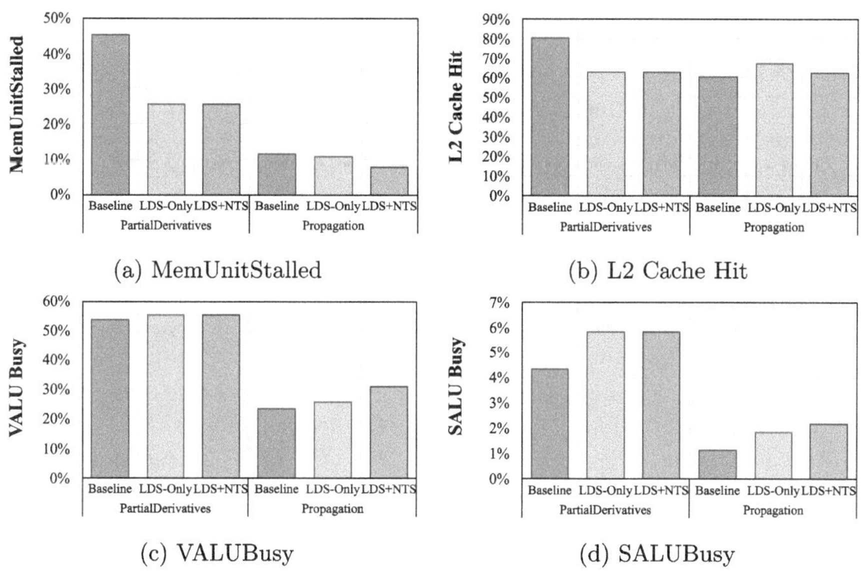

(a) MemUnitStalled (b) L2 Cache Hit

(c) VALUBusy (d) SALUBusy

Fig. 1. Hardware-level metrics for the execution of each configuration on the AMD MI250X.

Finally, `SALUBusy` quantifies the activity of the Scalar Arithmetic Logic Units (SALU), which are responsible for handling control logic and scalar computations. As observed in Fig. 1d, this metric increases with the use of LDS in both kernels. In `partialDerivatives`, it grows from $\approx$ 4.35% to $\approx$ 5.82%, while in `propagation`, it increases from $\approx$ 1.15% to $\approx$ 2.17%. These increases reflect the additional scalar instructions required for shared memory indexing and synchronization, particularly due to the use of LDS buffers and conditional execution. Despite the increase, SALU activity remains low overall and does not adversely impact performance.

5.3 Performance, Energy, and EDP Evaluation

In this section, we discuss the performance, energy, and the trade-off between both through the energy-delay product (EDP) metric. For that, we start by discussing the execution time for the `partialDerivatives` and `propagate` kernels across the three configurations, shown in Fig. 2a. For the `partialDerivatives` kernel, the baseline execution time is 1.398 seconds. The use of LDS in the *LDS-Only* configuration reduces this time to 1.115 seconds, representing a performance improvement of $\approx$ 20.2%. The addition of non-temporal store operations in the *LDS+NTS* configuration provides a marginal further gain, reducing the execution time to 1.114 seconds. This indicates that most of the performance benefit in this kernel stems from reduced global memory pressure due to shared memory usage, while non-temporal stores offer negligible impact, likely because the kernel is already dominated by wavefield accesses rather than coefficient reads.

In the `propagate` kernel, performance improvements are more significant. The baseline configuration executes in 9.71 seconds. When LDS is employed (*LDS-Only*), the time is reduced to 8.27 seconds, yielding a $\approx$ 14.8% improvement. The *LDS+NTS* configuration further reduces the execution time to 6.73 seconds, totaling a $\approx$ 30.7% reduction compared to the *baseline*. These results confirm that `propagate` benefits from both memory coalescing via LDS and cache efficiency improvements from bypassing the L1/L2 caches for non-reused coefficient data. To assess the impact of the memory optimizations on the overall application throughput, we report performance in terms of GSamples/s, which measures the number of samples computed per second. As shown in Fig. 2b, the baseline implementation achieves a throughput of 4.42 GSamples/s. When shared memory is introduced (*LDS-Only*), performance improves to 4.83 GSamples/s, representing a gain of $\approx$ 9.3%. The *LDS+NTS* configuration further increases throughput to 5.83 GSamples/s, a 31.9% improvement over the baseline.

In high-performance computing, achieving fast execution is important, but reducing energy consumption is also a key concern. In this scenario, we extracted the energy consumption of each configuration through the CrayPAT tool, which reports the total energy consumption of the node during the entire execution of the application. The results, in joules, are shown in Fig. 3a. When only local data sharing is enabled, energy usage drops about 12% compared to the *baseline*. This reduction comes from fewer memory stalls and better use of fast on-chip memory, and also the reduction on the execution time, which reduces the amount of static power consumed. The *LDS+NTS* configuration achieves the lowest energy consumption, spending 27% less energy compared to the *baseline*.

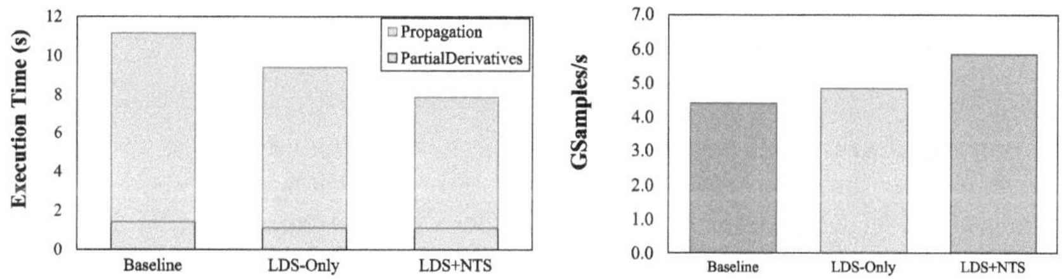

(a) Execution Time (s) (b) GSamples/s

Fig. 2. Performance results for each evaluated configuration. Execution time is split according to the HIP kernel, and the lower, the better. On the other hand, the GSamples/s are for the entire execution, and the higher, the better.

Finally, Fig. 3billustrates the EDP results, where a lower EDP indicates a better trade-off between performance and energy. The EDP of the *baseline* is improved by 25% when considering the *LDS-Only* configuration. With the combined use of local data sharing and non-temporal memory operations in the *LDS+NTS* version, the EDP drops even further to approximately half of the baseline.

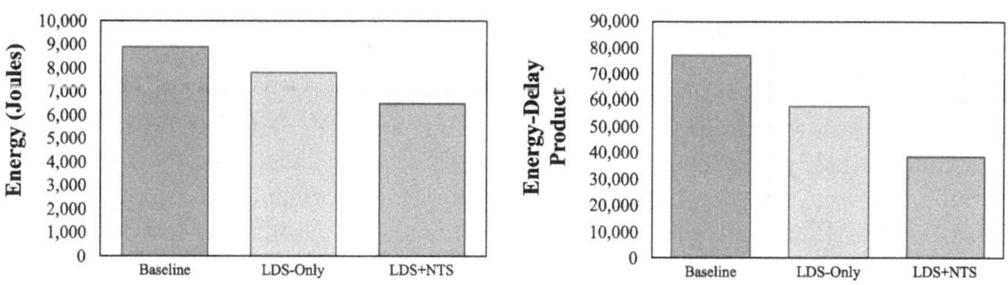

(a) Energy Consumption (b) Energy-Delay Product

Fig. 3. Energy and EDP results for each of the configurations. For both plots, the lower, the better.

6 Conclusion and Future Works

This work demonstrated the use of memory access optimizations in improving the performance and energy efficiency of stencil-based scientific applications on AMD GPUs. By leveraging the Local Data Share memory to reduce global memory traffic in stencil kernels and introducing non-temporal stores to minimize cache pollution, we achieved significant performance and energy gains of 31.9% and 27%, respectively, compared to a baseline version that relies on global memory accesses. In future work, we plan to extend our analysis to a broader set of GPU kernels, including those exhibiting diverse arithmetic intensities and memory access patterns.

Acknowledgments. This research used resources of the Oak Ridge Leadership Computing Facility at the Oak Ridge National Laboratory, which is supported by the Office of Science of the U.S. Department of Energy under Contract No. DE-AC05-00OR22725. This study was financed in part by the CAPES - Finance Code 001, FAPERGS - PqG 24/2551-0001388-1, and CNPq.

References

1. Anderson, J.E., Tan, L., Wang, D.: Time-reversal checkpointing methods for RTM and FWI. Geophysics **77**(4), S93–S103 (2012). https://doi.org/10.1190/geo2011-0114.1
2. Atchley, S., et al.: Frontier: exploring exascale the system architecture of the first exascale supercomputer. In: SC23: International Conference for High Performance Computing, Networking, Storage and Analysis, pp. 1–16 (2023). https://doi.org/10.1145/3581784.3607089
3. Bienz, A., Olson, L.N., Gropp, W.D., Lockhart, S.: Modeling data movement performance on heterogeneous architectures. Institute of Electrical and Electronics Engineers Inc. (2021). https://doi.org/10.1109/HPEC49654.2021.9622742
4. Fletcher, R.P., Du, X., Fowler, P.J.: Reverse time migration in tilted transversely isotropic (TTI) media. Geophysics **74**(6), WCA179–WCA187 (2009)
5. Garvey, J.D., Abdelrahman, T.S.: A strategy for automatic performance tuning of stencil computations on GPUs. Sci. Program. **2018**(1), 6093054 (2018). https://doi.org/10.1155/2018/6093054
6. Jin, Z., Vetter, J.S.: Evaluating unified memory performance in hip, pp. 562–568. Institute of Electrical and Electronics Engineers Inc. (2022). https://doi.org/10.1109/IPDPSW55747.2022.00096
7. Jung, J., Kim, J., Lee, J.: Deepum: tensor migration and prefetching in unified memory. In: Proceedings of the 28th ACM International Conference on Architectural Support for Programming Languages and Operating Systems, Volume 2, pp. 207–221. ASPLOS 2023, Association for Computing Machinery, New York, NY, USA (2023)
8. Jung, J., Park, D., Do, Y., Park, J., Lee, J.: Overlapping host-to-device copy and computation using hidden unified memory. In: Proceedings of the 25th ACM SIGPLAN Symposium on Principles and Practice of Parallel Programming, pp. 321–335. PPoPP '20, Association for Computing Machinery, New York, NY, USA (2020)
9. Knap, M., Czarnul, P.: Performance evaluation of unified memory with prefetching and oversubscription for selected parallel cuda applications on nvidia pascal and volta gpus. J. Supercomput. **75**(11), 7625–7645 (2019)
10. Liu, G.F., Meng, X.H., Yu, Z.J., Liu, D.J.: An efficient scheme for multi-GPU tti reverse time migration. Appl. Geophys. **16**(1), 56–63 (2019)
11. Liu, H., et al.: The issues of prestack reverse time migration and solutions with graphic processing unit implementation. Geophys. Prospect. **60**(5), 906–918 (2012)

12. Lorenzon, A.F., Beck, A.C.S., Navaux, P.O.A., Messer, B.: Energy-efficient GPU allocation and frequency management in exascale computing systems. In: ISC High Performance 2025 Research Paper Proceedings (40th International Conference), pp. 1–11 (2025)
13. Lorenzon, A.F., Navaux, P.O.A., Sardinha, A., Messer, B.: Towards performance portability of an oil and gas application on heterogeneous architectures. In: 2024 IEEE 36th International Symposium on Computer Architecture and High Performance Computing (SBAC-PAD), pp. 127–137 (2024). https://doi.org/10.1109/SBAC-PAD63648.2024.00019
14. Montella, R., et al.: Enabling the cuda unified memory model in edge, cloud and hpc offloaded GPU kernels, pp. 834–841. Institute of Electrical and Electronics Engineers Inc. (2022). https://doi.org/10.1109/CCGrid54584.2022.00099
15. Navaux, P.O.A., Lorenzon, A.F., da Silva Serpa, M.: Challenges in high-performance computing. J. Brazilian Comput. Society **29**(1), 51–62 (2023)
16. Okamoto, T., Takenaka, H., Nakamura, T., Aoki, T.: Accelerating large-scale simulation of seismic wave propagation by multi-GPUs and three-dimensional domain decomposition. Earth, Planets and Space **62**(12), 939–942 (2010). https://doi.org/10.5047/eps.2010.11.009
17. Pearson, C., et al.: Node aware stencil communication for heterogeneous supercomputers. In: 2020 IEEE International Parallel and Distributed Processing Symposium Workshops (IPDPSW), pp. 796–805. IEEE (2020)
18. Riahi, A., Savadi, A., Naghibzadeh, M.: Comparison of analytical and ml-based models for predicting CPU–GPU data transfer time. Computing **102**, 2099–2116 (9 2020). https://doi.org/10.1007/s00607-019-00780-x
19. Sabet, A.H.N., Zhao, Z., Gupta, R.: Subway: Minimizing data transfer during out-of-GPU-memory graph processing. Association for Computing Machinery, Inc (4 2020). https://doi.org/10.1145/3342195.3387537
20. Serpa, M., Mishra, P.: Performance evaluation and enhancement of the fletcher method on multicore architectures (2022)
21. Tabbakh, A., Annavaram, M., Qian, X.: Power efficient sharing-aware GPU data management. In: 2017 IEEE International Parallel and Distributed Processing Symposium (IPDPS), pp. 698–707 (2017). https://doi.org/10.1109/IPDPS.2017.106
22. Wang, P., Wang, J., Li, C., Wang, J., Zhu, H., Guo, M.: Grus: toward unified-memory-efficient high-performance graph processing on GPU. ACM Trans. Archit. Code Optim. **18** (3 2021). https://doi.org/10.1145/3444844
23. Zhang, Y., Hu, Y., Li, B., Peng, L.: Performance and power analysis of ATI GPU: a statistical approach. In: 2011 IEEE Sixth International Conference on Networking, Architecture, and Storage, pp. 149–158 (2011). https://doi.org/10.1109/NAS.2011.51

Profiling a Task-Based Molecular Dynamics Application with a Data Science Approach

Christian Asch[1(✉)], Lucas Mello Schnorr[2], and Esteban Meneses[1,3]

[1] National High Technology Center, San José, Costa Rica
{casch,emeneses}@cenat.ac.cr
[2] Institute of Informatics, Federal University of Rio Grande do Sul, Porto Alegre, Brazil
schnorr@inf.ufrgs.br
[3] Costa Rica Institute of Technology, Cartago, Costa Rica

Abstract. Charm++ is a parallel programming framework based on task-driven execution and global object references. It has been used successfully in various high-performance computing (HPC) applications, including the molecular dynamics simulator NAMD. While Charm++ includes built-in support for performance tracing and visualization through its Projections tool, the existing system offers limited extensibility and has no support for modern data science workflows. This work presents a new visualization and analysis pipeline for Charm++ trace data that emphasizes modularity, openness, and composability. Our toolchain leverages standard scripting languages and data formats - producing output in CSV and Parquet formats - to facilitate integration with data analysis ecosystems. We demonstrate the effectiveness of this approach using LeanMD, a proxy application derived from NAMD, and highlight specific types of custom visualizations that are difficult to achieve with Projections. Our system enables custom visualizations and streamlined analysis of chare-level execution behavior, offering researchers and tool developers improved capabilities for understanding program performance and identifying load imbalance. We discuss the architecture of our tool, its application to real-world traces, and potential extensions for other task-based frameworks.

Keywords: Charm++ · Trace Visualization · Performance Analysis

1 Introduction

Charm++ [5] is a task-based parallel programming framework designed to support high-performance distributed computing. It enables a global address space (GAS) model, which abstracts away the complexity of message-passing and allows developers to write parallel code more naturally and efficiently. Charm++ is the foundation for several large-scale scientific applications, most notably

K. Brown et al. (Eds.): CARLA 2025, CCIS 2750, pp. 140–155, 2026.
https://doi.org/10.1007/978-3-032-24923-4_10

NAMD [12], a widely used molecular dynamics simulator. Researchers have employed NAMD across a broad range of scientific domains, particularly in structural biology and drug discovery, where the need to model increasingly complex molecular systems has driven demand for more sophisticated simulations. The growing reliance on molecular simulations partly results from the expanding availability of high-performance computing resources [4]. This reliance has allowed scientists to run larger simulations and tackle various biological problems computationally. Consequently, NAMD has been ported and optimized for several leadership-class supercomputing platforms [1,7], allowing it to scale to hundreds of thousands of cores and support large biomolecular systems. Given the complexity and scale of Charm++ applications, a practical and effective performance analysis is critical. To that end, Charm++ includes support for detailed tracing and profiling, offering built-in mechanisms for generating and visualizing execution traces. However, the default tools provided are limited in flexibility, extensibility, and integration with modern data analysis ecosystems. This work presents an alternative approach to trace visualization that leverages standard, open-source, and composable tools for preprocessing and visualization. We aim to improve usability, extensibility, and analytical depth without sacrificing performance or scalability. We demonstrate the usefulness of our approach through an in-depth analysis of LeanMD, a proxy application derived from NAMD that implements a simplified molecular dynamics workload. By applying our toolchain to LeanMD, we highlight the advantages of our method and explore insights that would be much harder to obtain using the default Charm++ tools.

The paper has the following structure. Section 2 provides background on task-based parallelism, the Charm++ framework, the Projections trace visualizer, and the proxy app LeanMD. Section 3 presents related work. Section 4 details the design and implementation of our contribution to provide a new perspective for performance analysis of Charm++ applications. Section 5 presents the hardware and software environments of our experiments. Section 6 demonstrates the effectiveness of our method, while in Sect. 7, we delineate the main conclusions and future work.

2 Background

2.1 Task-Based Parallelism

Task-based parallel programming frameworks define a task as a sequential set of instructions that can execute concurrently with others, depending on control and data dependencies [16]. Graphs represent a model of tasks and their relationships, where nodes represent tasks, and directed edges represent relationships through tasks, usually data dependencies. Edges may also represent control flow directives. These graphs can be the Task Control Flow Graph (TCFG), where the edges represent a parent-child relationship between tasks, or a Task Dependency Graph (TDG), where the edges represent a predecessor-successor relationship, and both types of graph are directed acyclic graphs (DAG) [11]. Multiple libraries implement this paradigm in high-performance computing (HPC), such as StarPU, OmpSs, and, more relevant for our paper, Charm++.

2.2 Parallel Objects and Charm++

Within task-based parallel computing, the parallel objects model provides several sought-after features in HPC [2]. In this model, a parallel program consists of a collection of parallel objects, each holding a piece of the data and executing a piece of the computation. Objects interact, each publishing an interface of remote methods that any other object in the system might call. Objects are reactive; they remain idle unless another object calls a method upon them. The execution of a method may call other methods in different objects, effectively creating a message-driven execution. Hence, message exchanges occur in a global object space to implement a particular algorithm.

Parallel objects are *migratable*. Any object can serialize/deserialize its state and be moved from one processing element to another during execution. The collection of processing elements (a computing core in modern processors) forms the system. The processing elements (PEs) have an initial distribution of the parallel objects, but such an assignment can change during execution to address load imbalance or other runtime conditions. To achieve that level of sophistication, an introspective runtime system (RTS) is necessary to accomplish all operations. That runtime system will handle the routing and scheduling of messages. It will monitor computing and communication load to adjust the assignment of objects to processing elements dynamically. It is therefore necessary to have object *overdecomposition*, i.e., the number of parallel objects must surpass the number of processing elements. The optimal ratio of objects per processing element (virtualization ratio) is highly dependent on the application and dataset. With overdecomposition, the runtime system can offer latency hiding, load balancing, and general adaptivity to runtime conditions. Among the several load balancers algorithms, we employ `GreedyLB` and `GreedyRefineLB` strategies. The `GreedyLB` strategy relies on finding the heaviest chare and assigning it to the least loaded processing element [19], while `GreedyRefineLB` works similarly while also minimizing the number of migrations [3].

The Charm++ library [5] is an implementation of the parallel objects model. In active development since the 1990s, Charm++ is an ecosystem with a runtime system, applications, extensions to other programming languages, and debugging and performance analysis tools. The Charm++ nomenclature refers to objects as *chares*. Chare arrays are indexed containers of chares, having up to six dimensions. Charm++ builds on C++ and organizes programs into header, source, and special interface files. These interface files use a C-like grammar to define remote methods (entry methods) for all chares. In addition, the interface file also allows programmers to define global read-only variables. Proxies provide access to objects in the global object space. Consequently, a remote method invocation first contacts the proxy on the object on the local processing element. The runtime system will channel this invocation to the correct location of the object.

2.3 Projections

Projections [6] is a performance analysis framework integrated with Charm++. It has two sections: the instrumentation component and the analysis and visualization tool. The Charm++ framework integrates the instrumentation component with the RTS. It includes two important modes of tracing, `projections`, which allows for logs with a significant amount of detail but also with a greater size and a larger memory overhead, and `summary`, which records fewer data for each entry method, as well as average times and the number of executions, helping to reduce the storage needed for the logs.

The visualization component is written in Java and provides users with a set of ready-made visualizations that they can use to analyze the performance of their program, as well as some options for filtering out data, such as choosing which processing elements to see or the start and end time for a graph. These visualizations include timeline views, utilization graphs, communication patterns, and other standard performance metrics that provide insight into program behavior between processing elements. Although these built-in tools are helpful for many common performance issues, the framework offers limited flexibility for customization or extension. Figure 1a illustrates an example of a visualization generated using Projections. The "Overview" allows users to observe the activity of all processing elements over time. Each color represents a different type of chare, and the corresponding type appears with mouse hovering. Figure 1b presents a similar view, called the "Timeline", showing the same information in greater detail and in larger zoom.

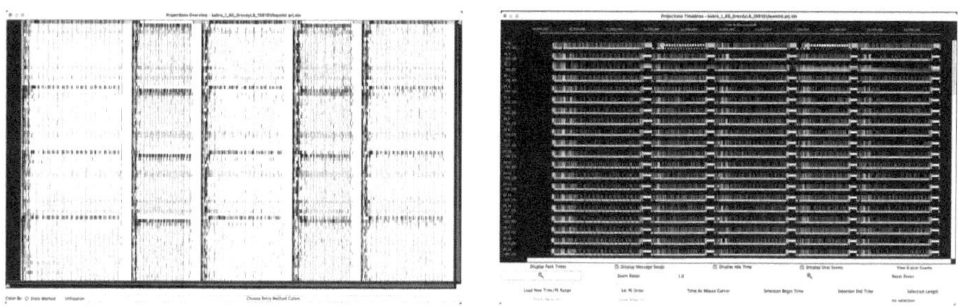

(a) Overview (b) Timeline

Fig. 1. Using Projections to visualize trace data in alternate ways.

2.4 Molecular Dynamics and LeanMD

Molecular dynamics is a simulation technique used in multiple areas, including biochemistry, biophysics, material science, and related fields [13]. These simulations allow scientists to study the structure and interactions of molecules for the development of new drugs, for example.

There are multiple tools for molecular dynamics; one is NAMD [12]. This simulation framework is written in Charm++ and solves the Newtonian equations of motion in 3D space. NAMD must calculate the force field that a potential energy generates to do this. They break down the potential energy into five components, including van der Waals forces, which they approximate using a Lennard-Jones 6-12 potential and the Coulomb potential for electrostatic interactions.

In this paper, we analyze a proxy app for NAMD called LeanMD [9], which is a molecular dynamics benchmark implemented in Charm++ that simulates molecular interactions using the Lennard-Jones potential and the Coulomb potential. These potentials theoretically apply to all pairs of particles in the system. However, computing interactions between all pairs of particles would scale quadratically with the number of particles, which is computationally prohibitive for large systems.

To mitigate this, LeanMD avoids evaluating all pairwise interactions. Instead, it exploits the short-range nature of the Lennard-Jones potential and the effectively localized contributions of the Coulomb potential. The simulation divides the domain into a grid of cubic cells, each represented by a Charm++ chare. Each cell maintains information about the molecules within its volume and interacts only with a fixed neighborhood of adjacent cells. This spatial partitioning restricts force computations to particle pairs within nearby cells, significantly reducing the number of interactions evaluated while maintaining physical accuracy.

Figure 2 illustrates this in one dimension. Each cell creates or shares a computation chare with a neighboring cell to evaluate inter-cell forces, ensuring that each chare computes each pairwise interaction exactly once. Molecules can migrate between cells as dictated by their trajectories. Computation chares distribute force calculations, and Charm++'s Structured Dagger (SDAG) constructs coordinate the overall simulation flow, facilitating asynchronous and data-driven execution.

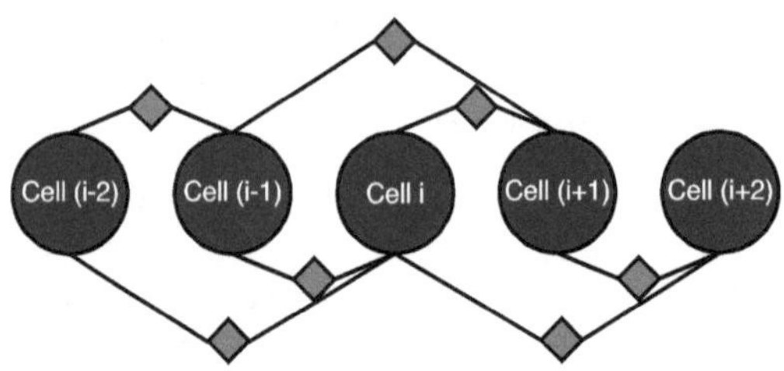

Fig. 2. How Cells create Compute chares.

3 Related Work

StarVZ [8] is a powerful R-based visualization tool, specifically designed for the analysis of traces generated by the StarPU runtime system. It provides a flexible and extensible framework for understanding the performance of task-based parallel applications that execute on heterogeneous architectures. Using the data science capabilities of R and various auxiliary tools, StarVZ enables researchers and developers to create insightful visualizations that reveal crucial performance characteristics, identify bottlenecks, and evaluate the impact of scheduling decisions and memory management strategies within StarPU applications. Although StarVZ itself does not collect trace data, it relies on StarPU's tracing capabilities to generate the necessary information for its analysis and visualization workflows. Although StarVZ offers a valuable data science-driven approach to performance analysis, particularly for StarPU-based applications, our work distinguishes itself by its specific focus on the Charm++ parallel programming model. Unlike StarVZ, which is a general tool for task-based systems that implement the sequential task flow, our approach is deeply integrated with Charm++ semantics, including its unique concepts of chares, messages, and remote method invocations. While sharing the data science-drive strategy, our focus on Charm++ allows us to provide a performance analysis workflow that understands and visualizes the behavior of Charm++ applications at a more granular and semantically rich level, capturing the intricacies of its object-based and message-driven execution model.

Compared to Projections, CharmVZ uses a preprocessing step to store trace data in the Parquet format, enabling rapid repeated analysis without having to reload the raw logs. On the other hand, Projections' workflow requires the reload of trace segments for each visualization. Additionally, creating bespoke visualizations only requires writing a script to consume the parquet dataset, while in Projections this would require the modification and recompilation of the entire Java tool. In [6], the authors demonstrate various analysis techniques using the Projections tool to visualize and diagnose multiple aspects of NAMD's performance and a program called CPAIMD. They also test new parallelization strategies in LeanMD and measure their effects. Our paper differs when using the Projections tool to visualize the behavior; instead, we used the CharmVZ visualization pipeline, proposed in this article, which enabled us to create bespoke visualizations tailored to our use case.

4 Design and Implementation

Charm++ can generate detailed trace files with the `projections` backend for a post-mortem analysis. The compilation of Charm++ applications must also consider specific flags to instrument the binary and generate the trace files during the execution. An execution with those options triggers the creation of three file types: `STS`, `log`, and `.projrc` files. There can be multiple `log` files, one for each processing element in the execution. The `STS` file contains metadata about the execution, including the number of processing elements and the indexed names of the charges, among other data. The `log` files contain the actual events, where each line represents an event type and contains information about that specific type, such as the processing elements involved, the timestamp, and the chare involved. The chare is referred to by its index, corresponding to the index in the `STS` file. Due to their size, Charm++ compresses `log` files with gzip. Finally, the

.projrc file contains configurations for the Projections graphical user interface (GUI), which we do not use in our project. How Projections works with the data is by first asking the user which visualization they want, then the user selects a subset of the data they want to analyze, for example, which processing elements and which interval of time, then Projections loads the data, and finally generates the desired visualization. This method has the advantage of avoiding having all the data in main memory, which could be unfeasible due to the size of the log files. However, it has the disadvantage of reloading the data each time the user wants another visualization, as well as the fact that the user is limited to the visualizations the software offers. We decided to take a different approach, summarized in Fig. 3, which relies on a series of smaller programs to create a reproducible workflow. The output of each of these programs becomes the input of the next in the pipeline. The purpose of designing the system in this way is to allow flexibility to change components later on to adapt the tool for other types of analysis. We also created a CharmVZ library to implement some of these programs, allowing code reuse when applicable.

In Fig. 3, in the print_csv.py step, we read the STS and log files, parsing each line of log files and writing it to a file descriptor, which can be an actual file or standard output. The paje_creator.sh step creates the necessary headers for the paje file, used as input for the pjdump step. This program is part of the PajeNG library [14], which is capable of filtering and structuring the data into a final csv file that contains the raw information for our analysis: the chare name, the start and end times of each chare execution, the processing element which executed it, and the duration. After that, we execute a final step to compress the CSV into a parquet file [18], a columnar and fast file format ready for data science tools.

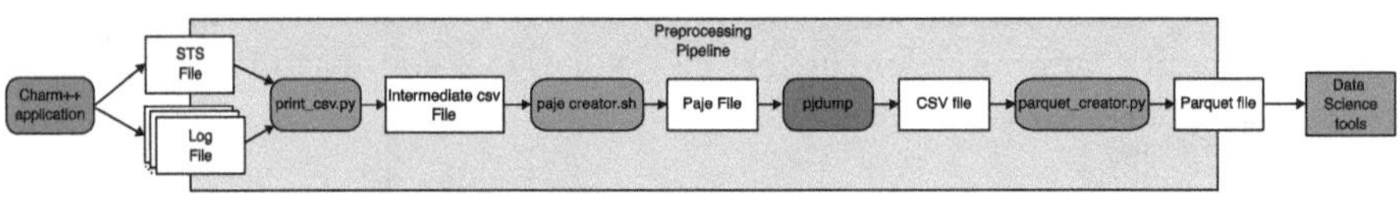

Fig. 3. CharmVZ workflow represented as a pipeline of data transformation.

To analyze the traces, we employ the Polars library to manipulate the data frames. Polars is often faster than the more traditional Pandas library because Polars is multithreaded and uses a columnar data format, already optimized for SIMD operations [17]. Additionally, it supports lazy evaluation, although we did not use this capability for the current paper. We used matplotlib [15] to create multiple types of plots as follows. **Chare duration plot**. A histogram showing the cumulative duration of a chare in all processing elements. We can see an example of this type of plot in the Results section (see Fig. 5a). **Chare frequency plot**. A histogram displays the number of times each chare appears (executed) across all processing elements. **Chare activity heatmap**. This type of plot shows which chares were the most active and in which processing element.

For example, Fig. 4a shows that the Compute chare was the most active in this execution, being the less active in each node's first few processing elements. Additionally, processing element zero did most of the processing related to the load balancing. **Timeline overview plot**. This plot, shown in Fig. 4b, is similar to the one provided by Projections (see Fig. 1a). The vertical axis shows the state of each processing element, while the horizontal axis shows the evolution over time, depicting chare execution. In the example, we can see that the Compute chare dominates the execution. However, we can also devise some structure, such as when the load balancer execution happens in the processing element zero. **Percent imbalance plot**. This plot, shown in Fig. 4c plots the percent imbalance at various points during the execution. The percent imbalance (λ) implementation uses Eq. 1 [10]. With this plot, it is possible to visualize the effects of the different events, especially the load balancer. We can combine this plot with the Timeline overview plot to see the effects more clearly, as in the results section (see Fig. 5c).

$$\lambda = \left(\frac{L_{max}}{\bar{L}} - 1\right) \times 100\% \tag{1}$$

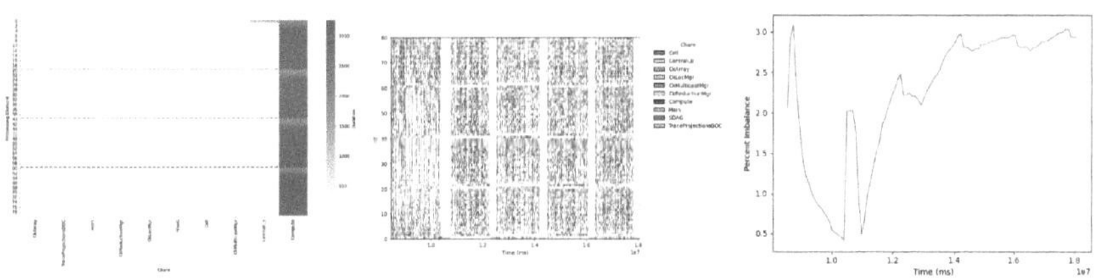

(a) Activity heatmap. (b) Timeline plot. (c) Percent imbalance.

Fig. 4. Examples of three visualizations created by the CharmVZ workflow.

5 Experimental Setup

5.1 Hardware and Software Environments

We conducted our experiments on the Kabré supercomputer at the National Supercomputer Center at the National High Technology Center of Costa Rica (CNCA-CeNAT). We used the Kurá general purpose partition, which has 12 nodes equipped with an Intel Xeon Silver 4316 CPU at 2.30 GHz, 20 cores, two threads per core, and 256 GB of memory. Table 1a lists the software environment used for the LeanMD executions. We list the versions of the runtime requirements for the CharmVZ pipeline in Table 1b. We implemented this pipeline in the PCAD infrastructure of the Federal University of Rio Grande do Sul (INF/UFRGS), using the `bali2` machine, with a dual Intel Xeon CPU E5-2650 at 2.00 GHz, 16 cores, two threads per core and 32 GB of main memory.

Table 1. Software environment of our experiments.

Software	Version
Linux distribution	Alma Linux 8
Kernel version	4.18.0553.22.1.el8_10.x86_64
Charm++	v6.10.2
LeanMD	dfb51
MPI (mpich)	3.3.2
gcc	9.3.0

(a) Software for LeanMD

Software	Version
pandas	2.2.3
polars	1.29.0
pyarrow	19.0.1
seaborn	0.13.2
matplotlib	3.10.3
PajeNG	a702c

(b) Software for CharmVZ.

5.2 Experimental Design

To showcase our tool, we executed and profiled LeanMD in different situations. The arguments used throughout our runs for the LeanMD proxy application are as follows:

- `dimX`, `dimY`, `dimZ`: The number of cells in the X, Y, and Z dimensions.
- `steps`: The total number of simulation steps.
- `firstLBstep`: The first step in which the load balancer is executed.
- `LBPeriod`: The number of steps between load balancer executions.

We can also configure the number of processing elements that are involved in the execution, as well as the choice of load balancer. For our setup, a processing element corresponds to a process in a node, and they are distributed in a blocked scheme across nodes.

The total number of chares created by LeanMD is determined by the total number of cells (Eq. 2) and the number of Compute chares per cell (Eq. 3) using Eq. 4. The 75 within Eq. 3 comes from the definition of the neighborhood size in the LeanMD source code.

$$Chares_{Cells} = dim_x \cdot dim_y \cdot dim_z \tag{2}$$

$$Chares_{Computes} = \left\lfloor \frac{75}{2} \right\rfloor + 1 \tag{3}$$

$$Chares_{total} = Chares_{Cells} \cdot Chares_{Computes} \tag{4}$$

Apart from these chares, there is an additional number of internal chares created by the Charm++ Runtime to control data migration, the load balancer execution, and similar background tasks.

We execute LeanMD with three input sizes (`Small`, `Medium`, and `Large`), as seen in Table 2. We compare the `GreedyLB` and the `GreedyRefineLB` load-balancing strategies for each level. We used a fixed number of processing elements for all these combinations, `steps`, `firstLBstep`, `LBPeriod` set to 80, 100, 20, and 20.

Table 2. Three experimental cases for the LeanMD executions.

Case	Dimensions	Total Chares
`Small`	$4 \times 4 \times 4$	2432
`Medium`	$6 \times 6 \times 6$	8208
`Large`	$10 \times 10 \times 10$	38000

6 Results

We investigate the influence of the Charm++ load balancer on execution time to effectively illustrate the value of a data science approach in the trace analysis of Charm++ applications. Our focus is on comparing GreedyLB and GreedyRefineLB, which shed light on general application behavior through a timeline plot that includes the percent imbalance metric. These plots highlight the relation between processing element activity and percent imbalance in the y-axis. Additionally, we utilize histograms to quantify the total time dedicated to computing the load balancer heuristics. These plots highlight the flexibility that CharmVZ affords over Projections to create different types of visualizations.

This section concentrates on the most active chares to maintain clarity and relevance. We analyze the three scenarios – `Small`, `Medium`, and `Large` – discussing the unique characteristics of each in a cumulative manner to provide a comprehensive understanding of the results.

`[Small]` Fig. 5a demonstrates that the Compute chare is the one that takes the most amount of time across all chares, which is positive, as this is the chare that does most of the job. Additionally, we can see that the Load Balancer does significantly more work in the GreedyRefineLB run. We can confirm this behavior by verifying that the CentralLB chare – which represents the time spent on each load balancing heuristic – takes significantly longer for GreedyRefineLB. Figures 5c and 5b show different phases during the execution, each triggered by the load balancer. In the GreedyLB run, most processing elements experience idle time during the transition, which is longer than in the GreedyRefineLB run. The plot also shows that the percent imbalance is lower at the end of the GreedyRefineLB execution. Wrapping up, the GreedyRefineLB execution

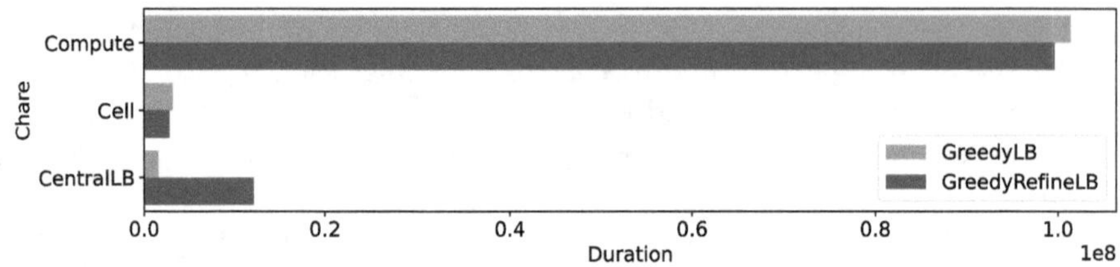

(a) Histogram of chare duration for both load balancing strategies.

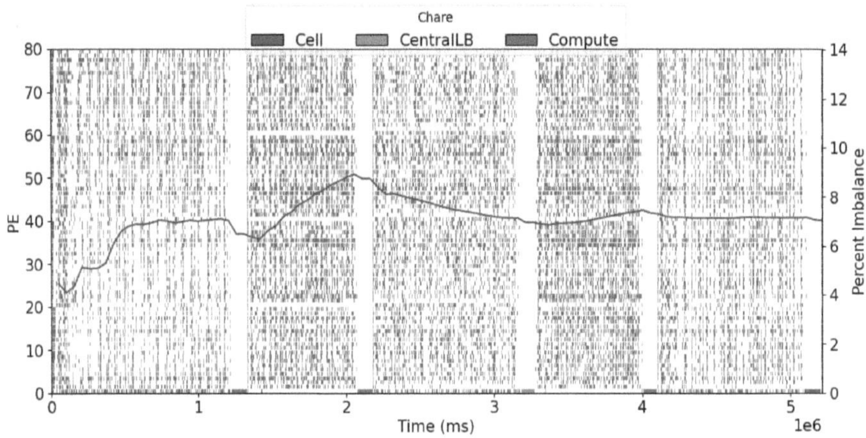

(b) Timeline view for the GreedyLB execution.

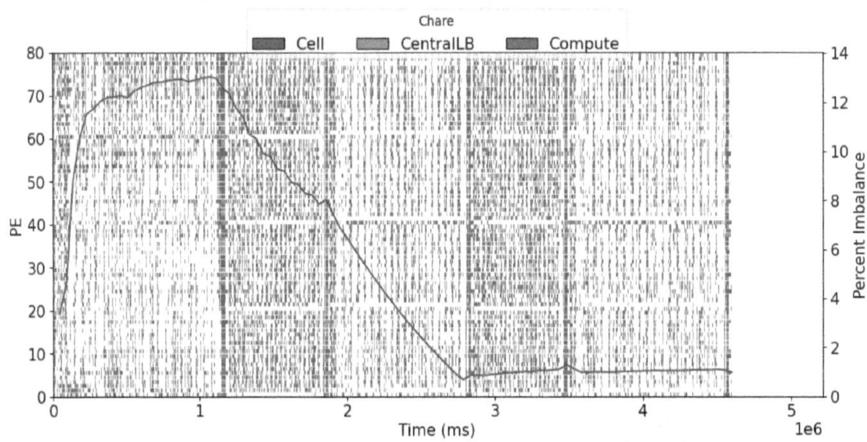

(c) Timeline view for the GreedyRefineLB execution.

Fig. 5. Comparison of load balancing strategies in the `Small` case.

finishes first with 4,599,663 ms. The GreedyLB execution finishes at 5,216,409 ms, so GreedyRefineLB is 11% faster for this execution despite having spent much more time in the heuristic.

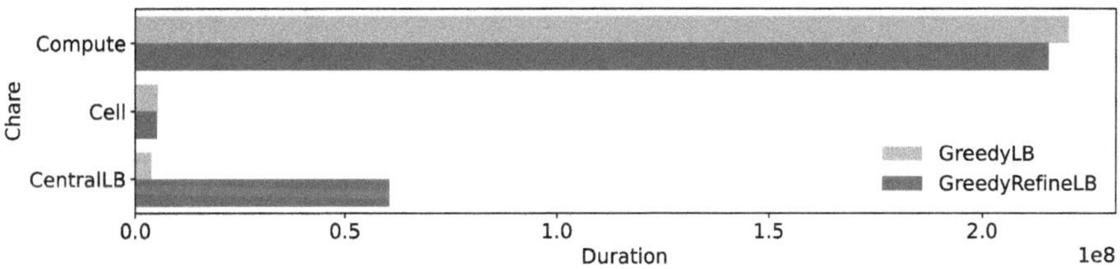

(a) Histogram of chares duration for both load balancing strategies.

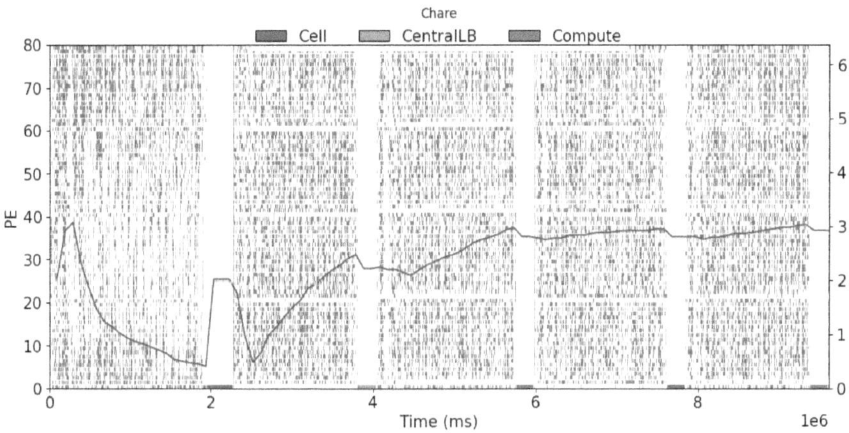

(b) Timeline view for the GreedyLB execution.

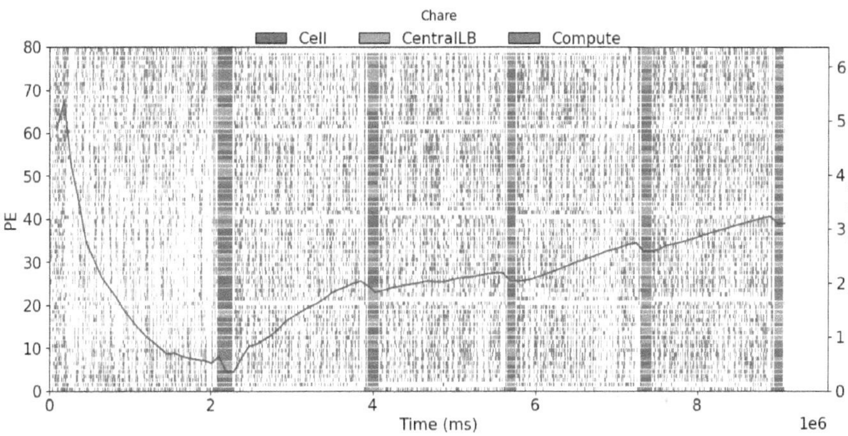

(c) Timeline view for the GreedyRefineLB execution.

Fig. 6. Comparison of load balancing strategies in the `Medium` case.

`[Medium]` Fig. 6a shows that the Compute chare is also the longest running chare in this execution in both load balancing strategies and that the GreedyRefineLB strategy once again has a higher level of activity in the load balancing chare. In

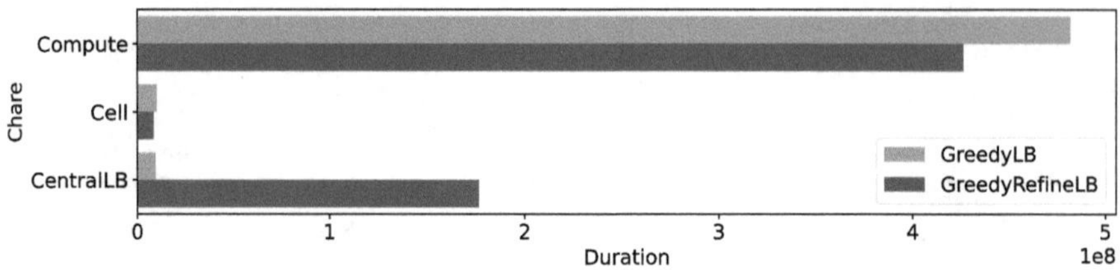

(a) Histogram of chares duration for both load balancing strategies.

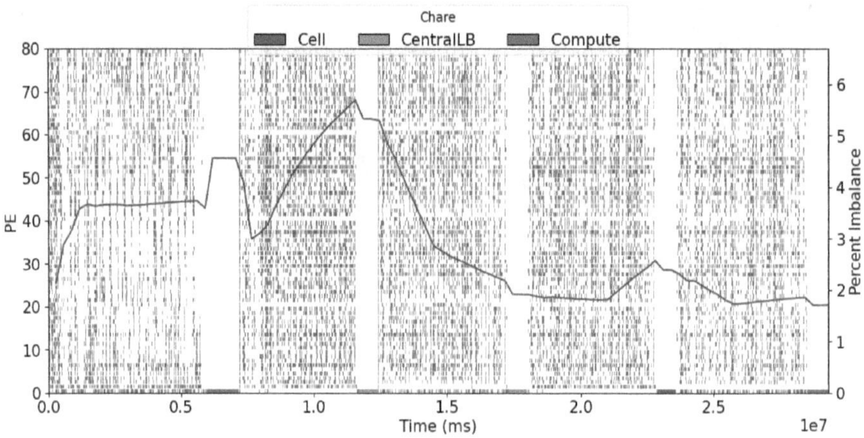

(b) Timeline view for the GreedyLB execution.

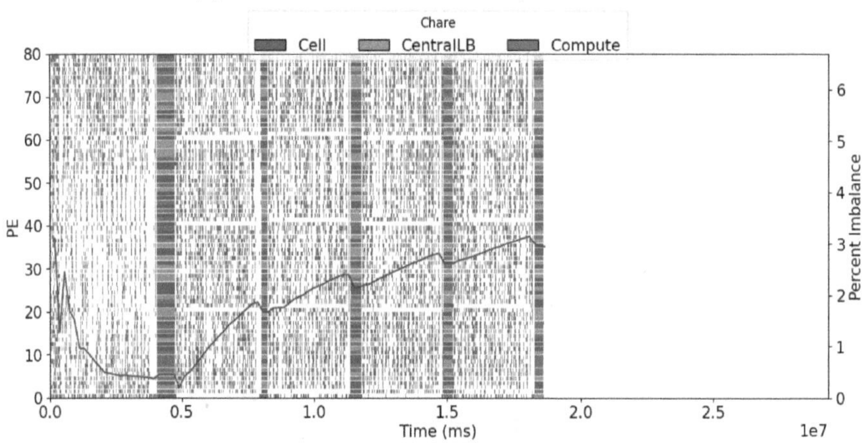

(c) Timeline view for the GreedyRefineLB execution.

Fig. 7. Comparison of load balancing strategies in the `Large` case.

Fig. 6c, we observe that the imbalance remains below 4% throughout the execution, comparable to Fig. 6b. However, GreedyLB execution had more idle time between transitions again. In the end, the makespan for GreedyLB execution was

9,624,284 ms, while for GreedyRefineLB was 9,081,315 ms (GreedyRefineLB is ≈5% faster).

[Large] Fig. 7a shows the same trend as in the other two cases, with the Compute chare taking most of the time for both strategies and the CentralLB chare taking significantly more time in the GreedyRefineLB execution. Something interesting to note in Fig. 7c and 7b is that the percent imbalance follows a similar trend than in Fig. 6c and 6b respectively, although with a different magnitude. The makespan for these executions was 29,314,810 ms in the case of the GreedyLB and 18,659,758 ms for the GreedyRefineLB execution. So, in a larger case with a more expressive workload, the increased effort in the GreedyRefineLB strategy pays off as the total execution time is 36% faster than the one obtained with GreedyLB.

7 Discussion and Final Remarks

This work described in this article introduced a new performance visualization and analysis tool based on data science tools for the Charm++ ecosystem. Our workflow enables researchers to study the performance of their Charm++ programs more effectively. It also provides a new tool for load balancer developers to see the impact of their tool on the system load imbalance more easily. In addition, the modular approach to the tool's design enables scientists to create visualizations tailored to their specific needs and lines of inquiry. This method highlights the usefulness of applying modern data science tools and techniques to the performance analysis of HPC software.

In alignment with open science principles, all data and software used in this study are openly available to the community. The complete dataset, along with instructions for reproduction of the figures of this manuscript in the form of computational notebooks, can be accessed at https://doi.org/10.5281/zenodo.15612154. CharmVZ source code is also hosted at https://github.com/caschb/charmvz. This ensures transparency, reproducibility, and facilitates further research based on our work.

As the work carried out in our efforts opens up numerous possibilities, we anticipate future work. First, it is necessary to optimize the CharmVZ pipeline further to handle larger traces, which would allow us to analyze more realistic cases. Several sound solutions for the scalability of data science workflows could represent possible solutions, such as using Apache's PySpark backend for our CharmVZ code. Another effort could be to work with field researchers to create specific visualizations for their use cases, using application data structures to inspire new visualizations. Finally, our modular approach to our tools enabled us to expand their use to other task-based parallelism frameworks.

Acknowledgments. We executed LeanMD on the Kabré Supercomputer at the National Center for High Technology, a program of the National Center of Deans of Costa Rica (CeNAT-CONARE). The data science pipelines in this work used the

PCAD infrastructure, https://pcad.inf.ufrgs.br, at the Informatics Institute at the Federal University of Rio Grande do Sul (UFRGS, Brazil). We thank the CAPES "Move La América" program for the scholarship granted to the first author.

Disclosure of Interests. The authors have no competing interests to declare that are relevant to the content of this article.

References

1. Acun, B., Hardy, D.J., Kale, L.V., Li, K., Phillips, J.C., Stone, J.E.: Scalable molecular dynamics with NAMD on the summit system. IBM J. Res. Dev. **62**(6), 4:1–4:9 (2018). https://doi.org/10.1147/JRD.2018.2888986
2. Acun, B., et al.: Power, reliability, and performance: one system to rule them all. Computer **49**(10), 30–37 (2016). https://doi.org/10.1109/MC.2016.310
3. Bak, S., Menon, H., White, S., Diener, M., Kale, L.: Multi-level load balancing with an integrated runtime approach. In: 2018 18th IEEE/ACM International Symposium on Cluster, Cloud and Grid Computing (CCGRID), pp. 31–40. IEEE (2018)
4. Hollingsworth, S.A., Dror, R.O.: Molecular dynamics simulation for all. Neuron **99**(6), 1129–1143 (2018)
5. Kalé, L., Krishnan, S.: CHARM++: a portable concurrent object oriented system based on C++. In: Paepcke, A. (ed.) Proceedings of OOPSLA 1993, pp. 91–108. ACM Press (1993)
6. Kalé, L.V., Zheng, G., Lee, C.W., Kumar, S.: Scaling applications to massively parallel machines using projections performance analysis tool. Futur. Gener. Comput. Syst. **22**(3), 347–358 (2006). https://doi.org/10.1016/j.future.2004.11.020
7. Kumar, S., et al.: Scalable molecular dynamics with NAMD on the IBM Blue Gene/L system. IBM J. Res. Dev. **52**(1.2), 177–188 (2008). https://doi.org/10.1147/rd.521.0177
8. Nesi, L.L., Pinto, V.G., Miletto, M.C., Schnorr, L.M.: StarVZ: performance analysis of task-based parallel applications (2020). https://inria.hal.science/hal-02960848
9. Mehta, V.: LeanMD: a Charm++ framework for high performance molecular dynamics simulation on large parallel machines. Ph. D. thesis, University of Illinois at Urbana-Champaign (2004)
10. Pearce, O., Gamblin, T., De Supinski, B.R., Schulz, M., Amato, N.M.: Quantifying the effectiveness of load balance algorithms. In: Proceedings of the 26th ACM International Conference on Supercomputing, pp. 185–194 (2012)
11. Pereira, R.: Efficient use of task-based parallelism in HPC parallel applications. Ph. D. thesis, Ecole normale supérieure de lyon - ENS LYON (2023). https://theses.hal.science/tel-04466797
12. Phillips, J.C., et al.: Scalable molecular dynamics with NAMD. J. Comput. Chem. **26**(16), 1781–1802 (2005)
13. Rácz, A., Mihalovits, L.M., Bajusz, D., Héberger, K., Miranda-Quintana, R.A.: Molecular dynamics simulations and diversity selection by extended continuous similarity indices. J. Chem. Inf. Model. **62**(14), 3415–3425 (2022). https://doi.org/10.1021/acs.jcim.2c00433
14. Schnorr, L.: Pajeng–paje next generation. https://github.com/schnorr/pajeng/
15. Team, T.M.D.: Matplotlib: visualization with python (2025). https://doi.org/10.5281/ZENODO.15375714

16. Thoman, P., et al.: A taxonomy of task-based parallel programming technologies for high-performance computing. J. Supercomput. **74**(4), 1422–1434 (2018). https://doi.org/10.1007/s11227-018-2238-4
17. Vink, R., et al.: Pola-rs/polars: Python polars 1.30.0 (2025). https://doi.org/10.5281/ZENODO.15481815
18. Vohra, D.: Apache Parquet, pp. 325–335. Apress, Berkeley, CA (2016). https://doi.org/10.1007/978-1-4842-2199-0_8
19. Zheng, G., Bhatele, A., Meneses, E., Kale, L.V.: Periodic hierarchical load balancing for large supercomputers. Int. J. High Perform. Comput. Appl. **25**(4), 371–385 (2011)

Artificial Intelligence at HPC Scale

Investigating the Impact of DVFS on the Energy Efficiency of AI Workloads on GPUs

Thiago dos Santos Gonçalves and Arthur Francisco Lorenzon(✉)

Institute of Informatics, Universidade Federal do Rio Grande do Sul, Porto Alegre, RS 91501-970, Brazil
{thiago.goncalves,aflorenzon}@inf.ufrgs.br

Abstract. The increasing scale of artificial intelligence (AI) models has led to unsustainable energy consumption in GPU-based systems, creating an important need for more efficient computing strategies. While Dynamic Voltage and Frequency Scaling (DVFS) can be an efficient technique, the combined impact of GPU core and memory frequencies is often not systematically evaluated. This paper presents a comprehensive analysis of how tuning both GPU core and memory frequencies affects performance, energy consumption, and the Energy-Delay Product (EDP) for AI workloads. We evaluate seven benchmarks with diverse computational demands on an AMD Radeon RX 7700XT GPU across 12 distinct frequency configurations. Our results reveal that memory-bound applications can benefit from the increase of memory frequency, reducing execution time by up to 80.7%, and compute-bound applications benefited more from higher core frequencies. In addition, by selecting appropriate operating frequencies, it is possible to reduce the EDP by up to 98.3% comparing to the worst-case scenario, highlighting the possible energy efficiency gains of choosing a balanced configuration that optimizes the energy-performance trade-off.

Keywords: AI workloads · DVFS · Energy Efficiency · GPU

1 Introduction

The rapid advancement of artificial intelligence (AI) workloads, particularly large-scale deep learning models, has significantly increased the demand for high-performance computing (HPC), with graphics processing units (GPUs) serving as the cornerstone of AI training and [9]. While GPUs deliver high performance due to their parallel architecture, their operation at scale often leads to substantial power consumption and environmental impact. This issue is exemplified by recent efforts such as the training of *Grok-3*, a state-of-the-art language model by xAI[1], which required over 200,000 NVIDIA H100 GPUs operating near peak

[1] https://x.ai/news/grok-3.

K. Brown et al. (Eds.): CARLA 2025, CCIS 2750, pp. 159–171, 2026.
https://doi.org/10.1007/978-3-032-24923-4_11

power levels of 700 watts each. The total power draw, including networking and cooling overheads, reached 100 megawatts (MW), a level of consumption comparable to that of a small city. Therefore, as AI models continue to grow in complexity and scale, ensuring energy-efficient operation of GPU-based systems is essential to sustaining future AI progress in an environmentally responsible manner.

In this context, improving the energy efficiency of AI workloads without sacrificing performance has become a research challenge. Among the various strategies under consideration, evaluating and adjusting GPU and memory operating frequencies has emerged as a promising technique. Unlike static hardware configurations or workload-specific autotuning, dynamic voltage and frequency scaling (DVFS) offers the potential to adapt GPU behavior to the computational intensity and memory bandwidth demands of each workload phase. Empirical evidence suggests that many AI workloads, especially during inference or when training sparse or smaller models, underutilize available GPU resources [10]. Operating these underutilized GPUs at their highest frequency results in unnecessary power consumption, reducing overall efficiency.

While tools such as NVIDIA's `nvmlDeviceSetApplicationsClocks()` and equivalent features in AMD's ROCm ecosystem enable manual control of GPU frequency settings, our work offers a complementary perspective by evaluating the impact of both core and memory frequency across diverse kernels and execution phases of AI workloads. In particular, memory frequency, though often less emphasized, can significantly influence whether a workload behaves as memory-bound or compute-bound. Hence, understanding this behavior can guide more effective tuning strategies that reduce energy consumption while maintaining performance.

Considering the aforementioned scenario, we investigate how tuning GPU and memory operating frequencies impacts performance, energy consumption, and the trade-off between both, represented by the energy-delay product (EDP) metric for representative AI workloads. In a nutshell, the contributions are as follows:

- An evaluation of the impact of both GPU compute unit and memory frequency scaling across seven AI benchmarks with different workload characteristics on an AMD Radeon RX 7700XT GPU.
- A detailed analysis demonstrating that for memory-bound applications, prioritizing memory frequency can reduce execution time by up to 80.7%, while for compute-bound applications, core frequency is the dominant factor, highlighting that not every operating frequency change on different workloads will bring the same results.
- A demonstration that workload-aware frequency scaling can yield significant improvements in overall performance-energy efficiency, reducing the EDP by up to 98.3% compared to the worst-case scenario.

The remainder of this work is organized as follows. In Sect. 2, we provide a background regarding the employment of DVFS on AMD GPUS and list the related work. Then, the description of the AI workloads and the experimental setup is provided in Sect. 3. The results are discussed in Sect. 4 while the conclusions are draw in Sect. 5.

2 Background

In this Section, we start by describing the employment of DVFS to manage the operating frequency of the core and memory parts of GPUs. Then, we discuss the related work and compare our contributions to it.

2.1 Dynamic Frequency and Voltage Scaling in GPUs

Dynamic Voltage and Frequency Scaling (DVFS) is a commonly adopted technique to optimize the trade-off between energy consumption and computational performance in modern computing systems, including GPUs. The concept involves modifying the supply voltage and clock frequencies of the hardware in response to the current workload characteristics. In this scenario, because power consumption is quadratically dependent on voltage and linearly dependent on frequency [7], decreasing these parameters can lead to significant energy savings. However, such reductions often result in lower computational throughput, which is especially relevant for GPUs due to their role in high-throughput parallel processing.

The impact of DVFS varies depending on the nature of the application. For compute-intensive workloads, reducing the core frequency tends to severely impact performance, limiting the applicability of aggressive DVFS policies. Conversely, memory-bound applications–where data transfer latency or memory bandwidth is the primary constraint, may tolerate lower core frequencies with minimal performance degradation. In these cases, DVFS can effectively reduce power usage while maintaining efficiency. Additionally, DVFS is not limited to the GPU cores; it can also be applied to the memory subsystem. Hence, tuning the memory frequency independently enables further optimization, particularly for workloads that exhibit low compute-to-memory ratios. GPUs from vendors such as NVIDIA, AMD, and Intel incorporate hardware-level DVFS mechanisms that respond dynamically to thermal conditions, power budgets, and workload profiles.

2.2 Related Work

Optimizing GPU frequency has become a key strategy for improving the energy efficiency of modern GPU-accelerated applications. Numerous studies have explored the impact of adjusting core and memory frequencies on power consumption and performance, and have proposed different methods for frequency tuning under diverse workload characteristics. Jiao et al. [4], for instance, develop power-performance models that guide the selection of kernel combinations for concurrent execution, applying DVFS (Dynamic Voltage and Frequency Scaling) to optimize energy usage. Guerreiro et al. [3] investigate the effects of both core and memory frequency scaling on overall GPU application behavior, highlighting the importance of coordinated tuning. Stachowski et al. [11] propose an autotuning framework that identifies energy-optimal GPU frequencies using DVFS, targeting efficient execution in varying conditions.

Additional efforts have explored the integration of frequency scaling with workload-specific optimization strategies. Seyed et al. [8] combine DVFS with dynamic batching in deep neural network (DNN) workloads to improve power management during training and inference. AccelWatch [6] provides a power modeling tool that predicts GPU power behavior under different DVFS configurations, while Ali et al. [1] introduce a deep neural network-based model to predict performance and power consumption across a range of frequency levels. Foster et al. [2] offer a comprehensive evaluation of machine learning benchmarks across multiple GPU architectures, examining trade-offs between performance and energy. More recently, Wang et al. [12] present a utilization-aware frequency scaling strategy for optimizing energy in heterogeneous GPU clusters.

In addition to these prior efforts, our work focuses specifically on understanding how GPU frequency settings, including both core and memory, affect performance, energy consumption, and the EDP for AI-centric workloads. Rather than proposing predictive models or automation frameworks, we provide an analysis that shows practical information about the behavior of applications under various frequency configurations. Our study aims to inform and assist end-users by offering guidelines for selecting the most suitable frequency combinations to optimize according to performance, energy efficiency, or EDP, thereby supporting more effective resource use on modern GPU systems.

3 Methodology

In this Section, we describe the AI algorithms used to evaluate the impact of GPU and memory operating frequency on the performance and energy efficiency. We also list the execution environment.

3.1 Target Applications

We considered seven parallel machine learning applications already implemented with HIP with distinct GPU compute units and memory demands from the HeCBench [5] benchmark suite:

- *Maxpool3D*: Three-dimensional max pooling operation commonly used in neural networks. The benchmark processes a batch of 96 input volumes of size 4096×4096, repeated over 1,000 iterations.
- *Relu*: Rectified Linear Unit (ReLU) activation function applied to a flat input array containing 10 million elements, executed over 50,000 repetitions to ensure sufficient workload granularity.

- *Pool*: Two-dimensional pooling operation for convolutional neural networks. The workload consists of a batch size of 256, 96 input channels, input feature maps of size 448 × 448, and output maps of size 108 × 108, repeated over 1,000 iterations.
- *KNN*: Implementation of the k-Nearest Neighbors algorithm with 5,000 classification queries, simulating repeated inference steps.
- *KMeans*: Clustering algorithm executed with default configuration parameters, representative of unsupervised learning workloads.
- *LDA*: Latent Dirichlet Allocation (LDA) topic modeling algorithm, executed over 5,000 iterations, emulating iterative probabilistic inference used in text mining tasks.
- *StdDev*: Standard deviation calculation over a dense matrix of dimensions 65,536 × 16,384, repeated for 500 iterations to simulate sustained statistical processing workloads.

Each application was compiled using the HIP compiler v.6.3.42134 and the $-O3$ optimization flag, with the *Stddev* application also being compiled with the *-ffast-math* and *-munsafe-fp-atomics* flags.

3.2 Execution Environment

The experiments were performed on an AMD Radeon RX 7700XT graphics card. This GPU has 54 Compute Units and 12 GB of GGDR6 RAM with a 192-bit memory bus, capable of operating at up to 2276 MHz and 1124 MHz, respectively. We considered four different operating frequencies for the GPU memory (96 MHz, 456 MHz, 772 MHz, and 1124 MHz) and three different operating frequencies for the GPU compute unit (500 MHz, 1645 MHz, and 2276 MHz), for a total of 12 frequency variations per application. Each combination of frequency configuration was executed 10 times, and the results presented in the following Sections are an average of these executions, with a standard deviation lower than 0.5%. We used the *rocm-smi* tool to collect the power draw metrics in intervals of 100 milliseconds, and the total energy consumption was calculated by integrating power with respect to time, as shown in Eq. 1. For the execution time, we considered the report from each benchmark. Also, the EDP is calculated by multiplying the execution time (in Seconds) by the total energy consumption (in Joules).

$$E = \int_{t_{start}}^{t_{end}} P(t)\, dt \qquad (1)$$

4 Experimental Results

In this Section, we discuss the results obtained from our experiments. For that, we first discuss the performance results in Sect. 4.1. Then, energy results are discussed in Sect. 4.2. Finally, Sect. 4.3 discusses the trade-off between performance and energy consumption. Finally, Sect. 4.4 provides guidelines to help end-users optimize the use of operating frequencies.

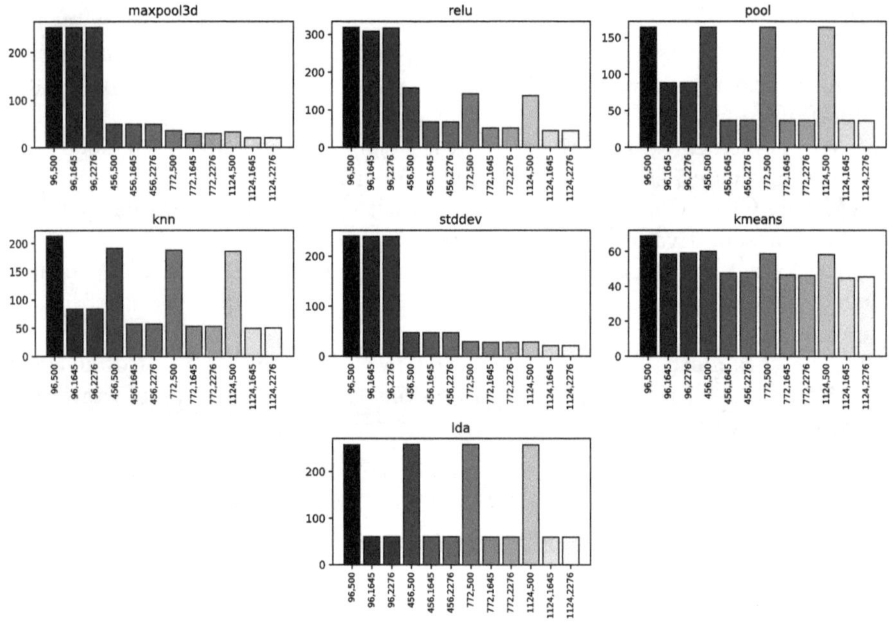

Fig. 1. Execution Time for each application in each operating frequency configuration. Low values mean better performance.

4.1 Execution Time Analysis

We start our analysis by discussing the performance results achieved when executing each benchmark across different memory configurations, previously defined in Sect. 3. For that, Fig. 1 illustrates the execution time for every benchmark on each combination of memory and compute unit frequency. From left to right, the plot starts with the lowest operating frequencies, organized as a tuple (memory, compute unit frequency), going up to their highest possible operating frequencies.

We start our analysis by highlighting that only increasing the GPU operating frequency does not yield uniform performance improvements across all configurations or workloads. As can be observed in Fig. 1, for memory-bound applications such as *Maxpool3D*, *Relu*, and *Stddev*, the impact of memory frequency scaling is significantly more pronounced than that of compute frequency scaling. Specifically, increasing the memory frequency from 96 MHz to 456 MHz, while keeping the compute unit frequency fixed at 500 MHz, leads to significant reductions in execution time: 80.7% for *Maxpool3D*, 50.6% for *Relu*, and 80.4% for *Stddev*. On the other hand, increasing the compute unit frequency from 500 MHz to 1465 MHz with memory frequency held constant at 96 MHz results in less than 1% performance improvements for Maxpool3D and *Stddev*, and only 3.3% for *Relu*. These kernels rely heavily on nested loops that traverse large input matrices, performing element-wise operations with limited data reuse. This access pattern leads to frequent and regular memory accesses, making them particularly sensitive to memory subsystem bottlenecks. As a result, when the memory frequency is low, the latency of accessing global memory dominates the execution time, and increasing compute throughput yields diminishing returns due to data starvation in the execution units.

A contrasting performance trend can be observed in applications where the dominant factor in execution time reduction is the increase in compute unit frequency. These workloads, including *Pool*, *Knn*, and *Lda*, benefit significantly more from enhanced compute throughput than memory bandwidth improvements. When increasing the compute frequency from 500 MHz to 1645 MHz while keeping the memory frequency fixed at 96 MHz, the execution time is reduced by 46.2%, 61.8%, and 76.7% for *Pool*, *Knn*, and *Lda*, respectively. This behavior highlights the compute-bound nature of these applications, where a larger proportion of execution time is spent performing arithmetic or logic operations rather than waiting for memory transactions.

The underlying computational patterns of these applications provide a further understanding of this behavior. The *Pool* application involves size-reduction operations over input matrices, often requiring multiple conditional and aggregation steps per output element, especially in max or average pooling variants. *Knn* is characterized by intensive distance calculations and subsequent sorting operations for nearest neighbor selection, exhibiting high arithmetic intensity. Similarly, *Lda* performs model training through iterative updates involving matrix-vector multiplications, dot products, and normalization steps, demanding significant computational resources per input sample. While all these applications include matrix traversal, the primary bottleneck shifts to computation per element rather than data access, making them highly responsive to increases in compute frequency.

Moreover, these workloads also exhibit moderate sensitivity to memory bandwidth, though to a lesser extent. For example, when increasing the memory frequency from 96 MHz to 456 MHz while keeping the compute frequency fixed at 1645 MHz, execution times are reduced by 58.6% for Pool and 32.1% for Knn. This indicates that while performance is predominantly constrained by compute throughput, memory subsystem enhancements still contribute to reducing latency in data fetch and intermediate result access, particularly in the early or final stages of computation.

In contrast to the previously discussed applications, *Kmeans* exhibits a more balanced sensitivity to both compute and memory frequency scaling, with smaller absolute performance gains observed when tuning either parameter in isolation. Specifically, increasing the compute unit frequency from 500 MHz to 1645 MHz while maintaining the memory frequency at 96 MHz yields a 15.5% reduction in execution time. Similarly, increasing the memory frequency from 96 MHz to 456 MHz while keeping the compute unit frequency fixed at 500 MHz results in a 13.1% improvement. However, when both frequencies are scaled simultaneously, the cumulative execution time reduction reaches 31.1%, indicating that the performance of Kmeans is jointly bounded by compute and memory subsystem limitations.

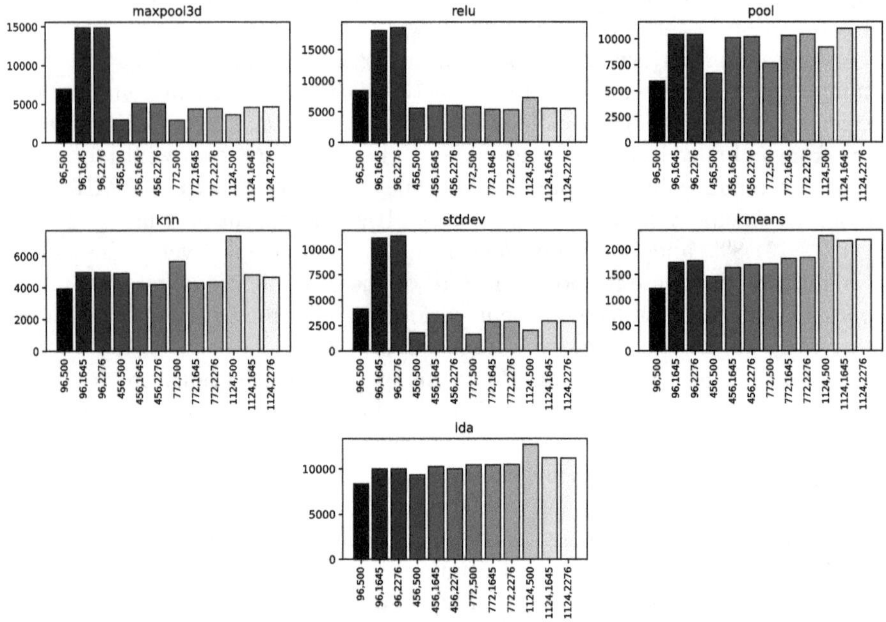

Fig. 2. Energy Consumption for every application in every possible frequency configuration. Low values are better

This behavior can be attributed to the algorithmic structure of *Kmeans*, which performs iterative centroid updates and distance computations over large datasets. In each iteration, the algorithm recalculates cluster memberships based on proximity, often requiring repeated traversal of input data and dynamic updates to centroid positions. In the GPU implementation under analysis, memory allocations and data movements are performed inside the main loop that iterates over clusters. This results in a mixed workload profile where memory operations (e.g., allocations and data transfers) coexist with arithmetic computations (e.g., distance calculations and centroid updates), leading to a dual sensitivity to both compute and memory performance.

4.2 Energy Consumption Analysis

Figure 2 shows the energy usage in Joules for each benchmark on every configuration, organized in the same manner as Fig. 1.

The *Maxpool3D*, *Relu*, and *Stddev* applications also have similar energy consumption patterns, consuming the most energy when keeping the memory frequencies low and the compute unit frequencies high. The best energy usage for the *Maxpool3D* and *Stddev* applications can be seen when executing them at 772 MHz for the memory frequency and 500 MHz for the compute unit frequency, and the worst is when they lower the memory frequency to 96 MHz and increase the compute unit frequency to 2276 MHz. For the *Relu* application, the worst case is on the same configuration, but the best case is when keeping the memory frequency at 772 MHz and the compute unit frequency at 2276 MHz. When comparing their best and worst cases, they have a 80.4%, 71.4%, 85.8% difference in energy usage for the *Maxpool3D*, *Relu*, and *Stddev* applications, respectively. This high energy consumption when executing these applications at a low memory frequency and a high compute unit frequency highlights again their high amount of memory accesses during execution, with many compute unit cycles spent waiting to find data in the GPU memory.

Now, in algorithms such as *Pool*, *Knn*, *Lda*, and *Kmeans*, there is a modest increase in energy consumption as the operating frequencies increase. First, it's important to reemphasize that not every frequency increase is equal. In the *Pool*, *Lda*, and *Kmeans* algorithms, there is an upwards trend in energy usage as the frequencies go higher, with higher energy usage increases when the compute unit frequencies also increase. In the *Knn* algorithm, there seems to be a trend reversal when increasing the memory frequency past 456 MHz. While the increase of compute unit frequency from 500 MHz to 1645 MHz with memory operating frequency at 96 MHz results in a 26.3% increase in energy consumption, the same compute frequency increase with the memory frequency at 456 MHz results in a 13.2% reduction in energy consumption. This is due to the application reaching an energy-optimized memory frequency at 456 MHz, allowing the compute unit to access data as soon as possible and minimizing the chance of memory bottlenecks. Also, these benchmarks' lowest energy consumption values were when both operating frequencies were at their lowest, but there is a significant difference between each benchmark when comparing their executions at the highest and lowest operating frequencies possible. While in the *Pool* application there is a 87.4% increase in energy consumption from the lowest to the highest frequencies, the *Knn* application only increases its energy consumption by 18.4% under the same circumstances. This further highlights the difference on the bottleneck profiles of each application and the importance of being mindful of the hardware level impact when choosing an optimal configuration to run an application.

4.3 Energy Delay Product Analysis

Finally, we analyze the EDP obtained on each benchmark, linking it to the previous execution times and energy consumption discussions. Figure 3 shows the EDP for each application on every configuration, organized like Figs. 1 and 2. When analyzing the *Maxpool3D*, *Relu*, and *Stddev* applications, the energy efficiency gains when increasing the memory frequency become even more apparent, and is due to both the high execution times and high energy consumption on low memory frequency configurations. In addition, when comparing worst and best cases, there is a 97.5%, 95.8%, and 98.3% difference on the *Maxpool3D*, *Relu*, and *Stddev* applications, respectively, demonstrating that in some applications,

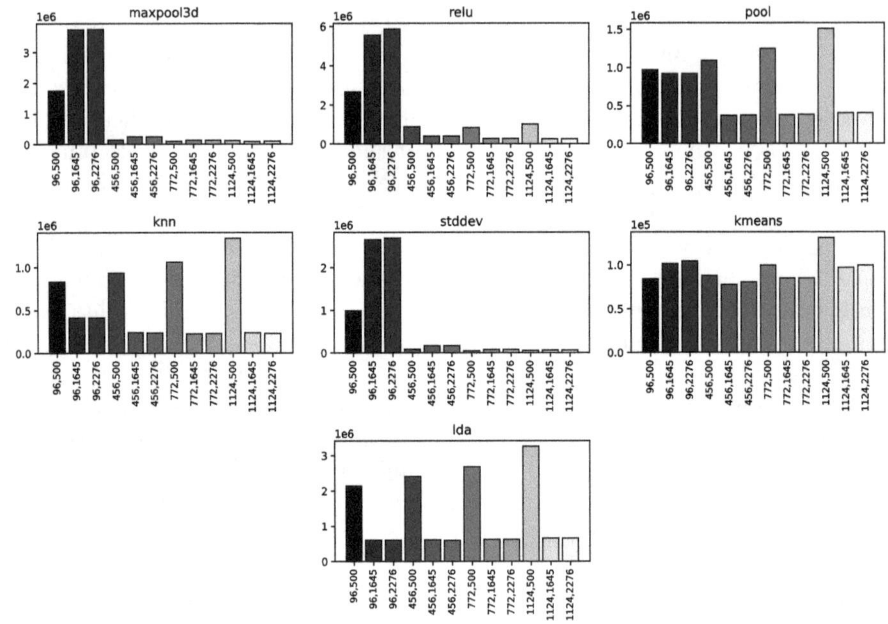

Fig. 3. EDP for every application in every possible frequency configuration. Y-axis values are in scientific notation. Low values mean better energy efficiency.

memory bottlenecks can result in a costly loss of energy efficiency. Lastly, both the *Maxpool3D* and *Relu* applications achieved their best EDP when executing with 1124 MHz memory frequency and 1645 MHz compute unit frequency, showing that for some applications, moderate operating frequencies can be the most energy efficient.

In contrast, the plot for the *Pool*, *Knn*, and *Lda* applications' EDP maintain similar patterns as their execution times. As such, they achieve the smallest EDP values with high compute unit frequencies because of their smaller amount of variation on the energy consumption of every configuration when compared to the last set of applications. On top of that, when comparing their EDP with the highest memory frequency and the lowest and highest compute unit frequencies, there is a 273.8%, 483.0%, 396.7% increase for the *Pool*, *Knn*, and *Lda* applications. This highlights again their heavy dependence on arithmetic operations, unnecessarily spending power with wasted instruction cycles when executing these applications with low compute unit frequencies.

Lastly, the *Kmeans* application maintains its balanced values when looking at its EDP plot, with a smaller 69.4% increase in EDP between the best and worst cases. The benchmark's balanced memory and compute unit usage also reflect on its EDP values, only showing a compute unit bottleneck when executing with the maximum possible memory frequency and the minimum possible compute unit frequency. It's also important to note that there is an apparent change on what worsens the EDP values depending on the executing frequency, because while there is a 20.2% increase on EDP when increasing the compute unit frequency from 500 to 1645 MHz and keeping the memory frequency at 96 MHz, the EDP decreases by 12.4% by doing the same frequency increase on the compute unit frequency but keeping the memory frequency at 456 MHz. Memory bottlenecks can explain this behavior, with the application only getting energy efficiency benefits by balancing the memory frequency and compute unit frequencies.

Table 1. Best operating frequency combinations for every benchmark, considering execution time, energy consumption, and energy delay product.

Benchmark	Time	Energy	EDP
maxpool3d	1124 Mhz,2276 Mhz	772 Mhz,500 Mhz	1124 Mhz,1645 Mhz
relu	1124 Mhz,1645 Mhz	772 Mhz,2276 Mhz	1124 Mhz,1645 Mhz
pool	772 Mhz,2276 Mhz	96 Mhz,500 Mhz	456 MHz,1645 Mhz
knn	1124 Mhz,1645 Mhz	96 Mhz,500 Mhz	772 Mhz,1645 Mhz
stddev	1124 Mhz,2276 Mhz	772 Mhz,500 Mhz	772 Mhz,500 Mhz
kmeans	1124 Mhz,1645 Mhz	96 Mhz,500 Mhz	456 MHz,1645 Mhz
lda	1124 Mhz,2276 Mhz	96 Mhz,500 Mhz	456 MHz,2276 Mhz

4.4 Optimizing Operating Frequencies

Table 1 shows the best operating frequencies in relation to execution time, energy consumption, and EDP. The operating frequencies are organized as a tuple (memory, compute unit frequency).

We would like to point out that no benchmark has a configuration that manages to get the best execution times and energy consumption simultaneously, and on top of that, only the *Relu* application manages to get the best execution times and EDP on the same configuration, and the *Stddev* application is the only one that gets the best energy consumption and EDP on the same configuration, reaffirming that there is no single frequency configuration that can get the best results for every criteria. Operating frequencies that decrease execution time often increase energy consumption, and most times aren't the best choice if energy efficiency is the main goal, as shown in Table 1.

For this reason, it's important to choose the best operating frequencies, being mindful of the application's workloads, and balancing them if a hardware bottleneck occurs. As we have seen in Fig. 2, memory-bottlenecked applications such as *Maxpool3D*, *Relu*, and *Stddev* often waste a lot of energy when executing with low memory frequencies, and Table 1 shows that, on the contrary of all other applications, their best energy consumption is achieved when the memory frequency is balanced. Furthermore, no application managed to get the best EDP values when executing at the maximum operating frequencies, and only the *Maxpool3D* and *Relu* applications managed to get their best EDP executing with the same frequencies.

5 Conclusion and Future Works

As artificial intelligence applications continue to grow in scale and computational demand, the resulting increase in GPU energy consumption has become a critical concern for sustainable high-performance computing. In this study, we examine how variations in core and memory frequency settings influence the performance, energy usage, and EDP of a modern AMD GPU across a range of representative workloads. The experimental results demonstrate that selectively increasing memory frequency can yield substantial performance gains, reducing execution time by up to 80.7% in certain memory-bound applications. Furthermore, configuring the system to minimize energy consumption, rather than maximizing performance, can lower energy usage by as much as 85.8%, highlighting the potential of frequency tuning for energy-aware computing. Furthermore, we observe that choosing the optimal frequency pair for energy efficiency can reduce the EDP by up to 98.3%, indicating a significant improvement in overall energy proportionality without compromising computational accuracy.

Future work includes broadening the scope of workloads and exploring a finer-grained space of frequency configurations. Additionally, we intend to investigate the impact of tuning other GPU subsystems, such as the Infinity Fabric interconnect and I/O controllers, to better understand their contribution to energy efficiency in heterogeneous architectures.

Acknowledgments. This study was financed in part by the CAPES - Finance Code 001, FAPERGS - PqG 24/2551-0001388-1, and CNPq.

References

1. Ali, G., Side, M., Bhalachandra, S., Wright, N.J., Chen, Y.: Performance-aware energy-efficient GPU frequency selection using DNN-based models. In: Proceedings of the 52nd International Conference on Parallel Processing, ICPP 2023, pp. 433–442. Association for Computing Machinery, New York, NY, USA (2023). https://doi.org/10.1145/3605573.3605600,
2. Foster, B., Taneja, S., Manzano, J., Barker, K.: Evaluating energy efficiency of GPUs using machine learning benchmarks. In: 2023 IEEE International Parallel and Distributed Processing Symposium Workshops (IPDPSW), pp. 42–50 (2023). https://doi.org/10.1109/IPDPSW59300.2023.00019
3. Guerreiro, J., Ilic, A., Roma, N., Tomás, P.: DVFS-aware application classification to improve GPGPUs energy efficiency. Parallel Comput. **83**, 93–117 (2019)
4. Jiao, Q., Lu, M., Huynh, H.P., Mitra, T.: Improving GPGPU energy-efficiency through concurrent kernel execution and DVFS. In: 2015 IEEE/ACM International Symposium on Code Generation and Optimization (CGO), pp. 1–11 (2015). https://doi.org/10.1109/CGO.2015.7054182

5. Jin, Z., Vetter, J.S.: A benchmark suite for improving performance portability of the sycl programming model. In: 2023 IEEE International Symposium on Performance Analysis of Systems and Software (ISPASS), pp. 325–327 (2023). https://doi.org/10.1109/ISPASS57527.2023.00041
6. Kandiah, V., et al.: Accelwattch: a power modeling framework for modern GPUs. In: MICRO-54: 54th Annual IEEE/ACM International Symposium on Microarchitecture, MICRO 2021, pp. 738–753. Association for Computing Machinery, New York, NY, USA (2021). https://doi.org/10.1145/3466752.3480063
7. Le Sueur, E., Heiser, G.: Dynamic voltage and frequency scaling: the laws of diminishing returns. In: Proceedings of the 2010 International Conference on Power Aware Computing and Systems, pp. 1–8 (2010)
8. Nabavinejad, S.M., Reda, S., Ebrahimi, M.: Coordinated batching and DVFS for DNN inference on GPU accelerators. IEEE Trans. Parallel Distrib. Syst. **33**(10), 2496–2508 (2022). https://doi.org/10.1109/TPDS.2022.3144614
9. Navaux, P.O.A., Lorenzon, A.F., da Silva Serpa, M.: Challenges in high-performance computing. J. Braz. Comput. Soc. **29**(1), 51–62 (2023)
10. Pan, B., et al.: Dense training, sparse inference: rethinking training of mixture-of-experts language models. arXiv:2404.05567 (2024)
11. Stachowski, M., Fiebig, A., Rauber, T.: Autotuning based on frequency scaling toward energy efficiency of blockchain algorithms on graphics processing units. J. Supercomput. **77**, 263–291 (2021)
12. Wang, S., Chen, S., Shi, Y.: Utilization-prediction-aware energy optimization approach for heterogeneous GPU clusters. J. Supercomput. **80**(7), 9554–9578 (2024)

High-Performance Computing Applications

A Scientific Data Integrity System Based on Blockchain

Gian Sebastian Mier Bello[1(✉)], A. Martínez-Méndez[1,2], Carlos J. Barrios H.[1,3,4], Robinson Rivas[5], and Luis A. Núñez[1,2]

[1] SC3UIS-CAGE, Universidad Industrial de Santander, Bucaramanga, Colombia
{gian2210073,alexander2198160}@correo.uis.edu.co,
{cbarrios,lnunez}@uis.edu.co

[2] GIRG, Universidad Industrial de Santander, Bucaramanga, Colombia

[3] LIG/INRIA DataMove, Grenoble, France

[4] CITI/INRIA SiNDY, Lyon, France

[5] Universidad Central de Venezuela, Caracas, Venezuela
robinson.rivas@ciens.ucv.ve

Abstract. In most High Performance Computing (HPC) projects nowadays, there is a lot of data obtained from different sources, depending on the project's objectives. Some of that data is very huge in terms of size, so copying such data sometimes is an unrealistic goal. On the other hand, science requires data used for different purposes to remain unaltered, so different groups of researchers can reproduce results, discuss theories, and validate each other. In this paper, we present a novel approach to help research groups to validate data integrity on such distributed repositories using Blockchain. Originally developed for cryptographic currencies, Blockchain has demonstrated a versatile range of uses. Our proposal ensures 1) secure access to data management, 2) easy validation of data integrity, and 3) an easy way to add new records to the dataset with the same robust integrity policy. A prototype was developed and tested using a subset of a public dataset from a real scientific collaboration, the Latin American Giant Observatory (LAGO) Project.

Keywords: Blockchain · HPC Application · Scientific collaboration · Integrity · Distributed HPC

1 Introduction

Almost all pieces of data published on the Internet today are at risk of being manipulated or viewed without prior authorization; data can be manipulated at different layers of the network. In this context, Blockchain appeared, which was initially conceived as a P2P transaction system, but thanks to its properties such as decentralization, immutability, and encryption, it has proven to be effective in ensuring the integrity and traceability of digital records. The most recognized application of this technology is Bitcoin. As per the observations made by Hirsh & Alman [1], Bitcoin facilitates secure monetary transactions without the need

K. Brown et al. (Eds.): CARLA 2025, CCIS 2750, pp. 175–190, 2026.
https://doi.org/10.1007/978-3-032-24923-4_12

for financial intermediaries. Nevertheless, they assert that the primary objective of this technology is to establish an immutable record of ownership and provenance. This characteristic is essential for ensuring the integrity of scientific data and, ultimately, the advancement of scientific research.

HPC has become essential in recent times for the advancement of new scientific knowledge and, consequently, for scientific research across various disciplines, as articulated by Silva et al. [2]. In consideration of modern computational capabilities, it is now possible to execute complex simulations with a degree of realism and precision unprecedented. Nowadays, numerous applications requires substantial computational resources encompass seismic analysis related to natural disasters, oil and gas exploration, climate and flood forecasting, computational fluid dynamics (CFD), Deoxyribonucleic Acid (DNA) sequencing, simulations of electromagnetic equations, analyses in the energy sector, materials science, and other related domains [3].

The applications and resources are optimized and calibrated to achieve superior performance in their execution, resulting in the generation of substantial volumes of data. Thus, it is imperative to manage these resources appropriately to facilitate research. A pertinent example of such projects is the Latin America Giant Observatory (LAGO) project [4]. Within this initiative, data are derived from a network of radio telescopes and subsequently processed utilizing high-performance computing (HPC) facilities in Latin American countries. It is of utmost importance that, for scientific purposes, the data remain unaltered and accessible, enabling various research groups to collaborate reliably and discuss findings. In instances such as the LAGO project, the substantial size of the data poses significant challenges in maintaining trustworthy copies of the entire datasets. The proposed system addresses this by adopting an off-chain storage model; only the cryptographic hashes and metadata of the scientific data are stored on the blockchain, while the large datasets themselves remain in their original distributed repositories. This approach ensures data integrity without overloading the blockchain, which is not designed to store large files, thereby avoiding constraints on block size. Therefore, in this work, we propose a prototype to support the integrity of the measurement and simulation data of the LAGO project.

Combining blockchain technology with high-performance computing (HPC) is an emerging field that could significantly change how computational resources are utilized and shared. This novel approach presents challenges in management and usage, including scalability, consensus mechanisms, blockchain architectures, and widespread adoption in large-scale scientific infrastructures. However, the benefits in trust, security, cost efficiency, and performance in heterogeneous systems (including levels in multiscale architectures such as Edge and Fog Computing) as well as decentralized advanced computing capabilities motivate the research, development, deployment, and implementation of this integration.

In this context, the proposed blockchain-based prototype contributes by addressing key challenges in data integrity and access control within distributed HPC environments. This can be achieved by leveraging Hyperledger Fabric's permissioned architecture, which restricts participation to authenticated entities and users using cryptographic identities (X.509 certificates) with **MSP**. Access policies are enforced through chaincode logic, allowing fine-grained control over who can register, query, or update metadata linked to scientific datasets. Regarding traceability, each transaction—including the registration of raw data, simulation inputs, and processed outputs—is immutably recorded in the ledger, providing a verifiable and timestamped audit trail of the entire data lifecycle. This enables researchers to reconstruct workflows, validate results, and attribute contributions across distributed HPC infrastructures. For tamper-evidence, the use of cryptographic hashing ensures that any alteration to input/output files or metadata would result in a mismatch with the stored hash, and the content block hash in the chain too, as a result signaling potential integrity breaches. This technique allows to ensure data has not being manipulated nor changed since the use by research groups. However, it doesn't prevent the data manipulation itself: only serves as a warrantee of data pureness if any other group wants to check for data integrity or compare sources.

This paper is structured as follows: Sect. 2 provides background on the LAGO project, which offers a public dataset emphasizing transparency, low cost, and heterogeneity integration; and the state of the art and key features revised to implement our proposal. Section 3 discusses the execution environment, considering the analysis to choose the optimal deployment strategies, designing the prototype, demonstrating the proof of concept, and validating and fine-tuning the deployed prototype. In Sect. 4, we present the most significant results, followed by a discussion in Sect. 5. Finally, we conclude with our findings and suggestions for further work in Sect. 6.

2 Background

In this section, we present the basis of our work: the LAGO initiative and their need for data, and some state-of-the-art on Blockchain technology and its relation with Scientific Data Management.

2.1 LAGO

The Latin American Giant Observatory (LAGO) constitutes a sophisticated astroparticle observatory established to examine space weather phenomena, extreme astrophysical events, and atmospheric radiation at ground level. It functions through a distributed network of Water Cherenkov Detectors (WCD) strategically deployed at thirty-one sites, encompassing a broad spectrum of latitudes, from Mexico to Antarctica, and altitudes ranging from sea level to 5000 m covering a wide range of geomagnetic rigidity cut-offs and atmospheric absorption/reaction levels. The LAGO WCD is simple and robust, and incorporates several integrated devices to allow time synchronization, autonomous operation, on-board data analysis, as well as remote control and automated data transfer [5,6]. These detectors collect substantial volumes of cosmic ray measurements across different environmental and geomagnetic conditions, yielding an extensive and unique scientific dataset.

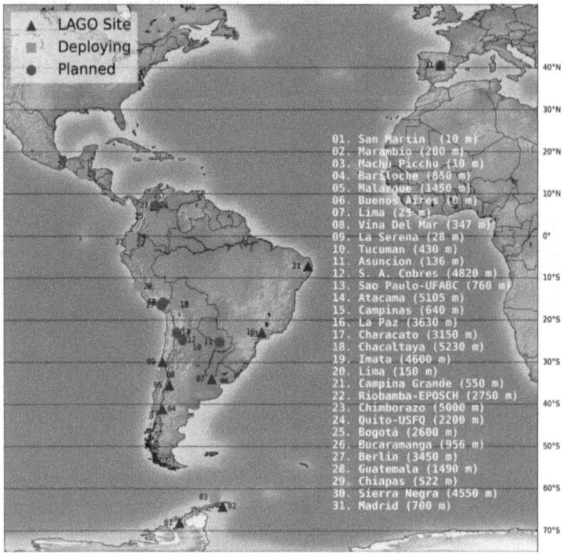

Fig. 1. Geographical distribution of LAGO Project WCD detectors. Taken from [7].

Figure 1 shows the different sites where detectors are placed, indicated by blue triangles. The orange squares represents the deploying sites where computing capabilities and data storage are available, and the red circles indicate the planned sites.

LAGO is coordinated by the LAGO Collaboration, which comprises over 90 researchers from 25 institutions across Latin America and Spain. In addition to collecting experimental data, the collaboration also produces simulation data using high-performance computational (HPC) frameworks. Both experimental and simulated datasets are organized into hierarchical layers according to their level of processing and intended scientific use, with higher layers significantly reducing the data volume.

One of LAGO's primary objectives [8] is to preserve both raw and processed data for potential reprocessing, particularly in the event of software errors, changes in analysis pipelines, or methodological updates. This is crucial given the computational cost, energy consumption, and complexity involved in regenerating degraded or lost data. Furthermore, as HPC environments are heavily used in LAGO for executing simulation and data analysis workflows, ensuring the integrity and verifiability of their outputs is fundamental for scientific reproducibility. In this context, this work proposes a blockchain-based solution designed to integrate with HPC workflows and support the secure registration of data products. By enabling tamper-proof, traceable, and verifiable records of datasets across the collaboration, the system contributes to more reliable data management, facilitating cross-institutional trust and reducing unnecessary reprocessing efforts.

2.2 State of the Art

Some works related to the use of blockchain in HPC to ensure data integrity and promote scientific collaborative environments were identified. However, no approach was found that simultaneously encompasses these issues.

A first relevant work is "A Blockchain-Based Architecture for Trust in Collaborative Scientific Experimentation [12] In this study, a cloud-hosted blockchain network with geographically distributed nodes was implemented to support and build trust in scientific collaborative environments. The solution leverages the immutability of records in blockchain to ensure data provenance and uses a decentralized application that collects key data based on a provenance model. Their case study focused on coronavirus genomic data, where access management was performed using certificates that guarantee the identity of contributors. Although this paper shares our vision regarding data integrity, we focus on supporting a high computation environment in different geographic zones.

Another relevant work is "SciLedger: A Blockchain-based Scientific Workflow Provenance and Data Sharing Platform" [13]. This solution implements a blockchain to support scientific workflows, with features such as handling multiple streams and an invalidation mechanism. It uses a Merkle tree to verify the provenance of data and allows public access to the stored data stream. While sharing the vision of ensuring data integrity, our approach differs by prioritizing the data flow support in every layer.

Finally, in "Earth Observation Data Provenance: A Blockchain-Based Solution" [14], the traceability and sharing of data related to observations of the Earth's surface and atmosphere are addressed. Due to the volume of data in petabytes, this work proposes an off-chain storage model, using the blockchain to store key information using hashes. In addition, it uses a voting-based consensus algorithm, optimizing performance and energy efficiency. In this case, many similarities are shared in terms of how to ensure traceability, store, and guarantee the integrity of the data using a decentralized application. Taken together, these works demonstrate the potential of blockchain technology to strengthen collaborative science. They provided the foundation for this proposal; however, none of them focused on verifying the integrity of the data.

3 Execution Environment

This work was developed based on "7 phases of Blockchain Implementation" [9]. The following steps were: review of the state of the art, analysis and selection, prototype design, proof of concept, and validation and adjustment.

3.1 Prototype Architecture

After a detailed study of the LAGO project and its data flow in the collaboration, the options were limited to network types with permissions. Table 1 provides a comparison of the leading permissioned blockchain platforms considered for this work.

Table 1. Comparison of blockchain platforms

Feature	Hyperledger Fabric [10]	Ripple [10]	Corda [10]	Quorum [10]
Privacy	Private channels for confidential transactions	Trust network based on credit relationships	Transactions visible only to involved parties	Private transactions via nodes and Tessera
Consensus	RAFT	Validator nodes	Validation by notaries	RAFT, IBFT
Smart contracts	Modular support with Chaincode	Not applicable	JVM with legal regulations	Compatible with Solidity and EVM
Automation	Chaincode for business rules	Limited to settlements	Based on legal contracts	Compatible with Ethereum tools
Main applications	General business sectors	Finance, remittances, and global payments	Financial institutions and legal sectors	Finance, logistics, and industries using Ethereum

Upon analyzing the other alternatives in the table—Ripple, Corda, and Quorum—it was observed that they all focus on the financial aspect. Therefore, Hyperledger Fabric 2.5 [11] is the most suitable option for the LAGO project, as its network with permissions structure ensures that only authorized participants can access the data. It also supports private channels and smart contracts, improving confidentiality and operational efficiency. Being open source allows for customization without licensing costs and makes it easy to adapt to the project's needs. Furthermore, its consensus mechanism, RAFT, operates by choosing a leader to validate transactions even in the event of communication failures. This reduces energy and hardware costs, making its implementation more sustainable in the long term.

The blockchain prototype shown in Fig. 2 uses Hyperledger Fabric as its base platform. Two member organizations of the LAGO Collaboration were taken into account: **Universidad Industrial de Santander** and **Escuela Superior Politécnica de Chimborazo**, since both had the necessary data for the test. To support the RAFT protocol based on Crash Fault Tolerance (CFT), an odd number of nodes per organization was chosen. The description of the components and the transaction flow is detailed below.

1. *Certificate Authority* is responsible for issuing MSP (Membership Service Provider) based digital identities to network participants. These identities are encapsulated in X.509 certificates, which are required to interact with the network.
2. *Chaincode* The chaincode defines the business logic and rules of the blockchain network, managing key-value pairs that represent the initial state and transactions of the system. Unlike traditional smart contracts, chaincode operates on authorized private networks within nodes rather than on decentralized

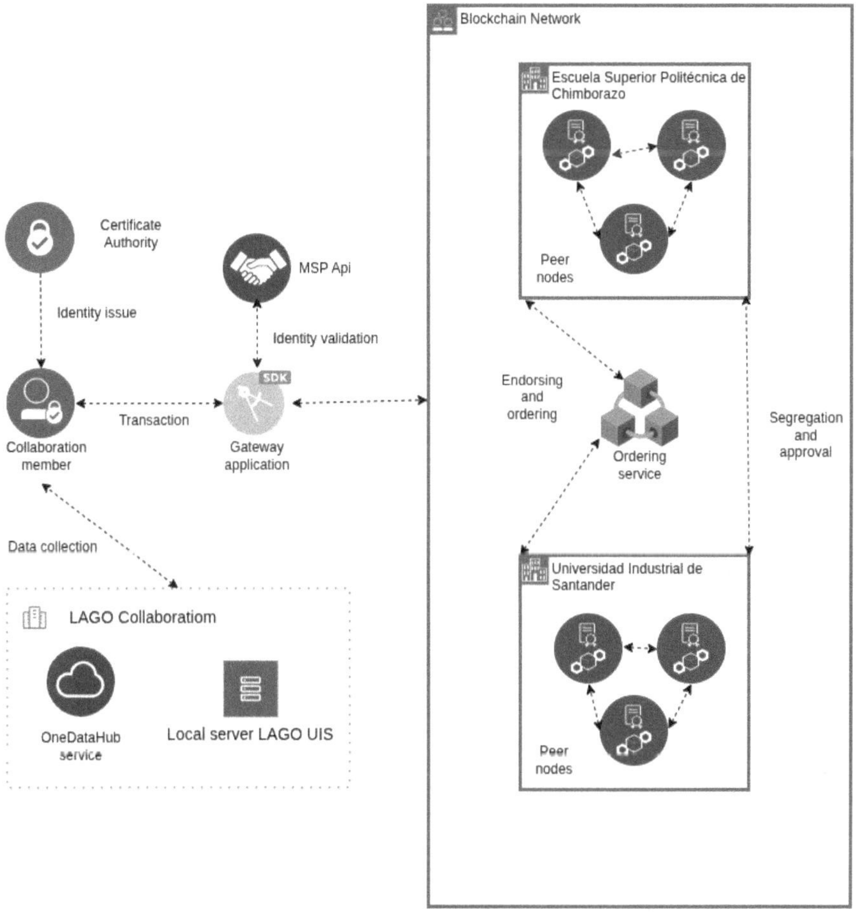

Fig. 2. Blockchain prototype architecture.

virtual machines, under specific endorsement policies that guarantee security and control.

3. *Gateway application (SDK)* is the bridge between users (collaboration members) and the blockchain network. It facilitates the submission of transaction proposals and identity validation using the MSP API. Transactions refer to Chaincode functions running on the nodes.
4. *Ordering service* It is responsible for receiving transactions proposed by users, assigning them a chronological order, and distributing the resulting blocks to peer nodes in both organizations.
5. *Peer nodes* Each organization has three peer nodes that validate the transactions according to the endorsement policies and store a copy of the updated blockchain. This ensures the decentralization of the recorded data.
6. *LAGO Collaboration* represents the integration of the data collection systems, such as the OneDataHUB Service and the local LAGO UIS server,

which receives the measurement data (L0), with the blockchain network. The measurement data and transactions by the collaboration members are processed and stored by transactions.

3.2 Data Scheme

The proposed data schema defines the generic structure of information recorded in the Hyperledger Fabric blockchain network to store scientific simulations and measurements of the LAGO project. Each record has an **Id**, which acts as a unique identifier and follows the DMP convention [8]; a **Type** field, which indicates whether it is a simulation or measurement and its level (L0, L1, S0, S1, etc.); **Metadata**, corresponding to the metadata of the raw data; **Raw data**, with the hash and location of the data obtained; **Input data** and **Input metadata**, which store the input data and metadata used in simulations; **Output data** and **Output metadata**, which record the processed results and their respective metadata. In addition, additional fields are included such as **Site name** (name of the site where data was generated), **Collaborator name** (name of the responsible collaborator), **ORC id** (ORCID identifier of the collaborator) and **Access url**, which provides the external address where the original file or related information can be consulted or accessed. This structure ensures that all elements of the scientific workflow are clearly defined, verifiable and accessible.

3.3 Materials

For the implementation of the prototype in Hyperledger Fabric we have a x86_64 GNU/Linux Debian 6.1.128-1 machine with 7.51 GB of RAM and 8 cores, along with the tools: **Docker** and **Docker Compose.**[1] essential for running different network services such as containers with the **images** of certificate authorities (fabric-ca), peers, noSQL CouchDB databases (couchdb) and orderers.

Digital identities were configured using X.509 certificates to ensure controlled access on the network. An inter-organizational communication channel was established, and the 'ScientificDataCollectContract' chaincode was deployed to manage scientific records with role-based access control.

It was identified that if a peer node falls out of sync with the network—due to connectivity loss or other faults—it may locally possess a divergent or outdated version of the ledger. Transactions submitted to such a node risk being rejected by the broader network during the ordering and validation phases because they are based on an inconsistent world state. This behavior is not an oversight by the protocol, but a fundamental security feature to prevent "double-spending" or the introduction of invalid data. To mitigate this, the client application was designed to halt transaction proposals to any peer whose ledger state is detected as corrupt or inconsistent, as detailed in Algorithm 1.

[1] Docker and Docker Compose are tools to manage containers: https://www.docker.com/.

Algorithm 1 Verify Block Integrity

```
procedure IntegrityVerification(contentHash, dataHashString, block, i)
    if contentHash ≠ dataHashString then
        blockDataList ← Get the list of transactions from the block.
        if blockDataList is not empty then
            for each bl in blockDataList do
                if bl is not empty then
                    signature ← Extract the transaction signature.
                    envPayload ← Get the transaction payload.
                    headerPayload ← Extract the transaction header.
                    txId ← Get the transaction identifier.
                    creatorBytes ← Extract the transaction creator's identity.
                    verifier ← Prepare the signature verification using the SHA-256 algorithm.
                    Validate the creator's signature with the transaction data.
                    isValid ← Sign envPayload with creatorBytes and compare with signature
                    if isValid = false then
                        Throw an error indicating that block i has been tampered with in the transaction with ID txId
                    end if
                else
                    Print No transaction data in block
                end if
            end for
        end if
    end if
end procedure
```

This **gateway** application was developed in **Node.js** to interact with the network. It verifies the integrity of a block on the blockchain by comparing the stored data with that calculated in real time. First, the hash of the content (contentHash) is compared with the hash recorded in the block header (dataHashString). If they do not match, it is considered that the block might have been tampered with. Then, the transactions within the block are extracted and verified.

For each transaction in the block, if it is not empty, the signature, payload, and header are extracted, along with the identifier (txId) and the identity of the originator. A signature verifier using SHA-256 is prepared and validated if the creator's signature is authentic. If the validation fails, an error is thrown indicating that the transaction with the txId in block i has been tampered with. If there is no transaction data, a message is printed indicating its absence. The implementation repository is available at[2]

Data Collection. The process started with the extraction of a subset of data from two main sources. On the one hand, the measurements stored in a local server of the LAGO project were selected and downloaded. On the other hand, the simulations were obtained from the centralized repository of One Data Hub, a platform for storage and access of scientific data. These two sources provided the base information to be processed.

The extracted data were processed using Python scripts, designed to convertthe measurements and simulations into a standard, lightweight JSON-like

[2] Implementation repository: https://github.com/GSMier/ProyectoLago.

structure. During this processing, the input and output files and their respective metadata were analyzed. To ensure data integrity, unique identifiers were generated using the hash function SHA-256, applied to each of the files and their contents to the original format. This approach allows verifying that the data have not been altered during or after processing.

Finally, the processed data and the scripts used for its transformation were stored in a GitHub repository. This repository, accessible at[3], contains the generated JSON, as well as the code used to transform the data. This centralized storage facilitates access to the processed data and allows other collaborators to replicate the process or adapt it to new needs.

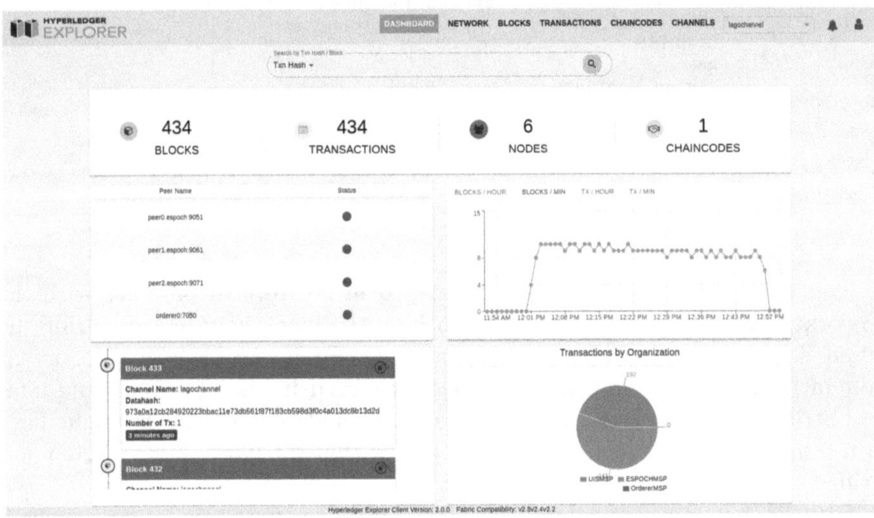

Fig. 3. Hyperledger Explorer Dashboard.

The storage in the blockchain was then carried out with previous data. With the help of **Hyperledger Explorer**, a web service developed by Hyperledger Fabric[4], network data such as blocks, nodes, transactions, chaincode, and channels can be visualized. As can be seen in Fig. 3, 434 transactions were performed, of which 430 were invoked by the chaincode "ScientificDataCollection" to store the data, which were distributed in different blocks, since each block accepts transactions in 2-second intervals. With an average of approximately 8 transactions/min, the scientific data of the 2 organizations were recorded. In Hyperledger Fabric, its structure is more complex, as each transaction includes digital signatures generated with the private keys of its creators. In addition,

[3] Link to the repository of scripts and processed data https://github.com/GSMier/LAGO-data.

[4] Hyperledger Explorer repository: https://github.com/hyperledger-labs/blockchain-explorer.

peer nodes that validate and approve these transactions also add their signatures to the blocks. Figure 4 illustrates this structure, where each block is linked to the previous one via cryptographic hashes.

3.4 Proof of Concept

The blockchain is the component where all transactions recorded on the network are stored. In Hyperledger Fabric, its structure is more complex, as each transaction includes digital signatures generated with the private keys of its creators. In addition, peer nodes that validate and approve these transactions also add their signatures to the blocks.

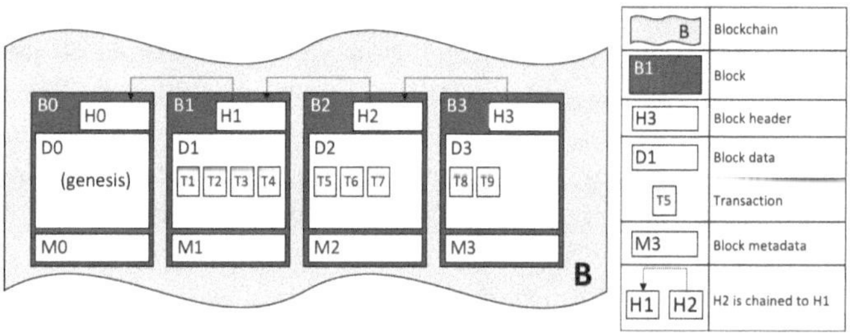

Fig. 4. Hyperledger Fabric blockchain structure—Taken from [16].

In Hyperledger Fabric, the integrity of the data in the blockchain is validated by verifying blocks and transactions. At the block level, the continuity of the chain is ensured by checking that the hash of the previous block matches the stored hash in the current block, avoiding alterations in the history. It also verifies that the hash of the current block corresponds to its content, ensuring that it has not been modified. In addition, metadata signatures and configurations are validated to confirm that the blocks have been issued by authorized entities and that the network configuration is consistent and legitimate. For transactions, checks are performed on the digital signatures on the headers and approvals, ensuring that the identities involved belong to authorized entities within the Membership Service Provider (MSP). It is validated that the signatures of the approvers are legitimate and correspond to the content approved in the transaction, ensuring that the consensus has been followed correctly.

In the Hyperledger Fabric blockchain structure, data integrity is enforced by specific cryptographic mechanisms. First, all blocks are cryptographically linked using **SHA256** hash keys, where every block header contains the hash of the previous block, creating an immutable chain[cite: 164, 165]. Second, every transaction is secured using the **Elliptic Curve Digital Signature Algorithm (ECDSA)**. Through the **Membership Service Provider (MSP)**, each participant is issued a public/private key pair. Transactions are signed with the creator's private key, ensuring both authenticity and integrity, as any alteration to the transaction data would invalidate the signature. To assess the integrity of the data, the on-chain records of measurements and simulations—such as the data hashes, metadata, and collaborator names—are directly modified within the file that stores the blockchain, and any alterations are verified using the Blockchain Verifier tool, developed by Hyperledger Fabric. This test simulates a direct attack on the ledger's integrity, while the large scientific data files themselves remain untouched in their off-chain storage locations.

4 Results

For integrity validation testing, the blockchain file was directly manipulated, which represents an extreme scenario in which the robustness of the data integrity mechanism can be demonstrated. By modifying the underlying ledger directly, the test bypassed application-level protections to challenge the blockchain's core safeguards. The resulting hash mismatches clearly exposed the tampering, demonstrating how blockchain ensures tamper-evidence through its cryptographic chaining of transactions. Moreover, since each block is interlinked and verified through consensus, even isolated changes disrupt the ledger's integrity and can be reliably flagged.

However, this type of tampering is unlikely in a real environment. For this experiment, thirteen pieces of data were randomly selected from all transactions. The results of the block-level verification are shown in Fig. 5, highlighting the hash mismatches that occur when on-chain data is tampered with.** The results are in format JSON[5].

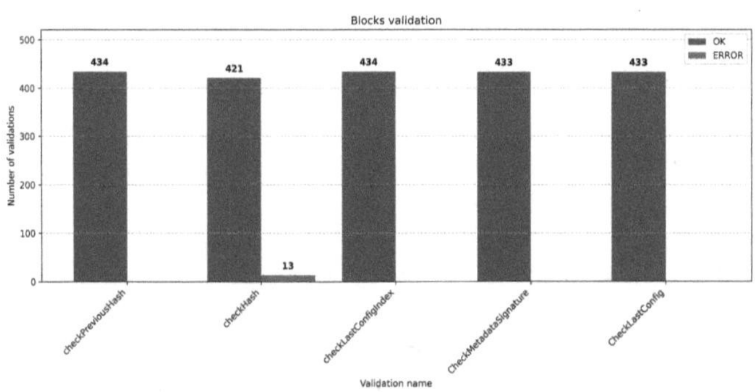

Fig. 5. Blocks validation.

When analyzing the manipulated data with **Blockchain Verifier**, several specific anomalies were detected that confirmed the tampering. First, it was evident that the hash of the manipulated block's content no longer matched the

[5] Results repository: https://github.com/GSMier/ProyectoLago/tree/main/resultados.

original data hash stored in its header, which is the primary indicator of a data breach. The tool also revealed an unexpected behavior in Hyperledger Fabric: the hash of the block stored in its own header was not recalculated after the content was modified, which could complicate tampering detection if not for other checks. Furthermore, as shown in Fig. 6, the tampering invalidated numerous transaction signatures. In this case, **65 digital signatures** failed validation, confirming that the integrity of individual transactions was also compromised.

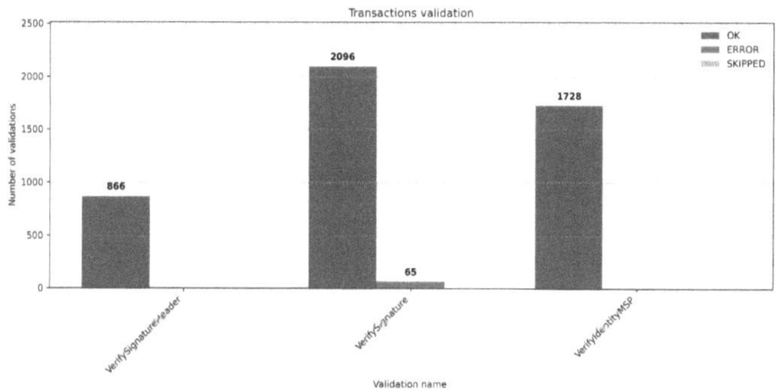

Fig. 6. Transactions validation.

The validation of transactions in **Hyperledger Fabric** heavily relies on the digital signatures generated via the **Membership Service Provider (MSP)**. The MSP is responsible for issuing cryptographic identities to all authorized participants. Each transaction is then signed using the private key associated with a participant's identity. These digital signatures, which are directly dependent on the transaction's payload, serve two critical functions. First, they provide authentication, proving the transaction was created by a legitimate network member. Second, they ensure integrity, as any change to the transaction data after it has been signed would cause the signature verification to fail. This adds a crucial layer of security, as each transaction contains individually verifiable proof from its endorsers and owner, allowing any alteration to be quickly detected by a signature mismatch.

In this case, 65 signatures did not pass validation. This is because each transaction may contain one or more signatures, depending on the number of passing signatures required for validation. In the case of the **ScientificDataCollection** chaincode, four signatures are required to approve a transaction. It is important to consider that there are other chaincodes in execution, such as the one corresponding to the life cycle for the implementation of a new **chaincode**.

5 Discussion

Blockchain, as a decentralized ledger technology, offers a promising solution to various challenges faced by large-scale scientific infrastructures by enabling and supporting high-performance computing (HPC) distributed systems. Blockchain improves the use of dormant computational resources across the entire range of an advanced computing continuum, from edge devices to cloud computing capabilities and storage. Regarding applications, deploying blockchain to establish decentralized HPC marketplaces, in alignment with other blockchain initiatives, promotes the sustainability and shared economy of computational power [17]. However, within this context, the contribution of resources and data remains a contentious topic, requiring further discussion to assess the value of these resources and data accurately. For instance, in terms of cost efficiency, blockchain capitalizes on underutilized resources by allowing blockchain-based HPC platforms to significantly reduce the expenses related to large-scale computation compared to traditional supercomputers or cloud computing services. However, to ensure the benefits, it is crucial to enhance trust and security, and the blockchain's inherent transparency and immutability guarantee that computational tasks are carried out securely, data integrity supported and that participants are compensated.

More work must be done in order to prevent data manipulation. Due to the size of data samples for LAGO and many other HPC projects around the world, it is not feasible to store all data in the Blockchain, but recording hashes and other metadata must serve as a way for scientists to check data integrity and validate all research groups are working with the same samples independently of time and place.

6 Conclusions and Further Work

The development of a blockchain-based prototype for scientific data integrity demonstrated the feasibility of using Hyperledger Fabric to enhance secure access, traceability, and tamper-evidence in the management of large-scale distributed datasets processed in HPC clusters. Applied to a subset of the LAGO project's public data, the prototype showed that blockchain can effectively support the immutability and verifiability of scientific records, even when stored in decentralized and heterogeneous environments.

The cryptographic mechanisms of the blockchain infrastructure ensure that any unauthorized alteration in the dataset is immediately detectable, fulfilling the requirements for scientific reproducibility and trust. By ensuring that the data has not been altered, it avoids the need to reprocess large volumes of information, a task that, in high-performance computing (HPC) contexts, involves a high energy cost. This benefit is particularly relevant in projects such as LAGO, where data is extensive and costly to generate.

During implementation, challenges arose in node synchronization and consistency, particularly when peers lost connectivity. This loss of connection directly impacted the prototype's reliability, creating a vulnerability where a node's local ledger could become inconsistent with the rest of the network. Submitting transactions to such a node resulted in errors due to the mismatch of data and hashes, threatening the system's integrity. These issues were addressed at the application level by implementing a mechanism to block transactions to peers in a corrupted state, while a re-initialization process was integrated to restore system consistency once connectivity was re-established. However, such challenges underscore the importance of further work in improving scalability, fault tolerance, and operational automation for deployment in full production environments.

Relying on other technologies in demand, such as Artificial Intelligence (AI), could benefit both in their weak points, in terms of traceability, interoperability, and scalability. Including AI with blockchain and HPC is part of our ongoing work.

Acknowledgments. The authors thank the CYTED co-funded LAGO-INDICA network (524RT0159-LAGO-INDICA: Infraestructura digital de ciencia abierta) and the Universidad Industrial de Santander (UIS), especially the research group Cómputo Avanzado y a Gran Escala (CAGE), for their institutional support and the resources provided for this work. AI technology was used to proofread and polish this manuscript (OpenAI, 2025; Gemini, 2025).

References

1. Fill, H.-G., Meier, A. (eds.): Blockchain. EH, Springer, Wiesbaden (2020). https://doi.org/10.1007/978-3-658-28006-2
2. Silva, G., Klôh, V., Yokoyama, A., Gritz, M., Schulze, B., Ferro, M.: SMCis: Scientific Applications Monitoring and Prediction for HPC Environments. In: Bianchini, C., Osthoff, C., Souza, P., Ferreira, R. (eds.) WSCAD 2018. CCIS, vol. 1171, pp. 69–84. Springer, Cham (2020). https://doi.org/10.1007/978-3-030-41050-6_5
3. Mantripragada, K., Binotto, A., Tizzei, L.P.: A Self-adaptive Auto-scaling Method for Scientific Applications on HPC Environments and Clouds. arXiv.org (2015)
4. LAGO Project Homepage. https://lagoproject.net/. Accessed 15 May 2025
5. Iván Sidelnik, Hernán Asorey
6. Sidelnik, I., Asorey, H., Guarin, N., Durán, M.S., Bessia, Horacio Arnaldi, L., Gómez Berisso, M., Lipovetzky, J., Pérez, M., Haro, M.S. Jerónimo Blostein, J.,
7. Rubio-Montero, A.J., Pagan-Munoz, R., Mayo-Garcia, R., Pardo-Diaz, A., Sidelnik, I., Asorey, H.: A novel cloud-based framework for standardized simulations in the Latin American giant observatory (LAGO). In: 2021 Winter Simulation Conference (WSC), pp. 1–12 (2021)
8. LAGO Collaboration (2022). *The LAGO Data Management Plan (DMP) document 1.1.* Accessed 10 May 2025
9. CompTIA: 7 Phases of Blockchain Implementation. https://www.mspinsights.com/doc/phases-of-blockchain-implementation-0001. Accessed 18 May 2025
10. Raj, P., Deka, G.C.: Blockchain technology: platforms, tools and use cases. Academic Press, an imprint of Elsevier, Cambridge, MA (2018)
11. What's New in Hyperledger Fabric v2.5. https://hyperledger-fabric.readthedocs.io/en/release-2.5/whatsnew.html#what-s-new-in-hyperledger-fabric-v2-5. Accessed 18 May 2025
12. Coelho, R., Braga, R., David, J.M.N., Stroele, V., Campos, F., Dantas, M.: BlockFlow: blockchain-based architecture for trust and traceability in collaborative scientific experimentation. J. (Dordrecht) (2022)

13. Hoopes, R., Hardy, H., Long, M., Dagher, G.G.: SciLedger: a blockchain-based scientific workflow provenance and data sharing platform. In: 2022 IEEE 8th International Conference on Collaboration and Internet Computing (CIC), pp. 125–134. IEEE (2022)
14. Zhang, F., Wang, Z., Guo, R., Qu, G.: Earth observation data provenance: a blockchain-based solution. IEEE Trans. Ind. Inf. **20**(7), 9548–9556 (2024)
15. Xu, H., Zhang, L., Liu, Y., Cao, B.: RAFT based wireless blockchain networks in the presence of malicious jamming. IEEE Wireless Commun. Lett. **9**(6), 817–821 (2020)
16. Hyperledger Fabric Documentation. https://hyperledger-fabric.readthedocs.io/en/latest/ledger/ledger.html. Accessed 14 May 2025
17. Griffin, M.: Entrepreneurs think Blockchain is the future of cloud computing and HPC. 311 Institute (2018)

A Scalable and Reproducible Parsl Framework for Molecular Evolutionary Analyses on HPC Systems

Rafael Terra[1(✉)], Hugo Oliveira[1], Daniel Janies[3,4], Hiago Rocha[1], Diego Carvalho[2], Carla Osthoff[1], and Kary Ocaña[1]

[1] National Laboratory for Scientific Computing, Petrópolis, RJ, Brazil
{rafaelst,hugodpo,mayk,osthoff,karyann}@lncc.br

[2] Federal Center for Technological Education Celso Suckow da Fonseca, RJ, Brazil
d.carvalho@ieee.org

[3] Center for Computational Intelligence to Predict Health and Environmental Risks, University of North Carolina at Charlotte, Charlotte, NC, USA
djanies@charlotte.edu

[4] Department of Bioinformatics and Genomics, University of North Carolina at Charlotte, Charlotte, NC, USA

Abstract. Codon-based model testing is fundamental to molecular evolution studies. The growing complexity of these analyses – driven by computationally intensive likelihood estimations, memory-demanding datasets, and the need to scale across hundreds or thousands of genes – necessitates efficient use of high-performance computing resources. To address this need, we present HighSPA, a scalable and reproducible framework that integrates two widely used tools for evolutionary analysis – CodeML and HyPhy – into parallel workflows using the Parsl library. We validated HighSPA using DENV genomes from Brazil (serotypes 14), applying six codon substitution models. When using the CodeML workflow, HighSPA identified high-confidence positively selected sites (PSS) with serotype-specific patterns. In contrast, the HyPhy workflow detected fewer PSS, likely due to its more conservative inference approach. In terms of performance, HighSPA-HyPhy significantly reduced makespan and increased throughput – by an average of 87× and 89×, respectively – compared to the sequential execution of the analyses. These results support the presence of adaptive evolution in key genes such as *E*, *NS3*, and *NS5*, and demonstrate HighSPA's effectiveness for large-scale evolutionary analysis.

Keywords: Scientific Workflows · High-Performance Computing · Evolutionary Analysis

1 Introduction

Bioinformatics plays a central role in modern biological research, providing computational tools and scalable workflows for large-scale genomic analysis [15].

K. Brown et al. (Eds.): CARLA 2025, CCIS 2750, pp. 191–205, 2026.
https://doi.org/10.1007/978-3-032-24923-4_13

Evolutionary analyses [18], including phylogenetic reconstruction, detection of positive selection, and molecular epidemiology, are essential for uncovering mechanisms of disease progression, immune escape, and drug resistance, as seen in studies of dengue and human immunodeficiency virus [9]. In this context, codon-based model testing, i.e., analysis of coding sequences to estimate substitution rates, is a fundamental approach in molecular evolution, widely applied to detect signatures of selection along phylogenetic branches [4,13].

As genomic data continues to grow exponentially, especially in virology and epidemiology, robust, scalable, and reproducible evolutionary inference becomes increasingly critical. Therefore, efficient use of HPC resources is essential to handle the large volume of computational tasks and intermediate data generated. Scientific workflows provide an effective solution by modeling the experiment as a set of interdependent tasks and can be executed and managed by Scientific Workflow Management Systems (SWfMS) [3], which orchestrate task execution, handle data dependencies, allocate computational resources, and ensure fault tolerance and reproducibility. Thus, SWfMSs enable parallel and scalable execution, making them well-suited for large-scale evolutionary analyses [18].

This work addresses the computational challenges of scaling positive selection analyses across large viral genomic datasets – a critical need in both evolutionary research and epidemic response. Traditional tools such as CodeML [18] and HyPhy [10] offer well-established models for detecting selection but employ orthogonal strategies to solve the problem. CodeML tends to be more time-consuming, especially for large alignments, but often produces more accurate results. In contrast, HyPhy is faster but yields more conservative outcomes due to stricter statistical thresholds.

To overcome these limitations, we present an HPC-aware framework, HighSPA (High-Performance Selection Pressure Analysis), which automates and parallelizes both tools across hundreds of alignments and gene partitions. HighSPA is built on Parsl [1], a parallel scripting library for orchestrating workflows in HPC environments. By assigning CodeML and HyPhy distinct analytical roles – one favoring model depth, the other computational efficiency – the framework balances exploratory breadth with statistical rigor, allowing users to choose based on their expertise, the characteristics of the input gene sequences, and the required accuracy for the analysis. This design enables high-throughput, reproducible analyses of selection patterns in viral genomes, even under real-time constraints such as outbreak monitoring.

In summary, our contributions with the HighSPA framework are threefold:

- **Workflow modeling**: The HighSPA framework defines two distinct workflows for selection pressure analysis, each leveraging the strengths of either CodeML or HyPhy, and selectable based on user preference.
- **Automated data and task management**: HighSPA simplifies execution on HPC resources by automatically managing intermediate data and task scheduling, requiring only initial configuration and input from the end user.
- **High-performance execution**: Results obtained using an HPC infrastructure consisting of 4 computing nodes show that HighSPA can manage the

execution of multiple input files in a single run. Using HyPhy, makespan is reduced by 87× and throughput increases by 89×, on average. With CodeML, makespan is reduced by 31× and throughput increases by 21×.

The remainder of this manuscript is organized as follows: Sect. 2 reviews related work; Sect. 3 provides background; Sect. 4 introduces the HighSPA framework; Sect. 5 describes the experimental methodology; Sect. 6 presents the results; and Sect. 7 concludes with a summary and future directions.

2 Related Works

There are many open-source software to explore insights in computational evolution data (see Table 1). However, leveraging these open-source technologies in a scalable way is still a challenge for analysts or users who are not familiar with HPC technologies. Motivated by that, we developed the HighSPA framework to be a reproducible, scalable, and shareable framework modeled with bioinformatics HPC workflow managers and environments.

Other groups have developed workflows to simplify molecular evolution analysis, including the workflows/software CodeML, SciEvol [8], EasyCodeML [4], SlimCodeML [13], FastCodeML [16], CuCodeML [11], BABAPPA [14], GWideCodeML [6], ete-evol [5], LMAP [7], and HyPhy/Datamonkey [10]. While these worflows/software have some characteristics and packages in common with HighSPA, features such as package management software or reporting functionalities can vary considerably. Table 1 presents a comparison of features in HighSPA workflows with other molecular evolution workflows. We manually extracted information on each workflow's computational environment, language, and organism from its original publication and homepage.

Our Contributions. As shown in Table 1, HighSPA and SciEvol are the only workflows using scientific workflow management systems (Parsl and SciCumulus, respectively), while the others are standalone pipelines. SciEvol runs in the cloud, which can lead to variable resource availability, data transfer delays, and higher costs, potentially impacting performance and reproducibility. Most other tools run locally or on clusters but lack full automation and scalability on HPC systems. HighSPA's Python-based Parsl workflows enable efficient, parallel execution and resource management on dedicated HPC infrastructure, supporting large-scale, reproducible selection pressure analyses beyond current approaches. Moreover, HighSPA is orthogonal to existing scientific workflows, meaning that CodeML and HyPhy tools can be replaced with minimal changes. HighSPA is a flexible, extensible framework that supports additional workflows while delivering performance and scalability benefits.

3 Background

This section introduces key concepts and tools used throughout the paper. It: (i) provides background on Dengue viruses (Sect. 3.1); (ii) describes the computational molecular evolution tools used in this work (Sect. 3.2); and (iii) explains Parsl, the SWfMS on which HighSPA is built (Sect. 3.3).

Table 1. Comparison of HighSPA with common selection pressure analysis tools.

Workflow	Reference	SWfMS	Environment	Language	Organism
CodeML	[18]	-	Local	ANSI C	-
SciEvol	[8]	SciCumulus	Cloud	-	Protozoans
EasyCodeML	[4]	-	Local/Cluster	Java	Primates
SlimCodeML	[13]	-	Local/Cluster	ISO C++ Standard 1998	Primates, *Euteleostomi*
FastCodeML	[16]	-	Local/Cluster	ISO C++ 2003	Primates, *Euteleostomi*
CuCodeML	[11]	-	Local	CUDA	Primates, *Euteleostomi*
BABAPPA	[14]	-	Local	Bash and Python	*Brassicaceae* species
GWideCodeML	[6]	-	Local	Python	*Saccharomyces*
ete-evol	[5]	-	Local	Python	-
LMAP	[7]	-	Local/Cluster	Perl	Turtle species
HyPhy/Datamonkey	[10]	-	Local/Cluster/Cloud	ANSI C++	-
HighSPA (Ours)	**Own**	**Parsl**	**Local/Cluster**	**Python**	**DENV**

3.1 Dengue Virus

Dengue viruses (family Flaviviridae) are the etiological agents of dengue fever, primarily transmitted by mosquitoes of the genus Aedes. Their widespread circulation in tropical and subtropical regions – particularly in endemic countries like Brazil – poses serious public health challenges, driven by recurrent outbreaks and the emergence of severe clinical forms such as dengue hemorrhagic fever and dengue shock syndrome [12]. Dengue viruses are grouped into four antigenically distinct serotypes (DENV-1 to DENV-4). Each serotype is subdivided into 21 recognized genotypes: six for DENV-1, six DENV-2, five DENV-3, and four DENV-4.

3.2 Computational Molecular Evolutionary Analysis

Understanding selective pressures on protein-coding genes is central to molecular evolution. A key metric in this context is the omega (ω) parameter, which represents the ratio of non-synonymous (d_N) and synonymous (d_S) substitutions in coding deoxyribonucleic acid (DNA) sequences. This ratio ($\omega = d_N/d_S$) provides insights into the selective pressures acting on genes, such as purifying selection ($\omega < 1$), neutral evolution ($\omega \approx 1$), or positive selection ($\omega > 1$) [2].

To identify site- or lineage-specific signals of selection, statistical frameworks like maximum likelihood estimation (MLE) are commonly used [13]. Likelihood Ratio Tests (LRTs) compare nested evolutionary models to detect positive selection and infer adaptive changes at specific sites or along particular branches. The widespread adoption of these approaches has resulted in the development of robust computational tools and extensively used, such as CodeML and HyPhy.

CodeML [18] is a widely used tool implementing codon-based evolutionary models; yet, it operates as a single-threaded, CPU-bound process. Analyzing an alignment of 100 sequences may take hours or even days on a high-performance machine, and processing hundreds of alignments serially can extend runtimes to days or weeks on a single workstation. In contrast, HyPhy [10] offers a more flexible and extensible platform that supports a broad range of selection detection methods with partial parallelization capabilities and is maintained by an active and contemporary user community. Despite their strengths and popularity, CodeML and HyPhy differ in workflow and interface, posing challenges to their integration into seamless, large-scale, and high-throughput evolutionary workflows [15]. Below, we briefly review the characteristics and methodologies of CodeML and HyPhy in the context of computational evolution analysis.

CodeML: Model-Based Inference. CodeML is a classic tool that implements a suite of codon substitution models for molecular evolutionary analysis. These models – including M0, M1a, M2a, M3, M7, and M8 – enable detection of selection by assuming different distributions of ω among codons [18]. The simplest model, M0, assumes a single ω across all sites, providing a baseline for overall selective pressure. In contrast, M3 allows for multiple discrete site classes with distinct ω values, capturing variation in selection along the sequence.

More powerful tests for detecting positive selection include the comparisons M1a (Nearly Neutral, allowing only $\omega \leq 1$) vs. M2a (Positive Selection, allowing $\omega > 1$), and M7 (beta-distributed $\omega \leq 1$) vs. M8 (beta + positive selection class). These model pairs are evaluated using the LRT, where twice the difference in log-likelihoods ($2\Delta\ell$) is compared to a chi-square distribution with degrees of freedom equal to the difference in the number of free parameters – typically 2. A significant LRT result suggests that the more complex model including positively selected sites provides a better fit to the data. Once a model with $\omega > 1$ is supported, CodeML identifies candidate sites under selection using the Bayes Empirical Bayes (BEB) method, which accounts for uncertainty in parameter estimates and is preferred over the simpler Naïve Empirical Bayes (NEB) approach [18]. Codons with BEB posterior probability ≥ 0.95 are interpreted as having strong evidence of positive selection.

Despite its methodological robustness, CodeML's scalability is hindered by its single-threaded, CPU-bound design. However, when executing multiple models, CodeML can benefit from the parallelization in HPC environments, where workflow orchestration tools like Parsl can enable scalable, automated execution.

HyPhy: Flexible Selection Models with Partial Parallelization. HyPhy (Hypothesis Testing Using Phylogenies) offers a more flexible and extensible platform for evolutionary analyses. Unlike CodeML, it includes a wide array of selection detection methods such as MEME (Mixed Effects Model of Evolution), FEL (Fixed Effects Likelihood), FUBAR (Fast Unconstrained Bayesian Approximation), aBSREL (Adaptive Branch-Site Random Effects Likelihood), NY (model based on the Nielsen-Yang framework), and SLAC (Single Likelihood Ancestor Counting), which are tailored to different types of evolutionary hypotheses, including episodic or pervasive selection [10].

HyPhy supports both *site-* and *branch-specific* analyses and provides a scripting language (Batch Language) and graphical user interface, in addition to its command-line mode. Due to its built-in parallelization, modular design and scripting capabilities make it well-suited for integration into distributed computing pipelines, especially when orchestrated using workflow tools like Parsl to coordinate large-scale, automated executions.

3.3 The Parsl Library

Parsl is a parallel programming library developed in Python that uses decorators to run functions and external software as *python apps* and *bash apps*, leveraging native language features. This design allows for intuitive workflow definition and configuration directly in Python [1]. Parsl is highly modular and portable, separating workflow logic from execution configuration through abstractions known as executors and providers. As a result, workflows can be executed across heterogeneous computing environments, such as local machines, clusters, and cloud platforms with little or no modification to the workflow logic. Additionally, Parsl includes a monitoring module that enables users to track workflow behavior and provides basic provenance of the executed tasks [1].

4 HighSPA Framework

HighSPA is a framework designed to perform large-scale evolutionary analyses of multiple models and inputs in a single run, using the computing power of HPC environments. The framework orchestrates a sequence of bioinformatics tasks, automating data processing steps such as sequence alignment, format conversion, phylogenetic inference, and evolutionary model testing. HighSPA supports two possible workflows: one based on CodeML and another based on HyPhy. The framework is highly modular, promoting portability, ease of use, and ease of maintenance, while also enabling component replacement and extension.

A conceptual overview of the framework is shown in Fig. 1. Since the framework focuses on selection pressure analysis, the two workflow models – HyPhy (top) and CodeML (bottom) – are specifically designed for this purpose. In the following sections, we provide a detailed explanation of the execution flow.

Inputs. Upon execution (*Start*), HighSPA receives input from the user in the form of a folder path (*Folder containing FASTA files*). This folder contains multiple files, each with several genetic sequences. HighSPA processes files in multi-FASTA format – a standard text-based format where each sequence is preceded by a header line. In addition to the input files, the user must specify which workflow to execute (either CodeML or HyPhy). This choice can be guided by the user's expertise, knowledge of the input gene characteristics, or desired accuracy of the selection analysis. Next, HighSPA executes multiple workflow instances in parallel using the selected model (CodeML or HyPhy), with one instance per input file. In the following sections, we describe the execution of each workflow individually.

HighSPA-CodeML Workflow. While there are input files to process (*∃ files to process?*), the CodeML workflow is executed in parallel (referred to as HighSPA-CodeML). Each instance receives a multi-FASTA file (*Multi-FASTA file*) and

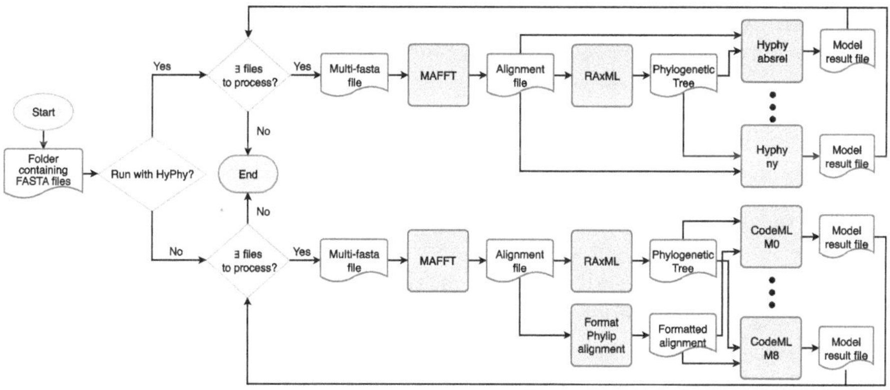

Fig. 1. Conceptual view of the HighSPA framework.

performs multiple sequence alignment (MSA) using MAFFT. This step produces a MSA file (*Alignment file*), which serves as input to two subsequent tasks: (*i*) RAxML and (*ii*)*Format phylip alignment.* In (*i*), RAxML reconstructs a phylogenetic tree from the aligned sequences using the maximum likelihood method, estimating the tree that best explains the observed genetic variations. Its output is a *phylogenetic tree* file representing the inferred evolutionary relationships among the sequences. On the other hand, in (*ii*), the format conversion task adapts the alignment file into PHYLIP format, which is required for CodeML execution. The outputs of both RAxML and the PHYLIP conversion – the phylogenetic tree and the formatted alignment – are then used as input for six distinct CodeML executions, each applying a specific codon substitution model: *M0*, *M1*, *M2*, *M3*, *M7*, and *M8*. The results of these executions are organized into model-specific directories for structured post-analysis (*Model result file*).

HighSPA-HyPhy Workflow. The execution flow of the HyPhy workflow (referred to as HighSPA-HyPhy) is similar to that of HighSPA-CodeML, with a key distinction: the output generated by MAFFT does not require reformatting before it can be used as input for HyPhy. Initially, the input multi-FASTA file (*Multi-FASTA file*) undergoes multiple sequence alignment using MAFFT, producing an *Alignment file*. Next, *RAxML* is executed to infer the phylogenetic relationships among the aligned sequences, generating a corresponding *phylogenetic tree* file. Such output is then passed to six distinct HyPhy analyses, each applying a different codon-based model designed to detect various patterns of natural selection: *NY*, *MEME*, *SLAC*, *FUBAR*, *FEL*, and *aBSREL*. As with CodeML, the results of each model are stored in dedicated directories to support structured downstream analysis (*Model result file*).

Output. As mentioned, the output of both workflows – HighSPA-CodeML and HighSPA-HyPhy – is a set of *model result files*, each corresponding to a specific evolutionary model applied. These files contain detailed statistical outputs and selection analysis metrics (e.g., dN/dS ratios, p-values), which are intended to be interpreted by the domain expert using HighSPA to draw biological conclusions about the evolutionary pressures acting on the input genetic sequences.

4.1 Software Availability

The HighSPA source code is openly available on its GitHub repository: https://github.com/karyocana/HighSPA, which also includes detailed instructions for executing it on both local machines and SLURM-managed HPC clusters. In addition to the inputs described in Sect. 4, HighSPA provides a set of configurable parameters, allowing users to customize their execution. These include enabling or disabling the monitoring module – which tracks resource usage and execution metrics (e.g., CPU utilization, memory consumption, task durations) throughout the workflow – selecting the execution environment (local or SLURM-based), and specifying the output directory for results. While these parameters do not alter HighSPA's core execution flow and are therefore not detailed in this paper, comprehensive documentation is available in the GitHub repository.

5 Methodology

In this section, we describe our experimental methodology. All the scripts and datasets will be available in the GitHub repository, as explained in Sect. 4.1.

5.1 Datasets

Our experimental evaluation utilizes dengue virus (DENV) genomes (serotypes DENV-1 to DENV-4) sampled in Brazil. These genomes were retrieved from the Bacterial and Viral Bioinformatics Resource Center (BV-BRC) database[1]. We performed manual curation to extract the coding sequences (CDSs) for each gene, *resulting in a collection of ten distinct datasets, one for each gene*: *C*, *prM*, *E*, *NS1*, *NS2A*, *NS2B*, *NS3*, *NS4A*, *NS4B*, and *NS5*. Considering the four dengue virus serotypes (DENV 1–4), our dataset comprises a total of 40 individual input files, covering all ten genes across each serotype.

5.2 Execution Setup

Experiments were run on a HPC cluster composed of four compute nodes. Each node is equipped with 2× 24-core Intel Xeon Gold 6248R CPUs @ 3.00 GHz (48 cores per node) and 48GB of RAM, totaling 192 cores and 384GB of memory across the cluster. The cluster employs SLURM as its workload manager for job scheduling and resource allocation. The software used to run HighSPA includes Parsl v1.2, MAFFT v7.525, RAxML v8.2.13, CodeML (from the PAML package v4.10.7), and HyPhy v2.5.67. All experiments were executed using Python v3.12.

[1] https://www.bv-brc.org/.

6 Results

This section presents our results in two parts: (i) HighSPA's performance based on makespan and throughput (Sect. 6.1); and (ii) the quality of HighSPA's execution on the DENV1-4 dataset (Sect. 6.2).

6.1 Performance-Wise

We begin by evaluating the **makespan**, i.e., the total time required to complete all tasks from start to finish, as achieved by HighSPA. We compare HighSPA to the sequential execution of all tasks in the workflow, which is equivalent to executing the workflow on a single-core machine or employing a single worker. Table 2 presents these results. Notably, HighSPA outperforms the sequential execution approach due to its ability to execute multiple tasks in parallel by distributing tasks across multiple nodes, with each node containing 48 workers. HighSPA is, on average, 87× faster and up to 109× faster when using 4 nodes for HighSPA-HyPhy, and 31× faster on average, reaching up to 35× with 4 nodes for HighSPA-CodeML, as presented in Fig. 2.

Table 2. Makespan (in minutes) and throughput (tasks per minute) achieved by HighSPA under different node configurations, using the DENV 1–4 dataset.

Node Configuration	Makespan HighSPA-HyPhy (min)	Throughput HighSPA-HyPhy (tasks/min)	Makespan HighSPA-CodeML (min)	Throughput HighSPA-CodeML (tasks/min)
Sequential	2148.18	0.17	51523.30	0.01
2-Nodes	30.30	11.88	1661.55	0.22
3-Nodes	23.43	15.36	1860.50	0.19
4-Nodes	19.65	18.32	1445.92	0.24

Now, regarding **throughput** – which measures the number of tasks completed per unit of time (e.g., tasks/min), and is shown in the second and fourth columns of Table 2 – HighSPA also outperforms the sequential execution. This improvement is expected, as HighSPA is capable of executing multiple tasks simultaneously. On average, the throughput increases by 89×, reaching up to 107× when executed on 4 nodes for HighSPA-HyPhy, and by 21× on average, up to 24×, for HighSPA-CodeML.

To further investigate HighSPA's throughput and utilization of HPC resources, Fig. 3 shows the number of CPU cores used by HighSPA throughout the workflow execution (y-axis) over time in seconds (x-axis). Figure 3a corresponds to CodeML, and Fig. 3b to HyPhy. Each figure presents results for different numbers of compute nodes, distinguished by different colors. These results, together with those in Table 2, further highlight HighSPA's ability to scale with increasing computational resources, particularly when running CodeML.

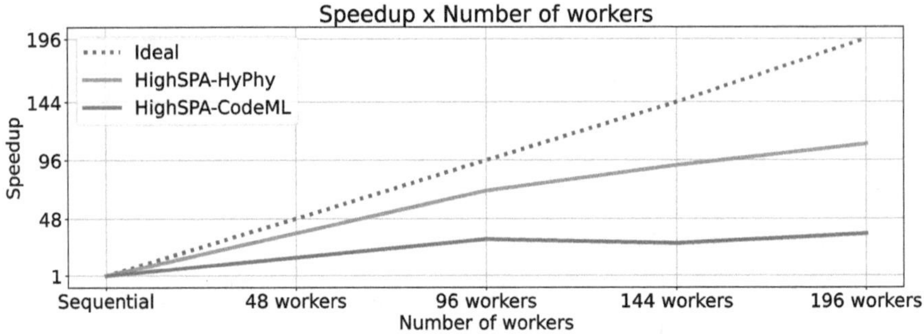

Fig. 2. Speedup by the number of workers for the HighSPA execution.

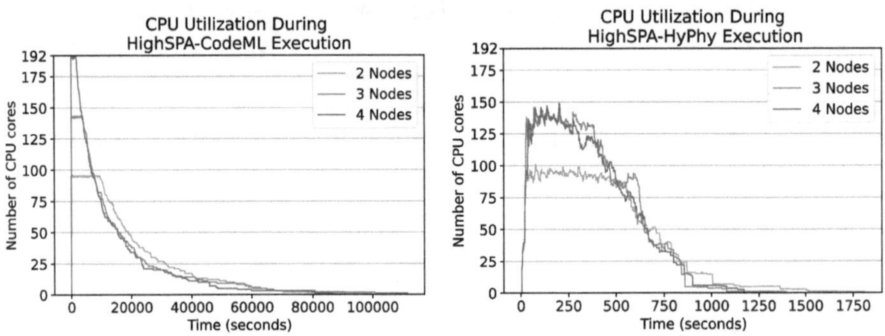

(a) (b)

Fig. 3. Comparison of CPU usage in HighSPA-CodeML (left) and HighSPA-HyPhy (right) throughout the workflow execution.

Due to CodeML's longer execution time, the parallel execution environment provided by HighSPA-CodeML benefits significantly from a high-performance network infrastructure, which helps explain its maximum throughput when executed on four nodes. The dataset consists of 40 input files, each with 6 models, resulting in a total of 240 CodeML tasks (6 tasks per file $\times$ 40 files) that are distributed efficiently across 4 nodes, each with 40 cores.

On the other hand, it is worth noting that HighSPA's execution with CodeML takes longer than with HyPhy (HighSPA-CodeML takes, in average, 60$\times$ longer to execute.). The performance of HighSPA when executing HyPhy stagnates with 3 nodes, *i.e.*, there are almost no improvements when using more than 3 nodes. This behavior occurs because the workload used in the experiment is insufficient to fully utilize the available resources. Although the same task distribution is maintained (6 tasks per file $\times$ 40 files $=$ 240 HyPhy tasks), the input data, which originates from a real-world scenario, resulted in shorter execution times for the HyPhy tasks. Consequently, the number of available cores exceeds the number of parallelizable tasks running simultaneously, limiting the degree of parallelism and causing the use of additional nodes beyond three to be largely ineffective in terms of performance gains.

As previously discussed, CodeML tends to be more time-consuming, particularly for large alignments, but it often produces more accurate results. In contrast, HyPhy executes faster but yields more conservative outcomes due to stricter statistical thresholds, as will be shown in the solution quality evaluation in Sect. 6.2. In fact, the average execution time of a single task using CodeML is 408.30 minutes, compared to just 15.10 minutes for HyPhy.

Finally, to illustrate the high degree of parallelism enabled by HighSPA, Fig. 4 shows the Directed Acyclic Graph (DAG) from CodeML execution on the DENV1-4 dataset. A similar DAG is also produced for HyPhy and across other datasets. In this figure, each colored circle represents a task that HighSPA must execute (refer to Fig. 1 for a one-to-one correspondence), and the straight lines indicate dependency relationships between tasks. Notably, all tasks in the same frontier (e.g., red, purple, green, or yellow) can be executed simultaneously, as they are independent of each other. As our results demonstrate, HighSPA exploits this high degree of parallelism to execute tasks as early as possible, thereby making more efficient use of HPC resources and significantly improving both makespan and throughput in sequence alignment workflows.

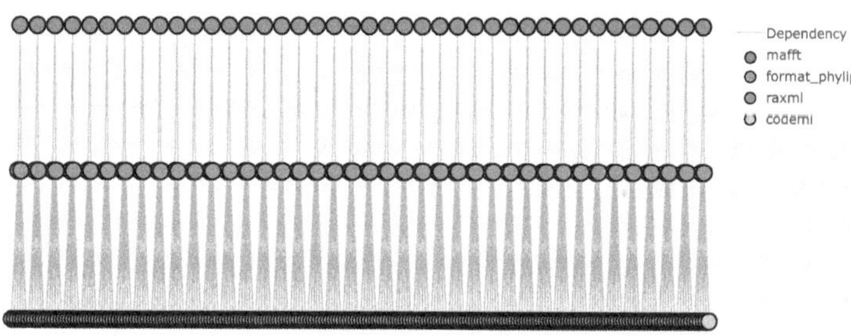

Fig. 4. HighSPA-CodeML workflow Directed Acyclic Graph (DAG) generated during the execution on the DENV1-4 datasets.

6.2 Solution-Wise

Table 3 summarizes the key positively selected sites (PSS) identified by both HighSPA-CodeML and HighSPA-HyPhy workflows within the HighSPA framework. This comparison highlights the complementary detection patterns of the two methods and demonstrates the effectiveness of our framework in executing multiple models in parallel for robust, genome-wide evolutionary analyses.

We used HighSPA-CodeML with the M8 model to detect PSS in complete Brazilian DENV genomes. High-confidence PSS (BEB $\geq$ 0.95) were identified in both structural and non-structural genes, with notable serotype-specific

Table 3. PSS detected by CodeML (M8) and HyPhy (FUBAR and NY) models across DENV genes and serotypes using HighSPA. Sites with BEB ≥ 0.90 are shown in **bold**; * indicates BEB ≥ 0.95, ** indicates BEB ≥ 0.99. Blue rows mark DENV-2 *NS3* and DENV-3 *E*, discussed in the text. Entries with BEB ≤ 0.75 or no positive selection were omitted. Full table is on the HighSPA GitHub.

Serotype	Gene	CodeML model	HyPhy model	
		M8	FUBAR	NY (M8)
DENV-1	*C*	26 G 0.890	**26 (0.900)**	**26 (0.999**)**
	E	297 M 0.797	None	None
	NS1	48 K 0.598, 77 Y 0.688, 93 A 0.870, 105 R 0.540, 131 A 0.623, 146 D 0.538, 175 H 0.694, 251 I 0.726, 293 Y 0.676	None	None
	NS2A	41 L 0.609, 67 R 0.699, 81 F 0.813, 158 F 0.522, 213 K 0.761	**213 (0.918)**	None
	NS3	252 H 0.771, 474 I 0.708	None	None
	NS4B	**34 R 0.964***	None	**34 (0.994**)**
	NS5	370 V 0.602, **629 S 0.916**, 893 E 0.672	None	None
DENV-2	*E*	93 K 0.750, 129 I 0.631, **160 K 0.939**, 203 D 0.610, 347 V 0.644, 363 S 0.634	**93 (0.907),** **160 (0.986*)**	None
	NS1	5 I 0.688, 164 T 0.865	None	None
	NS2A	40 F 0.599, 51 R 0.532, 62 A 0.515, 63 T 0.748, 116 - 0.580, 133 A 0.517	None	**63 (0.992**),** **116 (0.952*)**
	NS3	**14 G 0.994****, 385 L 0.775, 418 K 0.618, 549 K 0.701	**14 (0.996**)**	**14 (0.999**),** **549 (0.996**)**
	NS4A	23 N 0.746, **39 K 0.976*, 41 Y 0.969***, 42 T 0.635	None	None
	NS5	267 I 0.727, **271 I 0.952***, 335 V 0.692, 429 G 0.702, 521 E 0.567, 523 G 0.636, 553 V 0.800, 641 I 0.880, 878 G 0.767, 895 E 0.593	None	None
DENV-3	*C*	None	**45 (0.915)**	None
	E	**124 P 0.980*, 132 Y 0.918,** 169 T 0.662, 171 A 0.664, 278 A 0.574, 301 T 0.857	**124 (0.968*),** **132 (0.934)**	**124 (0.999**),** **132 (0.982*),** **301 (0.983*)**
	NS2A	**37 F 0.954***, 40 F 0.701	**37 (0.969*)**	None
	NS3	**356 A 0.954***	**356 (0.979*)**	**356 (0.999**)**
	NS4A	95 L 0.767, 99 E 0.552	None	None
	NS5	288 N 0.639, 365 S 0.768, 374 E 0.628, 382 R 0.528, 639 P 0.721, 675 A 0.710, 835 N 0.637	None	None
DENV-4	*E*	149 H 0.683, 163 T 0.792, 233 Y 0.708, 238 V 0.552, 252 V 0.581, 290 E 0.509, 324 V 0.582, 393 R 0.534, 455 I 0.558, 461 F 0.876	None	None
	NS5	141 D 0.531, 224 A 0.883, 227 N 0.538, 423 G 0.608, 826 I 0.667	None	**224 (0.968*)**

patterns. For example, in DENV-1, codon 34 (R, BEB = 0.964*) of *NS4B* showed strong evidence of selection. In contrast, DENV-2 and DENV-3 exhibited broader signals, particularly in DENV-2 at codon 14 (G, BEB = 0.994**) of *NS3*; codons 39 (K, BEB = 0.976*) and 41 (Y, BEB = 0.969*) of *NS4A*; and codon 271 (I, BEB = 0.952*) of *NS5*. In DENV-3, strong signals were observed at codon 124 (P, BEB = 0.980*) of *E*, codon 37 (F, BEB = 0.954*) of *NS2A*, and codon 356 (A, BEB = 0.954*) of *NS3*. Several additional sites with moderate support (BEB 0.50–0.90) suggest episodic and potentially lineage-specific selection.

In contrast, the HighSPA-HyPhy workflow detected far fewer high-confidence sites. Most signals came from FUBAR and MEME (PSS BEB ≥ 0.95), with some overlap with CodeML—for instance, codons 124 and 132 in DENV-3 *E*, and codon 14 in DENV-2 *NS3*. The discrepancy likely stems from the conservative nature and distinct statistical assumptions of HyPhy's models, especially FEL and SLAC, which prioritize robustness over sensitivity. These results corroborate previous findings of adaptive evolution in DENV genes related to immune evasion, vector interaction, and host adaptation [9,17]. The *E*, *NS3*, and *NS5* genes showed the strongest signals, while *NS4A* and *NS4B* exhibited limited or no selection. Although DENV-4 showed fewer high-confidence sites, some codons met relaxed thresholds, suggesting potential lineage-specific adaptation.

When considering PSSs (BEB $\geq$ 0.95) independently identified by M8 (CodeML), FUBAR (HyPhy), and MEME (HyPhy), the DENV serotype with the highest number of PSSs was DENV-2 (7), followed by DENV-3 (5), DENV-1 (2), and DENV-4 (1) (Table 3). The genes with the most PSSs, regardless of serotype, were *E*, *NS2A*, *NS3*, and *NS4A* (3 each), followed by *C*, *NS4B*, and *NS5* (1 each). These results remained largely consistent when considering PSSs simultaneously identified by CodeML and at least one HyPhy model. Under this stricter criterion, the serotypes with the most PSSs were DENV-3 (3), DENV-1 (1), DENV-2 (1), and DENV-4 (0). At the gene level, *NS3* showed the highest number of PSSs (2), followed by *E*, *NS2A*, and *NS4B* (1 each).

Codon model comparisons (M0 vs. M3, M1a vs. M2a, M7 vs. M8) for DENV-2 *NS3* and DENV-3 *E* revealed codon 14 (G) in *NS3* as a high-confidence PSS (BEB $\geq$ 0.99), with additional support for codons 385, 418, and 549. In *E*, codon 124 (P) showed strong selection (BEB = 0.98), and codons 132, 169, 171, and 301 had moderate support. These findings highlight M8's effectiveness in detecting adaptive signals in DENV genes. Figure 5 shows BEB probabilities; full results are on the HighSPA GitHub.

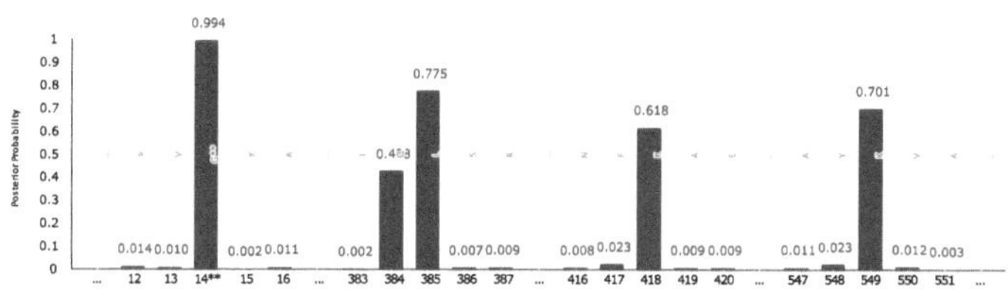

(a) DENV-2 *NS3* region.

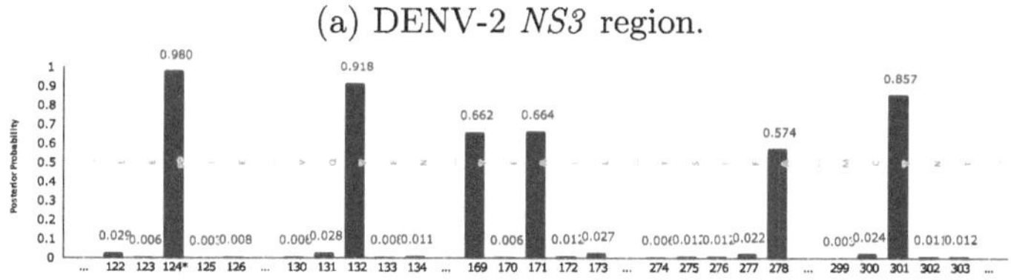

(b) DENV-3 *E* region.

Fig. 5. BEB Posterior Probabilities of PSS ($\omega > 1$) under CodeML M8 model.

7 Conclusion

We present HighSPA, a framework integrating HyPhy and CodeML for fast, scalable selection pressure analysis on HPC with expert-defined alignment quality. Experiments using datasets from four Dengue virus (DENV 1–4) serotypes, targeting 10 protein-coding genes, on an HPC cluster with four computing nodes demonstrated its effectiveness: HighSPA significantly reduces makespan and increases throughput. Using HyPhy, makespan is reduced by 87× and throughput increases by 89×, on average when compared to the sequential execution. With CodeML, makespan is reduced by 31× and throughput increases by 21×. Additionally, it detected adaptive evolution in key genes such as *E*, *NS3*, and *NS5*, confirming HighSPA's suitability for large-scale molecular evolutionary analyses. As future work, we plan to conduct an in-depth performance analysis of the software components, exploring parallelism strategies for shared and distributed memory environments, as well as an I/O profiling study to evaluate the impact of data generation on execution efficiency.

Acknowledgements. This research was funded by CNPq (grants 440360/2022-6, 444558/2024-1) and partially supported by FAPERJ (E-26/202.302/2024).

References

1. Babuji, Y., et al.: Parsl: Pervasive parallel programming in python. In: Proceedings of the 28th International Symposium on High-Performance Parallel and Distributed Computing. pp, 25–36 (2019). https://doi.org/10.1145/3307681.3325400
2. Álvarez Carretero, S., Kapli, P., Yang, Z.: Beginner's guide on the use of paml to detect positive selection. Mol. Biol. Evol. **40**(4) (2023). https://doi.org/10.1093/molbev/msad041
3. Cohen-Boulakia, S., et al.: Scientific workflows for computational reproducibility in the life sciences: Status, challenges and opportunities. Futur. Gener. Comput. Syst. **75**, 284–298 (2017). https://doi.org/10.1016/j.future.2017.01.012
4. Gao, F., Chen, C., Arab, D.A., Du, Z., He, Y., Ho, S.Y.W.: EasyCodeML: a visual tool for analysis of selection using CodeML. Ecol. Evol. **9**(7), 3891–3898 (2019). https://doi.org/10.1002/ece3.5015
5. Huerta-Cepas, J., Serra, F., Bork, P.: ETE 3: reconstruction, Analysis, and Visualization of Phylogenomic Data. Mol. Biol. Evol. **33**(6), 1635–1638 (2016). https://doi.org/10.1093/molbev/msw046
6. Macías, L.G., Barrio, E., Toft, C.: GWideCodeML: a python package for testing evolutionary hypotheses at the genome-wide level. G3 Genes—Genomes—Genetics **10**(12), 4369–4372 (2020). https://doi.org/10.1534/g3.120.401874
7. Maldonado, E., Almeida, D., Escalona, T., Khan, I., Vasconcelos, V., Antunes, A.: LMAP: lightweight multigene analyses in PAML. BMC Bioinf. **17**(1), 354 (2016). https://doi.org/10.1186/s12859-016-1204-5
8. Ocaña, K.A.C.S., de Oliveira, D., Horta, F., Dias, J., Ogasawara, E., Mattoso, M.: Exploring Molecular Evolution Reconstruction Using a Parallel Cloud Based Scientific Workflow. In: de Souto, M.C., Kann, M.G. (eds.) BSB 2012. LNCS, vol. 7409, pp. 179–191. Springer, Heidelberg (2012). https://doi.org/10.1007/978-3-642-31927-3_16

9. Pollett, S., et al.: Understanding dengue virus evolution to support epidemic surveillance and counter-measure development. Infect. Genet. Evol. **62**, 279–295 (2018). https://doi.org/10.1016/j.meegid.2018.04.032
10. Pond, S.L.K., Frost, S.D.W., Muse, S.V.: HyPhy: Hypothesis testing using phylogenies. Bioinformatics **21**(5), 676–679 (2005). https://doi.org/10.1093/bioinformatics/bti079
11. Ren, M., Huang, X., Wu, Z., Stones, R.J., Liu, X., Wang, G.: CuCodeML: GPU-Accelerated CodeML for the Branch-Site Model in Phylogenetics. In: 2020 IEEE International Conference on Parallel & Distributed Processing with Applications, Big Data & Cloud Computing, Sustainable Computing & Communications, Social Computing & Networking, pp. 67–75. IEEE (2020). https://doi.org/10.1109/ISPA-BDCloud-SocialCom-SustainCom51426.2020.00035
12. Roy, S.K., Bhattacharjee, S.: Dengue virus: epidemiology, biology, and disease aetiology. Can. J. Microbiol. **67**(10), 687–702 (2021). https://doi.org/10.1139/cjm-2020-0572
13. Schabauer, H., et al.: SlimCodeML: an optimized version of codeml for the branch-site model. In: 2012 IEEE 26th International Parallel and Distributed Processing Symposium Workshops & PhD Forum, pp. 706–714. IEEE (2012). https://doi.org/10.1109/IPDPSW.2012.88
14. Sinha, K.: Babappa: An automated pipeline for codeml mediated selection analysis integrating prank and iq-tree2. bioRxiv, pp. 2025–04 (2025). https://doi.org/10.1101/2025.04.27.650835
15. Beerenwinkel, N., Siebourg, J.: Scalable Workflows and Reproducible Data Analysis for Genomics. In: Anisimova, M. (ed.) Evolutionary Genomics. MMB, vol. 1910, pp. 33–70. Springer, New York (2019). https://doi.org/10.1007/978-1-4939-9074-0_24
16. Valle, M., et al.: Optimization strategies for fast detection of positive selection on phylogenetic trees. Bioinformatics **30**(8), 1129–1137 (2014). https://doi.org/10.1093/bioinformatics/btt760
17. Waman, V.P., Kale, M.M., Kulkarni-Kale, U.: Genetic diversity and evolution of dengue virus serotype 3: a comparative genomics study. Infect. Genet. Evol. **49**, 234–240 (2017). https://doi.org/10.1016/j.meegid.2017.01.022
18. Yang, Z.: PAML 4: phylogenetic analysis by maximum likelihood. Mol. Biol. Evol. **24**(8), 1586–1591 (2007). https://doi.org/10.1093/molbev/msm088

Performance and Energy Consumption Prediction of Scientific Workflows Using Machine Learning

Felipe Barbosa[1(✉)], Erick Damasceno[2], Fellipe Queiroz[2], Josiany Brito Guimarães[2], Daniel Cordeiro[3], Josivaldo de Souza Araújo[1], and Marcos Amaris[1]

[1] Institute of Exact and Natural Sciences, Federal University of Pará, Belém, Brazil
felipe.barbosa@icen.ufpa.br, {josivaldo,amaris}@ufpa.br

[2] Amazon Development Center in Engineering, Federal University of Pará, Tucuruí, Brazil
{erick.silva,fellipe.queiroz,josiany.guimaraes}@tucurui.ufpa.br

[3] School of Arts, Sciences and Humanities, University of São Paulo, São Paulo, EACH–USP, Brazil
daniel.cordeiro@usp.br

Abstract. In High Performance Computing (HPC), large-scale scientific workflows are essential for modern discoveries but lead to significant energy consumption. This work explores predictive models to estimate both energy consumption and performance, to support sustainable computing in HPC environments. We used WfCommons to generate workflows, Wrench to simulate the supercomputing environments, and Scikit-learn to implement machine learning algorithms. Regression models, including ensemble techniques, were developed and evaluated using widely adopted scientific workflows such as BLAST, Montage, and Epigenomics. For training, features included IO time (in seconds) and the amount of bytes read and written. In energy consumption prediction, the Gradient Boosting Regressor (GBR) achieved high R^2 scores, such as 0.8556 for Epigenomics and 0.7143 for BLAST. For performance prediction, GBR also showed superior accuracy, with MAE and MAPE as low as 0.0257 and 0.0068, respectively, in the BLAST workflow. These results confirm the effectiveness of ensemble models in energy efficiency and performance, contributing to sustainable scientific computing.

Keywords: HPC · Scientific Workflow · Energy Consumption · Performance · Ensemble Learning · Sustainable Computing

1 Introduction

Scientific workflows (SWs) are structured representations of complex computational experiments, commonly used in various domains such as bioinformatics, astrophysics, and climate science [7]. Some of their roles are to automate and scale data processing, making them essential for modern scientific discovery.

K. Brown et al. (Eds.): CARLA 2025, CCIS 2750, pp. 206–220, 2026.
https://doi.org/10.1007/978-3-032-24923-4_14

Lately, High Performance Computing (HPC) has become essential for the execution of large-scale SWs [2], allowing faster and more detailed analyses. However, increasing computational demand also leads to significant energy consumption [9,12], raising concerns about sustainability and operational costs [9].

Energy estimation in SWs is critical because it allows researchers and system administrators to make informed decisions [2] about resource allocation, scheduling, and energy-efficient execution. Despite its importance, a study by Aldinucci et al. [2] found that only 12% of the workflow tools in Italian research projects addressed energy efficiency, highlighting a global research gap.

Therefore, predicting the energy consumption of a workflow before execution allows proactive strategies [17] to optimize energy use without compromising performance [6]. This is notably relevant as the rise of artificial intelligence (AI) and data-intensive applications amplifies the energy footprint of HPC systems [9].

However, this work proposes a predictive model based on Machine Learning (ML) to estimate both the energy consumption and the performance of SWs, for example, BLAST, Montage, and Epigenomics, executed in HPC environments. The goal is to contribute to more sustainable computing practices by enabling better planning and scheduling of scientific experiments.

2 Theoretical Background

2.1 Synthetic Scientific Workflow

Scientific Workflows are a powerful abstraction that is used to model large-scale scientific applications [2]. They have become ubiquitous in many scientific fields and are a pillar of modern scientific computing [7]. They are commonly represented as Directed Acyclic Graphs (DAGs), with tasks as vertices and dependencies as edges, helping to identify parallel paths and efficient execution planning [11]. Increasing DAG complexity demands advanced scheduling.

Tools such as Pegasus map workflows to various computational infrastructures, optimizing resource use [12,17]. This complexity heavily burdens distributed infrastructures [10,12]. Due to their intensive nature, workflows run in HPC environments, where GFLOPS/watt is a key metric.

Synthetic data offers advantages for workflow testing, being easier to generate and covering diverse conditions [11,14]. WfCommons generates synthetic DAGs to study scalability, efficiency, and energy [7,10,11]. On the other hand, synthetic workflows have the disadvantage of deficits in fidelity, as they often present excessive structural and logical simplifications, given that, in some cases, part of the complexity of the DAGs is not captured [10,11,14]. An example of a scientific workflow is Montage [5] (Fig. 1), which performs a series of automated steps, such as resampling, projection, background correction, and composition of sky images, to generate high-precision mosaics [5,20].

Synthetic scientific workflows are crucial for efficient modern computational experiments, ensuring performance, reproducibility, scalability, and energy efficiency [10].

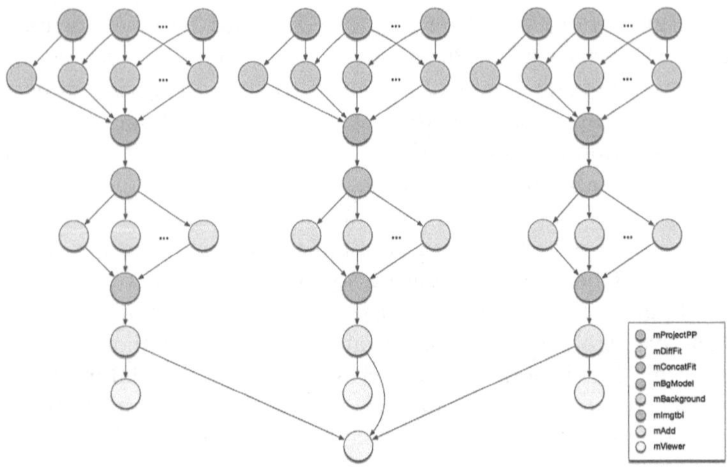

Fig. 1. Montage modular stages (top-down): image reprojection (`mProjectPP`), difference calculation and adjustment (`mDiffFit`, `mConcatFit`), background modeling and correction (`mBgModel`, `mBackground`), metadata extraction (`mImgtbl`), combination of reprojected images (`mAdd`), and visualization of the final result (`mViewer`) [12].

2.2 WfCommons Framework

WfCommons is a framework designed to facilitate large-scale computing experiments by generating synthetic workflows in graph format that simulate real-world applications. Figure 2 illustrates its main components and their relationships [7]. WfCommons builds models from logs of real workflow executions, which are processed by the WfInstance module to create structured and reusable workflow representations [7,13]. These models support analysis, simulation, and performance prediction [12].

WfCommons is grounded in real scientific workflow instances to build synthetic generators through WfChef, which extracts structural patterns and performance characteristics from production execution data [11,12]. Validation is performed by quantitatively comparing structural and execution behavior aspects between real and synthetic workflows, using metrics such as approximate edit distance, type hash frequency, and makespan discrepancy [11]. Results show that WfCommons produces more realistic workflows than previous approaches, including the replication of specific energy consumption patterns, thereby validating its effectiveness in extrapolating scenarios beyond the available real execution data.

The framework integrates with simulation tools such as Wrench [8], enabling scalable simulations on HPC platforms [16,19]. By combining WfCommons with Wrench, researchers can simulate complex workflows and assess strategies or configurations before deploying them in the real world, thereby reducing development time and costs.

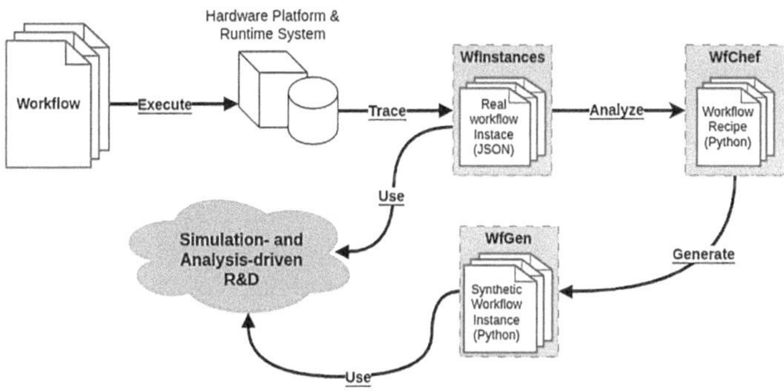

Fig. 2. A brief view of the WfCommons framework and its components. Adapted from the image on the site: https://docs.wfcommons.org/en/latest/.

2.3 Performance and Energy Consumption

Studies have analyzed the energy consumption in HPC systems and the energy expenditure of scientific workflows, reflecting the growing concern for energy efficiency due to the complexity and scale of these systems. This concern drives in-depth analyses of their effects on carbon footprint and CO_2 emissions [4].

Therefore, with the increasing complexity of simulations, analyses, and computational applications, workflows have become increasingly utilized in High-Performance Computing as an effective way to orchestrate and automate these tasks [9,21]. Despite their efficiency in coordinating tasks, the adoption of scientific workflows in HPC environments brings to light a recurring challenge: the balance between performance and energy consumption.

The relationship between workflow size and the number of nodes in the cluster directly influences queue wait time, execution time, and application energy consumption [9,21]. This relationship is nonlinear, and performance improvements do not always imply greater energy efficiency, highlighting the importance of scheduling strategies and predictive models that simultaneously consider time and energy metrics. Unlike the traditional energy consumption model found in the literature on energy-aware workflow scheduling, it is observed that energy consumption is affected in a non-linear way by CPU usage and task allocation between cores and sockets [9].

Faced with these scenarios, the text argues that simply maximizing the utilization of computational resources does not ensure energy efficiency. Moreover, the distribution of tasks across cores and sockets can lead to unbalanced energy consumption, affecting both energy costs and overall system performance. Therefore, the development of predictive models becomes essential to achieving a balance between performance and energy efficiency in HPC environments.

2.4 Machine Learning

In the context of predicting performance and energy consumption in SWs executed on supercomputers, different machine learning models have proven effective. Linear Regression (LR), despite its simplicity and limitation in capturing nonlinear relationships, presents consistent results when associated with feature extraction techniques, achieving average errors of less than 3% in predicting GPU kernel execution time [3], as well as good accuracy in estimating energy consumption in HPC workloads [6].

Random Forest (RF), in turn, stands out as an ensemble method based on decision trees, capable of handling heterogeneous data and reducing the variance of predictions [3]. On the other hand, Gradient Boosting Regressor (GBR), including its variants such as XGBoost, CatBoost, and LightGBM, is considered one of the most robust methods because it iteratively combines multiple "weak learners", adjusting errors from previous models through gradient descent [15,18]. This technique is particularly well-suited to capturing complex, nonlinear patterns, resulting in more accurate predictions across different energy consumption domains [15].

LR, RF, and GBR will be used to predict the performance and energy consumption of scientific workflows, with the aim of supporting the construction of more efficient scheduling and energy management systems on HPC platforms.

3 Method

3.1 Data Collection Procedures

Data from the WfCommons[1] framework was used in this study. WfCommons provides open-source datasets of scientific workflow instances and tools for generating synthetic workflow instances with a significant volume of tasks.

For this study, synthetic scientific workflows were generated using three core modules of the WfCommons framework [13]: WfInstances (workflow collection and grouping), WfChef (recipe generation), and WfGen (workflow synthesis). This modular approach allowed the creation of a dataset with controlled and relevant characteristics for the investigation [12,13]. The workflows are detailed in Table 1.

The study utilized three distinct workflows, each with a specific scientific purpose. BLAST compares nucleotide or protein sequences against database entries and evaluates the statistical significance of the matches [22]. Montage is an astronomical tool designed to create mosaics of customized scientific images by assembling multiple FITS input images [5,20]. Finally, Epigenomics workflows automate complex Big Data pipelines for genome sequencing data processing, enabling efficient handling of various computational tasks in genomics [1].

The synthetic workflow data, including task counts, dependencies, and allocated resources, was structured in JSON files. These served as input for computational simulations that collected performance metrics, which were then saved as CSV files for analysis.

[1] More information about WfCommons: https://wfcommons.org/.

Table 1. Summary of the workflows used in this research, detailing the number of instances evaluated, the range of tasks per workflow, and their computational characteristics. The final column classifies each workflow as CPU-bound, IO-bound, or balanced (CPU + IO), reflecting the primary resource demand during execution.

Workflow	Instances	Nºtasks	CPU load	IO Load	Class
BLAST	2,549	11–14,048	High	Moderate	CPU-bound
Montage	2,549	11–14,036	Moderate	Very High	IO-bound
Epigenomics	2,549	11–14,047	Moderate	High	CPU + IO

3.2 Simulator Implementation for Data Collection

The Wrench[2] framework was used to simulate synthetic scientific workflows through a C++ simulator and XML scripts. The infrastructure was described using SimGrid-compatible XML files[3], emulating the Apollo 2000 supercomputer[4] with 31 nodes, 868 cores, 3,392 GB of RAM, and 156 TB of storage. Due to Wrench limitations, the NVIDIA Tesla V100 GPU was replaced by four additional cloud-provisioned nodes. A WMSHost node was included for workflow management (Fig. 3).

Three virtual machines (CloudNode1–3), each with 28 cores and defined memory, were provisioned via a cloud computing service and registered in a core utilization map for management during simulation. Pilot jobs were employed to dynamically request cores when none were active, expanding available resources. The list of compute services was built at runtime and included both VMs and active pilot job resources. Task scheduling uses the conservative backfilling algorithm at the core level (conservative_bf_core_level), ensuring efficient resource usage under time constraints.

Finally, the energy consumption data collected in joules was converted to power in watts using the basic formula[5], as shown in Formula 1.

$$Power(W) = \frac{Energy(J)}{Time(s)} \tag{1}$$

3.3 Data Collection and Explanation of Attributes

Data was collected on a laptop with an AMD Ryzen 7 processor with 16 threads, 8 GB of RAM, and an Nvidia GeForce GTX 1650 graphics card with 4 GB of dedicated memory. For the experiments, a Docker container was used with the Wrench image (version 2.3), responsible for running the simulations, and the WfCommons framework (version 1.5), used to generate the synthetic workflows.

[2] More information about Wrench: https://wrench-project.org.

[3] SimGrid enables the development of simulators for distributed applications. More information in: https://simgrid.org.

[4] Apollo 2000: https://www.ccad.ufpa.br/cluster/hardware/.

[5] See: https://courses.lumenlearning.com/suny-physics/chapter/7-7-power/.

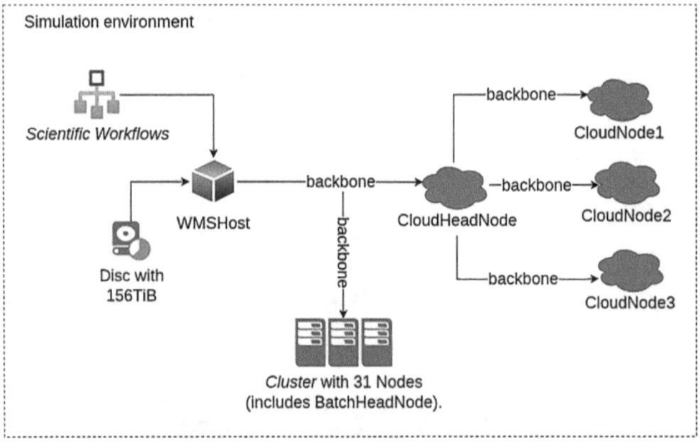

Fig. 3. Infrastructure diagram extracted from the Wrench Simulator XML file, illustrating the components and their configuration.

During the simulation runs, a C++ script was responsible for recording information into a CSV file, utilizing the language's standard library.

Based on the features in Table 2, the variables `io_input_time`, `io_output_time`, `total_bytes_read`, and `total_bytes_write` were selected as input features for training and testing the models of ML [12]. These variables are directly related to data movement and input and output (IO) operations, which are critical factors that influence both the duration (`completion_date`) and energy consumption (`power`) of workflow executions.

Table 2. This table shows some of the main features extracted from the simulation, which were duly processed and then submitted to the ML models.

Feature Name	Description	Type
`sum_cores_allocated`	Total number of CPU cores allocated for workflow execution.	integer
`avg_task_execution` (s)	Average execution time of the tasks.	float
`compute_time` (s)	Total time spent on computation by tasks on a host.	float
`io_input_time` (s)	Total time spent on input (read) operations by tasks.	float
`io_output_time` (s)	Total time spent on output (write) operations by tasks.	float
`total_bytes_read` (B)	Total bytes read from the workflow.	integer
`total_bytes_write` (B)	Total bytes write from the workflow.	integer
`comm_comp_ratio`	Ratio between communication time and computation time.	float
`completion_date` (timestamp)	Time at which the workflow execution completed.	float
`power` (W)	Power consumption of the host during execution.	float

To streamline the execution of Wrench and WfCommons within the container. All developed code and Jupyter notebooks are available in the project's GitHub repository[6].

3.4 Data Processing and Machine Learning

The data preprocessing was performed using Python with the `Pandas`, `Seaborn`, and `NumPy` libraries. Feature engineering techniques were applied to prepare the data for analysis and modeling. The variables were aggregated by `run_id` using "`groupby`", and specific transformations such as a base-10 logarithmic transformation on the conclusion time were used to improve data quality and reduce skewness.

Machine learning refers to a set of techniques for understanding data and making predictions [3]. These techniques are implemented in various software libraries, with Scikit-learn being a prominent and widely adopted open-source tool in Python. It provided a comprehensive suite of tools for various machine learning tasks, including regression, which is pertinent here. The metric to evaluate errors in performance prediction using regression techniques is commonly the Mean Absolute Percentage Error (MAPE) [3], which can be analyzed in Eq. 2.

$$\text{MAPE} = \frac{1}{n}\sum_{t=1}^{n}\left|\frac{A_t - F_t}{A_t}\right| \tag{2}$$

In addition to MAPE, other metrics will be used to evaluate the regression models, including Mean Absolute Error (MAE), Mean Squared Error (MSE), and the Coefficient of Determination (R^2).

The learning models used for this study were as follows: Gradient Boosting Regressor (GBR), Linear Regression (LR), and Random Forest (RF).

4 Results and Discussion

We evaluated the execution of the prediction model in three different scenarios. In these scenarios, the performance of the workflow and the energy consumption for the BLAST, Montage, and Epigenomics workflows were measured using the Mean Absolute Percentage Error (MAPE), as defined in Eq. 2.

4.1 BLAST Prediction Results

Figure 4 shows the learning curves for the Performance (Fig. 4(a)) and Power (Fig. 4(b)) GBR models, depicting MSE over boosting iterations for training (solid) and test (dashed) sets.

For Performance GBR, the training MSE dropped from ~0.82 to ~0.14, with the test MSE stabilizing at 0.1905 between 150~200 estimators and a generalization gap of ~0.05 ($MAPE = 0.0701$, $MAE = 0.3279$, $R^2 = 0.6658$). Power

[6] https://github.com/feliperafaelbarbosa/energy-consumption-simulator.

GBR achieved lower errors, with training MSE reaching ~0.0022 and test MSE ~0.0028, showing a smaller gap (~0.0006) and better balance ($MAPE = 0.0068$, $MAE = 0.0257$, $R^2 = 0.7143$).

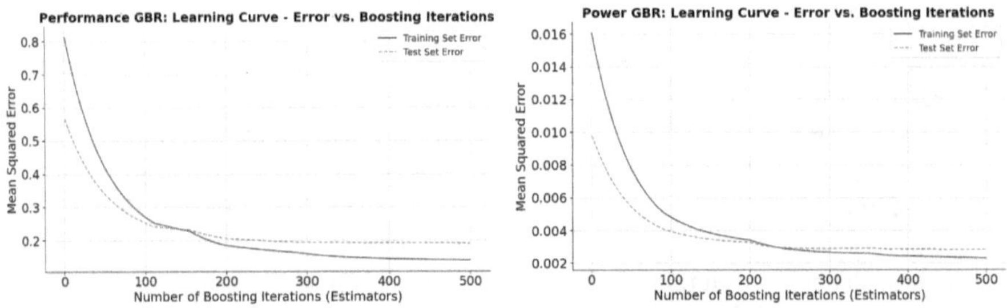

(a) BLAST Performance GBR model curves

(b) BLAST Power GBR model curves

Fig. 4. Learning curves for the Gradient Boosting Regressor models. (a) Performance GBR. (b) Power GBR. The plots show the MSE evolution for training (solid line) and test (dashed line) sets over the number of boosting iterations.

The Power GBR model outperformed the Performance GBR in all error metrics. For both models, the test error stabilized between 150~200 estimators, indicating an optimal range without signs of overfitting up to 500 estimators.

Figures 5 and 6 present the importance of features for each model, using MDI and the importance of permutation on the test set.

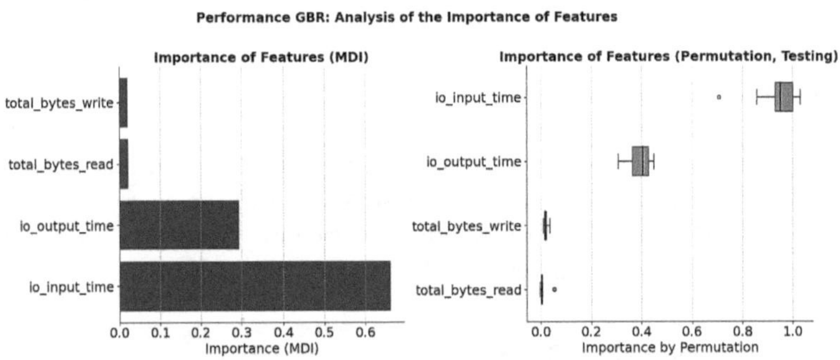

Fig. 5. The `io_input_time` feature stands out, with an MDI of ~0.65 and the highest median in the permutation analysis (~0.9), despite high variability and an outlier, as indicated by the boxplot.

Figure 7 shows scatter plots that compare the actual and predicted values of the LR models on the test set. For the Performance LR (Fig. 7(a)) and Power LR (Fig. 7(b)) models, the data points (actual vs. predicted), the test regression line

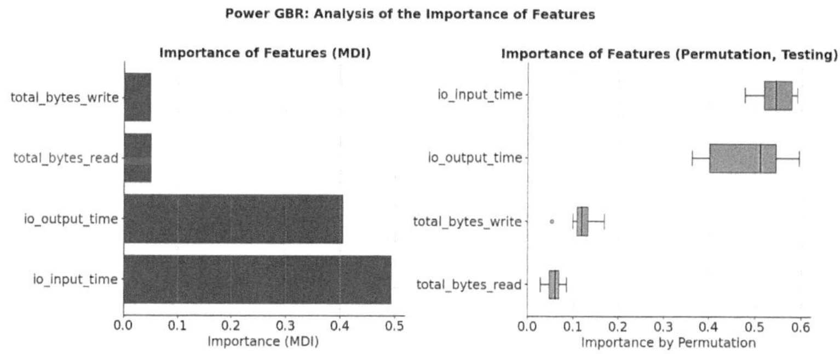

Fig. 6. The `io_input_time` feature is the most influential, with an MDI of ~0.48 and the highest median in the permutation analysis (~0.6). `io_output_time` follows closely in both metrics, while `total_bytes_write` and `total_bytes_read` show minimal impact across both importance evaluations.

(dashed line) with confidence interval (shaded area) and the perfect prediction line ($y = x$, continuous line) are shown.

The Performance LR model (Fig. 7(a)) showed high dispersion and low explanatory power ($R^2 = 0.2277$), with systematic errors. In contrast, the Power LR model (Fig. 7(b)) had better alignment with the $y = x$ line, lower error metrics ($MAPE = 0.0113$, $MSE = 0.0055$, $MAE = 0.0428$), and a higher R^2 (0.4371), indicating better suitability for modeling power consumption.

For the RF models (Fig. 8), the Performance RF (Fig. 8(a)) followed the trend of the data but showed more uncertainty for lower values ($R^2 = 0.6577$, $MAPE = 0.0596$). Power RF (Fig. 8(b)) outperformed all others, with tightly clustered predictions, narrow confidence intervals, and superior metrics ($R^2 = 0.7371$, $MAPE = 0.0071$), confirming its effectiveness for power prediction.

Overall, the Power RF model outperformed the Performance RF model. The R^2 value increased by 12.1% (from 0.6577 to 0.7371), indicating a higher proportion of explained variance. The error metrics also showed substantial improvements: MAPE decreased by 88.1%, MSE by 98.7%, and MAE by 92.2%. These results highlight the higher accuracy and generalizability of the Power RF model.

4.2 Beyond Workflow BLAST

In addition to the BLAST workflow, learning models were applied to the Montage and Epigenomics workflows to predict their performance in HPC environments. The results (Table 3) demonstrate notable variations in model effectiveness across different workflows.

Therefore, for the Montage workflow, the GBR achieved the most balanced performance, with an MAE of 0.4195, an MSE of 0.3163, and an R^2 of 0.5297. The RF model followed closely, yielding slightly higher error values ($MAE = 0.4451$, $MSE = 0.3524$), but a relatively high R^2 of 0.4759, suggesting generalizability. Nevertheless, the LR model performed significantly worse, with an R^2 of only

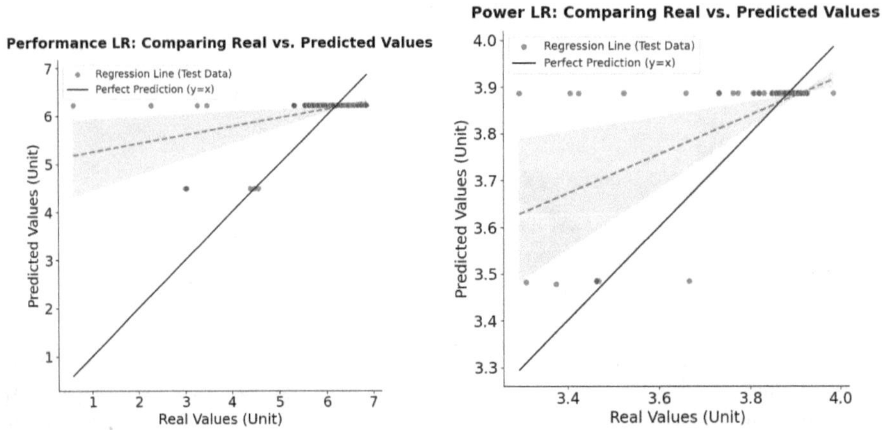

(a) BLAST Performance LR: Real vs Predicted (b) BLAST Power LR: Real vs Predicted

Fig. 7. Actual vs. predicted values for the Performance LR (a) and Power LR (b) models on the test set. Each plot shows data points (purple circles), the fitted regression line (teal dashed line with confidence interval), and the perfect prediction line ($y = x$, solid black).

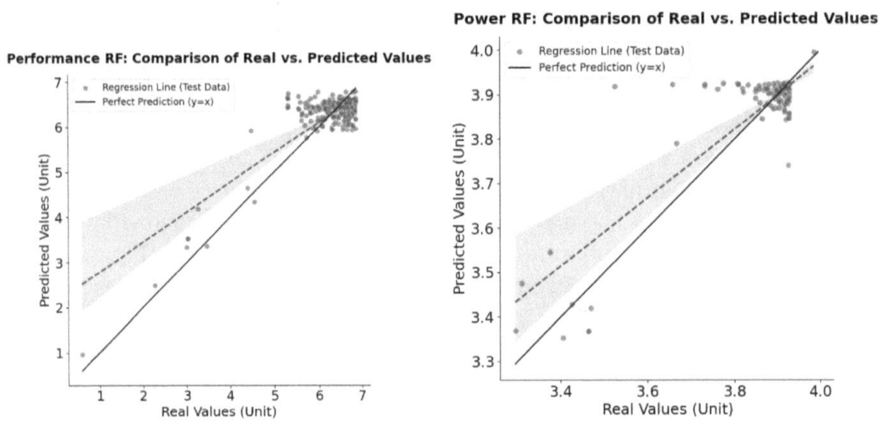

(a) BLAST Performance RF: Real vs Predicted (b) BLAST Power RF: Real vs Predicted

Fig. 8. Actual vs. predicted values for the Performance RF (a) and Power RF (b) models on the test set. Each plot shows data points (blue-gray circles), the fitted regression line (purple dashed line with light purple confidence interval), and the perfect prediction line ($y = x$, solid black). (Color figure online)

0.1638 and higher prediction errors, indicating its inadequacy in capturing non-linear patterns.

In the Epigenomics workflow, ensemble models demonstrated superior predictive capabilities. Across all workflows, MAPE also helped to demonstrate that the ensemble models performed better than the linear model. GBR and RF consistently yielded lower MAPE values, particularly in the Epigenomics workflow, where RF achieved the lowest score, followed closely by GBR. LR, on the other hand, exhibited substantially higher MAPE values across all workflows.

Table 3. Performance prediction results for scientific workflows in HPC environments using three machine learning models with four evaluation metrics. The best results are highlighted in magenta, the worst in blue, and the average in yellow.

Workflow	ML Model	MAE	MSE	R^2	MAPE
BLAST	GBR	0.3279	0.1905	0.6658	0.0701
	LR	0.4219	0.4403	0.2277	0.1106
	RF	0.3430	0.1951	0.6577	0.0596
Montage	GBR	0.4195	0.3163	0.5297	0.0793
	LR	0.4963	0.5623	0.1638	0.1215
	RF	0.4451	0.3524	0.4759	0.0766
Epigenomics	GBR	0.1801	0.0840	0.8556	0.0395
	LR	0.5437	0.5206	0.1046	0.1307
	RF	0.1862	0.0963	0.8344	0.0369

Table 4 presents an evaluation of the prediction of energy consumption. In the context of the Montage workflow, the GBR model stood out as the most effective, showing the best values for all four metrics. It should be noted that once again, the LR model was the model with the lowest predictive capacity, registering an R^2 of only 0.0411 and the highest errors in the other metrics. The R^2 values for this workflow were generally the lowest of the three workflows analyzed, suggesting greater complexity or less linearity in the relationship between the predictor variables and energy consumption.

The GBR model applied to Epigenomics achieved the best indicators in all metrics. However, the RF model continued with an intermediate performance ($MAE = 0.0895$, $MSE = 0.0155$, $R^2 = 0.4812$, $MAPE = 0.0247$). Linear Regression consistently showed the most limited performance, with an R^2 of 0.0600 and the highest errors, as shown in Table 4.

Table 4. Energy prediction results for scientific workflows in HPC environments using three machine learning models with four evaluation metrics. The best results are highlighted in magenta, the worst in blue and the average in yellow.

Workflow	Model ML	MAE	MSE	R^2	MAPE
BLAST	GBR	0.0257	0.0028	0.7143	0.0068
	LR	0.0428	0.0055	0.4371	0.0113
	RF	0.0267	0.0026	0.7371	0.0071
Montage	GBR	0.1050	0.0210	0.4714	0.0291
	LR	0.1680	0.0381	0.0411	0.0460
	RF	0.1116	0.0257	0.3538	0.0309
Epigenomics	GBR	0.0825	0.0130	0.5668	0.0228
	LR	0.1388	0.0281	0.0600	0.0377
	RF	0.0895	0.0155	0.4812	0.0247

5 Conclusion and Future Works

In this work, we develop a model capable of predicting energy consumption and performance when executing scientific workflows in HPC environments. We evaluated the application of three machine learning models in three different workflows, namely, BLAST, Montage, and Epigenomics, each with distinct computational characteristics.

The experimental results demonstrated that ensemble learning models, particularly GBR and RF, consistently outperformed the Linear Regression model across all workflows. GBR achieved the highest accuracy in most scenarios, with lower error rates and higher R^2 values, especially in the Epigenomics workflow, where it obtained an R^2 of 0.8556. This success can be attributed to the model's ability to handle strongly nonlinear relationships and complex I/O iterations in workflows that require massive amounts of data. MAPE further confirmed this trend, with GBR and RF yielding significantly lower values than LR. These findings highlight the importance of selecting robust, nonlinear models for predictive tasks involving complex workload behavior in HPC environments.

In future work, we intend to apply predictive models to task-level execution within workflows and integrate energy and performance predictions into dynamic resource allocation strategies.

Acknowledgments. This work was partially supported by the São Paulo Research Foundation (FAPESP), procs. #2019/26702-8, #2023/00811-0, and by the Science Center for Development "Carbon Neutral Cities" (FAPESP #2024/01115-0).

References

1. Ahmad, W., Alam, B., Sharma, S., Kushwaha, A.: Epigenomics scientific big data workflow scheduling for cancer diagnosis in health care using heterogeneous computing environment. Braz. Arch. Biol. Technol. **66**, e23210795 (2023). https://doi.org/10.1590/1678-4324-2023210795
2. Aldinucci, M., et al.: A systematic mapping study of italian research on workflows. In: Proceedings of the SC '23 Workshops of the International Conference on High Performance Computing, Network, Storage, and Analysis, pp. 2065–2076. SC-W '23, Association for Computing Machinery, New York, NY, USA (2023). https://doi.org/10.1145/3624062.3624285
3. Amaris, M., Camargo, R., Cordeiro, D., Goldman, A., Trystram, D.: Evaluating execution time predictions on GPU kernels using an analytical model and machine learning techniques. J. Parallel Distributed Comput. **171**, 66–78 (2023). https://doi.org/10.1016/j.jpdc.2022.09.002
4. Benhari, A., Trystram, D., Dufossé, F., Denneulin, Y., Desprez, F.: Green HPC: an analysis of the domain based on top500. arXiv preprint arXiv:2403.17466 (2024)
5. Berriman, G.B., et al.: Montage: a grid-enabled engine for delivering custom science-grade mosaics on demand. In: Optimizing scientific return for astronomy through information technologies. vol. 5493, pp. 221–232. SPIE (2004). https://doi.org/10.1117/12.550551
6. Carastan-Santos, D., da Costa, G., Poquet, M., Stolf, P., Trystram, D.: Lightweight prediction for improving energy consumption in HPC platforms (2024). https://hal.science/hal-04566184, working paper or preprint
7. Casanova, H., Berney, K., Chastel, S., Da Silva, R.F.: Wfcommons: data collection and runtime experiments using multiple workflow systems. In: 2023 IEEE 47th Annual Computers, Software, and Applications Conference (COMPSAC), pp. 1870–1875 (2023). https://doi.org/10.1109/COMPSAC57700.2023.00290
8. Casanova, H., Pandey, S., Oeth, J., Tanaka, R., Suter, F., Ferreira da Silva, R.: Wrench: a framework for simulating workflow management systems. In: 2018 IEEE/ACM Workflows in Support of Large-Scale Science (WORKS), pp. 74–85 (2018). https://doi.org/10.1109/WORKS.2018.00013
9. Coleman, T., Casanova, H., Gwartney, T., da Silva, R.F.: Evaluating Energy-Aware Scheduling Algorithms for I/O-Intensive Scientific Workflows. In: Paszynski, M., Kranzlmüller, D., Krzhizhanovskaya, V.V., Dongarra, J.J., Sloot, P.M.A. (eds.) ICCS 2021. LNCS, vol. 12742, pp. 183–197. Springer, Cham (2021). https://doi.org/10.1007/978-3-030-77961-0_16
10. Coleman, T., et al.: Wfbench: Automated generation of scientific workflow benchmarks. In: 2022 IEEE/ACM International Workshop on Performance Modeling, Benchmarking and Simulation of High Performance Computer Systems (PMBS), pp. 100–111. IEEE (2022). https://doi.org/10.1109/PMBS56514.2022.00014
11. Coleman, T., Casanova, H., da Silva, R.F.: Wfchef: Automated generation of accurate scientific workflow generators. CoRR **abs/2105.00129** (2021). https://arxiv.org/abs/2105.00129
12. Coleman, T., Casanova, H., Pottier, L., Kaushik, M., Deelman, E., Ferreira da Silva, R.: Wfcommons: a framework for enabling scientific workflow research and development. Fut. Gener. Comput. Syst. **128**, 16–27 (2022). https://doi.org/10.1016/j.future.2021.09.043

13. Da Silva, A.A., Pablo Hong Enriquez, R., Rattihalli, G., Thurimella, V., Da Silva, R.F., Milojicic, D.: Enabling HPC scientific workflows for serverless. In: SC24-W: Workshops of the International Conference for High Performance Computing, Networking, Storage and Analysis, pp. 110–125 (2024). https://doi.org/10.1109/SCW63240.2024.00022
14. Hao, S., et al.: Synthetic data in AI: Challenges, applications, and ethical implications (2024). https://arxiv.org/abs/2401.01629
15. Hussain, I., Ching, K.B., Uttraphan, C., Tay, K.G., Noor, A.: Evaluating machine learning algorithms for energy consumption prediction in electric vehicles: A comparative study. Sci. Rep. **15**(1), 16124 (2025). https://doi.org/10.1038/s41598-025-94946-7
16. Kalam Azad, M.A., Iqbal, N., Hassan, F., Roy, P.: An empirical study of high performance computing (HPC) performance bugs. In: 2023 IEEE/ACM 20th International Conference on Mining Software Repositories (MSR). pp. 194–206 (2023). https://doi.org/10.1109/MSR59073.2023.00037
17. Mellone, G., De Vita, C.G., Caramiello, D., Singh, D.E., Blas, J.G., Ciaramella, A.: Workflows' applications in computational environmental science: a survey. In: Proceedings of the 2nd Workshop on Workflows in Distributed Environments, pp. 1–7. WiDE '24, Association for Computing Machinery, New York, NY, USA (2024). https://doi.org/10.1145/3642978.3652833
18. Mitchell, R.: Gradient boosting, decision trees and xgboost with cuda. NVIDIA Developer Blog (2017). https://developer.nvidia.com/blog/gradient-boosting-decision-trees-xgboost-cuda/, acessado em 2026/04/29 10:05:40
19. Raj, R.K., et al.: High performance computing education: Current challenges and future directions. In: Proceedings of the Working Group Reports on Innovation and Technology in Computer Science Education, pp. 51–74. ITiCSE-WGR '20, Association for Computing Machinery, New York, NY, USA (2020). https://doi.org/10.1145/3437800.3439203
20. Triendl, S., Ristov, S.: Peeking behind the serverless implementations and deployments of the montage workflow. In: Companion of the 15th ACM/SPEC International Conference on Performance Engineering, pp. 196–203. ICPE '24 Companion, Association for Computing Machinery, New York, NY, USA (2024). https://doi.org/10.1145/3629527.3651420
21. Warade, M., Schneider, J.G., Lee, K.: Towards energy-aware scheduling of scientific workflows. In: 2022 International Conference on Green Energy, Computing and Sustainable Technology (GECOST), pp. 93–98 (2022). https://doi.org/10.1109/GECOST55694.2022.10010634
22. Wheeler, D., Bhagwat, M.: Blast quickstart: example-driven web-based blast tutorial. In: Bergman, N.H. (ed.) Comparative Genomics: Volumes 1 and 2, chap. 9. Humana Press, Totowa (NJ) (2007). https://www.ncbi.nlm.nih.gov/books/NBK1734/

Optimizing the Energy-Efficiency of QMCPACK on Aurora Supercomputer via GPU Sharing

Matheus Costa[1], Philippe O. A. Navaux[1], Silvio Rizzi[2], and Arthur Francisco Lorenzon[1](✉)

[1] Institute of Informatics, UFRGS, Porto Alegre, Brazil
{mmcosta,navaux,aflorenzon}@inf.ufrgs.br

[2] Argonne National Laboratory, Lemont, IL, USA
srizzi@anl.gov

Abstract. As high-performance computing advances toward the exascale, energy efficiency has become a primary concern. However, complex scientific applications often underutilize GPU hardware, such as GPUs, leaving valuable resources idle. In this scenario, this paper investigates GPU sharing as a strategy to improve resource utilization and energy efficiency for the QMCPACK application on the Aurora supercomputer. We evaluate Intel's Multiple Compute Command Streamers (CCS) technology across a scale of 1 to 16 nodes on Aurora, comparing a baseline single-rank-per-GPU-tile configuration (1-CCS) against multi-rank setups with two (2-CCS) and four (4-CCS) ranks per tile. Our results demonstrate that GPU sharing via the 2-CCS mode yields significant performance improvements regarding the Figure of Merit (FOM) by an average of 17% and enhances energy efficiency (FOMe) by 32% compared to the baseline configuration that uses 1-CCS only. We also show that the 4-CCS configuration suffers from increased MPI communication overhead and lower vectorization efficiency, being worse for performance and energy than running with only 1-CCS. On the other hand, 2-CCS achieves a better balance between higher compute unit engagement and reduced memory system stalls. We also show that exploiting GPU sharing can be an effective strategy for boosting both throughput and sustainability on modern HPC systems, but over-partitioning can introduce overheads that cancel out the benefits.

Keywords: High-performance computing · Energy efficiency · GPU sharing · Green HPC

1 Introduction

The rise of high-performance computing (HPC) towards exascale capabilities has intensified the focus on energy efficiency as a main concern alongside raw

K. Brown et al. (Eds.): CARLA 2025, CCIS 2750, pp. 221–234, 2026.
https://doi.org/10.1007/978-3-032-24923-4_15

computational power. As scientific applications scale to exploit increasingly complex architectures, achieving high throughput with reduced energy consumption has become essential for enabling sustainable large-scale simulations [14]. Quantum Monte Carlo (QMC) methods, in particular, are both computationally demanding and scientifically valuable, offering accurate solutions to complex many-body problems in materials science and condensed matter physics. Among these applications, QMCPACK [9] is a widely used QMC application designed to run efficiently on leadership-class systems, making it a relevant benchmark for evaluating energy-aware execution strategies.

QMCPACK has been extensively optimized for modern supercomputers, supporting GPU acceleration through backends such as CUDA, HIP, and SYCL, and scaling efficiently across nodes using MPI. Despite these optimizations, the application exhibits phases of execution where GPU utilization is not ideal due to variability in workload characteristics, memory-bound kernels, and synchronization overhead, which can result in periods of low computational activity and leave parts of the GPU resources idle. In particular, GPU sharing techniques, where multiple workloads or processes utilize a single GPU concurrently, have emerged as a promising approach to increase hardware utilization and reduce energy-per-task metrics. By enabling multiple QMCPACK instances to run concurrently on the same GPU, it becomes possible to reclaim idle cycles and improve overall energy efficiency. However, the performance implications and energy trade-offs of such configurations, especially in multi-node executions, are not yet well understood.

Recent developments in Intel GPU architecture have introduced support for the concurrent execution of multiple workloads on a single GPU. A key feature enabling this capability is the use of multiple Compute Command Streamers (CCSs), which allow the GPU to divide its execution units into independent partitions. Each CCS can manage its own stream of commands, enabling multiple applications or processes to issue work concurrently with minimal interference. This design allows for improved hardware utilization, particularly in scenarios where individual workloads do not fully occupy the available computational resources.

Considering the aforementioned scenario, we investigate the employment of GPU sharing strategies to improve the energy efficiency of QMCPACK through an extensive set of experiments on up to 16 nodes from the Aurora supercomputer. The three main contributions of this paper are: (*i*) a comprehensive performance and energy efficiency evaluation of Intel's CCS technology for a large-scale scientific application; (*ii*) a hardware-level analysis using the Intel® VTune™ Profiler that identifies the root causes of performance variations, including MPI overhead, memory stalls, and compute unit utilization; (*iii*) a characterization of the performance trade-offs of spatial GPU sharing, demonstrating that its effects extend beyond the GPU to impact CPU-side memory pressure and communication overhead, while revealing the potential drawbacks of over-partitioning.

The findings show that a moderate sharing approach with two MPI ranks per GPU tile (2-CCS) is highly effective, improving performance by an average of 17% and energy efficiency by 32% over the baseline configuration. The paper provides a hardware-level analysis using the Intel® VTune™ Profiler to explain these results, attributing the success of the 2-CCS mode to superior compute unit engagement and memory management. At the same time, the analysis reveals that the degraded performance of a four-rank configuration (4-CCS) is caused by bottlenecks such as increased MPI communication overhead and lower vectorization efficiency. By identifying this ideal configuration, the work offers guidance on resource utilization, demonstrating that while spatial partitioning can improve GPU utilization and reduce memory stalls, there is an optimal balance that avoids the counterproductive effects of over-subscribing the GPU.

The remainder of this paper is structured as follows. In Sect. 2, we present the QMCPACK application, describe the GPU sharing strategies used in this work, and list the related work. Then, the methodology employed during the experiments is described in Sect. 3. Experimental results are discussed in Sect. 4, while the conclusions are drawn in Sect. 5.

2 Background

In this Section, we describe QMCPACK and its parallel implementation. Then, we discuss the GPU-Sharing techniques, emphasizing the model employed by Intel GPUs, as they are our target hardware. Finally, we list the related work and compare our contributions to it.

2.1 QMCPACK

QMCPACK [9] implements several QMC algorithms, including Variational Monte Carlo (VMC) and Diffusion Monte Carlo (DMC). These methods randomly sample the many-body electronic wavefunction. The core computational entity in these simulations is called "*walker*", which represents a configuration of electron coordinates in the simulation space.

The DMC algorithm in QMCPACK refines the stochastic sampling of the many-body wavefunction by propagating walkers through imaginary time evolution. Each Monte Carlo generation involves a sequence of single-particle moves for each electron within a walker. New electron positions are proposed based on a combination of stochastic diffusion and deterministic drift terms derived from the gradient of the trial wavefunction. These proposed moves are evaluated via the Metropolis-Hastings criterion, accepting or rejecting them based on the computed ratio of the trial wavefunction at the new and old configurations. Accepted moves trigger computationally expensive updates, such as matrix inversions associated with the Slater determinants. Once all particle moves for a walker are completed, the local energy is evaluated, and walkers are reweighted and branched based on their relative energies to maintain population control and statistical balance. This process is iteratively performed over multiple generations.

The primary mode of parallelism exploitation in QMCPACK is achieved by distributing these walkers across available resources. Recent versions of QMCPACK include batched driver designs, where walkers are grouped into "crowds" to maximize data locality and GPU utilization, where walkers in different crowds remain asynchronous, further improving performance portability and scalability across heterogeneous computing systems [11]. In a typical hybrid MPI+GPU setup, walkers are divided among MPI ranks, and within each rank, the local energy and walker update steps are offloaded to GPUs, where further parallelism can be exploited. Moreover, QMCPACK exhibits minimal communication between MPI processes, which contributes to its near-ideal parallel efficiency when scaled across distributed-memory systems. Despite the low inter-process communication, the application is highly sensitive to memory bandwidth within each walker and is significantly affected by cache architecture, including cache size and type. As a result, optimization efforts are often directed toward improving intra-node resource utilization and memory hierarchy efficiency [13].

2.2 GPU Sharing

GPU sharing is generally achieved through either temporal or spatial methods. Temporal sharing enables multiple processes to share a GPU over time. It operates by granting one process exclusive access to the GPU's resources using preemption and context switching. However, for large and demanding workloads, the process of preemption and context switching can lead to considerable overhead, reducing overall efficiency [18]. Spatial sharing divides the GPU's physical resources among multiple processes, allowing them to run concurrently within isolated partitions. This method aims to improve resource utilization by enabling true parallelism, especially when individual workloads do not fully saturate the GPU, allowing the unused resources from one workload to be leveraged by others.

Intel GPUs use multiple CCSs to spatially partition the GPU [7]. Each CCS serves as an independent engine within the GPU architecture, responsible for fetching, decoding, and dispatching compute kernels to a group of compute units. The newer Intel micro-architecture uses the X^e-core as the compute unit, containing vectors and matrix Arithmetic Logic Units (ALU). Each core has 8 vector and 8 matrix engines and shares a 512KB L1 cache. Once a kernel is submitted to the CCS, it is divided first into work groups and then into threads, which are subsequently dispatched to a X^e-core for parallel execution. The CCSs can be configured in three different modes (see Fig. 1): (*i*) 1-CCS mode, in which a single active CCS controls all X^e-cores. This configuration is the default. (*ii*) 2-CCS mode, where the cores are evenly and exclusively assigned to each of the two active CCSs; and (*iii*) 4-CCS mode, which is the same as the previous, but there are four CCSs. This spatial partitioning allows applications to use 1-CCS for large kernels or multiple CCSs for parallel execution of smaller, concurrent kernels on dedicated core partitions. Importantly, this multi-CCS capability enables a higher density of MPI ranks to be effectively mapped to each GPU, with each rank targeting independent X^e-core partitions, simplifying parallelism at the MPI level.

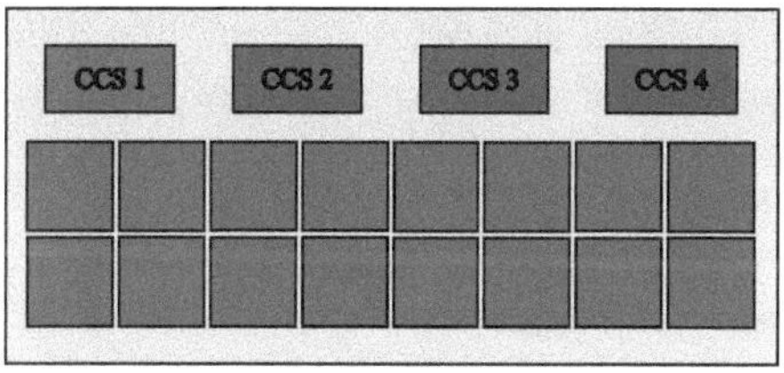

(a) 1-CCS mode utilizing all X^e-cores.

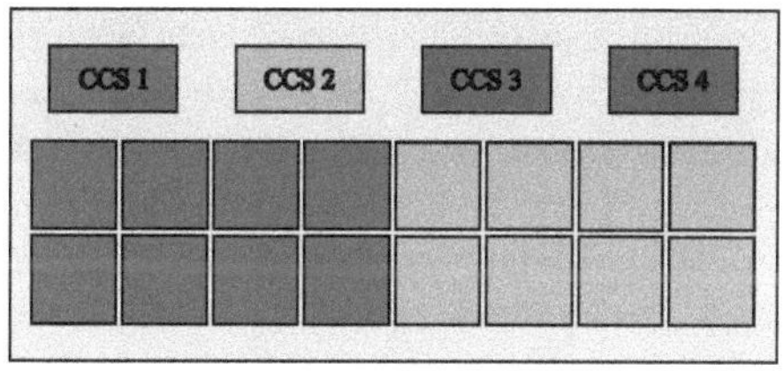

(b) 2-CCS mode distributing workload across half of the X^e-cores per CCS.

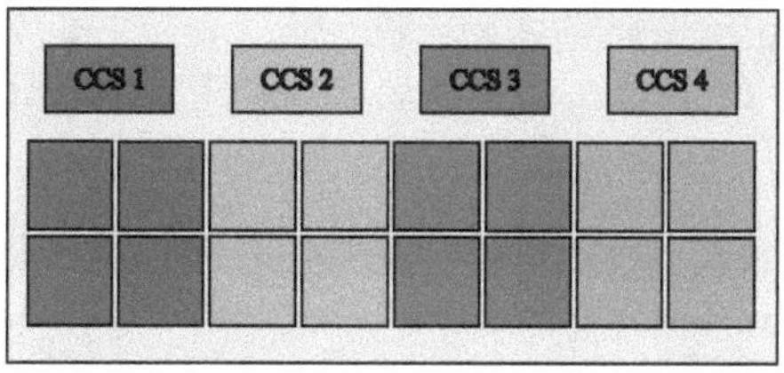

(c) 4-CCS mode distributing workload across one-quarter of the X^e-cores per CCS.

Fig. 1. Illustration of workload distribution across X^e-cores with varying numbers of CCSs.

Other GPU vendors have also introduced mechanisms to support resource sharing across multiple workloads, enabling improved utilization and concurrency. NVIDIA, for instance, provides a combination of temporal and spatial sharing strategies. Time-slicing allows multiple processes to share the GPU in a serialized manner, while the Multi-Process Service (MPS) [16] enables concurrent kernel execution by multiple MPI ranks or processes. Additionally, NVIDIA's Multi-Instance GPU (MIG) technology [15] supports hardware-level spatial partitioning by dividing a single physical GPU into multiple isolated instances, each with its own dedicated compute, memory, and cache resources. AMD GPUs similarly support fine-grained spatial sharing through the use of Asynchronous Compute Engines (ACEs) and Compute Units (CUs), which can be assigned to independent command queues. Techniques such as CU masking allow subsets of compute units to be allocated to specific workloads, enabling true concurrent execution with hardware-enforced separation [17].

2.3 Related Work

Underutilization of compute resources in modern GPUs is often caused by imbalances within parallel executions units. Common bottlenecks include memory latency, register and shared memory contention, pipeline stalls and synchronization overheads. These issues often leave parts of the GPU underutilized, reducing overall performance and efficiency [6,19]. Optimizing resource utilization is even more challenging in heterogeneous architectures. Maloney et al. [12] conducted a resource utilization study on the JUWELS supercomputer, highlighting these inefficiencies. Their work identified significant underutilization of key components, observing that for GPU-intensive jobs, host CPUs and a significant portion of the host memory capacity are often left idle.

GPU idle times, ofter caused by waiting for data due to communication overheads and poor data locality, has been identified as one of the main contributors to energy inefficiency [2]. Also, non-uniform memory access (NUMA) effects, if not carefully managed, can significantly decrease both performance and energy efficiency by increasing memory traffic in multi-GPU systems [8].

Energy costs are also increased when higher precision computing is employed in comparison to lower precision alternatives. This highlights the increasing importance of treating energy efficiency as a primary design constraint, not only in hardware architectures but also in software design decisions [20].

QMCPACK supports mixed-precision computation, which reduces memory footprint at the cost of lower numerical accuracy. This trade-off enables higher walker count on the GPU, leading to improved time-to-solution and reduced energy consumption [5]. Tramm et al. [21] has shown that the utilization of multiple MPI ranks per GPU can improve performance and simplify concurrency across heterogeneous systems from NVIDIA, AMD, and Intel. This approach has been applied in portable Monte Carlo particle transport applications to optimize resource utilization across architectures.

Byun et al. [3] highlight how MPS improves GPU utilization, particularly for AI/ML workloads, demonstrating an increase in both efficiency and throughput when applying GPU-sharing techniques. In addition, Adufu et al. [1] demonstrate that the combination of MPS and MIG enhances execution time and memory bandwidth in comparison to the use of MIG alone, allowing for more effective concurrent execution of multiple applications. ParvaGPU [10] explores GPU sharing in cloud environments, specifically for deep neural network inference. Their approach maximizes the number of MIG instances and the number of concurrent processes per instance, although MPS is only employed for identical workloads.

3 Methodology

This section details the experimental setup, including the application and input configuration, the hardware platform, and the specific execution configurations.

3.1 Application

We consider the QMCPACK v4.0.0, sourced from the ALCF-4 benchmark suite[1]. It has been compiled with the Intel® oneAPI DPC++/C++ Compiler version 2025.0.4, with linked support for MPICH 5.0.0. Build options included enabling

[1] https://github.com/argonne-lcf/alcf4_benchmarks.

GPU offload features for both OpenMP and SYCL, as well as support for mixed-precision calculations. All simulations used an input designed for a DMC simulation of a *fcc* phase *NiO* system consisting of a 256-atom cell, as provided by the ALCF-4 benchmark suite. To support the analysis of the results, further investigation of hardware-level metrics is conducted using the Intel® VTune™ Profiler 2025.0.1.

3.2 Hardware

For the evaluation, we consider the Aurora supercomputer, an exascale system at the Argonne Leadership Computing Facility (ALCF). Aurora is a 10,624-node HPE Cray-Ex-based system. Each node is equipped with two Intel® Xeon® CPU Max 9470C Series processors and six Intel® Data Center GPU Max 1550 Series accelerators. Each GPU features two independent compute tiles and 128 GB of HBM2e memory (64 GB per tile), presenting 12 independently addressable GPU tiles per node. The GPUs are interconnected in an all-to-all topology using Intel Xe Link interfaces, enabling high-bandwidth, low-latency communication within the node. The experiments were performed utilizing a range of 1 to 16 nodes of this system.

3.3 Testbed

Our methodology centered on a GPU affinity strategy, binding one MPI rank to each of the 12 available GPU tiles per node for the baseline **1-CCS** mode. This default 1-CCS configuration assigns all X^e-cores of a tile to its rank via a single active CCS. We then evaluated two additional configurations, **2-CCS** and **4-CCS**, by using the `ZEX_NUMBER_OF_CCS` environment variable to activate two and four CCS instances per tile, respectively. Activating multiple CCSs ensures an even and dedicated partitioning of a tile's X^e-cores, halved for 2-CCS mode and quartered for 4-CCS mode. This allows for an increase in MPI rank density per tile, with each MPI rank then utilizing its own dedicated CCS. The three possible configurations (1-CCS, 2-CCS, and 4-CCS) were compared to evaluate the impact of spatial partitioning on performance and energy efficiency.

Application parameters were configured to maintain a consistent workload distribution across all experimental setups. Each GPU tile was assigned a constant computational load equivalent to managing 256 walkers. This was achieved by setting 256 walkers per MPI rank in the baseline 1-CCS mode (corresponding to one MPI rank per tile), 128 walkers per MPI rank for the 2-CCS mode (two MPI ranks per tile), and 64 walkers per MPI rank for the 4-CCS mode (four MPI ranks per tile). This setup ensures that when comparing different CCS modes on a fixed number of nodes, the total computational workload processed by those nodes remains identical. Furthermore, when evaluating performance across an increasing number of compute nodes, this per-node workload was kept constant. The goal of this weak scaling methodology is to assess how the system performs as both the problem size and allocated resources are increased, ideally maintaining constant computational effort and efficiency per node.

Energy consumption data was collected using the Global Extensible Open Power Manager (GEOPM) [4] tool. For each execution, two readings of the `BOARD_ENERGY` signal were taken, before and after the execution, using the command `geopmread BOARD_ENERGY board 0` on each node. This command returns the accumulated energy consumed by the node in joules. The total energy consumption was calculated as the difference between the two readings summed across all nodes. To ensure statistical reliability, each experimental configuration described above was executed 10 times. The performance metrics collected from these runs consistently exhibited a standard deviation below 5%.

4 Evaluation

This section presents a detailed performance and energy efficiency analysis of QMCPACK under multiple CCS configurations. We investigate the impact of 1-CCS, 2-CCS, and 4-CCS modes on the Figure of Merit (FOM) and Energy-Based Figure of Merit (FOMe), as well as GPU utilization and memory system interactions.

4.1 Overall Performance and Energy Efficiency

To evaluate both computational speed and energy efficiency, we employ two complementary metrics. Throughput performance is measured by the FOM, which captures the cost of moving walkers forward at each step:

$$FOM = \frac{number\_of\_MPI\_ranks \times walkers\_per\_rank \times steps}{walltime} \tag{1}$$

While FOM reflects raw computational throughput, modern HPC environments require understanding energy efficiency as well. Therefore, we introduce an energy counterpart to FOM, denoted as FOMe, which replaces wall time with total energy consumption to capture how much computation is performed per unit of energy:

$$FOMe = \frac{number\_of\_MPI\_ranks \times walkers\_per\_rank \times steps}{energy} \tag{2}$$

This dual-metric approach provides insight into both speed and energy efficiency of each CCS configuration, commonly referred to as "science per energy".

The scaling of the FOM across different node counts provides insights into the raw computational throughput achieved by each CCS configuration, as depicted in Fig. 2. The 1-CCS configuration, serving as the baseline, generally demonstrates good FOM scaling with an increasing number of nodes. For instance, at 1 node, the average FOM is approximately 77, and this scales up to roughly 1180 at 16 nodes, corresponding to 96% weak scaling efficiency.

Building on this baseline performance, the comparison between CCS modes reveals a clear performance hierarchy. As shown in Table 1, the 2-CCS mode

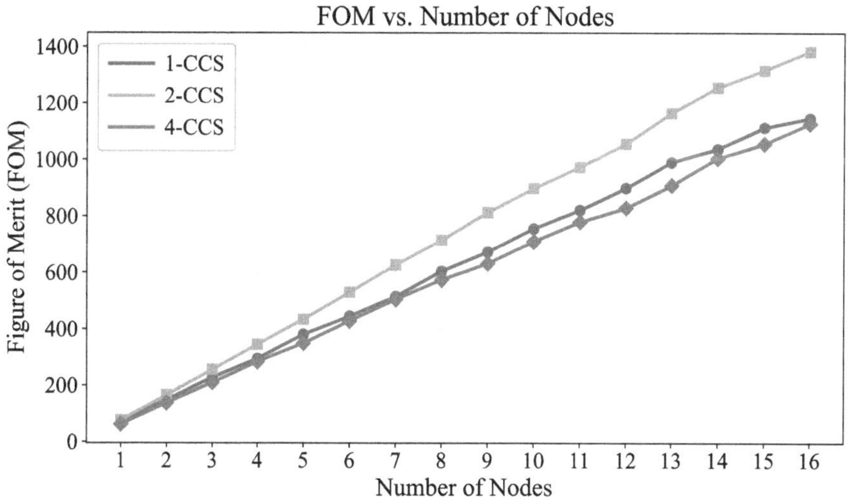

Fig. 2. FOM scaling (higher is better).

consistently outperforms the other configurations, with an average FOM ratio of 1.17× over the 1-CCS mode across all tested node counts. The peak improvement for 2-CCS is observed at 7 nodes, where it reaches 1.22× the FOM of 1-CCS.

In contrast, the 4-CCS mode consistently underperforms the baseline, averaging only 0.94× the performance of 1-CCS. Even at its best relative performance of 0.98× at 7 and 16 nodes, 4-CCS still falls short of the baseline. This performance degradation indicates that excessive GPU partitioning introduces more overhead than benefit, revealing the limits of GPU sharing.

From an energy efficiency perspective, the FOMe improvement ratio shown in Table 1 further highlight the benefits of the 2-CCS mode. The 2-CCS mode shows even greater improvements in energy efficiency than in raw performance, averaging 32% better FOMe compared to 1-CCS. The most significant energy efficiency gain for 2-CCS is also seen at 7 nodes, with an 1.41× improvement in FOMe. This suggests that 2-CCS offers even greater improvements in energy efficiency than performance alone.

In the 4-CCS mode, similar to its FOM trend, shows reduced energy efficiency, with an average FOMe ratio of 0.90× relative to the baseline. The best FOMe is 0.97×, also occurring at 7 and 16 nodes, but still falling short of the 1-CCS baseline. These results suggest that while 2-CCS enhances both throughput and science per energy, 4-CCS tends to be less beneficial to both.

An additional insight into the energy efficiency scaling is provided by Fig. 3, which illustrates the absolute FOMe, for each CCS configuration across the tested node counts. The 1-CCS mode produces a relatively stable FOMe across the evaluated range.

However, both the 2-CCS and 4-CCS configurations exhibit a similar scaling pattern characterized by an initial decrease in FOMe at very low node counts

Table 1. FOM and FOMe improvement ratio over 1-CCS configuration

Nodes	FOM Ratio		FOMe Ratio	
	2-CCS	**4-CCS**	**2-CCS**	**4-CCS**
1	1.05	0.85	1.08	0.73
2	1.12	0.93	1.22	0.86
3	1.12	0.91	1.22	0.85
4	1.17	0.96	1.32	0.93
5	1.14	0.92	1.26	0.86
6	1.19	0.96	1.36	0.93
7	**1.22**	**0.98**	**1.41**	**0.97**
8	1.18	0.95	1.34	0.91
9	1.21	0.94	1.39	0.90
10	1.19	0.94	1.36	0.90
11	1.19	0.95	1.35	0.92
12	1.17	0.92	1.32	0.87
13	1.18	0.92	1.33	0.87
14	1.21	0.97	1.40	0.95
15	1.18	0.95	1.34	0.92
16	1.21	**0.98**	1.38	**0.97**
Avg.	1.17	0.94	1.32	0.90

(e.g., 2 nodes) before achieving stabilization from 4 nodes onwards. The 2-CCS mode not only recovers from its initial drop, but consistently outperforms the 1-CCS baseline, making it an effective strategy even at smaller scales. Meanwhile, the 4-CCS mode, despite showing some improvement from its 1-node performance and peaking between 4 and 7 nodes, never matches the energy efficiency of the baseline configuration.

These scaling patterns suggest that the benefits of GPU sharing are not uniform across all scales, but 2-CCS provides consistent advantages while 4-CCS consistently underperforms, with the performance gap widening as it scales.

4.2 Hardware Metrics and CCS Impact

To further investigate the influence of CCS mode and the associated MPI rank density, this subsection provides an analysis using the Intel® VTune™ Profiler Application Performance Snapshot (APS). The snapshots, captured for 8-node runs, reveal several key hardware-level differences.

One of the findings concerns MPI communications patterns, which help to understand the performance ceiling observed in 4-CCS. While 1-CCS and 2-CCS show similar absolute MPI time (54 s each), 4-CCS mode shows a significant penalty, with its time increasing to 67 s. This overhead becomes apparent when examining the dominant MPI function, `MPI_Allreduce` contributes

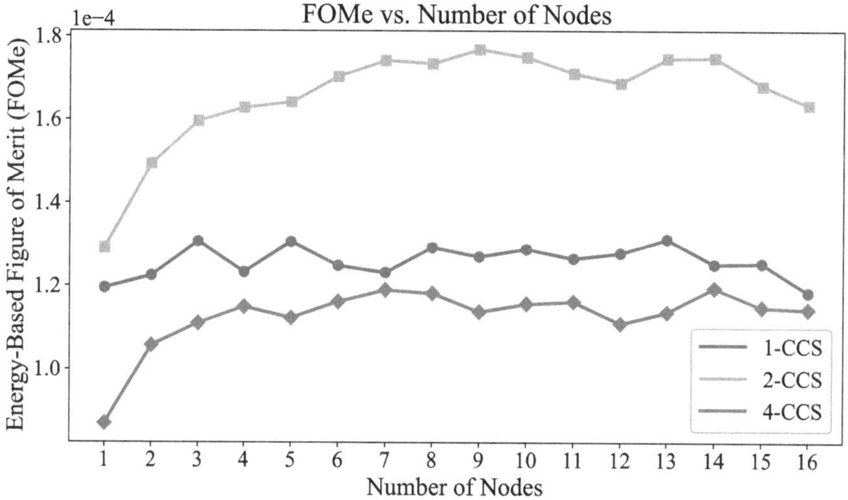

Fig. 3. FOMe scaling (higher is better).

16.98%, 17.09%, and 19.45% to the elapsed time for 1-CCS, 2-CCS, and 4-CCS, respectively. The increase in communication overhead suggests that the rank density increases with 4-CCS outweighs the potential benefits of improved resource utilization.

An analysis of memory system behavior indicates that increased GPU sharing through higher CCS counts reduces some memory pressure. Memory stalls, represented as a percentage of slots where pipeline could be stalled due to demand load or store instructions, decrease from 52.21% in 1-CCS mode to 43.71% in 2-CCS, and further to 38.35% in 4-CCS. Similarly, cache stalls (as a percentage of time the machine was stalled on L1, L2, and L3 caches) also show a descending trend: 48.74% for 1-CCS, 39.42% for 2-CCS, and 38.34% for 4-CCS. This reduction in both memory and cache stalls suggests that partitioning the GPU allows concurrent ranks to potentially hide memory latencies more effectively or make better use of aggregated cache resources. Despite each rank having a smaller individual share of compute resources, the ability of partitioning to help reduce memory pressure aligns closely with established optimization goals for this application, as pointed by Mathuriya et al. [13].

While higher CCS counts improve memory operations, compute utilization presents a more complex picture that helps explain why 4-CCS fails to take advantage of memory improvements. Vectorization efficiency shows a decline with increased GPU sharing, 84.88% for 1-CCS, 84.49% for 2-CCS, and 80.79% for 4-CCS. This degradation, particularly for 4-CCS, suggests that the smaller problem slices handled by each rank in higher CCS modes might lead to less efficient vector unit utilization, potentially due to shorter vector lengths or increased scalar operations for managing smaller workloads.

However, the GPU activity metrics reveal why 2-CCS achieves better performance despite some vectorization losses. The percentage of active Xe Vector Engines (XVEs) is highest for the 2-CCS mode, achieving up to 15%, compared to 9% for 1-CCS and 10% for 4-CCS. This indicates that 2-CCS achieves better overall engagement of compute units, effectively balancing vectorization efficiency with resource utilization.

Another GPU metric that had impact was XVE State Idle, representing the normalized sum of all cycles on all XVEs that were not spent actively executing instructions, showed variation across different CCS configurations. In both 1-CCS and 2-CCS modes, XVE State Idle was 56%, while 4-CCS mode increased to 59%. This suggests that further partitioning the data may result in an imbalance, potentially reducing the efficiency of the GPU by overly partitioning the workload.

Taken together, these hardware metrics explain the observed performance hierarchy: 2-CCS achieves the optimal balance between memory improvements and compute utilization, while 4-CCS suffers from excessive communication overhead and workload fragmentation that diminishes its memory advantages. This evaluation reveals that the advantages of GPU sharing through multiple CCS are not limited to isolated GPU performance enhancements. The reduction in CPU-side memory and cache stalls, as observed with APS, indicates that a more efficient GPU operation, achieved by appropriate spatial partitioning, can lower pressure on the CPU's memory subsystem. This suggests that strategic GPU sharing can lead to a more balanced and efficient utilization of the entire node's resources.

5 Conclusion

The evaluation of QMCPACK performance and energy efficiency under multiple CCS configurations on the Aurora supercomputer reveals distinct trade-offs associated with GPU spatial partitioning and MPI rank density. The 2-CCS mode, which assigns two MPI ranks to each GPU tile, with each rank managing half of the tile's X^e-cores via an independent CCS, consistently comes out as the best configuration. It delivers the highest FOM, indicating maximum computational throughput, and the highest FOMe, meaning superior energy efficiency across the range of 1 to 16 nodes. This optimal performance is attributed to an effective balance: the increased concurrency (two ranks vs. one) improves GPU occupancy by allowing for better latency hiding and pipeline utilization while minimizing memory/cache stalls, thereby reducing idle resources and improving overall system efficiency.

This whole-system perspective reveals that GPU sharing strategies can be leveraged not only to improve GPU utilization but also to enhance CPU memory utilization efficiency. By creating more concurrent memory access patterns through spatial partitioning, the system can better utilize available memory bandwidth and reduce contention across the entire node architecture, suggesting that GPU sharing techniques represent a broader approach to system-level optimization. Future work should explore the applicability of these findings to other applications and investigate adaptive CCS selection based on workload characteristics. Additionally, analyzing the interaction between GPU sharing strategies and emerging memory architectures, such as high-bandwidth memory hierarchies, could further optimize energy efficiency.

Acknowledgments. This research used resources of the Argonne Leadership Computing Facility, a U.S. Department of Energy (DOE) Office of Science user facility at Argonne National Laboratory and is based on research supported by the U.S. DOE Office of Science-Advanced Scientific Computing Research Program, under Contract No. DE-AC02-06CH11357. This study was financed in part by the CAPES - Finance Code 001, FAPERGS - PqG 24/2551-0001388-1, and CNPq.

References

1. Adufu, T., Ha, J., Kim, Y.: Exploring the diversity of multiple job deployments over GPUS for efficient resource sharing. In: International Conference on Information Networking, pp. 777–782. IEEE Computer Society (2024). https://doi.org/10.1109/ICOIN59985.2024.10572198
2. Arunkumar, A., Bolotin, E., Nellans, D., Wu, C.J.: Understanding the future of energy efficiency in multi-module GPUS. In: 2019 IEEE International Symposium on High Performance Computer Architecture (HPCA), pp. 519–532. IEEE (2019)
3. Byun, C., et al.: GPU sharing with triples mode. arXiv preprint arXiv:2410.22254 (2024)
4. Eastep, J., et al.: Global extensible open power manager: a vehicle for HPC community collaboration on co-designed energy management solutions. In: Kunkel, J.M., Yokota, R., Balaji, P., Keyes, D. (eds.) High Performance Computing, pp. 394–412. Springer International Publishing, Cham (2017)
5. Godoy, W.F., et al.: Characterizing GPU energy usage in exascale-ready portable science applications (2025). https://arxiv.org/abs/2505.05623
6. Hestness, J., Keckler, S.W., Wood, D.A.: GPU computing pipeline inefficiencies and optimization opportunities in heterogeneous CPU-GPU processors. In: 2015 IEEE International Symposium on Workload Characterization, pp. 87–97 (2015). https://doi.org/10.1109/IISWC.2015.15
7. Intel Corporation: Advanced topics — Intel ®oneAPI GPU Optimization Guide (2025). https://www.intel.com/content/www/us/en/docs/oneapi/optimization-guide-gpu/2025-0/advanced-topics.html
8. Khairy, M., Nikiforov, V., Nellans, D., Rogers, T.G.: Locality-centric data and threadblock management for massive GPUS. In: 2020 53rd Annual IEEE/ACM International Symposium on Microarchitecture (MICRO), pp. 1022–1036. IEEE (2020)
9. Kim, J., et al.: QMCPACK: an open source ab initio quantum monte carlo package for the electronic structure of atoms, molecules and solids. J. Phys. Condensed Matter **30**(19), 195901 (2018). https://doi.org/10.1088/1361-648X/aab9c3
10. Lee, M., et al.: ParvaGPU: efficient spatial GPU sharing for large-scale DNN inference in cloud environments . In: SC 2024.,pp. 1–14. IEEE, Los Alamitos, CA, USA (2024)

11. Luo, Y., Doak, P., Kent, P.: A high-performance design for hierarchical parallelism in the QMCPACK monte carlo code. In: 2022 IEEE/ACM International Workshop on Hierarchical Parallelism for Exascale Computing (HiPar), pp. 22–27. IEEE (2022)
12. Maloney, S., Suarez, E., Eicker, N., Guimarães, F., Frings, W.: Analyzing HPC monitoring data with a view towards efficient resource utilization. In: 2024 IEEE 36th International Symposium on Computer Architecture and High Performance Computing (SBAC-PAD), pp. 170–181 (2024). https://doi.org/10.1109/SBAC-PAD63648.2024.00023
13. Mathuriya, A., Luo, Y., Benali, A., Shulenburger, L., Kim, J.: Optimization and parallelization of b-spline based orbital evaluations in QMC on multi/many-core shared memory processors. In: 2017 IEEE International Parallel and Distributed Processing Symposium (IPDPS), pp. 213–223. IEEE (2017)
14. Navaux, P.O.A., Lorenzon, A.F., da Silva Serpa, M.: Challenges in high-performance computing. J. Braz. Comput. Soc. **29**(1), 51–62 (2023)
15. NVIDIA: Nvidia a100 tensor core GPU architecture (2020). https://www.nvidia.com/content/dam/en-zz/Solutions/Data-Center/nvidia-ampere-architecture-whitepaper.pdf
16. NVIDIA: Multi-process service (2025). https://docs.nvidia.com/deploy/pdf/CUDA_Multi_Process_Service_Overview.pdf
17. Otterness, N., Anderson, J.H.: Exploring AMD GPU scheduling details by experimenting with "worst practices". In: Proceedings of the 29th International Conference on Real-Time Networks and Systems, pp. 24–34. RTNS 2021, Association for Computing Machinery, New York, NY, USA (2021). https://doi.org/10.1145/3453417.3453432
18. Pratheek, B., Jawalkar, N., Basu, A.: Improving GPU multi-tenancy with page walk stealing. In: 2021 IEEE International Symposium on High-Performance Computer Architecture (HPCA), pp. 626–639 (2021). https://doi.org/10.1109/HPCA51647.2021.00059
19. Sethia, A., Mahlke, S.: Equalizer: dynamic tuning of GPU resources for efficient execution. In: 2014 47th Annual IEEE/ACM International Symposium on Microarchitecture, pp. 647–658 (2014). https://doi.org/10.1109/MICRO.2014.16
20. Shankar, S., Reuther, A.: Trends in energy estimates for computing in AI/machine learning accelerators, supercomputers, and compute-intensive applications. In: 2022 IEEE High Performance Extreme Computing Conference (HPEC), pp. 1–8. IEEE (2022)
21. Tramm, J., et al.: Performance portable monte carlo particle transport on intel, NVIDIA, and AMD GPUS. In: EPJ Web Conference, vol. 302, pp. 04010 (2024)

Driving Computational Efficiency in Large-Scale Platforms Using HPC Technologies

A Martínez-Méndez[1,2(✉)], Carlos J. Barrios H.[1,3,4], Antonio J. Rubio-Montero[5], Hernán Asorey[5], Rafael Mayo-García[5], and Luis A. Núñez[2]

[1] SC3UIS-CAGE, Universidad Industrial de Santander, Bucaramanga, Colombia
alexander2198160@correo.uis.edu.co, cbarrios@uis.edu.co
[2] GIRG, Universidad Industrial de Santander, Bucaramanga, Colombia
lnunez@uis.edu.co
[3] LIG/INRIA DataMove, Grenoble, France
[4] CITI/INRIA SiNDY, Lyon, France
[5] Centre for Energy, Environmental and Technological Research (CIEMAT), Madrid, Spain
{antonio.rubio,rafael.mayo}@ciemat.es, hernan@piensas.xyz

Abstract. The Latin American Giant Observatory (LAGO) project utilizes extensive High-Performance Computing (HPC) resources for complex astroparticle physics simulations, making resource efficiency critical for scientific productivity and sustainability. This article presents a detailed analysis focused on quantifying and improving HPC resource utilization efficiency specifically within the LAGO computational environment. The core objective is to understand how LAGO's distinct computational workloads—characterized by a prevalent coarse-grained, task-parallel execution model—consume resources in practice. To achieve this, we analyze historical job accounting data from the EGI FedCloud platform, identifying primary workload categories (Monte Carlo simulations, data processing, user analysis/testing) and evaluating their performance using key efficiency metrics (CPU utilization, walltime utilization, and I/O patterns). Our analysis reveals significant patterns, including high CPU efficiency within individual simulation tasks contrasted with the distorting impact of short test jobs on aggregate metrics. This work pinpoints specific inefficiencies and provides data-driven insights into LAGO's HPC usage. The findings directly inform recommendations for optimizing resource requests, refining workflow management strategies, and guiding future efforts to enhance computational throughput, ultimately maximizing the scientific return from LAGO's HPC investments.

Keywords: LAGO · Astroparticle Physics · High-Performance Computing (HPC) · High-Throughput Computing (HTC) · Resource Efficiency · Workload Characterization

K. Brown et al. (Eds.): CARLA 2025, CCIS 2750, pp. 235–248, 2026.
https://doi.org/10.1007/978-3-032-24923-4_16

1 Introduction

The Latin American Giant Observatory (LAGO) project [1] represents a significant advancement in the field of astroparticle physics. It focuses on the detection of secondary particles generated by high-energy astrophysical events such as gamma-ray bursts [2], solar flares, and cosmic rays [3]. These phenomena provide crucial insights into the universe's most energetic processes and are essential for understanding fundamental questions in physics and astrophysics. Given the complexity and scale of these research objectives, LAGO relies heavily on sophisticated simulations to model particle interactions, atmospheric effects [4], and the responses of detection instruments.

The computational demands of LAGO simulations are substantial, requiring extensive processing power to analyze large datasets and perform intricate physical calculations, a common characteristic in this scientific domain as highlighted by research on high-performance computing for astrophysical simulations and astroparticle observations [5]. As the volume of data generated grows, the efficient utilization of high-performance computing (HPC) systems becomes critical to ensure timely, accurate, and cost-effective results. These substantial computational challenges in simulation, data processing, and analysis are characteristic of modern large-scale scientific facilities, shared by experiments across domains, from particle astrophysics observatories like LAGO and the Pierre Auger Observatory [6] to next-generation radio astronomy projects such as the Square Kilometre Array (SKA) [7]. Optimizing HPC resource efficiency, in addition to raw performance, is not merely a technical necessity. It is essential for enabling sustainable scientific exploration and for meeting the project's ambitious research goals within existing computational budgets.

LAGO has established multiple detector sites across Latin America to effectively coordinate these efforts, each contributing valuable data to the overarching research objectives. (Fig. 1) shows the locations of all LAGO detector sites. This visualization highlights the project's wide geographical reach and collaborative structure. This geographical distribution not only enhances the diversity of data collected but also underscores the need for efficient computational strategies to integrate and analyze results from these varied locations effectively.

In this context, this article emphasizes the importance of moving beyond basic performance tuning to a more comprehensive analysis of HPC resource efficiency tailored to LAGO's specific computational tasks. Understanding how different types of LAGO simulation workloads consume resources—such as CPU time, storage I/O, and network bandwidth—is fundamental. This work presents an analysis framework aimed at characterizing typical LAGO workloads and evaluating their resource utilization efficiency on HPC platforms, primarily using data extracted from execution logs and system monitoring tools. By assessing the alignment between the demands of these workloads and their actual resource consumption, we aim to identify patterns of both efficient and inefficient usage. This analysis seeks to pinpoint opportunities for optimization in areas like job configuration, resource requests, and workflow management, ultimately contributing

Fig. 1. Map of LAGO Detector Sites across Latin America, illustrating the geographical distribution and collaborative network contributing to astroparticle physics research. Source: [8]

to enhanced computational throughput and the overall sustainability of LAGO's scientific endeavors in astroparticle physics.

2 Background

Effective resource efficiency analysis requires understanding workload paradigms. High-Performance Computing (HPC) typically addresses tasks needing intensive, tightly-coupled parallel computation over short periods. Conversely, High-Throughput Computing (HTC) manages numerous independent, loosely-coupled tasks, often over extended durations, ideal for problems divisible into smaller units (e.g., large dataset processing or ensembles of independent simulations). While distinct, both are vital, and understanding their characteristics is key for optimizing large-scale Advanced Computing systems. The LAGO project, with its diverse computational demands, operates within this landscape.

2.1 Brief Overview of LAGO Simulations and Their Computational Complexity

LAGO simulations cover various astroparticle phenomena (e.g., detection of gamma-ray bursts [9], space weather studies [10]), demanding advanced computational methods for particle interactions, atmospheric effects, and modeling detector responses and calibration [11,12]. High computational demands arise from processing extensive datasets and intricate physical calculations via sophisticated algorithms [13]. There are three main types of simulations in production, each corresponding to a specific type of data product. S0, S1, and S2. These represent, respectively: raw simulated observations in the detectors, calculated with ARTI/CORSIKA; secondary particles processed with ARTI; and simulated detector response, using Meiga/ARTI/Geant4. In addition, machine learning techniques are being developed to classify the particles that arrive at the detectors, which will constitute the future S3 data.

A cornerstone of LAGO's simulation capabilities is the ARTI framework [14], integrating tools like CORSIKA [15], Meiga [16] and Geant4 [17] for atmospheric showers and detector responses. These varying computational tasks represent distinct workloads with different resource profiles. In addition, machine learning techniques are being developed [18] to classify the particles that reach the detectors.

LAGO's architecture (Fig. 2, source: [8]) uses Docker images for efficiency and reproducibility [8]. These images encapsulate core simulation functionalities, enabling automated checks, DataHub storage/publication with standardized metadata (PiDs), and B2FIND integration [19]. Researchers access resources via the LAGO Virtual Organization (VO) (managed by eduTEAMs [20]). DataHub uploads are restricted to official Docker images for metadata consistency. This self-contained approach enables flexible deployment on cloud and private clusters. However, it also requires thorough efficiency analysis across different platforms. This architecture streamlines data management and collaborative research, making efficient processing key to advancing astroparticle physics [13]. Understanding resource efficiency within this framework is vital for maximizing its potential.

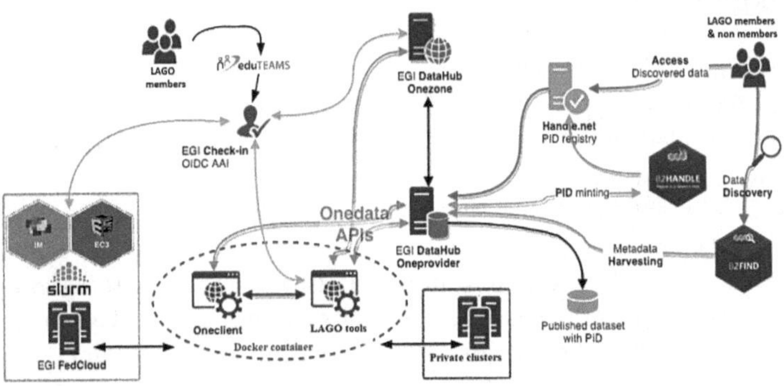

Fig. 2. Overview of the LAGO Simulation Architecture. Source: [8]

3 Methodology

This study employs an analysis framework to evaluate HPC resource utilization efficiency for LAGO's computational tasks, considering its prevalent coarse-grained, task-parallel execution model. The methodology relies on analyzing historical job data and system logs, interpreted with expert knowledge of LAGO workflows [13], to gain insights into resource consumption patterns and identify optimization areas.

3.1 Analysis Environment and Data Sources

The analysis used job accounting data and system monitoring logs from the EGI FedCloud infrastructure supporting the "lagoproject.net" Virtual Organization [21], leveraging experiences from LAGO's integration with cloud services via initiatives like EOSC-Synergy [22]. LAGO's significant computational activity on this infrastructure resulted in high resource consumption (e.g., Top 10 VO usage, Top 1 scratch I/O during the period) [13]. Key data sources included:

- **Job Scheduler Logs (Slurm):** Provided data on submitted task-jobs, requested resources (CPU cores, walltime, requested memory), allocated nodes, execution time, completion status, and basic CPU usage summaries.
- **LAGO VO Metadata:** Information linking jobs to simulation types (e.g., CORSIKA, Geant4/Meiga), LAGO sites, workflow stages, or identifying test runs.
- **Expert Knowledge from the LAGO Collaboration:** Crucial for interpreting task-parallel structures, understanding workflows (e.g., those using ARTI [14]), identifying site-specific variations, distinguishing test/development jobs, and validating findings [13].
- **Filesystem Logs/Monitoring (Selective):** Used for insights into I/O patterns for representative workloads.

The software environment involved standard LAGO simulation codes in Docker containers, often managed by wrapper scripts orchestrating numerous task-jobs [8].

3.2 Workload Characterization

A primary step was categorizing dominant computational workloads by computation type and usage patterns, achieved by:

- Analyzing job submission patterns, parameters, and LAGO metadata.
- Clustering jobs by resource usage profiles (CPU time per task) and duration.
- Explicitly differentiating production simulation campaigns (many task-jobs) from data processing and shorter 'test' or development runs using heuristics and expert input.
- Noting, where possible, site-specific simulation variations influencing resource needs.

This defined workload profiles (W1: 'MC Simulation Tasks', W2: 'Data Processing Tasks', W3: 'User Analysis/Development/Testing') for efficiency assessment. The workload categories previously identified were:

- **W1: Large-Scale Monte Carlo (MC) simulations (e.g., CORSIKA):** Many small to medium jobs (14 cores), often generated via toolchains like ARTI [14]. Represented ∼40% of total core-hours. Efficiency stems from granular submission, avoiding idle reservations.
- **W2: Data Processing/Reconstruction:** Medium-duration jobs (2–12 h), often arrays or sequential task-jobs. Varied resource requests per task, sometimes fewer cores but significant I/O. Accounted for ∼35% of core-hours.
- **W3: User Analysis, Development, and Testing:** Heterogeneous mix including interactive jobs, analysis scripts, and frequent short "test" submissions. Variable requests, making up ∼25% of core-hours but more of total job count.

Site-specific simulations add further heterogeneity.

3.3 Resource Efficiency Metrics and Analysis

To assess workload efficiency, we focused on standard metrics per task-job, interpreted within the overall campaign/activity context:

- **CPU Efficiency:** $\frac{\text{Actual CPU Time Used}}{\text{Allocated CPU Time}}$. Indicates CPU activity.
- **Walltime Efficiency:** $\frac{\text{Actual Walltime Used}}{\text{Requested Walltime}}$. Measures runtime estimation accuracy.
- **Job Completion Rate:** Percentage of successful task-jobs.
- **I/O Patterns (Qualitative/Quantitative):** Data volume read/written per task/campaign.

We calculated metrics for each task-job and then aggregated them by workload type. The analysis focused on metric distributions to better understand variability and the effect of outliers such as test jobs. High per-task CPU efficiency with granular submission contributes to overall campaign efficiency.

3.4 Analysis Workflow

The analysis workflow (Fig. 3) involved:

1. **Objective Definition:** Analyze and improve LAGO's HPC resource efficiency, considering its execution patterns.
2. **Data Collection:** Gather job accounting, system monitoring, LAGO metadata, and expert input.
3. **Data Preprocessing:** Clean, integrate data. Standardize formats. Apply heuristics/metadata flags to identify potential test jobs.
4. **Workload Characterization:** Classify workloads considering task-parallel structure, test jobs, and site variations (see Sect. 3.2).
5. **Efficiency Metric Calculation:** Compute per-task-job metrics.
6. **Trend Analysis & Efficiency Assessment:** Aggregate metrics by workload. Analyze distributions, assess impact of test jobs/site variations. Correlate efficiency with job parameters. Interpret results in the coarse-grained model context.

7. **Identify Optimization Opportunities:** Pinpoint improvement areas (e.g., resource requests, test job practices, task-internal bottlenecks, workflow management).
8. **Strategy Validation (Conceptual):** Propose strategies and future measurement approaches.

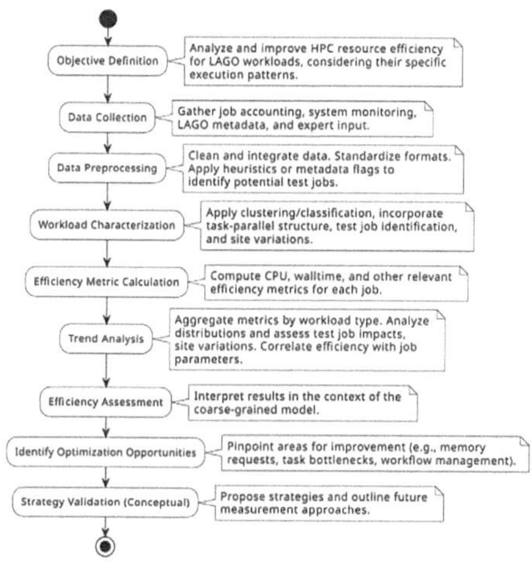

Fig. 3. Conceptual Workflow for Analyzing HPC Resource Efficiency in the LAGO Framework, highlighting the steps from objective definition and data collection to workload characterization, efficiency analysis, and identification of optimization strategies.

4 Resource Efficiency Analysis Results

This section presents HPC resource efficiency findings for LAGO tasks on the EGI FedCloud infrastructure from the beginning of simulation activities until September 2024. LAGO simulations often use a coarse-grained parallelization, decomposing into many independent task-jobs managed semi-manually, influencing efficiency metric interpretation.

Importantly, each simulation task may represent a different physical runtime, depending on the complexity of the simulated particle. Consequently, even with abundant resources, the total execution time for a simulation campaign is determined by the slowest (most complex) individual task.

Although LAGO simulations follow a standardized structure in terms of software tools and general workflow (e.g., using CORSIKA or Geant4), parameter-level variations are common across sites. These include differences in the total simulated time, the number of particles per job, or specific physics configurations. Such variability reflects the scientific goals of each site or campaign and contributes to the observed heterogeneity in workload profiles and resource usage.

Additionally, the computational cost and runtime of each simulation can depend on physical characteristics of the phenomenon and the site being modeled, particularly altitude, which influences the development of particle showers and thus affects simulation depth, granularity, and duration.

The job records also revealed the submission of test simulations, characterized by shorter runtimes and simplified configurations. While necessary for validation and debugging, these jobs tend to skew average efficiency metrics and should be considered separately in future performance analyses.

Finally, although tools like CORSIKA and Geant4 support internal parallelization (e.g., multi-threading or MPI), integration with site-specific orchestration scripts remains poorly documented. This has limited the adoption of fine-grained parallelization strategies. Resolving these issues could improve performance by enabling better intra-task parallelism and more efficient resource usage.

To illustrate the variability in execution times for tasks within a large simulation, two examples are presented showing how tasks associated with different types of particles can have significantly different execution times. These graphs highlight the impact of particle complexity on simulation times and how this can affect the total runtime of the simulation campaign (Fig. 4).

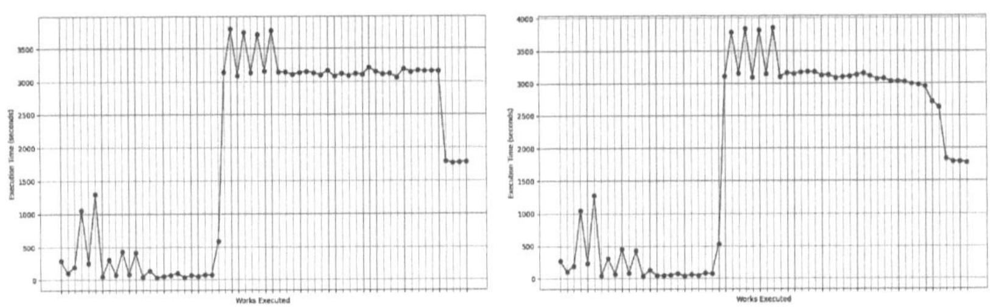

Fig. 4. Examples illustrating the variability in execution times per task or particle within a single simulation job. These differences reflect the complexity of individual particle simulations, which are independent and submitted as separate tasks.

4.1 Resource Utilization Patterns

Each workload exhibited distinctive efficiency profiles:

- **CPU Efficiency:** W1 (MC Simulations) tasks exhibited near-perfect CPU efficiency (∼100%), as resources are requested only when jobs are ready to run and released immediately upon completion. This on-demand strategy eliminates idle time and ensures optimal core utilization. W2 (Data Processing) jobs had moderate efficiency (∼60–75%), suggesting the presence of I/O waits or serial phases. W3 (User Analysis/Testing) showed variable and often low CPU efficiency (avg. ∼40%), due to interactivity, development cycles, suboptimal scripting, and numerous test runs.

- **Walltime Efficiency:** W1 tasks also achieved near-perfect walltime efficiency (∼100%), as jobs are launched just-in-time and terminate as soon as computation finishes, minimizing waste. W2 and W3 jobs showed lower efficiency (∼50–60%), significantly impacted by short 'test' jobs with conservative walltime requests. Filtering out test jobs would likely improve these averages. Particle complexity also contributes to runtime spread in W1/W2.
- **Job Failures:** About 15% of W1/W2 failures were due to exceeding walltime (some complex particle tasks take longer), and ∼10% to out-of-memory errors (indicating issues with absolute limits or actual requirements).

Below are four examples of the temporal distribution of jobs in the simulation. These graphs demonstrate that there is no over-reservation of resources; instead, jobs only request the resources necessary for each specific task. As shown, each task has its own execution window and does not depend on the completion of other tasks to execute (Fig. 5).

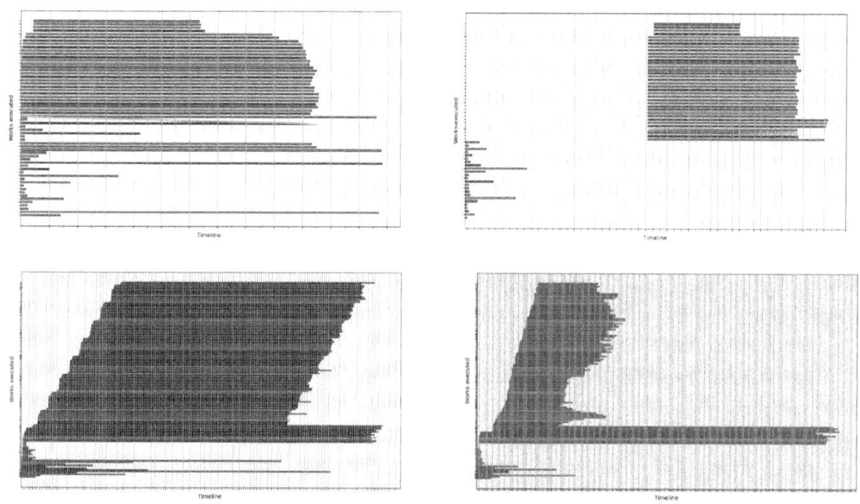

Fig. 5. Examples showing the distribution of simulation jobs in time. These graphs demonstrate the task-parallel execution strategy in which only the resources required by each task are requested, without idle reservations or inter-task dependencies.

Future work should focus on (i) improving documentation and integration of fine-grained parallelization features within CORSIKA and similar tools, (ii) promoting harmonization of simulation parameters across LAGO sites where possible, and (iii) filtering test jobs in performance assessments to avoid distortions in global efficiency metrics.

4.2 Identification of Key Inefficiencies and Challenges

Key areas based on observed patterns and operational context include:

1. **Impact of Test Jobs on Averages:** Frequent short test jobs (esp. W3) skew average walltime and potentially CPU efficiency metrics, masking production run efficiency.
2. **Suboptimal CPU Utilization in Specific Tasks/Workloads:** Moderate W2 and low W3 (excluding tests) CPU efficiency suggest tasks need optimization (I/O, serial sections), possibly compounded by difficulties leveraging internal parallelism of core simulation engines.
3. **Heterogeneity and Lack of Standardization:** Site-specific simulation variations complicate developing universal optimization strategies.
4. **Workflow Management Overhead:** Manual management of numerous interdependent task-jobs can add overhead and complexity, affecting time-to-solution. Campaign duration is often dictated by the longest tasks (due to particle complexity).
5. **Altitude-Specific Simulation Needs:** Adapting simulations for LAGO's diverse detector altitudes (sea level to >5000 m.a.s.l.) alters particle interactions and computational load, impacting performance baselines across sites.
6. **Runtime Variability due to Particle Complexity:** Within MC campaigns (W1), simulation time per primary particle varies significantly by type, energy, and shower complexity, challenging precise walltime requests.
7. **Challenges with Internal Parallelism Integration:** Integration of internal parallelism (multi-threading/MPI in CORSIKA/Geant4) with site-specific scripts is poorly documented, limiting fine-grained parallelization and potential intra-task performance gains.

These findings provide concrete targets for optimization efforts aimed at improving overall HPC resource utilization within the LAGO project.

5 Discussion and Further Work

This analysis, focusing on HPC resource efficiency for LAGO's task-parallel workloads, provides insights for improvement by moving beyond raw performance to how effectively resources are used.

5.1 Summary of Efficiency Findings

LAGO's task-parallel approach inherently promotes efficiency by minimizing idle resource reservations, seen in high W1 per-task CPU utilization. However, issues like variable walltime estimation accuracy persist. Test jobs significantly impact aggregate metrics, and site-specific simulation heterogeneity complicates standardized assessment. Moderate W2 CPU efficiency suggests task-internal bottlenecks.

5.2 Implications for LAGO Computational Strategy

The identified inefficiencies and operational characteristics have direct implications for LAGO's computational strategy:

- **User Guidance/Training:** For realistic walltime requests, general resource awareness, best practices for test job submission (e.g., specific queues/annotations), and understanding task duration variance.
- **Targeted Profiling/Optimization:** For W2 tasks, focusing on I/O or serial sections, and understanding task complexity variance.
- **Resource Policy Adjustments:** Policies encouraging accurate requests; queue structures better handling many short/medium task-jobs.
- **Workflow Management Tools:** Adopting sophisticated tools to automate task-job management and dependency tracking.
- **Standardization Efforts:** Encouraging standardized setups for common tasks across sites where feasible.

Addressing these points can lead to more effective use of allocated time and resources, enhancing LAGO's scientific output.

5.3 Challenges and Limitations

This analysis faces challenges inherent in interpreting system-level logs for task-parallel workflows:

- **System-Level View Limitations:** Scheduler logs offer a limited view (e.g., peak memory accuracy, CPU time attribution in parallel jobs).
- **Attributing Campaign Efficiency:** To assess the efficiency of an entire campaign, both per-task efficiency and the effectiveness of task-parallel decomposition must be considered. However, job metrics capture only part of this picture.
- **Impact of Heterogeneity and Test Jobs:** Site-specific simulations and test jobs complicate average efficiency calculations and global recommendations.
- **Manual Workflow Aspects:** Manual work distribution hinders automatic capture of full campaign structure from logs.
- **Challenges with Internal Parallelism Integration:** While core simulation tools like Geant4 and CORSIKA offer internal parallelism options (e.g., multi-threading), their integration with site-specific orchestration scripts remains poorly documented within the LAGO framework. This has limited the adoption of fine-grained parallelization strategies, due to potential conflicts with existing custom scripts and the established coarse-grained, multi-job execution model. This limitation hinders potential intra-task performance gains.

5.4 Future Directions for Efficiency Improvement

Future work should focus on overcoming these limitations and proactively improving efficiency within LAGO's operational model:

- **Enable Finer-Grained Parallelism:** Resolve conflicts to document and enable internal parallelism (e.g., multi-threading in Geant4) in core simulation engines, complementing the coarse-grained approach.
- **Develop Resource Estimation Tools:** For users to better estimate runtime and other key resource needs.
- **Integrate Application-Level Monitoring:** Using lightweight profiling/monitoring in LAGO Docker containers for granular application behavior data.
- **Enhanced Logging/Metadata:** Methods for users to tag "test" vs. "production" jobs and link task-jobs to campaigns/sites.
- **Workflow Analysis Tools:** For multi-job, task-parallel workflows using scheduler data and enhanced metadata.
- **Promote Workflow Management Systems:** Evaluate and promote adoption of systems like Snakemake, Nextflow for LAGO.
- **Explore Container/Task Optimizations:** Reduce startup times or overheads of many containerized task-jobs.

In conclusion, systematically analyzing HPC resource efficiency, while adapting interpretation to LAGO's specific task-parallel strategy, yields crucial insights. Understanding how resources are used—beyond just raw metrics—makes it possible to apply targeted optimizations. This improves throughput, supports sustainable resource use, and ultimately accelerates scientific discovery. Implementing strategies from this analysis is vital for maximizing LAGO's HPC return on investment.

Acknowledgments. The authors thank the CYTED co-funded LAGO-INDICA network (524RT0159-LAGO-INDICA: Infraestructura digital de ciencia abierta) and the EL-BONGO physics project for their support and collaboration initiatives. We also acknowledge the Universidad Industrial de Santander (UIS), especially the research groups Cómputo Avanzado y a Gran Escala (CAGE) and Grupo de Investigación en Relatividad y Gravitación (GIRG), for their institutional support and resources provided for this work. AI technology was used to proofread and polish this manuscript.(OpenAI, 2025. Gemini 2025).

References

1. Sidelnik, I., Asorey, H., Collaboration, L., et al.: LAGO: the Latin American giant observatory. Nucl. Instrum. Methods Phys. Res., Sect. A **876**, 173–175 (2017)
2. Sidelnik, I., et al.: The capability of water Cherenkov detectors arrays of the LAGO project to detect Gamma-Ray Burst and high energy astrophysics sources. Nucl. Instrum. Methods Phys. Res., Sect. A **1056**, 168576 (2023)

3. Santos, N.A., et al.: First measurements of periodicities and anisotropies of cosmic ray flux observed with a water-Cherenkov detector at the Marambio Antarctic base. Adv. Space Res. **71**(6), 2967–2976 (2023)
4. Asorey, H., Suárez-Durán, M., Mayo-García, R.: ACORDE: a new application for estimating the dose absorbed by passengers and crews in commercial flights. Appl. Radiat. Isot. **196**, 110752 (2023)
5. Becerra, L.M., Sarmiento-Cano, C., Martínez-Méndez, A., Dominguez, Y., Núñez, L.A.: High-performance computing for astrophysical simulations and astroparticle observations. In: Barrios H., C.J., Rizzi, S., Meneses, E., Mocskos, E., Monsalve Diaz, J.M., Montoya, J. (eds.) High Performance Computing, vol. 1887, pp. 184–196, Communications in Computer and Information Science. Springer Nature Switzerland,Cham (2024). https://doi.org/10.1007/978-3-031-52186-7_13
6. Allekotte, I., et al.: The surface detector system of the Pierre auger observatory. Nucl. Instrum. Methods Phys. Res., Sect. A **586**(3), 409–420 (2008)
7. Dewdney, P.E., Hall, P.J., Schilizzi, R.T., Lazio, T.J.L.: The square kilometre array. Proc. IEEE **97**(8), 1482–1496 (2009)
8. Rubio-Montero, A.J., Pagan-Munoz, R., Mayo-Garcia, R., Pardo-Diaz, A., Sidelnik, I., Asorey, H.: A novel cloud-based framework for standardized simulations in the Latin American giant observatory (lago). In: 2021 Winter Simulation Conference (WSC). IEEE (2021)
9. Allard, D., et al.: Use of water-Cherenkov detectors to detect gamma ray bursts at the large aperture GRB observatory (LAGO). Nucl. Instrum. Methods Phys. Res., Sect. A **595**(1), 70–72 (2008)
10. Asorey, H., Núñez, L.A., Suárez-Durán, M.: Preliminary results from the Latin American giant observatory space weather simulation chain. Space Weather **16**(5), 461–475 (2018)
11. Calderón-Ardila, R., Jaimes-Motta, A., Sarmiento-Cano, C., Suárez-Durán, Vásquez-Ramírez, A., et al.: Modeling the lago's detectors response to secondary particles at ground level from the Antarctic to Mexico. In: 36th ICRC (2019)
12. Galindo, A., et al.: Calibration of a large water-Cherenkov detector at the Sierra Negra site of Lago. Nucl. Instrum. Methods Phys. Res., Sect. A **861**, 28–37 (2017)
13. Núñez-Chongo, O., Asorey, H., Rubio-Montero, A.J., Suárez-Durán, M., Mayo-García, R., Carretero, M.: Convergent data-driven workflows for open radiation calculations: an exportable methodology to any field. J. Supercomput. **81**, 465 (2025)
14. Sarmiento-Cano, C., Suárez-Durán, M., Calderón-Ardila, R., et al.: The ARTI framework: cosmic rays atmospheric background simulations. Eur. Phys. J. C **82**, 1019 (2022)
15. Heck, D., Knapp, J., Capdevielle, J., Schatz, G., Thouw, T., et al.: Corsika: a monte carlo code to simulate extensive air showers (1998)
16. Taboada, A., Sarmiento-Cano, C., Sedoski, A., Asorey, H.: Meiga, a dedicated framework used for muography applications. J. Adv. Instrum. Sci. **2022**, 266 (2022)
17. Agostinelli, S., et al.: Geant4—a simulation toolkit. Nuclear instruments and methods in physics research section A: accelerators, spectrometers, detectors and associated equipment, vol. 506, no. 3, pp. 250–303 (2003)
18. Torres, T.J., LAGO Collaboration, et al.: Enhanced particle classification in water Cherenkov detectors using machine learning: modeling and validation with monte carlo simulation datasets. Atmosphere **15**(9) (2024)

19. Widmann, H., Thiemann, H.: Eudat B2find: a cross-discipline metadata service and discovery portal. In: EGU General Assembly Conference Abstracts, pp. EPSC2016–8562 (2016)
20. Coulouarn, T.: Eduteams un service géant pour les équipes virtuelles. In: JRES (Journées réseaux de l'enseignement et de la recherche) 2017 (2017)
21. European grid infrastructure: EGI fedcloud (2022). Accessed 30 Apr 2025. https://www.egi.eu/egi-infrastructure/
22. Rubio-Montero, A., Pagán-Muñoz, R.: et al.: The EOSC-synergy cloud services implementation for the Latin American Giant Observatory (LAGO). In: 37th ICRC, vol. 395, Berlin, Germany, 2021, p. PoS(ICRC2021)261

Author Index

K. Brown et al. (Eds.): CARLA 2025, CCIS 2750, pp. 249–250, 2026.
https://doi.org/10.1007/978-3-032-24923-4

FSC
www.fsc.org
MIX
Papier | Fördert gute Waldnutzung
FSC® C083411

Zeitfracht Medien GmbH
Ferdinand-Jühlke-Straße 7
99095 Erfurt, Deutschland
produktsicherheit@kolibri360.de